Craig Baehr
Kelli Cargile Cook

THE AGILE COMMUNICATOR

Principles and Practices in Technical Communication

Second Editon

Kendall Hunt
publishing company

Cover image © Shutterstock, Inc.

Kendall Hunt
publishing company

www.kendallhunt.com
Send all inquiries to:
4050 Westmark Drive
Dubuque, IA 52004-1840

Copyright © 2016, 2017 by Craig Baehr and Kelli Cargile Cook

PAK ISBN 978-1-5249-3391-3
Text Alone ISBN 978-1-5249-3393-7

Kendall Hunt Publishing Company has the exclusive rights to reproduce this work, to prepare derivative works from this work, to publicly distribute this work, to publicly perform this work and to publicly display this work.

All rights reserved. No part of this publication may be reproduced, stored in a retrieval system, or transmitted, in any form or by any means, electronic, mechanical, photocopying, recording, or otherwise, without the prior written permission of the copyright owner.

Printed in the United States of America

Contents

CHAPTER 1 **Communicating Agilely in the 21st Century Workplace** 1
Twentieth Century Workplaces: Working the Line 3
The 21st Century Work Model: Rapid Change, Iterative Cycles, and Agility 6
Chapter Summary 10
Chapter Assignments 10

CHAPTER 2 **Managing Projects as an Iterative Process** 13
Iterative Process and Project Management 15
Technical Communication Iterative Process: The Four Phases 17
Chapter Summary 26
Chapter Assignments 26

CHAPTER 3 **Planning Your Communication Product** 29
Defining Your Audience 30
Managing and Scoping the Project 37
Resource Planning 48
Completing the Planning Phase 53
Chapter Summary 54
Chapter Assignments 54

CHAPTER 4 **Determining Your Technical Communication Product** 57
Document Genres and Types 58
Conventions and Stylistics 61
Developing a Document or Project Plan 72
Chapter Summary 77
Chapter Assignments 78

CHAPTER 5 **Building Teams and Improving Processes** 81
Distributed Workplaces and Teams 83
Team Process Improvement 93
Strategies for Improving Team Processes and Value Added 101
Chapter Summary 103
Chapter Assignments 104

CHAPTER 6   Researching Content   107

Formulating Problem Statements and Research Questions   108
Choosing Research Methods   111
Research Reporting Responsibilities   125
Chapter Summary   130
Chapter Assignments   130

CHAPTER 7   Writing Content, Technical Style, and Editing   133

A Brief Introduction to Content Authoring   134
Words, Sentences, Paragraphs: The Building Blocks of Style   138
Reviewing and Editing Your Own and Others' Content   157
Chapter Summary   161
Chapter Assignments   161

CHAPTER 8   Developing Information and Instructional Content   165

Content Management Concepts and Practices   166
Information Modeling and Structure   168
Content Reuse and Single Sourcing   172
Developing Meaningful Metadata for Your Documents   176
Reusability and Usability Considerations   179
Information Development for Instructional Purposes   182
Chapter Summary   193
Chapter Assignments   194

CHAPTER 9   Designing Visual Information   197

Visual Design Theories   199
Design Principles   207
Developing Visual Information Graphics   210
Developing Design Style Sheets, Templates, and Visual Identities   215
Chapter Summary   217
Chapter Assignments   217

CHAPTER 10   Corresponding   219

Writing and Critiquing Professional Correspondence   221
Formatting Correspondence   229
Writing Electronic Correspondence   233
Writing Socially Mediated Communication   235
Chapter Summary   237
Chapter Assignments   238

Contents   **v**

CHAPTER 11   **Reporting Status and Progress**   **241**
    Instance Reports   241
    Status Reports   249
    Chapter Summary   251
    Chapter Assignments   252

CHAPTER 12   **Instructing**   **255**
    Writing Instructional Documents   257
    Instructional Document Types   265
    Chapter Summary   273
    Chapter Assignments   274

CHAPTER 13   **Developing Web Sites and Electronic Content**   **275**
    Developing Electronic Documents   277
    Choosing Authoring Tools and Methods   285
    Chapter Summary   291
    Chapter Assignments   291

CHAPTER 14   **Proposing**   **293**
    Guidelines and Strategies for Writing a Winning Proposal   296
    Writing and Drafting Proposals   298
    Reviewing and Revising the Proposal   302
    Submitting the Proposal   302
    Chapter Summary   308
    Chapter Assignments   308

CHAPTER 15   **Reporting Research and Project Results**   **311**
    Reporting Results   312
    Chapter Summary   336
    Chapter Assignments   336

CHAPTER 16   **Developing Professional Profiles and Job Search Materials**   **341**
    Assessing Your Skills   342
    Creating and Maintaining a Professional Profile   343
    Locating Available Positions   360
    Applying for Positions   363
    Interviewing   368
    Chapter Summary   371
    Chapter Assignments   372

CHAPTER 17 Presenting   375
　　　　　Professional Presentations   375
　　　　　Planning, Developing, and Delivering Presentations   379
　　　　　Evaluating Presentations   396
　　　　　Chapter Summary   397
　　　　　Chapter Assignments   398

CHAPTER 18 Writing Technical Definitions and Descriptions   399
　　　　　Writing Technical Definitions   400
　　　　　Writing Technical Descriptions   403
　　　　　Documents That Use Technical Descriptions   405
　　　　　Organizational Patterns   408
　　　　　Persuasive Stylistics   412
　　　　　Using and Applying Standards   413
　　　　　Chapter Summary   416
　　　　　Chapter Assignments   417

References   419

Index   421

Communicating Agilely in the 21st Century Workplace

CHAPTER OVERVIEW

This chapter introduces you to the methods and practices that characterize the 21st century workplace. It compares and contrasts the 20th and 21st century models, and it discusses the importance of agile communication and iterative processes as emerging themes in the 21st century workplace. After reading this chapter, you should be able to meet the following objectives:

- Define and describe the changing role of technical communication in the workplace.
- Compare and contrast the 20th and 21st century workplace models and practices.
- Define and describe the importance of agile communication and iterative processes to technical communication.

Effective communication has always been necessary for effective workplaces, but never more so than in the 21st century. Today's workplaces require you to understand and adapt to many communication challenges, such as global communication, cross-functional and cross-cultural teaming, fluctuating information environments and technologies, rapid writing assignments, short turnarounds or deadlines, and client involvement in project development and implementation.

To meet these challenges, you must be responsive to change by carefully assessing communication situations and adapting quickly and effectively to them. You must target incoming challenges, employ your research and knowledge management skills to understand them, and adapt your communication skills to respond to them. Whether you are preparing for a career as a technical communicator or as a professional in another field, you will find that understanding technical communication processes and practices will help you succeed.

What does technical communication mean in the 21st century? Technical communication is information expressed in words (spoken and written) and images that allows individuals to perform work. These words and images may be conveyed using multiple forms of media,

Figure 1.1. Technical communication is information expressed in words and images that allows individuals to perform work.

> **EXERCISE 1.1**
>
> ## Will You Be a Professional Who Communicates or a Communication Professional?
>
> In the United States, the Bureau of Labor Statistics (BLS) maintains the *Occupational Outlook Handbook* (*OOH*), which is available online at http://www.bls.gov/ooh/ and updated annually. Visit the *OOH* and look up your future occupation. Note the kinds of communication work that your future occupation requires. Now look up "Technical Writer" in the *OOH*. Using the information you gather from this research, compare and contrast the differences between professionals who communicate as part of their job and professional communicators.
>
> **Tasks to be completed:**
>
> 1. Access the Bureau of Labor Statistics (BLS) *Occupational Outlook Handbook (OOH)* online at http://www.bls.gov/ooh/ using a Web browser.
> 2. Look up your future occupation and make note of the communication work described for that occupation.
> 3. Look up Technical Writer and make note of the communication work described for that occupation.
> 4. Compare and contrast the differences and discuss your findings.

ranging from print to electronic, and they can be performed in equally varied locations: from the shop floor to the front office, from the kitchen to the garage, from spaceships to submarines. Technical communication is used to plan, design, make, test, and use products. It is also the information we use to communicate with others about these products.

Agile communicators in the 21st century also use **technologies**—tools, methods, mechanisms, or processes used to solve problems—to produce information solutions. While they use technologies to do their work, they also frequently work in technological settings.

What do technical communicators do? Many technical communicators not only support the development of technological products, but they also use their knowledge about and competencies with technology to create technical documents to accompany these products. Technical communicators work in diverse organizations, such as information technologies, engineering, medicine, science, public relations, manufacturing, design, and non-profits. Information products they produce range from technical manuals to Web sites and proposals.

What are technical communicators' job titles? Because their work can be located in many sectors, technical communicators' job titles also vary: content manager, information developer, information architect, technical communicator, visual designer, illustrator, and usability expert are just a few examples of the titles technical communicators may possess. Additionally, terms, such as "professional communication," "business communication," "technical writing," "scientific writing," and "medical writing," are often used synonymously with technical communication. We view these terms as variations of technical communication situated within specific professions. For example, proposals written to gain scientific research funding, reports of research findings, and presentations of these findings are all examples of scientific writing, which falls under the larger umbrella term "technical writing." Similarly, accountants engage in financial (or business) writing when they create annual reports, write email to clients, and produce tax reports. In both examples, the scientists and accountants are engaging information and using it to create documents that communicate with others, such as funding agencies, other scientists and accountants, and clients. They are professionals who communicate.

Unlike scientists, accountants, and other professionals who communicate as *part* of their job, technical communicators communicate as their job; they are information specialists. They specialize in creating information products. They "work at the intersection of technology and people, migrating back and forth between technology and communication as they design products for specific audiences" (Pringle and Williams, 2005, p. 369). The range of skills and jobs in technical communication today includes technical writers and editors, indexers, information architects, instructional designers, technical illustrators, globalization and localization specialists, usability professionals, visual designers, Web designers, teachers, researchers, and corporate trainers, among others (STC Web site).

Whether you are a professional who communicates or a communication professional, this book will help you to prepare and build related skills and practices for creating technical documents in your future career. In the following sections of this chapter, we describe how the work of technical communication, whether conducted as part of one's job or as one's specialty, has changed as work models have changed over the past century.

TWENTIETH CENTURY WORKPLACES: WORKING THE LINE

When you think of 20th century production models in the United States, you may recall images of assembly lines and industrialists, such as Henry Ford, the automotive giant whose company implemented these processes. Assembly line production, however, was not the beginning of the product development process; initially, product designs started at drafting boards where engineers created blueprints for either products or the technology needed to manufacture those products. In fact, product designs included construction logic. Construction logic designated how larger components could be manufactured along

Figure 1.2. Photographed in 1913, early Ford automobiles roll off an assembly line.

> # EXERCISE 1.2
>
> ## *Learning More about Workplace Production Models*
>
> Visit the Internet Moving Image Archive (http://www.archive.org/details/movies) or conduct an internet image search to find pictures or videos of production lines. Use keywords, such as "mass production," "assembly line," or "manufacturing." Find at least one image from the early to mid-20th century (1900–1950) and from later in the century or the beginning of the 21st century (1951 to present day). Do the processes illustrated in these images differ? How? Describe what is being produced and note any similarities with or differences from the processes described in this chapter. Write a short 250-word comparative description of these images. Include a citation for both images in your description.
>
> **Tasks to be completed:**
>
> 1. Search the Internet Moving Image Archive, from the URL provided above, for images or videos of production lines, using keywords such as mass production, assembly line, or manufacturing.
> 2. Find at least one image from 1900–1950 and one from 1990 to the present.
> 3. Compare and contrast the images to determine the similarities and differences.
> 4. Write a short description of your findings.

one main assembly line. The main line was connected to smaller subassembly lines. The subassembly lines were responsible for building smaller, more modular parts that were then incorporated into the larger components. In early mass assembly products, most, if not all, of the components—large and small—were manufactured or produced on site. Figure 1.2 provides a brief glimpse into early automotive production lines.

Extensive prototyping tested designs and, in doing so, tested the construction logic, the manufacturing technologies, and processes needed to implement and incorporate parts. Once prototypes were deemed successful, production lines were carefully constructed to reflect the prototyped processes. Consumer products, such as cars, tractors, chain saws, and toasters, were manufactured in linear progression, humans and tools working together completing one task after another. On assembly lines, workers were stationed at each step of the process, and they completed the same procedures repetitively for hours on end, each one completing a single task and then passing the product along to the next person down the line. One after another, workers performed their tasks until the product was finally complete and rolled off the line. Whereas a single worker might take days, weeks, or months to assemble a product like a car, an assembly line could put together tens, hundreds, or even thousands of identical products daily. To profit, this production model relied on a cohesive process for a stable product design, expedited with low-cost human capital and dependable technological tools. If changes were required or occurred at any stage in the process—customer requests, consumer needs, design modifications, mechanical breakdowns, worker inefficiencies—the process slowed or stopped completely. A single modification might take hours or even weeks to reconfigure the line.

This method of manufacturing was mirrored in mid- to late 20th century information technology design and production as well. Although software programming developed much later in the 20th century than automotive manufacturing, its early development cycle—a process known as waterfall (or plan-driven) development—was quite similar. In simple terms, Figure 1.3 illustrates a five-step waterfall development process in software engineering: proposing; analyzing and specifying; implementing; testing and

Figure 1.3. The waterfall work model follows a linear process from start to finish.

troubleshooting; and producing and maintaining. This process is likened to a waterfall because the proposed idea and specifications (the plan) drive the entire process, and a clear line separates idea development and construction. The process is predictive, starting from a plan and sequentially progressing through the plan. That is, construction flows downward from the plan and its specifications, and steps are followed sequentially. New steps begin after the previous step is completed. Like the assembly line process, waterfall development relies on a strong design that is as viable at the end of production as it was at its beginning. If changes occur, workflow (the downward progression of the waterfall) is obstructed.

As Figure 1.3 demonstrates, the waterfall model always includes information exchanges: proposals, specifications, design documents, and reports. These exchanges, though, are typically between similar audiences: manufacturers and vendors communicate with one another, engineers communicate with other engineers, programmers report to other programmers. Each type of communication is specialized and uses technical jargon, language specific to an expert audience. At the end of the cycle, however, information about the new product needs to be conveyed to the consumer.

By the 1940s and 1950s, technical writers were hired to produce these documents. Typically, technical writers were given the product and told to learn how to use and share this knowledge with consumers. Technical writers were advised to translate the technical jargon of the developers into easy-to-understand, clear-as-a-windowpane instructions for consumers. In essence, as Slack, Miller, and Doak (1993) explain, technical communicators transferred and translated technical documentation so that consumers could understand and use it. They "cleaned up" the writing of the engineers and programmers, and they corrected spelling and grammar errors. In effect, they were clerical workers whose primary job was to simplify expert technical information into easy-to-understand consumer information. Technical writers' work began at the end of the waterfall process as products were rolling off the line. Their challenges were to learn to use technologies, to produce documentation that effectively supported consumers, and to produce that documentation quickly. Failing to work quickly resulted in delays or products shipped without documentation.

What these examples from manufacturing and software programming illustrate is the predictive nature of 20th century production models. The plan (which includes both the product design and the production or assembly design) defines the process: the final product results from the successful implementation of both. The plan and process predict, in other words, the success of the product. If the plan is well designed and the technologies are effectively developed to complement production, then the actual production progresses in the expected or predicted way.

However, when production models emphasize processes and plans over the product itself, then change becomes more challenging. Linear processes can easily be disturbed, and a disturbed progression disrupts the entire process or workflow. These processes also depend on local, situated production, where parts and components are manufactured or developed within close proximity to each other, and they rely on human resources that work as dependably and automatically as their technological counterparts. Humans are part of the machine, in a sense. As long as they are consistent, dependable, and inexpensive to compensate, the product is productively and cheaply produced. What is unaccounted for in these production models and what cannot be accounted for is change.

THE 21ST CENTURY WORK MODEL: RAPID CHANGE, ITERATIVE CYCLES, AND AGILITY

The stability of early- and mid-20th century production models has changed in the 21st century as the work of U.S. manufacturing, production, and economic development has shifted. The job stability of both blue- and white-collar workers has evaporated. Many jobs and processes associated with them have moved overseas to reduce labor and production costs. Organizations are no longer locally, regionally, or even nationally defined; more and more, they are global, either through workforce or production diversification. The development of information technologies now allows for easy communication between workforces located anywhere and working anytime.

Cross-cultural teaming is commonplace. Even within the United States, the increased employment of individuals from varied gender, racial, and ethnic groups has diversified teams. Teams are not only **cross-cultural**; they are also often **cross-functional**, meaning that scientists, engineers, accountants, marketing personnel, and project managers all work on a single team from project conception to completion. At the same time, consumers' desires and abilities to purchase more highly customized products have required quicker turnarounds and design adaptations.

These are only a few of the changes that have dramatically affected assembly line and waterfall development processes. By the late 1970s, Isaac Asimov (1978), who was both a scientist and science writer, predicted: "It is change, continuing change, inevitable change, which is the dominant factor in society today. No sensible decision can be made any longer without taking into account not only the world as it is, but the world as it will be...."

To address the paradox that organizations must expect change and adapt to it, new production models were first introduced in the late 1990s. Known as agile development models, they emphasized teamwork, working deliverables, customer collaboration, and responsiveness to change. Other key values, described in the *Agile Manifesto* (2001), are short development cycles; frequent testing; trust and frequent communication among team members; adaptation to changing circumstances; and reflecting in order to learn. These principles are called **adaptive** (or sometimes called **agile**), in contrast to waterfall development's **predictive** product development cycle. In other words, these processes are designed to expect and respond quickly to change rather than be obstructed or delayed by it.

EXERCISE 1.3

Visualizing Waterfall and Agile Development Cycles

Working with a partner, conduct an internet search for images of the waterfall development cycle and the agile development cycle, and note where you find images that appear to describe these cycles, as discussed in this chapter. What is standard in the illustrations of the waterfall cycle? Where do illustrations of the waterfall cycle vary? What is standard in the illustrations of the agile development cycle? Where do illustrations of the agile cycle vary? Which cycle seems more standardized? Why? Discuss the similarities and differences in these two models and their depictions.

Tasks to be completed:

1. Conduct an online search for images of both the waterfall development and agile development cycles.
2. Examine key features that appear consistent or standard across each model.
3. Compare and contrast the similarities and differences in the two models in the images you find.
4. Discuss your findings with others.

In a sense, they are both adaptive and predictive because they begin with a preliminary plan, which adapts as the project encounters change. They focus less on early detailed plans, specifications, or documentation and more on getting started on the product, learning and adapting as the product design develops, and working in teams to check, validate, and test design efficiencies and functions. Equally important, customers or product consumers are invited frequently to interact as team members along with developers, providing input and advice, engaging in testing as the product develops, and suggesting modifications along the way. The production model then develops through feedback and short, **iterative** (repeated) development cycles—design, develop, test, seek feedback, respond to feedback.

While this process may sound similar to the 20th century development model, the key difference is timing: 21st century processes are conducted in short, productive bursts, which are then connected with other short productive bursts. The cycle moves in a short, spiraling fashion, looping or cycling through the development process again and again. Throughout these cyclical processes, people and their input are valued over strict plans or

> ### EXERCISE 1.4
>
> ### *Understanding Workplace Change*
>
> Conduct a short 10–15 minute interview with a friend or family member who has retired or is near retirement age. Ask them to describe the kinds of jobs they have had in their careers. How did their workplaces change over the course of their career? For example, how have services or products changed or how have technologies been integrated into workplaces? Also, ask them what role communication (writing, speaking, talking with team members) played in their first jobs, and what role it played in their later jobs. Write a short summary about what you learned from your interview.
>
> **Tasks to be completed:**
>
> 1. Speak with a friend or family member who is retired or nearing retirement and interview that person about workplace changes they have experienced over time.
> 2. Ask questions regarding changes in the role communication, technologies, and work processes they experienced.
> 3. Write a short summary of your findings and prepare to discuss it.

process designs. Working with others—seeking input and responding to it—is required, and, at the end of design cycles, teams reflect on what they have learned and document this learning to improve future cycles.

These principles and key values relate directly to 21st century technical communication and the teams who produce it. Teams often manage and manipulate complex and diverse texts that are authored by culturally and educationally diverse individuals. Individuals and teams work with various information technologies in order to create solutions to messy communication problems. To succeed in these technical communication situations, everyone needs to be able to develop texts quickly; collaborate with others, such as peers, supervisors, and subject-matter experts; and manage information in print and electronic formats. Whereas technical communicators of the past were primarily concerned with grammatical and mechanical skills, today's communicators rely not only on traditional writing and speaking abilities but also on social skills, organizational knowledge, and technological know-how. Assembly line use of standard formats and templates that once were sufficient for writing technical documentation are less viable and require adaptation to address specific organizational needs and problems.

Twenty-first century skills and the competencies required have been well researched and documented in recent technical and professional communication literature (See Hart-Davidson, 2001; Whiteside, 2003; Allen and Benninghoff, 2004; Rainey, Turner, and Dayton, 2005; Paretti, McNair, and Holloway-Attaway, 2007; Slattery, 2007). Employing the skills and competencies necessary to perform 21st century work requires communicators who can adapt to change, manage multiple texts in a variety of formats, and work well with others.

Agility in the 21st Century Workplace

If you already know the word agile, you probably associate it with the performance of an athlete or perhaps a sports car. People and objects that are agile are able to change directions swiftly and easily. They are flexible, quick, and graceful. In this book, the word **agile** refers to a communication aptitude or skill, specifically the ability to analyze a communication problem and adjust to changes that arise during the problem-solving process. It includes not only an understanding of the situation and its projected outcomes but also the ability to respond effectively when the situation changes. More specifically, it refers to the communicator's response to today's workplace and its challenges, such as global communications; cross-functional and cross-cultural teaming; fluctuating information environments and technologies; rapid writing assignments; short development cycles or turnarounds; and the need for client involvement in project development and implementation. Like the athlete or the sports car driver, agile communicators know their skills, possess quick reflexes under pressure, and use the technological tools they need to support high-performance.

As Figure 1.4 illustrates, iterative processes are inherently agile. An iterative process accommodates change during the development of a technical product in many ways. For example, when reviewing or testing draft documents during the development or quality assurance phases, problem areas or changes might be identified, which require you to return to earlier work completed, such as planning goals or features, and make necessary adjustments. Iterative processes allow developers to loop back and forth between tasks and phases to make changes, with the goal of producing a more effective and higher quality end product.

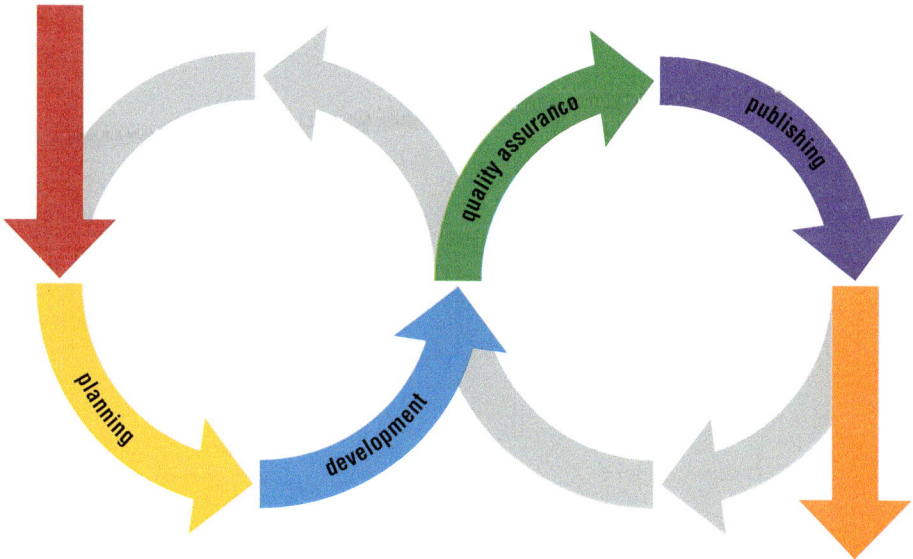

Figure 1.4. Iterative process cycle and repeat as needed.

Agile communication begins with knowledge of plan-driven design and acknowledges the need for forethought and planning when addressing an assignment. At the same time, agility allows communicators to respond to the complexities and change inherent in today's workplace. Communicators who are agile are able to assess situations as they change and adapt quickly and effectively. They target the incoming changes, employ their research and knowledge management skills to understand it and its effects, and then adjust and flex their communication skills to encompass or work with it. Whether you are preparing for a career as a technical communicator or as a professional in another field, you will find that understanding agile communication practices will help you succeed.

Chapter Summary

Technical communication is ubiquitous in today's 21st century workplace. Technical communicators use their knowledge and competencies with technology to create technical documents for a diverse range of industries, including information technology, engineering, medicine, science, public relations, manufacturing, design, and non-profit organizations. Information products they produce range from technical manuals to Web sites and proposals, and their job titles are equally vast, including content manager, information developer, information architect, technical communicator, visual designer, illustrator, and usability expert.

Twentieth century processes often followed a waterfall model, a predictive, sequential process. Twenty-first century processes are more agile (or adaptive) and iterative, in that these processes are designed to expect and respond quickly to change rather than be obstructed or delayed by it. While the same tasks are involved in producing technical documents, the overall process accommodates change more effectively.

Chapter Assignments

The exercises in this section ask you to apply what you have learned in this chapter as well as explore how this knowledge applies to and connects with other information in the textbook.

1. Think of a very familiar object that you know how to create or make. Design your own construction logic for product development using: (1) the waterfall development cycle and (2) the agile development cycle. Create a design for this process, and write a protocol or plan for each process.

2. Use your institution's library to locate and read a copy of one of the articles referenced in this chapter. (References for chapters are located at the end of the book.) Based on your reading, what are the three most important skills that a communicator should have to succeed today? How do these skills apply to the concept of agility described in this chapter?

3. Interview someone with a job similar to one you will seek after you graduate. Ask the person about the kinds of communications, such as reporting, presenting, and talking to others, required in the job. Does the person use specific technologies (mobile phones, email, or other hardware or software) to produce or deliver these communications? What were these technologies? How much time does the person spend on communication tasks each day or each week? How often does the person work with others to write (to get information, to get reviews or approval for the document)? Write a short 1–2 page memo that reports your findings.

Figure Credits

Figure 1.1. © Monkey Business Images/Shutterstock.com

Figure 1.2. "Ford factory, first moving assembly line, 1913, Highland Avenue, Detroit, MI." 1913. American Landscape and Architectural Design, 1850-1920, Frances Loeb Library, Graduate School of Design, Harvard University.

Figure 1.3. © dinsor/Shutterstock.com

Figure 1.4. © AlexAranda/Shutterstock.com

Managing Projects as an Iterative Process

2

CHAPTER OVERVIEW

This chapter provides an overview of iterative processes in creating technical communication products and documents, including tasks for each phase of the process. After reading this chapter, you should be able to meet the following objectives:

- Explain the iterative process of developing technical communication documents, including planning, development, quality assurance, and publication.
- Discuss the planning phase, including activity cycles, document ecologies, and creation processes for technical documents.
- Discuss the development phase, including the concepts of information modeling and single-sourcing in creating technical documents.
- Discuss the quality assurance phase, including continuing evaluation and assessment, or quality control, in developing technical documents.
- Describe the publishing phase, including technical, editorial, and managerial tasks associated with the final production and delivery of technical documents.

As you learned in Chapter 1, communication in today's workplace is often project-based. An important part of project planning is developing sustainable, mature processes that will help the team most effectively develop the communication product. Developing high maturity processes means following consistent standards and practices that result in the desired level of quality for the **end user,** the person who actually reads or uses the communication product.

The reality of many technical document projects is that the processes followed to complete a project are rarely accomplished in a linear progression without change. While smaller tasks may require following a linear set of instructions, the overall process for a project is ideally iterative. An **iterative** process cycles, rather than progresses linearly. Figure 2.1 illustrates how iterative processes cycle. While a project plan may outline tasks for a given project, it should allow enough agility and flexibility to revisit previous tasks and revise as needed. Iterative work processes typically involve continual assessment, or quality assurance, and revision of previous work as important components of the overall working process.

There are a number of causes and needs for iterative work processes in the 21st century workplace. Electronic publishing technologies have created the ability for most individuals and teams to produce documents more rapidly, make changes quickly, produce professional desktop publishing products, and upload new versions for online distribution.

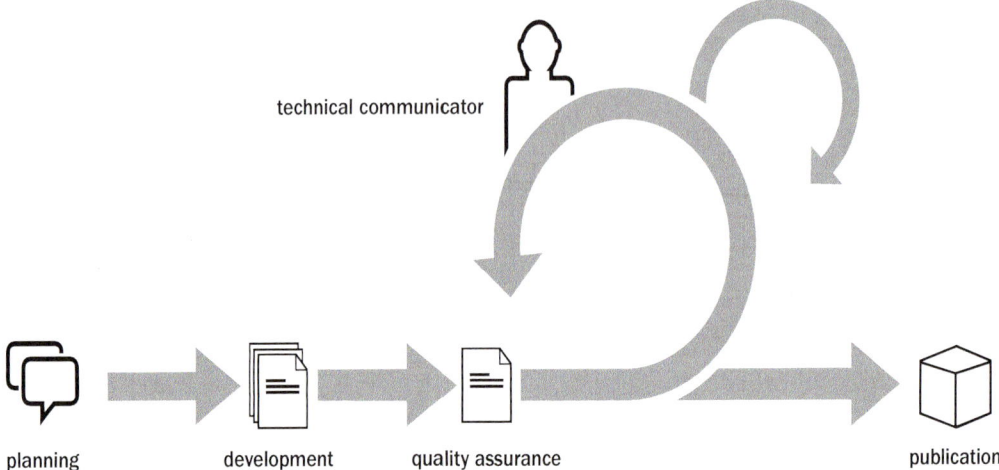

Figure 2.1. Technical communication processes are typically iterative, not linear.

The features of publishing software and tools used to collaborate, edit, design, and manage content have created authoring environments that encourage continual revision and updating. **Single-sourcing**, or **content reuse**, has become a cornerstone of online publication, where content is continually delivered based on the users' needs when they access it. (You will learn more about these kinds of content development in later chapters.) Higher levels of process maturity in organizations and workgroups support more agile approaches to working processes, including the ability to continually revise and update an information product's development and production cycles. And finally, the desire to work smarter and faster encourages teams to continually revise as they write and produce technical documentation.

While there are many advantages, there are also some challenges when working iteratively on a technical information product. Essentially, when a phase of the project ends, work may not be complete. For example, after a set of instructions is written, it may move on to a testing phase, which uncovers potential errors that must be fixed, requiring writers to edit and revise based on testing results. Iterative processes can potentially add more time on the development of documents, in revisiting and revising during development.

Figure 2.2. Iterative processes improve collaborations and encourage process maturity.

Another challenge of iterative processes is they require developers to consider the impacts of current tasks on previous ones; consequently, they must make appropriate changes before a document is complete. Additionally, iterative processes may rely on previous skills, work experience, and/or familiarity with organizational or discipline specific standards. As a result, new team members may require additional training or mentoring to adapt to rapid change and development.

Despite the associated challenges, there are also several advantages of incorporating an iterative approach to developing technical documents. First, work in one phase of the project can affect other phases. An iterative process allows communicators to address some of these changes during project development and production. Second, iterative processes mirror electronic publication characteristics. Third, while following a structured process provides stability for a project, the ability to revisit previous work and revise can save time in later development phases. Thus, iterative processes encourage flexibility and enhance collaboration practices. Fourth, iterative processes have the potential for reduced errors and higher quality in the finished product. Finally, iterative processes encourage process maturity by focusing on continual improvement and refinement of the information product.

ITERATIVE PROCESS AND PROJECT MANAGEMENT

Project management is as an iterative activity. For example, a team with the task of researching and developing a feasibility study, which looks at different approaches to addressing a problem or specific need, will have several tasks to manage simultaneously. They must research the problem, identify available solutions, interview subject matter experts, write progress reports, and eventually produce the feasibility report. The individual tasks to accomplish the goal are often overlapping and may require revisiting previous work along the project timeline. Since iterative processes require some back and forth activity, it is important to track **metrics**, such as resources, time, task completion, dependencies (or problem areas), and so forth, as part of project management. As a result, team members must track, document, and make records of ongoing work to ensure it is consistent with the project plan and overall content strategy for the project. **Content strategy** involves (1) analyzing users, content, information needs, process, and technologies, and (2) developing an organized, sustainable, and standardized process (Rockley & Cooper, 2012).

Process-mature and customer-focused products will consider user needs, expectations, and feedback throughout the management and development of a project. While the user preferences may not be the ultimate deciding factor in making choices for project content, tools, and platforms, they should be another source of information in making important decisions for products and their distinguishing characteristics and features. Integrating a user-centered approach will also help ensure savings of time, costs, errors, revisions, and customer frustration after delivery of the final product.

Document Ecologies and Activity Cycles

Document ecologies is a term used to describe content that gets recycled from one document to another. This term is comparable to the concept of **information ecologies**, information and documents that are closely related to one another (Nardi & O'Day, 1999). For example, a company profile might be used for marketing purposes but also for grant proposals. Another example would be the reuse of content from a goods and services proposal to progress reporting to the final report, where the content of sections is modified slightly for each document, but essentially much of the content of these documents contains similar information. These documents can be seen as related or existing within a similar information ecology and activity cycle. Figure 2.3 below illustrates how an activity cycle might work:

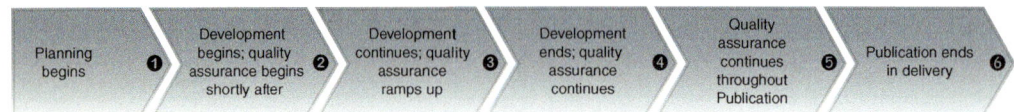

Figure 2.3. Document development flows through a typical activity cycle. This cycle may be iterative, doubling back when necessary to repeat steps along the way.

Depending on a variety of factors, work on a project often involves writing multiple document types as part of a process or cycle. For example, a team might first produce a series of research reports, then conduct and write an analytical (or feasibility) report that compares options discussed in the reports, and finally write a proposal that recommends the best choice. During the course of this document or activity cycle, the team might also write different documents such as memoranda, progress reports, usability assessments, and other types of shorter, supporting documents. Another example involves the process of developing a Web site, which might include writing and editing reports, marketing materials, technical descriptions of products and services and developing page layouts, stylesheets, forms, and usability assessments, in addition to the finished product. And again, during the course of this project, several shorter documents may support the project cycle. In these examples, you can see how text is first generated, modified as needed for other texts, and possibly cycled and recycled through various iterations, depending on the communication need at any given point in the project. At each point in the process, the team iteratively decides what is needed, determines how that information should be presented and designed, assures the quality of the content and design, and finally releases or publishes the version.

EXERCISE 2.1

Document Ecologies and Social Media

Identify a recent high-profile local, regional, or national news story, and locate how a new source uses and reuses information to push the information to its readers or viewers. For example, you might document the initial news notification sent to mobile devices, a detailed report on the media website, a video created on location, tweets, and Facebook posts. After you have gathered these examples, prepare to discuss how, in a project setting, this information might be developed iteratively as part of a larger publications process.

Tasks to be completed:

1. Identify a high-profile news story from a single news source.
2. Locate multiple examples of information released by this source to its readers or viewers. Copy or bookmark these examples for presentation.
3. Evaluate these examples to identify what information is contained in each one.
4. Respond to these questions:
    a. What information is constant?
    b. What information changes?
    c. What determines which information is constant and which changes?

TECHNICAL COMMUNICATION ITERATIVE PROCESS: THE FOUR PHASES

As the previous section discussed, technical communication documentation projects ideally incorporate project management practices, including a consistent content strategy, where work from one phase to the next follows an iterative process. This process includes four major phases, including planning, development, quality assurance, and publishing, across which various tasks and activities are completed (see Figure 2.4).

Figure 2.4. Technical communication products typically go through a four-phase process.

The **planning phase** involves developing goals, tasks, milestones, project scope, schedule, team roles, and resource allocation. The **development phase** includes the tasks of researching, organizing, writing, editing, designing, and producing content. The **quality assurance phase** involves testing, tracking, and reviewing drafts, prototypes, resources, tasks, goals, and other project metrics. Finally, the **publication phase** includes preparing documents and products for delivery, including the various technical and logistical tasks involved in completing a project. Each of these four phases will be discussed in the following sections.

Planning Phase

The planning phase is an essential first step in the iterative process of developing technical documentation. Effective teams always engage in good planning activities. These activities involve the creation process and often outline an overall content strategy, including types of documents to be created and organizational processes related to the project. The

> ### EXERCISE 2.2
>
> ### *Planning a Documentation Project*
>
> Your project team has been asked to propose a strategy for redesigning a corporate Web site's home page. As part of the project planning, you have been asked to identify and describe the roles of your individual team members who will perform this task. Additionally, you have been tasked to research background on the project, some of its competitors, and users.
>
> To help you determine what roles your team will need, you might browse *The Web Style Guide*'s article on site development teams (http://webstyleguide.com/wsg3/1-process/2-development-team.html).
>
> **Tasks to be completed:**
>
> 1. Select a corporate Web site to use for the task and familiarize yourself with it.
> 2. Identify a list of roles and skill sets required for redesigning the home page. Write a list of job titles including short descriptions of duties for each role.
> 3. Compile a list of potential research tasks and information resources for the project. Write a paragraph or two describing these tasks and resources, including how you will collect information on typical users and competing Web sites.

main planning document produced in this initial phase is the project plan, which serves as the roadmap for the project and its individual team members. The project plan will be discussed later in Chapter 4. During the planning phase, you can expect to complete the following tasks:

- Develop a project plan, including a discussion of project scope, goals, resources, tools, schedule, budget, team roles, milestones, and deliverables.
- Determine team roles and individuals working on a project.
- Conduct benchmarking research on past products, competing products, standards, best practices, and processes.
- Conduct user research and collect user data including analytics, feedback, focus group, error reports, user profiles, and use cases.
- Research tools and technologies to be used in the project development and delivery.

Documenting Planning Phase Activities

The main tasks involved in project planning includes defining the scope of the project, researching, and decision-making. These tasks involve writing descriptions of the information resources, tools, and types of users that will read or use your document. In addition to these descriptions, an effective way of completing planning tasks is to identify specific tasks to be completed and place them on a chronological chart. Each planning task might take the form of a shorter document or information graphic. For example, a project schedule might be an information graphic, such as a Gantt Chart, which you develop using a spreadsheet tool (see Figure 2.5).

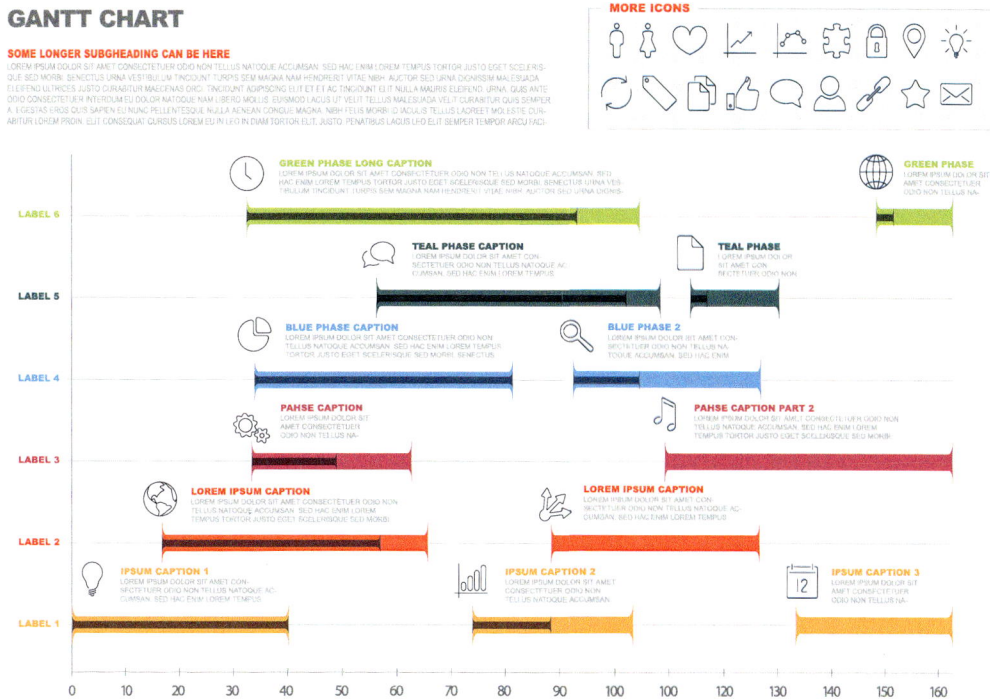

Figure 2.5. Gantt charts graphically map team tasks and individual team roles necessary to meet deadlines.

Research on software tools and technologies might be best summarized in a table, comparing features. User research might take the form of short descriptions, or use scenarios, that describe different groups of users and their preferences or uses of your document or product. As you complete each planning task, think of ways you can document or record your decisions and findings. Doing so will facilitate more effective communication among your team members and ensure they are well informed about various aspects of the project scope.

Development Phase

Whether you call it information development, content development, content management, information design, or information architecture, all of these tasks suggest a similar set of roles in producing technical documentation. The development phase involves the actual execution of the project or technical document, including its writing, design, and various drafts and milestones associated with creating and producing the product. The development phase typically includes the following tasks, each of which is introduced here but discussed in more detail in later chapters:

- Researching and writing content.
- Outlining content (information modeling, structuring content topics) and other relational aspects of content (metadata, tagging, cross-referencing, and hyperlinking).
- Developing drafts (and prototypes) of content, information graphics, navigation tools, forms.
- Considering user experience, instructional design, learning styles and related factors.
- Revising, editing, and single-sourcing content appropriate to the technology platform, delivery method, and user needs for information.

Two critical tasks that are part of the development phase involve information modeling and single-sourcing, which are briefly introduced below.

Outlining and Information Modeling

An important task in the development phase is to create information structures, models, maps, or outlines that best organize content for improved access, use, and readability. **Information models** can include site maps for Web sites, directory structures, help topic lists, table of contents, or other methods of outlining the organization of content. Information modeling considers the relationship between individual content topics within a document, and often these relationships are communicated through their placement in the overall structure or outline of the document. Equally important is your choice of terminology, titles, naming conventions, and items in the information model; you should choose terms, titles, naming conventions, and other items in the model that are familiar to both the type and purpose of the document and its user.

Figure 2.6 provides an information map for the Technical Communication Body of Knowledge (TCBOK) Project. It illustrates how the portal is designed with one main topic—the map—which is then divided into four subtopics (about, managing, producing, and researching). In turn, these subtopics are further subdivided into three to seven topics. Some of these seven topics are then divided into additional subtopics once or twice more. The model thus provide a visual design for the content of the document as well as the hierarchy of information within the document. In this way, the information model briefly summarizes hundreds of pages of content into a clear hierarchical structure than is easy to understand and follow during the next project process.

Single-sourcing and Content Reuse

One of the realities of publishing today is the need to reuse content in various configurations and forms, often based on factors such as product use, purpose, user, and search parameters. **Content reuse**, or **single-sourcing** of content, involves a range of strategies and methods. Ann Rockley (2001) proposes four levels of single-sourcing content, which range from cutting and pasting to dynamic content delivery. Table 2.1 provides a modified illustration of the four levels, discussing some of the methods and features of each level.

Content reuse should be a part of an overall effective content strategy, where the types and methods of reuse are planned according to project and user specifications. Content reuse is also essential to document cycles, where a project may involve reusing content from a technical paper, in other technical documents such as a feasibility study, proposal, and formal presentation. Some important guidelines to consider in effective content reuse include:

Chapter 2 Managing Projects as an Iterative Process

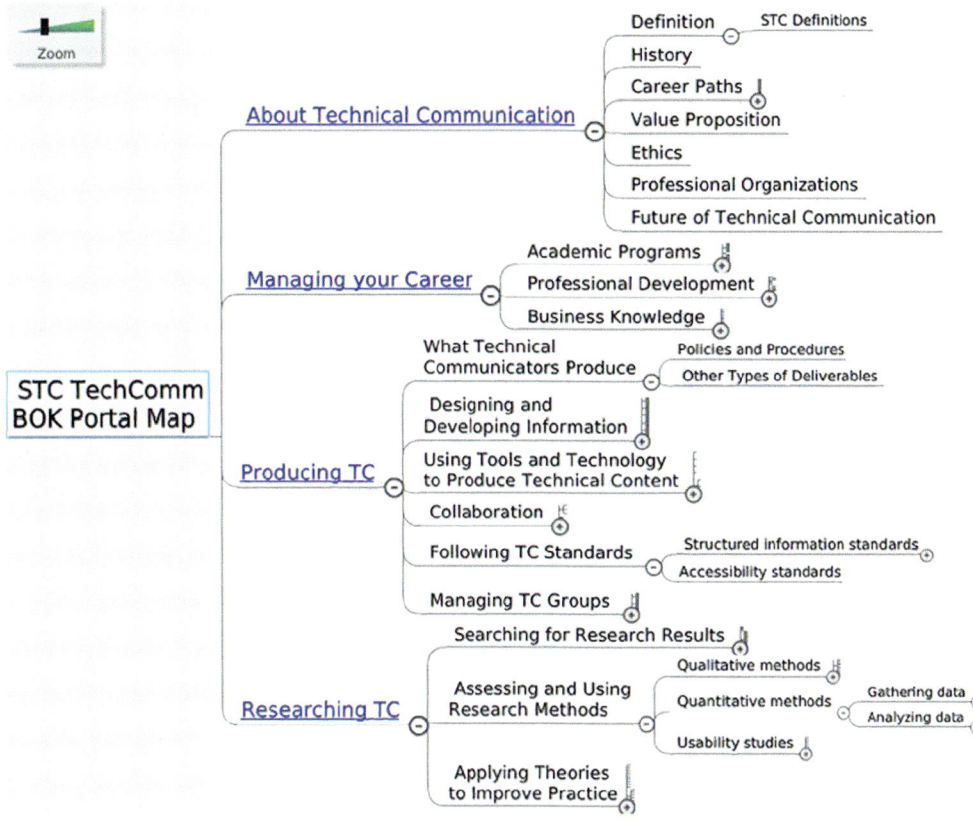

Figure 2.6. The Technical Communication Body of Knowledge (TCBOK) Wiki information model organizes content into four distinct sections.

Content reuse level	Method	Features
Level 1 Identical content	Cut and paste	Same content repurposed for a different use.
Level 2 Static content	Edited content	Edited content repurposed for multiple uses or media types.
Level 3 Dynamic content	Edited reusable content chunks	Edited content repurposed based on user searching and browsing.
Level 4 Customized content	Edited reusable content that anticipate user needs.	Edited content repurposed based on anticipated user needs.

Table 2.1. Content reuse levels and features

- Select the appropriate level of content reuse.
- Consider a user's need-to-know when reusing or repurposing information.
- Consider what information is necessary to accomplish the intended use of the product.
- Edit and rewrite reusable content for other iterations of technical documents.
- Reuse only what is necessary and only for a specified purpose.
- Select a tool or software program that will enable you to reuse content effectively.

> **EXERCISE 2.3**
>
> ## *Information Modeling*
>
> You have been hired as a consultant to revise and edit either the main navigation menu or site map for a university or college Web site. Part of this exercise involves looking for existing problems in the site's organization and identifying some of the expectations of typical users. Your goal is to find a way to improve the organization of content in the site, so the navigation tool and/or site map is easier to use by its intended audience.
>
> **Tasks to be completed:**
>
> 1. Select a Web site for a university or college and explore the main navigation menus, or, if available, site map.
> 2. Identify any potential problems in the current organization of information on the Web site by looking at the order and arrangement of pages in the site.
> 3. Make a list of potential users of the site and identify what information needs are most important to each group of site visitors.
> 4. Develop an improved information model for the navigation menu or site map, which considers the problems and potential users you identified.

An important consideration when reusing content is the issue of plagiarism and citation. Electronic content can be copyrighted and subject to intellectual property laws the same as any content in print, but in the workplace, you are often writing on behalf of your organization, which can have additional legal implications. As a rule of thumb, you should ensure that whatever content you are single-sourcing is appropriately cited and permissions for reuse are obtained to avoid any potential legal issue with regard to copyrighted material. Getting permission for reuse may involve some research to obtain points of contact and proper procedures for acquiring permissions for reuse.

Quality Assurance Phase

As work progresses in the development phase and drafts or prototypes are produced, the quality assurance tasks of reviewing and testing begin. Quality assurance is an important phase in the process of developing technical documents and products. This phase involves performing formal and informal reviews, establishing and tracking quality metrics, revising, editing, reflecting on processes through innovation and improvement, and documenting obstacles, solutions, and changes to the overall process. An effective work team considers quality assurance throughout the development cycle. Often, a significant portion of quality assurance occurs after the development phase commences. Typical tasks that are part of the quality assurance phase of a project include the following:

- Coordinating and managing formal reviews from subject matter experts, customers, and other formal entities.
- Testing formal prototypes of products in development.
- Developing heuristics, or specific criteria for evaluation and assessment purposes.

- Developing and tracking metrics for quality assurance activities, such as progress reporting.
- Recommending adjustments to scope, tasks, team contributors, milestones, etc., based on metrics results.
- Collecting feedback from team members and users.
- Maintaining a list of lessons learned and best practices.

Reviewing, Testing, and Editing

Metrics are criteria used to track various aspects of the project, including resources, tasks, and quality, in an attempt to monitor overall progress on a project. Metrics are used in many project management document types, such as the project plan, progress reports, and presentations. Metrics should be defined in terms of what they are attempting to measure, how it will be measured, and what values or quantities will be used. As a result, they are often presented using information graphics and short narrative descriptions. While most metrics can be tracked and assessed by the project manager, reviews require additional support. Metrics can also be used to test or evaluate drafts or prototype documents. Editorial reviews are one way of tracking progress on a project, in terms of the levels of accuracy, completeness, revisions, and errors of a particular document. Reviews often rely on the expertise of others, such as subject matter experts, consultants, users, or specialists to determine these factors. Regardless of the type of metrics or reviews you decide to conduct as part of your quality assurance activities, it is important to define, document, track, and report your findings throughout the project development process. Later chapters discuss methods of reviewing, testing, and editing documents prior to their publication.

Publishing Phase

Publishing technical documents is a much more complex process, due largely to technical software tools and electronic publishing demands. Some of these include the use of content management systems, structured authoring methods, online publishing platforms, distributed work teams, and increasingly rapid distribution cycles for technical documents. The ultimate goal of this final phase is preparing documents for release and customer distribution.

Typical tasks during the publishing phase include the following:

- Perform activities on final punch list or production checklist prior to delivery to ensure content accuracy, comprehensiveness, and usefulness.
- Publish or upload content and product deliverables to electronic publication platforms.
- Conduct final technical usability tests of products to eliminate any potential minor errors related to accessibility, usability, and readability for the final product.
- Distribute product.
- Advertise publication of product.
- Collect initial user feedback and error reports.

> **EXERCISE 2.4**
>
> ## *Identifying Quality Assurance Activities*
>
> You have been identified as the quality assurance manager on a project to develop a presentation to students and professionals on successful project planning strategies. Part of this role is managing the review process. Towards that goal, you have been tasked with organizing three different reviews for the presentation (a content review, a technical review, and a copyediting review), and developing the list of questions each reviewer will use to assess the presentation's slides and script.
>
> **Tasks to be completed:**
>
> 1. Determine what content should be included in the presentation and develop an outline, using this chapter as a resource.
> 2. Determine what software, tools, or technologies are required for the presentation.
> 3. Develop a set of review questions related to the presentation's content, for the content review expert.
> 4. Develop a set of review questions related to the technical aspects of the presentation, for the technical review expert.
> 5. Develop a set of review questions related to general editing, style, and use of language, for the copyediting review expert.

Regardless of the actual published form of your information product—print or electronic—genre expectations will determine its organization, content, and design. When publishing technical documents in online or electronic forms, additional related concepts such as information modeling, content reuse, user experience, and information design become important considerations in the overall the writing and publishing process.

Figure 2.7. Technical roles typically have increasing responsibility during the publishing phase.

Technology Issues

Because of the wide range of electronic publication tools, software, platforms, and writing and publication methods available, technology challenges have a significant impact on the publishing phase of technical documentation products. Accessibility, usability, and readability are all concerns during the publishing phase. These areas involve specific variables such as browser compatibility, file formats, readability, uploading, and conversion issues. An important part of the publication process may be to develop a checklist of these potential issues to ensure successful product delivery and to minimize troubleshooting problems and error

> ### EXERCISE 2.5
> ### *Production and Publication*
>
> A significant part of the production and publication process involves coordinating technological aspects of a project, including delivery. You have been tasked with researching and writing the section on final production and publication for a project plan on creating a Web site for a new company. This section should briefly (2–3 paragraphs) identify specific final production tasks (such as a checklist) and technical details required to publish the site online for the customer.
>
> **Tasks to be completed:**
>
> 1. Consult with your other team members and/or conduct research to determine what kinds of final production tasks and technical information is required to prepare a new Web site for publication, including uploading it for access on the Internet.
> 2. Develop a checklist of 8–10 specific final production tasks for the project.
> 3. Develop a list of technical issues and information required to prepare and upload the new Web site.
> 4. Write the short section for the project plan and include your production checklist as part of your submission.

reports. Often, this phase places additional responsibility on the technical role, such as a systems administrator or programmer, to oversee these tasks. Some of the issues to consider when developing a publishing checklist may include the following checklist items:

Accessibility

- Ensure server protocols and folders are properly set to facilitate uploading and updating of content by the development team.
- Validate user access credentials, such as login and password information.
- Provide alternate file formats or download links for viewers or plug-ins.
- Ensure compliance with appropriate laws and regulations for users with disabilities.

Usability

- Test the functionality of search tools, menus, links, and forms.
- Ensure correctness and accuracy of information provided to help users complete tasks and information searches.
- Collect and incorporate user feedback from tests into the revision process.

Readability

- Ensure content renders correctly in different Web browsers and screen settings.
- Verify and test that stylesheets and templates display properly in Web browsers.
- Conduct final copyediting checks of content.

Post-Publication

After publishing, effective organizations continue to collect feedback and data from users, use statistics (such as analytics), team members, and technical support staff. Another activity that may follow publishing is the post-project review meeting, and/or report. This activity typically involves the entire team compiling data, including metrics (hours spent, costs, etc.) and suggestions (formal and informal) that would comprise lessons learned and best practices. Compiling this information benefits future iterations of projects or may simply be generalizable enough to help team members improve performance and process in future projects. Post-publication activities also suggest another example of the iterative development process, where quality control evaluation and assessment continues, in perhaps different iterations, after the publication of information products.

Chapter Summary

Technical communication documentation development processes are iterative, involving planning, development, quality assurance, and publishing activities, where work in each phase necessitates continual revision and updating in the production of successful information products. Planning involves developing goals, tasks, milestones, project scope, schedule, team roles, and resource allocation. Development includes researching, organizing, writing, editing, designing, and producing content. Quality assurance involves testing, tracking, and reviewing drafts, prototypes, resources, tasks, goals, and other project metrics. Publication includes preparing documents and products for delivery. The advantages of iterative processes include reduced errors, improved project quality, enhanced collaboration, and process flexibility. The information provided about each phase and associated activities and tasks within this chapter applies to and will be covered in detail in later chapters.

Chapter Assignments

The exercises in this section ask you to apply what you have learned in this chapter as well as explore how this knowledge applies to and connects with other information in the textbook.

1. In technical documentation projects, what are some examples of how work on one task may affect previously completed work tasks? For example, how might work on a website affect a proposal or a Web site affect a presentation? For each example, identify a list of changes that would be required. How do these scenarios differ from one genre, or type of document, to another?

2. Discuss larger projects you have worked on in a group setting. Make a list of the document genres, or types, the project team developed as part of an activity cycle. Categorize the documents into one of three types: decision-making, technical information, and general correspondence. Draw a visual diagram to represent the cycle and its various categories. Present and discuss your diagram with your peers.

3. After completing the chapter exercises, combine your results into a single document as part of the first draft of a project plan. Read through the draft report and identify any sections that are missing or that should be included. Share your results with others for ideas of any sections or ideas you may have missed or would include.

4. Accessibility for users with disabilities is an important consideration of many online technical documents, such as Web sites, help systems, and other online media. As part of the publication phase, checking technical information products for compliance with accessibility laws and guidelines may be an important part of many projects. Research the following two accessibility standards sites: U.S. Government Section 508 Accessibility Guidelines and the W3C Web Content Accessibility Guidelines. Familiarize yourself with the guidelines and briefly summarize the major issues or concerns you would need to address if you were working on a Web site or other online media project.

Figure Credits

Figure 2.1. © Bakhtiar Zein/Shutterstock.com

Figure 2.2. © Rawpixel/Shutterstock.com

Figure 2.3. © John T Takai/Shutterstock.com

Figure 2.4. © Janos Timea/Shutterstock.com

Figure 2.5. © Petr Vaclavek/Shutterstock.com

Figure 2.6. http://www.tcbok.org/

Figure 2.7. © Pressmaster/Shutterstock.com

Planning Your Communication Product 3

CHAPTER OVERVIEW

This chapter introduces three key tasks you should complete when planning technical communication documents. After reading this chapter, you should be able to meet the following objectives:

- Conduct an audience analysis by creating user profiles and use scenarios.
- Manage and scope a project by completing a task analysis, including stating your objectives; detailing, organizing, and assigning tasks; and establishing project milestones.
- Take stock of needed resources for a project by allocating resources and creating a schedule and budget.
- Understand how planning tasks define your project, contribute to the development of a variety of planning documents, and develop your process maturity and sustainable practices.

If you took a basic composition course in high school or college, you may recall planning your documents by analyzing the audience for your essay, brainstorming ideas, creating mind maps and outlines, and then drafting and revising the essay. While these strategies are effective for writing individual academic essays, they are not able to describe and respond to the more complex communication documents you will complete in the workplace. This chapter provides you with specific strategies and practices for developing preliminary writing plans for a variety of workplace communication situations. It focuses on the planning stage in iterative design that you read about in Chapter 2.

The content of this chapter is based on several underlying assumptions. In the workplace, you will typically be completing multiple projects at the same time. Because you will be working on multiple projects, you will have competing demands on your time and resources. These competing demands will require effective time and resource management. As you complete these projects, you will learn from them, and your project management processes will mature. As they mature, you will increase your knowledge and identify metrics (or performance standards) that will improve the ways you scope and manage future projects.

Finally, this chapter is, at its most basic level, plan-driven. The steps in this chapter are designed to result in a document or project plan. You can develop the plan sequentially, from beginning to end, by working through the chapter:

- **Defining your task's audience** helps you to articulate and describe a complex of users who will engage with your task deliverable.
- **Analyzing your task** shows you how to state task objectives, establish your task requirements, analyze the key steps necessary to complete the task, sequence and evaluate these steps, and establish milestones.
- **Taking stock of resources** shows you how to estimate, allocate, and report the time, effort, and materials your project will require.

Having a preliminary plan for every communication deliverable you complete is useful for mapping progress. Your knowledge of project requirements and audience will determine how detailed the plan will need to be.

No matter the detail of the plan, you should consider any plan you make malleable and responsive to changes that occur as your project develops. As you become more comfortable with these stages in the planning process, you will find that these steps are not necessarily sequential but iterative. Rather than planning to work through the advice in this chapter in rote order, once for each project, you will probably cycle through planning and management phases several times as your work progresses. Your response to these changes and your ability to modify your plan accordingly are indicative of your increasing skills as an agile technical communicator.

DEFINING YOUR AUDIENCE

If a communication document is a response to specific needs or problems, then it follows that someone (an individual or individuals) must see, hear, or read that deliverable in order for change or action to occur. By definition, that "someone," "individual," or "individuals," are the **audience** with whom you are communicating. A communication theory, developed by Claude Shannon in the 1940s and based on telephone transmission, described the communicator as the *sender* of the message and the audience as the *receiver* of the message. Although the transmission theory works at the most basic levels of communication, both the "sender" and "receiver" terms lack the complexity to describe the audiences you may be addressing in the workplace. To begin to understand this complexity, consider the different ways an audience might access your communication product, as a *reader*, a *listener*, or *viewer*. For example, readers might read an instruction manual to complete a task, listeners might hear the instructions delivered in a podcast, and viewers might watch the same information described in a video. These generic identifiers can help you to choose the media to deliver your message:

- A **reader** is most often associated with a document constructed primarily of written words;
- A **listener**, with a speech or presentation of spoken words; and
- A **viewer**, with a document that is primarily graphic or image-based; and
- A **user** may be any or all of these identifiers.

These terms, however, become harder to apply if your communication is electronically delivered. For example, what would you call the audience of a multimedia product like a scientific documentary or the audience of a web-based instructional video? And think how you would need to adapt any of these documents if your audience included a person with a disability, such as a visual impairment or deafness. If the person with a visual impairment listens to the text, is that person a reader or a listener? And why does it matter? To deliver communication messages in these formats, you need to think not only about the images and texts but also about *how* words are displayed and sounds are played. Most importantly, you need to consider how the technologies your audience uses to access your deliverable support or hinder their abilities to use your document. As a final note, be aware that the people this textbook refers to as "audiences" can be identified with many other terms, depending on the writer's purpose. Audiences are also known "users," "consumers," and "clients," to name a few.

Figure 3.1. Audiences for technical documents may access your content through a variety of formats.

Writing Content for Different Audiences

As a college student, you probably have considerable experience modifying the same message for different audiences. For example, the messages and photos you text a friend during a Saturday afternoon football game probably vary greatly from the details you give your parents about the game in a phone conversation on Sunday afternoon. While both conversations are delivered from your mobile phone and report experiences of the same event, you are adept at deciding, in the moment, which details are appropriate for one audience but not for the other, and you understand how texting and telephoning constrain the information you can provide in these situations.

However, you may experience problems when adjusting your communication from your personal conversations to the classroom or to the workplace. In the classroom, most of your communications (written, oral, and visual) are intended for your instructor or your classmates. Even tasks that ask you to imagine another audience (such as an employer for a résumé) lack authenticity if you do not send the résumé to an actual employer. In reality, most essays and reports you write in college are written for classroom instructors who evaluate your knowledge rather than to an external audience who would take actions based on your writing.

Workplace communications strongly contrast with this college classroom model. Workplace communications have definite, identifiable audiences. In fact, they are often a complex of audiences ranging from your coworkers to your immediate supervisor to legal counsel. Complicating this issue is the fact that audiences change over time. Identifying these audiences, discovering how best to provide them with the information they need, and determining how to deliver information to them effectively are just a few of the challenges you must consider.

The following three examples depict different workplace communication documents and their complex audiences. The first, the speeding citation, illustrates the multiplicity of audiences a documents can have; the second, job search materials, how content can be modified for different audiences; and the third, marketing materials, how the same content can be expanded and abridged for different deliverable purposes.

The Speeding Citation

To illustrate the multiplicity of audiences a deliverable can have, consider a document that, unfortunately, many automobile drivers see at some point—the speeding citation. The purpose of the speeding citation, the deliverable in this case, is a violation of the speed limit. An officer uses a form to create the citation. After questioning the driver and checking the driver's license and sometimes other information, the officer completes the form, describing the current violation, and gives it to the driver.

So far, the deliverable—the citation—is apparently a communication solely between the officer and the driver, but that is a simplistic view of the citation's audience. At the roadside scene, drivers passing the two receive a clear message from the situation: slow down or you will be ticketed. After the roadside scene, audiences who review or read the citation become even more complex. The officer files the citation in the precinct where it is electronically recorded in a city or county database. The recorded information is then available to clerks who may read it when the driver pays the fine, or, if the driver does not pay on time, the information is available to other officers who may encounter this individual at a later date. The driver's copy may also have a life of its own, potentially being read, discussed, and acted upon by family members, lawyers, and even insurers.

Figure 3.2. Even speeding citations have multiple audiences.

Later, as part of an aggregated weekly or monthly report, the citation may be compiled along with all other traffic citations the department has issued. Readers of that report could be even more widely disseminated, including individuals in local and government offices or newspapers as well as researchers who study traffic patterns, accidents, and violations. In fact, some metropolitan police departments have frequently updated, interactive Web sites that inform drivers where citations are most commonly given; that is, they provide information that collects and counts traffic citation and accident locations. This information is then reported electronically to drivers so they can be especially careful in these higher risk areas. Each of these readers—from the driver of the car to the driver who checks the traffic Web site—will view and respond to information from the citation in different ways.

As you can see, the citation's audience is much broader than you might expect. While this speeding citation illustration describes a document that has personal, legal, civic, and even research implications, it is not an unusual example of workplace documents that have multiple audiences, some of whom you, as the writer, cannot personally know.

Job Search Materials

In some workplace communications, you will find a different issue when documents have common information, but they are shaped differently to meet audience expectations. You may encounter this situation when you prepare professional job search materials for the first time. The purpose behind these materials is simple enough: you need to find a permanent job that allows you to use your skills and abilities. Among the documents you prepare to address this purpose are résumés, cover letters, and interview answers. Résumés and cover letters are typically designed as printed materials, although you might deliver them to employers in either print or electronic formats. If you use employment-networking sites, you may even input résumé content into an electronic database. Interview answers are delivered verbally and most often in person, although telephone and videoconference interviews are becoming more commonplace. Each of these documents—whatever the format or delivery method—has a significant action or response they seek to elicit: to persuade the employer to hire you. Each of these documents also contains similar information about your education and work experiences, but this information must be packaged, extended, or abridged to meet the audience's expectations:

Figure 3.3. Job search materials are highly persuasive: they persuade the employer to hire you.

- Your résumé will summarize your education and job experiences in a quickly readable and scannable page layout.
- Your cover letter will contextualize your education and work experiences into a narrative that illustrates how these experiences have prepared you for the job.
- If your résumé and cover letter earn you an interview, your interview answers will need to be focused and directed to respond to specific questions the employer asks. Some of these answers may require you to elaborate on past experiences while other answers may ask you to project or predict how you would respond in a new situation.

All of these documents, whether spoken or written, must be tailored to persuade and demonstrate that you are a good fit for the position the employer is filling. To complicate this picture, you should also consider that you will probably be applying for multiple jobs when you graduate, so each of these documents—résumés, cover letters, and interview answers—must be modified slightly for each position to which you are applying. You will reuse most of the information in these documents when you apply for different jobs, but some of the information will need to be reworked to meet the expectations of each individual employer. Résumés, cover letters and other job search materials are discussed in detail in a later chapter.

Marketing Documents

Like individuals who must market themselves through résumés and cover letters to different employers, organizations have to develop comparable marketing information that they can reuse not only for similar purposes but also for different audiences. For example, a description of the services a non-profit organization provides might be summarized in a sentence or two in a letter asking for donations or expanded to 10 to 20 pages for its annual report. On the non-profit's *About Us* page on their Web site, one might find the description's length might be somewhere in between these lengths. Why the differences? In this case, the description's length changes because of audience expectations—the letter's reader who may or may not know about the non-profit will want to know immediately who is writing and why. The annual report's readers will understand that these texts are detailed and expansive in their descriptions while the Web site's text will be shorter to promote quick on-screen reading.

As you can see from these three extended examples, audiences can be complicated and hard identify. You will always know at least one person with whom you are communicating, but you may be unable to identify everyone who will eventually engage with the documents you produce. Even audiences you expect to engage with your texts can change. Nevertheless, you should take some time to consider who will use the communication documents, and, equally as important, why and how each of these audiences will use them.

Analyzing Your Audience

Audience analysis is a method for gathering information about your audience's knowledge, preferences, and intentions. **User profiles**, descriptions of typical users, and **use scenarios**, descriptions of actual working contexts of use, are two approaches that technical communicators take to conduct these analyses, to better understand their users' needs and expectations, and to shape their documents to meet audience needs. The word "use" in both of these approaches refers to a variety of communication activities, such as reading, viewing, or listening to a deliverable. User profiles and use scenarios can be completed independently or together, depending on the time and detail of information you need to understand the audience with whom you are communicating. When they are used together, the combined audience analysis is called a **persona**.

Figure 3.4. A user profile is a audience research tool that allows you to gather information about your audience.

User Profiles

User profiles are a planning strategy that prompts you to research individuals who belong to your audience. A user profile is an audience research tool that allows you to gather key information about your audience, whether your audience is someone you know or someone you do not know but anticipate may use the deliverable. User profiles can be abbreviated or extensive. For example, some user profiles may contain only two kinds of information: the user's expertise and subject domain knowledge (Hughes and Hayhoe, 2009). You might only need to identify how much knowledge and expertise the user has in the content (subject domain) of your deliverable. More extensive profiles would include more in-depth information:

- **Personal attributes**, such as age, gender, education, reading level, cultural expectations.
- **Attitudes and preferences**, such as attitudes and preferences about your subject matter, technology in general, or delivery methods.

- **Employment information**, such as position, years of experience, kinds of experience, knowledge of subject matter if related to work.
- **Knowledge and expertise**, such as knowledge as related to deliverable subject, method of gaining this knowledge, other kinds of expertise beyond workplace experience.
- **Deliverable expectations**, such as content, design layout and format, location of use, costs.

In some cases, you may gather this information through direct contact with your audience members. For example, if your deliverable is a report to your supervisors, then you will have the opportunity to question and observe the audience directly to develop the user profile. In other cases, you will have to conduct research, such as interviews and focus groups, to flesh out the details of the user profile. You may develop individual user profiles for known audience members, and, if the audience is not yet known, you can develop profiles that stand-in for potential audiences.

EXERCISE 3.1

Evaluating a User Profile

Visit the Society for Technical Communication Body of Knowledge (TCBOK) Portal at http://stcbok.editme.com/AboutUs and review the personas that were created to inform the TCBOK project. Choose one to evaluate using the characteristics described in the previous section. How well does the persona describe the user and use scenario?

Tasks to be completed:

1. Choose one of the personas found on the STC TCBOK Portal.
2. Read the persona carefully and identify any of the following information include in the person: personal attributes, attitudes and preferences, employment information, knowledge, and deliverable information.
3. After identifying content, evaluate how well the persona describes a potential TCBOK user.
4. Prepare to report your findings to your peers.

Use Scenarios

A second approach to audience analysis is use scenarios, which take user profiles one step further, requiring you to develop narratives or stories about how each user (audience member) will engage with the deliverable. Each use scenario is a little story, often a paragraph or two. Since users may engage in more than one way with a deliverable, you may have multiple user scenarios for a single audience. These scenarios provide you with a way to predict the user's expectations, motivations, actions, behaviors, and desires, related to the deliverable. To create a use scenario, recall what you know about your user profile, consider how the user will use the deliverable you are creating, and create a narrative describing that scene. As noted in the previous exercise, a good example of user profiles and use scenarios is found in the Technical Communication Body of Knowledge (TCBOK). One of the personas, Jennifer Bennett, is described as a technical communication student. Her persona description includes the following details about how she might use the TCBOK to get specific information. These informational needs are listed below:

- Wants to attend graduate school in technical communication.
- Seeks to help volunteer organization find funding for literacy projects.
- Interested in learning more about the achievement gap and how it pertains to technical communication

(TCBOK. http://stcbok.editme.com/Jennifer-Bennett-Technical-Communication-Student).

With multiple user profiles and use scenarios, in hand, you are then able to better shape your deliverable to meet each of the user's or users' needs. These profiles and scenarios also help you to evaluate the effectiveness of your final deliverable: does it work with the scenarios you imagined? If not, how might it be revised to do so? Use profiles and scenarios also come into play when conducting research, as discussed in detail in a later chapter.

EXERCISE 3.2

Use Scenarios and the TCBOK

Revisit the Technical Communication Body of Knowledge (TCBOK) Portal at http://stcbok.editme.com/Personas-and-the-STC-TCBOK and review other personas described there. What uses are listed for other personas visiting the TCBOK? Do you think all the users or user types that will visit the TCBOK are listed there? If not, what other personas are needed and for what uses might they visit the TCBOK? Create a persona for an additional TCBOK user.

Tasks to be completed:

1. Return to the TCBOK and review the persona use scenarios there.
2. List the uses that described in the use scenarios.
3. Evaluate the personas' profiles and use scenarios, and answer these questions:
    a. Do you think all the users or user types that will visit the TCBOK are listed there?
    b. If not, what other personas are needed?
    c. For what uses might these additional personas visit the TCBOK?
4. Write a brief persona to be added to the TCBOK.

Responding to Cultural Differences

A final but critical audience consideration is cultural difference. The users of technical documentation vary widely, and the products they use are manufactured and distributed across nations and continents. Even within organizations—from small businesses to global conglomerates—cultural differences come into play. For these reasons, agile communicators must think seriously about breakdowns that can occur when differences arise.

Cultural difference can affect the way users interpret and read text. For example, readers in Western countries read from left to right while readers from some Middle East and Eastern countries, such as readers of Japanese, Hebrew, and Arabic, read from right to left. This difference can affect page design and layout. As another example, cultural interpretation of images also varies. Nancy Hoft (1995) identifies four categories of images that can be problematic across cultures: images of people, animals, everyday objects, and religious symbols. She notes that "some may be offensive, others sacred or simply inappropriate for the context, while others may not mean what you think they mean in a target country" (264).

While cultural differences can make creating documents for varied audiences quite challenging, effective cross-cultural communication is possible and desirable. Your audience analysis should include research about the cultures represented in your audience as well as conversations with individuals who are members of the cultures different from yours. Identifying and discussing cultural differences with individuals in different cultures will give you first-hand insights and help you to prevent stereotyping. Discovering potential cultural differences prior to developing your technical document is the best path to understanding your audience's context and responding to it effectively.

EXERCISE 3.3
Researching Cultural Differences

Visit at least two of the following international culture websites, and research the culture of a country where you would like to visit or work. After reading about the culture of the country you have chosen, write a brief summary to share with your peers.

Intercultural Learning websites:

1. Country Insights, the Centre for Intercultural Learning: http://goo.gl/LcnS5N
2. Geert Hofstede's Countries: http://geert-hofstede.com/countries.html
3. BBC's Country Profiles: http://news.bbc.co.uk/2/hi/country_profiles/default.stm
4. CIA World Fact Book: https://www.cia.gov/library/publications/the-world-factbook/index.html
5. Another website of your choice

Tasks to be completed:

1. Choose a country to research.
2. Read about that country's culture at two different country profile pages.
3. Write a summary of key aspects of that country's culture.

MANAGING AND SCOPING THE PROJECT

Equally important to understanding and analyzing your audience is scoping the project you are about to undertake. The **scope** describes all the specifications and requirements for a project, including an analysis of the tasks you have been given and decisions on how and when to complete them. This section explains how to manage your project and scope it.

Managing Technical Communication Projects

Managing projects involves documenting and monitoring all the tasks that a team performs in developing and producing technical documents and products. Successful project management strategies include tracking and coordinating tasks and resources for an information project through its planning, development, production, and post-production phases. One important project management responsibility is to track metrics, or define, measurable quantities related to the project. Tracking **metrics** includes measuring and recording quantities of resources used, time spent, tasks completed, problems encountered, and solutions discovered. Project management is an ongoing function throughout the development of a project and ultimately impacts its success. Project management activities can be applied whether you are working on a project as an individual or as part of a larger team. Successful project managers typically have prior project experience, technical expertise in multiple areas, and good oral and written communication skills. As such, project managers have a wide range of responsibilities, including (but not limited to) communicating, ensuring quality assurance, planning, managing resources, and managing technical oversight (see Table 3.1).

Responsibilities	Tasks
Communicating	Conduct meetings. Write team memoranda and emails. Coordinate and write reports.
Quality assurance	Assess and track project metrics. Coordinate and conduct reviews. Report progress. Track dependencies.
Planning	Develop and update project plan. Schedule tasks. Set goals and milestones. Define scope of deliverables.
Managing resources	Track costs, hours, and labor. Coordinate with Subject Matter Experts (SMEs). Assign tasks and roles. Manage conflicts.
Technical oversight	Serve as a backup for team members. Provide technical supervision.

Table 3.1. Project management responsibilities and tasks.

SCOPING THE PROJECT WITH TASK ANALYSIS

Task analysis is a planning process you can use to describe, prepare for, and manage work to be completed. In this textbook, we use the term **task** to describe work-related assignments. Developed originally in manufacturing sectors, task analysis is commonly used today in design, engineering, education, training, and communication professions. Simply put, **task analysis** is a method used to state the goals of your task and to describe the steps (either physical or mental) that need to be completed to produce the promised deliverable.

You have worked with tasks if you have ever successfully followed a recipe, read instructions to assemble a bicycle or piece of furniture, scanned an annual report, followed the steps to install software, or used embedded help instructions to set up a media device on your television or computer. All of these documents—the recipe, the instructions, the report, and the embedded help—were designed for a purpose to complete a specific task. Some help you complete a task by walking you through a series of subtasks necessary for success; others, like reports, help you to make decisions.

EXERCISE 3.4
Task Analysis across Disciplines

To understand how widely task analyses are used across disciplines, take a few minutes to read about their uses on these Web sites:

- In usability research: Usability.gov's "Task Analysis," http://www.usability.gov/how-to-and-tools/methods/task-analysis.html
- In education: Virginia Department of Education's Training and Technical Assistance Center's "Task Analysis: Teaching Multistep Skills Made Easy," http://www.ttacnews.vcu.edu/2012/08/task-analysis-teaching-multistep-skills-made-easy/
- In human resources/management: Energy.gov's "NREL Job Task Analysis: Energy Auditor," http://energy.gov/sites/prod/files/2014/01/f7/51672.pdf

Tasks to be completed:

1. Visit Web sites listed above.
2. Read about task analysis in various disciplines.
3. Take notes and prepare to discuss task analysis as a process.

Although task analysis is most often employed to create communications that assist users in completing tasks, you can use this process to guide any work task—from tasks as simple as planning your day to those as complex as planning an extended research and development process. In communication design and planning, task analysis typically includes the following activities:

- Stating and confirming the purpose of the task.
- Defining the task requirements and documents.
- Stating the task objectives.
- Identifying the components (or steps) that must be completed to reach the desired outcome or objective.
- Sequencing the steps for accuracy, economy, and efficiency.
- Setting timelines or benchmarks for step and task completion.
- Evaluating the analysis for accuracy and completeness of the steps and their descriptions.
- Documenting lessons learned from the completed process to establish metrics and milestones for later projects.

After completing the task analysis, you will have a solid understanding of the project. You will know what the task is asking you to accomplish, what steps are necessary to accomplish the task, and in what order you will mostly likely complete these steps. Combined with other planning analyses, your task analysis will allow you to create a document or project plan that will guide you as you work. Such plans are particularly important if you find that you have multiple or overlapping work projects and teams. Tracking your progress with a detailed document or project plan will help you to stay on track with each project and adjust, as necessary, as steps and entire projects are completed. A task analysis will also assist you in determining what metrics, or measurable criteria, are important to track for the project as a whole.

As you have learned in Chapters 1 and 2, while your plan is intended to guide your project from start to finish, you should not consider it unalterable from your project's beginning to its end: technical communicators cycle through the project processes multiple times, refining their work as they learn more. Like all planning processes, task analysis and plans that derive from it are rarely exact. As you complete the steps in your task, you may discover that you missed steps along the way or inaccurately estimated the time or effort needed to complete them. Additionally, workplace situations, such as staff reductions or additions, variable resource availability, and foreshortened or extended deadlines, may also require you to modify your original plan. Even with changes, however, a solid task analysis allows you to manage your time, achieve goals, and complete projects with a set time and allocated resources.

What is Your Deliverable's Purpose?

To begin the process of task analysis, your first consideration is your deliverable's **purpose**. As noted earlier in this chapter, communication documents arise from needs or problems that require a response. Communication documents have purposes that drive them, such as informing a decision, recommending an action, or promoting a change. These documents that fulfill the task purpose can vary greatly in length and format. Sometimes the deliverable will be spoken words, as in a short informal oral report; at other times, written or visual texts are necessary to fulfill the task's purpose, such as emails, technical illustrations, or proposals.

The need or problem that creates a purpose for communication can be indirect and seem relatively unimportant, such as a sound that notifies you of an email's arrival or simply a difference of opinion between two people expressed in a water cooler conversation. Other needs or problems are more direct, urgent, and explicit calls for action, such as a discovery that makes a medical or scientific breakthrough or a mechanical or technological failure that requires immediate investigation and reporting. The time and technologies necessary to respond can be equally as varied: you might reply verbally to a question, write a quick email or instant message, compose an extended report, produce an instructional video, or design a Web site. Some of these activities take less than a minute while others can require years to complete.

As a technical communicator, then, when you receive a task, your first duty is to understand its purpose, the problem or need that drives the deliverable. If you do not understand the purpose, then you cannot address it. Consequently, your project is likely to fail before it ever gets started. To document the purpose, verbally state the reason for the task, either aloud to yourself or to a co-worker, or write it down on a notepad or in an electronic file to which you can refer.

What are the Requirements, Specifications, and Constraints that Situate the Task?

After you have a clear understanding of your task's purpose, then you are ready to define the task requirements and documents:

- Is a specific deliverable required (an email response, a proposal, or a report)? Check the wording of the task to see if you have an identified deliverable.
- Is the content or design of the deliverable specified? Some tasks clearly delineate the organization, format, and design of the documents. Make special note of these requirements and specifications: how long should the deliverable be? Is there font size or line-spacing requirement? Must the deliverable be submitted in print or through electronic means?
- What are the potential obstacles or actual constraints of your communication task? Are timeline or budgetary limitations stated? If so, what are they?

Among the most challenging aspects of understanding your task is identifying obstacles and constraints. **Constraints** are limits within which you must work. Examples of common project constraints are available time, money, and human resources. Constraints include limitations that can affect your preparation, development, and delivery of the completed task. Think of constraints as obstacles that can impede or halt your communication efforts. Sometimes they can seem innumerable. Lack of access to information, technologies, and experts can all lead to obstacles that hamper progress. Inadequate or undependable resources, such as money, time, and equipment, can limit your effectiveness.

Constraints may also be interpersonal or cultural. As we discussed in Chapter 1, 21st century workplaces may employ individuals who reside in different cities, regions, and even countries, and the organization's products or services may also be widely distributed. Distributed work means that some communications or texts you produce will need to address culturally different individuals. If you do not take these cultural differences into account, you may use words, images, examples, or even gestures that hinder your audience's ability or willingness to act.

Issues can also arise when individuals from different cultures team to complete tasks. Understanding and responding effectively to potential cultural differences can facilitate task completion, saving time and money and preserving collegiality between coworkers from different cultures. For example, culturally different coworkers or team members may have very different concepts of acceptable physical contact, language, gestures, and tones of voice. These kinds of difference are important to recognize and acknowledge so that all team members feel respected.

Answering questions about requirements, specifications, and constraints involves close reading or listening to task instructions and knowing your workplace and co-workers. Over the course of the project, knowing this information establishes boundaries for the final deliverable(s), and gives you a clear picture of the scope of the deliverable necessary to meet the task's purpose.

What are your Task's Objectives?

After you have stated your task's overall purpose, constraints, and general scope of your documents, you are ready to begin to define your task's **objectives**. These objectives will guide your progress throughout the project. Depending on the jargon (or professional language) of your field, objectives are also called "outcomes," "end results," "end-products," or "goals." Whatever they are called, objectives are statements that identify what you plan to accomplish in order to complete the task. For this reason, objectives always include a "strong" or "active" verb that describes your intentions and the rhetorical situation in which the task will be completed. For example, your intentions might be to "investigate," "determine," or "design." Different communications result in different end results, so their objectives differ, too: proposals persuade someone to buy a product or a service, reports support a decision or recommend an action, and instructions guide users as they complete a process. To determine the best strong or active verb for your objectives, articulate the problem or need your work is addressing. What actions are necessary to resolve the problem?

Your objectives will vary depending on what you want to accomplish. When you first begin writing or thinking about objectives, it is often helpful to have a template that you can modify for your specific situation. Templates for objectives commonly have four components:

1. **When** will successful completion be evaluated (time)?
2. **What** is being done (action)?
3. **Who** is completing the task (person)?
4. **How** will successful completion be determined?

Here is an example of a template objective for an analytical report:

> "After completing this analysis (*when?*), I (*who?*) will have produced an analytical report (*what?*). To be successful, this report will convince my audience to do _____ (_____, and _____). (*how?*)"

Note that each objective should have a performance metric (or observable and measurable action) that allows you to determine that the objective is complete or fulfilled.

Given the template, objectives may seem easy to write, but do not be fooled. Objectives can multiply and branch, and it is sometimes challenging to decide which ones are most important, or primary, and which ones are less important, or secondary. **Primary objectives** are overall or overarching goals that drive task completion. **Secondary objectives** are less important and necessary, in that they usually must be completed in order to achieve primary objectives.

Objectives can also be described as either **sequential** (linear, completed one after another) or **hierarchical** (objective that is impossible to complete without completing a prerequisite objective first). Because of their potential complexity, start the process of objective writing by working with the objective template and focusing on the most obvious indicators of measureable, demonstrable success for your task.

> ### EXERCISE 3.5
> ### *Analyzing Objectives*
>
> Using this template, a communication objective for this section of the textbook might be stated this way:
>
> > *"After reading this section on objectives, students will be able to state objectives for writing products they will produce this semester. Each student's objectives will contain the four identifiable components of good objectives."*
>
> The communication objective for the next section of this chapter might be as follows:
>
> > *"After reading this section, students will be able to identify a process they can follow to divide a task into subtasks and apply this process to a particular task they would like to complete."*
>
> Can you identify all four of the objective components in each of the examples? Discuss you findings. Now think about an upcoming communication assignment you have in this or another class, and write an objective for that task.
>
> **Tasks to be completed:**
>
> 1. Read the objective above, and identify the four objective components in it.
> 2. Discuss your findings with a partner or others.
> 3. Review a communication assignment you have pending or have recently completed.
> 4. Write an objective for the completion for that assignment.
> 5. Discuss your objective with a partner or others.

To illustrate how purpose, requirements, and objectives work together, consider this example: your instructor assigns this section on task analysis to you and asks you to summarize its contents:

- **What is the purpose of this task?** To allow you to gain a deeper understanding task analysis.
- **What are the requirements of the task?** The task deliverable is a summary that condenses or describes key points of this section on task analysis. Summaries vary in length and complexity, so what are your teacher's expectations for this summary—one sentence, one paragraph, one page, or more? And are there any requirements for the delivery, such as design, layout or delivery method? To understand the requirements, you will need to inquire more about task requirements and time, effort, and resource expectations.
- **What are your objectives to complete this task?** Once you have clarified your task, you might write an objective like this one: After reading this section, I will be able to summarize the key steps in task analysis in a single paragraph.

With this information, you are ready to move to the next step in the planning process: identifying the steps necessary to achieve these objectives.

What Steps are Necessary to Complete the Project?

Stating your communication objectives allows you to envision the end result of your work. The next problem in this process is to determine what work (or steps) is required to complete the task. Determining steps involves two key actions:

- Identifying and listing steps necessary to complete each task objective.
- Deciding if these steps can be classified into related groups.

You can start to identify steps by carefully reviewing the task you have been given. Often the task itself will outline or identify the steps required for successful completion. If not, then you have several options for gathering this information:

- If you have completed the task previously, then you can rely on your past experience to guide you as you list the steps.
- If you know someone who has completed a similar task, interview him or her, asking for detailed descriptions of past experiences with the same or comparable task.
- If you know more than one person who has completed the same or comparable tasks, conduct a focus group to gain multiple insights into the process.
- If someone is available to complete the task for you, observe him or her to see how to complete the task. Observing more than one person will help you to see if there are alternative ways for task completion.
- If the task involves a product, test or play with the product to see how it works, identifying the steps involved in using it.

EXERCISE 3.6

Reverse Engineering a Safety Video to Analyze Tasks

Search for and watch the five-minute video "Car Safety: The Science of Speed" in the National Science Foundation (NSF) Multimedia Gallery. Describe the video's objectives, steps, and step sequence. Evaluate your task analysis by comparing it to other students' analyses of the same video.

Tasks to be completed:

1. Search for and view "Car Safety: The Science of Speed."
2. After viewing the video, complete a task analysis of its content by answering these questions:
    a. What are the video's objectives?
    b. What are the steps described in the video?
    c. What is the sequence or order of steps in the video?
3. After answering the questions, compare your answers to these questions with your peers, and discuss any differences.

As you gather information about the steps necessary to complete a communication task, be sure to note both physical and mental steps. Physical steps are concrete, visible actions that are observable; mental steps are less easily seen but important actions, such as to *decide, consider, or evaluate*. In general, steps in task completion are typically written as imperative statements beginning with an "action" verb. Imperative statements often omit the subject of the sentence. The subject of the sentence, "you," is unstated. For example, "List the steps in the communication task" is an example of an imperative statement: "List" is the active verb; "you" is the understood subject.

Recalling the reading and summarizing illustration in the previous section, you might list the following steps to complete this task:

1. Read the section on task analysis carefully.
2. Take notes on steps in the task analysis process.
3. Review the chapter quickly with a second read-through and check my notes for accuracy.
4. Write the summary of steps in task analysis.

At this point in the task analysis, you should have a working list of steps that you can follow to accomplish each task objective.

What is the Best Organization for Task Completion?

After you have a list of steps necessary to meet your task objectives, you are ready to organize the objectives and their related steps. Sometimes this organization is obvious, but sometimes, especially when you have more than one objective, you must decide how best to accomplish each objective and thus the entire task. If you have more than one objective, you will first need to rank or list objectives in an order that works logically within your task constraints. With objectives that must be completed one after another, you will use a **chronological** or **sequential** order (Figure 3.5).

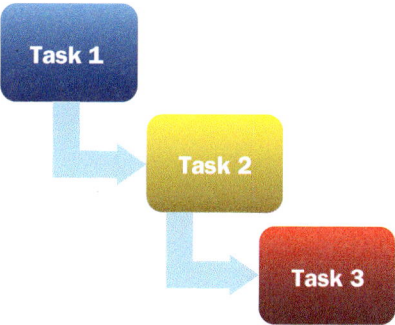

Figure 3.5. The flowchart illustrates a simple chronological or sequential order for completing tasks, similar to the Waterfall process model.

Other objectives that can be completed simultaneously and are not dependent on the completion of prior objectives can be listed in **parallel** order or in **tandem**. Parallel objectives and tasks are useful for team projects, as you can accomplish more if individuals are working on different tasks at the same time. Figure 3.6 illustrates how parallel or tandem tasks are completed.

Figure 3.6. When tasks iteratively overlap or require team members to complete them simultaneously, a parallel or tandem organization is effective.

Similarly, steps to accomplish each objective can be organized in sequential or parallel order. How you organize these items depends on your task. With some tasks, the best way to sequence them is to list them in chronological order, from the step that needs to be completed first to the step that is completed last. When steps are parallel, you can group steps by order of importance, where the primary or most important steps are prioritized over secondary, less important steps. When more than one person is assigned to a project, you may find that steps in the task are best prioritized and divided among team members, yet, once assigned to team members, steps are completed in chronological order.

> ## EXERCISE 3.7
> ### Conducting a Task Analysis
>
> Find an instructional video on YouTube.com or EHow.com. You can easily locate one using search terms, such as "task analysis," "how-to," "or "procedural analysis." Identify the objective of the analysis, the steps in the process, and the step sequence. Finally, evaluate the analysis: how well was it organized? Could you complete the instructions by following the video?
>
> **Tasks to be completed:**
>
> 1. Find an instructional video by conducting an internet search.
> 2. View the video.
> 3. Identify at least one objective for the video.
> 4. Identify the steps in the instructional process.
> 5. Order the steps as they are presented in the video.
> 6. Evaluate the video:
>   a. How well is it organized?
>   b. What organizational improvements might you suggest?
>   c. Could you successfully complete the video considering the steps and their organization?
> 7. Prepare a short written analysis to share with the class or a partner.

After you have organized your objectives and steps, you may find it useful to create a visual representation of your plan, to this point. Simple outlines are effective for visually deciding on and representing sequential orders. A numbered list designates chronologically ordered steps, while bulleted lists can be used to designate parallel objectives or steps. Flowcharts are also useful for graphically depicting steps in a chronological process. More complicated plans may require a Gantt chart to depict all tasks and steps required. Gantt charts are discussed in more detail in later chapter; however, Figure 3.8 provides you with a glimpse into how they work.

If You Follow the Steps, Will You Actually Accomplish the Larger Task?

After you have identified, organized, and ordered the steps in your task, your final steps in task analysis are evaluative. To evaluate your communication task analysis, answer the following questions:

- If you complete the steps you have outlined, will you meet your task objective(s)?
- Have you adequately identified and described each step of the process, to the best of your current knowledge? Are any steps missing?
- Have you organized the steps in a way that you will get from task beginning to assigned end successfully?
- What have you learned from completing this process?

The evaluation step is one that you should apply multiple times during task completion because situational changes and new information may require revision and reworking of the original plan.

EXERCISE 3.8

Searching the Internet to Learn More

To learn more about task analysis, you can conduct an internet search using these search terms: "task analysis" or "procedural analysis." You will also find many additional resources on writing objectives using these search terms: "writing objectives," "writing learning objectives," "writing behavioral objectives." You can find many examples of project postmortems searching with either of these terms: "project postmortem" and "lessons learned review." Work with a partner to complete the following research and reporting tasks.

Tasks to be completed:

1. Choose one of these terms to research, and search for information on the internet.
2. Compare and contrast the information you find on different sites.
3. Create a short (3–5 minute) oral presentation about your findings. Use screenshots and presentation software to deliver your presentation.

If you have evaluated your plan carefully and feel ready to move forward with it, then you have one additional task to add to the list. Plan a time, at the project's end, to reflect on the lessons you have learned. Many teams conclude their projects with a **final project postmortem** (also called a **Lessons Learned Review**). In a project postmortem, team members briefly record their project experiences, updating and annotating the original document plan, thus creating an institutional memory that future teams may use for similar projects. Postmortems identify steps taken, obstacles encountered and resolved, and issues left unresolved. In the postmortem, you should also note how effectively you allocated resources (did you use more or less than you estimated?) and whether your time estimates when scheduling were accurate. Involving the entire team in this process allows the group to record both its successes and its failures and passes important information forward to groups that tackle similar problems in the future. After you have completed multiple projects, you will begin to see patterns and trends in your project management. These patterns and trends will allow you to create milestones and metrics for projects. **Milestones** are clusters of tasks that are often completed together. By identifying and tracking milestones, you will eventually have a reliable means of planning tasks, their order, and their time requirements.

RESOURCE PLANNING

Another key task in planning your project is taking stock of resources. Project planning and management typically begin with analyzing your audience as well as identifying your communication purpose, objectives, and steps to completion, but nothing can be accomplished without resources. Taking stock of your resources before you begin a technical communication task means that you identify the materials your task requires, the time or amount of the resource needed, and costs associated with these uses.

This section is designed to help you think about the resources you will need to complete projects. It begins with a definition and overview of the resources you will need when completing communication tasks and explains why you should allocate these resources early when you are first planning your project. It concludes with suggestions for visualizing your resource allocations as well as overseeing their use throughout the project's duration.

What are Resources and Resource Allocation?

Technical communication tasks require a variety of **resources** to be completed. At the very least, they require you to budget time, effort, and materials to do the work. When you combine time and effort, you are estimating the labor required to complete the task. Materials include office supplies, technologies, and equipment expenses. Space considerations are also common budget items, especially if you need special facilities or laboratories for completing the task. At first, it will be challenging to arrive at numbers for quantifying these resources, but as your experience with communication projects and their management increases, you will develop metrics that you can apply quite readily when you allocate resources.

Even the simplest kinds of technical communication tasks, such as writing a grocery list, require time to write the items as well as a writing instrument and paper (or mobile device and apps) for recording the items. While you may not consider the time it takes to make a grocery list valuable, that is, worth anything, it does require you to expend time, effort, and materials to complete it. At the same time, if creating a grocery list saves you even 10 minutes that you would spend wandering the aisles of a grocery store, then you have profited from it by gaining time to do other chores or relax. Obviously, a single use of pencil or pen and a sheet of note paper may be negligible expenses, but the cost for a notepad and box of pens adds up when multiplied over time and number of users. Other resources that you should consider when allocating resources are costs associated with technology (e.g., expenses associated with computers, mobile devices, internet and Wi-fi access, and software or apps). Accounting for task costs in terms of both labor and materials is even more important in the workplace where you or your employer will want to minimize costs and maximize profit.

EXERCISE 3.9
Researching Project Management Applications

Conduct an internet search for project management software applications. Review the features of two project management software or mobile device applications. What kinds of resource allocation do these applications allow or support? Would either of these applications be good choices for technical communicators? Why or why not?

Tasks to be completed:

1. Conduct an internet search and locate two different project management software applications. You may choose applications for either computer or mobile use.
2. Identify the features of each application. What kinds of resource allocation do these applications allow or support?
3. Compare and contrast these features.
4. Evaluate the features to determine if either one would be good choices for technical communicators. If so, which one would you recommend? Why?
5. Discuss your findings with a partner or the class.

Why Allocate Resources so Soon?

Allocating resources early in the planning stages of project management is invaluable when you are working on or planning multiple projects. Early allocation of project resources can help you to determine when you might need additional labor, such as a student intern or temporary worker, and when you can request support from other team members, who are also working on multiple projects. You can determine when you need additional funding for materials or technology purchases that accompany new projects or the combination of a new project with old ones. The sooner you can estimate what resources are needed, how much of each resource is needed, and when they are needed, the better able you will be to have these resources available.

How Do you Estimate Resource Allocation?

Like other project management and planning you have considered in this chapter, allocating resources is easiest when you have completed a similar project and can estimate expenses based on metrics from projects you have already completed. If you have not completed the task before, then you should ask if anyone in your organization has completed a similar task and seek recommendations and suggestions from that person or persons. You might even be able to find examples of budgets and schedules in **legacy documents** (previous planning documents that have been filed away). If these options are not available, then you will have to estimate allocations beginning with a timeline or schedule, then fitting scheduled tasks within your own or your team's schedule, and finally determining what resources you will need to complete each task.

A timeline or schedule helps you to visualize the order of tasks needed to be completed. If you completed a task analysis earlier, then begin the process with that analysis and list its steps in reverse order. For example, if your task begins in September and must end by December, start a timeline beginning with December and work backwards. List items that need to be completed in November, October, and September. As you work backwards through the timeline, schedule the steps that must be completed, estimating the time it will take to complete each task. When you are working with a large team on a complex task, you may need to develop your timeline as Gantt chart. When working alone or with a small team, a simple chart, as depicted in Table 3.2, will suffice. When you have the timeline in hand, you have a good estimate of the time-on-task it will take to complete the task.

Task	Description	Assigned to	Due Date
Present poster	Prepare brief project presentation	Marcus, Gillian, and Alyce	Dec. 3
Edit and revise poster	Check over poster using rubric and make changes, if necessary	Gillian and Alyce	Dec. 5

Table 3.2. This simple timeline table identifies the task, describes it, assigns tasks to specific team members, and notes the due date.

Once you have estimated a timeline or schedule, then you should consider who will complete each task. If you are working alone, then this is a simple process: you fit the task and its steps within your own calendar. If you are working with a partner or a team to complete the process, then you will need to coordinate time-on-task tasks with your teammates. This can be challenging, and it may require you to adjust the timeline somewhat.

As noted earlier in the task analysis section, when you work with your teammates and their availabilities, consider which tasks must be completed in sequence and which ones can be completed in tandem or parallel. Having different individuals work in tandem allows projects to move forward more quickly and, if you can avoid overlap in tasks, you and your team will be much better able to complete the project within the deadline. When making task assignments, another key consideration is which method for writing collaboratively is best for this project. Here are three collaborative options that your team might consider when making tasks:

Team completion of each task. As a group, all members work together to plan, research, write, and edit. This option is the most time-consuming because all members are engaged in every task, and only one task at a time can be completed. When team members engage in this option for drafting, they may sit together at the same computer, or they may exchange drafts electronically, cycling the draft from individual to individual until it is complete. Choose this option only if you have a small team and sufficient time to make it work.

Team plans; individual team members research and write; one team member compiles individual contributions into a single document; team reviews. In this option, the team plans as a group; then individual team members accept tasks to research and write. When all members have completed their tasks, one team member compiles all the individual contributions into a single document, which everyone reviews and edits. This option works for well for large teams with varied expertise;

it also works well for projects like the ones you may complete in this class because each person has a specific task for which they are responsible.

Team planning; individual research and writing; individual review. This option is similar to the previous one, except that one individual, rather than the team, completes the final review of the document. This option works well when one team member has particularly strong editing skills.

Of course, these are not the only configurations possible. In some workplaces, for example, teams plan and review the final document, but one individual or a subgroup does all the writing. This configuration does not work well for class projects, but it is often used in workplaces where technical communicators do most of the team's writing and editing while others do research. Team leaders are typically familiar with the most common configurations in specific workplace and will recommend what has worked well in the past; nevertheless, knowing several writing teams' configurations can provide you with other options, if necessary.

With your tasks made, you can add up hours each person will need to expend, and multiply hours by labor costs. Adding up these numbers will give you a good estimate of the labor costs for the project.

Finally, after you have created a timeline and made tasks, then you are ready to estimate other resource expenses. Ask yourself what supplies, technologies, and other materials are needed for each task, and coordinate the resource needs with your time schedule and tasks. Then estimate what each of these resources will cost. (Even if the resources are available or on-hand, you should still estimate these costs because resources that are used must eventually be replaced.) Add up the various resource expenses, and combine this cost with your labor expenses. Together these numbers will give you a good estimate of the costs of your project, and the resources that must be allocated to complete it.

How Do you Document and Report Resource Allocation Estimates?

Several graphic aids are quite valuable when you are estimating resource allocations. A simple budget table allows you to indicate expenses. Table 3.3, a simple table originally developed for a student team project, illustrates budget expenses for a project that requires nothing more than time and transportation costs.

Item	Cost	Number	Total
Labor costs	$10.00/hour	25 hours	$250.00
Gasoline	$2.50/gallon	2 gallons	$5.00
		Grand Total	$255.00

Table 3.3. A table is a simple way to design a budget. Budget tables should include items, cost, quantity or number of items, and total costs.

In contrast to Table 3.3's simple tabular format with only two budget items, Table 3.4 provides a more detailed example of a budget. This budget was included in a proposal for a new computer classroom in an English building on a university campus. It includes requests for funds for items, such as space, furniture, mechanical upgrades, equipment, and labor. It also illustrates how these items are categorized and itemized and how expenses are sub-totaled and then totaled as overall expenditure. The upper part of the budget itemized the budget request items while the lower part describes the department's contributions to the proposed project.

Operating Expenses Budget Request	Cost	Total Cost
Facilities		**$7,765.00**
Electrical drops (5 at $370 each)	$1,850.00	
Wiring solution	$3,000.00	
Network drops (3 at $250 each)	$750.00	
Window coverings	$815.00	
Painting	$850.00	
Removal of existing equipment and reinstallation	$500.00	
Furniture		**$19,400.00**
Chairs (21 at $350)	$7,350.00	
Multi-configurable workstations	$10,000.00	
Printer stand	$750.00	
Laptop cart	$1,300.00	
Instructional equipment		**$47,009.00**
20 dual-boot capable Macbooks with upgrades and 3-year warrantees	$33,480.00	
Mice for interface control	$880.00	
External monitors and docking stations for high-end graphics stations	$1600.00	
Instructor computer	$2,300.00	
Mobile, interactive whiteboard	$5,249.00	
Document camera	$3500.00	
Software		**$2,197.00**
GenevaLogic Vision 5 classroom management software	$700.00	
Windows XP Professional	$1,197.00	
DeepFreeze Enterprise (security software)	$300.00	
Total Fund Request		**$76,371.00**

Distribution of Shared Costs (Department of English)		
Personnel		$12,000.00
Assistant Director (graduate instructor course release (1-1-1))	$12,000.00	
Software		$8,400.00
Adobe CS3 Design Premium	$6,510.00	
Microsoft Office (Win/Mac)	$1,890.00	
Total Distribution of Shared Costs		$20,400.00

Table 3.4. This table provides accounting for a more complex budget. It uses headings and white space within each section to delineate different types of expenses.

COMPLETING THE PLANNING PHASE

After you review your work carefully and make any necessary additions, revisions, or modifications, you should have a working plan for completing your task. You know what you are trying to achieve (your objectives), you know the steps you need to accomplish each objective, and you have a definitive order for completing objectives and the steps within them. Depending on the complexity of your project, tasks and milestones allow you (and your team) to check your progress. Moving through milestones points you toward successful project completion. Taken as a whole, these milestones become your working plan for accomplishing and completing a project. You can call this working plan your methods for completing the task, including the set of objectives, steps, and evaluations you will conduct to produce the task deliverable that fulfills the task purpose. Although you may encounter events that require you to revise your methods, the preliminary planning you have done here will provide a useful guide for your own work as well your team's work. The final deliverable for your plan can vary in formality and genre, ranging from an informally sketched plan sent in an email to a lengthy feasibility report or proposal.

Writing a Project Plan

Although you may not be familiar with the terms "document plan" or "project plan," you have certainly worked through the processes of completing both. If you have ever sketched a mind map or jotted a quick outline for answering a question or essay assignment, you created a document plan, a general guide for writing or completing the assignment. The difference between document and project plans is scope. Shorter assignments that can be completed with a simple communication require a document plan while a project plan details more complex, detailed, and time-consuming assignments. In some organizations, these plans are called "specifications" or "specs."

 Whichever approach you take, this chapter discussed key components that you should consider when planning a communication document or project. A project plan is a type of informational instance report, which you will read about more in the next chapter.

Chapter Summary

Planning a technical communication project effectively requires you to consider your deliverable's audience, schedule tasks necessary for completion, and allocate resources. At the end of this planning phase, you will have a better understanding of who will read your deliverable and what that audience expects from it. You will know what tasks need to be completed, who will complete these tasks, and when. You will also have a working budget that outlines what it will cost in time, money, and other resources to complete the project. Your initial plan will evolve over the project's duration, but you can avoid costly project creep, or uncontrolled expansion of a project, if you monitor progress continuously. And finally, you will want to be sure to document your planning specifications and project scope in a written document, called a project plan.

Chapter Assignments

The exercises in this section ask you to apply what you have learned in this chapter as well as explore how this knowledge applies to and connects with other information in the textbook.

1. Most higher education institutions have university tutoring centers where students and faculty can go to receive tutoring in writing, math, or other subjects. Imagine that you are developing a Web site for one of your university tutoring centers, and create use scenarios for at least three types of users who would access the Web site.

2. Cultural differences are present even in seemingly homogenous groups like your classroom, where most students will be about the same age and have the same purpose for being together—to complete this course; and these cultural differences can help or hinder the success of a deliverable. This exercise asks you to describe eight of your cultural attitudes on a continuum. After you have identified where your attitudes lie on the continuum, your instructor will gather your responses and map similarities and differences in the class' attitudes as a whole. Based on the group attitude map, you will create use profiles for two or three user "types" that represent the class's prevailing attitudes.

◀◀◀ Your behavior or attitude leaning ▶▶▶						
Check the box closest to your behavior or attitude.							
I strive to be on time to appointments.					I am late to appointments.
Abiding by laws is more important than personal loyalty.					Personal loyalty is more important than abiding by laws.
People must respect and follow authority.					People should question and ignore most authorities.
Promises are made to be broken.					A promise made is a promise kept.
To be affluent, you must be born with a certain background and status.					Anyone can become affluent, regardless of circumstances.

I prefer direct criticism to improve my work.				I prefer indirect criticism to improve my work.
The goals of the group outweigh the needs of the individual.				The goals of the individuals outweigh the needs of the group.
Logic and rationality should guide decisions.				Intuition and feelings should guide decisions.

3. Identify two of the leading project management software products or applications currently available. Based on criteria that you develop, compare and contrast the features of both products and recommend the product that would be most useful to help college students track their course projects. Present your findings in a visual format, such as a table.

4. Task analyses are used in many industries. Below are links to descriptions of how task analysis is used in Information Sciences, Mining, and Usability Studies. These resources will provide you with insights into how task and task analysis are used in government and private workplaces. With a partner, visit these sites and discuss how task analyses compare across industries:

   a. **Information and Library Sciences**: Crystal, A., & Ellington, B. (2004). Task analysis and human-computer interaction: approaches, techniques, and levels of analysis. *Proceedings of the Tenth Americas Conference on Information Systems, New York, New York*. Retrieved July 23, 2011 from http://www.ils.unc.edu/~acrystal/AMCIS04_crystal_ellington_final.pdf

   b. **Mining Engineering**: NIOSH Mining: Task Analysis | CDC/NIOSH. (n.d.). Retrieved July 23, 2011, from http://www.cdc.gov/niosh/mining/topics/ergonomics/taskanalysis/taskanalysis.htm

   c. **Usability Studies**: Task Analysis | Usability.gov. (n.d.). Retrieved July 23, 2011, from http://www.usability.gov/methods/analyze_current/analysis.html

5. Watch a movie that depicts project management and teamwork. You can choose from this list or select another of your instructor's or your choice: *The Wizard of Oz* (1939), *The Dirty Dozen* (1967), *The Italian Job* (1969 or 2003), *Aliens* (1986), *Mission Impossible* (1996), *The Incredibles* (2004), *The Great Debaters* (2007), or Guardians of the Galaxy (2014). As you watch the film, analyze a character's or a team of characters' project planning and management. Use your findings to create an imaginary project plan.

Figure Credits

Figure 3.1. © Rawpixel/Shutterstock.com

Figure 3.2. © Photographee.eu/Shutterstock.com

Figure 3.3. © King/Shutterstock.com

Figure 3.4. © Andrey_Popov/Shutterstock.com

Figure 3.5. © Kendall Hunt Publishing Company

Figure 3.6. © Kendall Hunt Publishing Company

Determining Your Technical Communication Product

4

CHAPTER OVERVIEW

This chapter introduces you to various technical communication document genres, conventions, styles, legacy documents, copyright, and intellectual property issues. It concludes with instructions for writing a document plan. After reading this chapter, you should be able to meet the following objectives:

- Discuss various technical communication document genres, including stabilized formats and use of templates, and the value of legacy documents.
- Explain the impact and importance of disciplinary conventions and professional style directives, including the importance of using style guides and manuals.
- Discuss the importance of version control, naming conventions, localization, and translation, and their role in creating new technical communication products.
- Understand related copyright and intellectual property considerations when writing on behalf of an organization.
- Create a document plan for an individually or collaboratively created technical communication product.

Technical communicators produce and participate in the creation of technical products. These products include a wide range of document types, such as reports, proposals, presentations, Web sites, and other informational and educational documents. They also encompass a wide range of purposes or intents, such as to inform, to explore, to research, to propose, to illustrate, and to decide. Making the decision on the type of product is often dependent on a wide range of factors including audience, purpose, and contexts or constraints, including ones specific to the discipline and organization. Changes in research findings and teaming configurations can also affect document type (Figure 4.1).

Figure 4.1. Deciding on document type often requires collaboration with others and research.

When making informed decisions on determining specific guidelines and standards to follow for particular kinds of document types, it is important to consider a number of factors: genres, specific document types, legacy content, conventions, style guidelines, and copyright or intellectual property issues. This chapter will introduce you to the different types of document genres, conventions, styles, and intellectual property issues. It also considers how some genres are generated through a combination of other documents and practices. To illustrate how a genre may draw from a combination of other information development practices and skills, Figure 4.2 provides you with a visual overview of some of the documents and practices, represented as icons that encompass the work of web usability and accessibility. Icons, such as usability testing, user research, interview, focus group, and user surveys, represent research practices included in web usability and accessibility work. Other icons, such as concept maps, style guides, and personas, are examples of documents generated during this work. These practices and documents as well as others not visualized here illustrate how complex a genre or type of technical communication work can be.

Figure 4.2. These web usability and accessibility icons illustrate how documents and practices are often interrelated in genres.

DOCUMENT GENRES AND TYPES

Genres are document categories based on their purpose or use, such as analytical reports, instructional documents, memoranda, presentations, and status reports. Genres include technical documents that inform, instruct, persuade, make decisions, propose, and report progress or status. Books and movies have different genres, including mystery, science fiction, drama, and comedy, to name a few. Figure 4.2 illustrates the familiar literary genres you might find in a bookstore. Each genre is comprised of several different kinds of documents with a similar purpose. For example, in status reports, there are many types of reports that address status, such as progress reports, annual reports, final reports, and so forth. Table 4.1 identifies common technical communication genres and types.

Genre	Types
Analytical reports	Analysis reports Feasibility studies Proposals Recommendation reports Research reports
Instructional documents	Instructions Procedures Technical descriptions Training materials White papers Instructional videos, screencasts, and podcasts
Correspondence	Emails Letters Memos Instant messages Texts
Presentations	Lectures Chalk talks Electronic slide shows Screencasts Podcasts Vidcasts
Status reports	Periodic reports (annual, quarterly, and monthly) Progress reports Final or completion reports

Table 4.1. Like literary genres, technical communication can be categorized by its genre or type.

Genres provide familiar structures and organizational patterns for documents with a specific purpose. They provide consistency for the users that read the documents as well as for the individuals who are responsible for writing and contributing to them. Genres are like recipes; they can be modified to fit a particular audience, purpose, or organizational needs and contexts. Across various workplaces and organizations, genres are easily recognized and help readers understand what information they will find within a specific document and in what order to expect that information.

Variations of Document Types within Genres

Document types used within specific genres vary based on a number of reasons. First, the purpose of the document may dictate which specific type is needed. For example, an analytical report may research a given problem and provide possible solutions, while a feasibility study or recommendation report may look at one solution or recommend one from multiple proposed solutions. Second, company or organizational policies or standards may inform the decision to use a specific document type. For example, an organization may insist on the use of a specific presentation software program for all of its internal and external presentations. Software programs typically use standardized templates that define the organization, structure, and delivery of presentation materials. This standardization can be a benefit to less experienced professionals and help reinforce consistent standards because it requires everyone in the organization to comply with a specific form or format. It can also be a hindrance because standardization limits creative or innovative approaches. Third, repeated practices may be the deciding factor in using the same type or genre for a specific project or purpose. Also, other factors such as audience, context, and use may dictate the use of different document types to suit a specific scope or needs.

EXERCISE 4.1

Learning More about the Analytical Report Genre (Feasibility Studies)

Feasibility studies focus on a given problem and often explore one or more possible researched solutions. To learn more about the scope and stylistics of this type of technical document, perform an online search using "feasibility study" as your keywords. Read or skim a few sample reports found online and make sure to look at a few reports on different subjects. Make a list of consistent features of each report and also note a few differences.

Tasks to be completed:

1. Search online for 2–3 report samples using the keywords "feasibility study." If necessary, you may also include specific topic names with your keywords to narrow your searches.
2. Skim each report, looking at the organization, content sections, use of information graphics, and variety of topics.
3. Make a list of similarities and differences among the reports you find.
4. Share your findings with others and discuss some of the important trends.

Legacy Documentation

Selecting the appropriate document genre and type is the first part of getting started in producing a technical document, but there are a number of other factors that influence how and what you write and how you adapt each form for the task at hand. Many times, when you start to write a document for an organization, chances are other documents have come before it. For example, technical communicators write proposals, annual reports, procedures, and other document types as part of their day-to-day operation and on specific frequencies. Even if they are writing a document for the first time, they will likely be able to seek out other sources of information or similar document types to inform the development of this work. Additionally, most technical documents and genres incorporate content from other sources, whether it comes from published research or from previous versions of reports that have been single-sourced or reused.

Legacy documentation, existing content sources, is often used to develop a new document. Using legacy documentation is an essential part of writing and developing technical documents. These documents can be external (sources outside of an organization) or internal (sources within an organization). Legacy content sources can vary widely, ranging from print to online sources; they can also be as varied as text, graphics, templates, documents, quotations, statistics, and other kinds of textual and visual information. These sources include internal reports or previous versions of reports from which content is single-sourced into future versions. Data sources that provide statistical evidence or information can be used as legacy resources to create information graphics that show trends, comparative values, or serve as valuable background information. Other types of legacy sources are published research papers, articles, book chapters, and presentations. In addition, templates and style guides provide guidance on the organization, consistency, and formatting of specific document types and genres.

When selecting legacy content sources, consider under what contexts and constraints they can be used. These contexts and constraints include disciplinary and organizational conventions, style guidelines, and citation issues. The following sections will address each of these issues more specifically.

EXERCISE 4.2
Conducting Legacy Content Research

You have been given the task of writing a technical description on the topic of selecting a new graphics card for computers in your office. While you may not have specific expertise on the topic, your manager is confident in your ability to research and report on the topic and to help make an informed recommendation. Ideally, the document should include a discussion of the following factors: speed, memory, compatibility, and cost. To prepare to write this report, conduct a series of online searches on graphics cards specifications and review instructional documents about these different factors. Collect this information into a working bibliography of sources about graphics cards.

Tasks to be completed:

1. Search online for information on graphics cards specifications, including the importance of speed, memory, compatibility, and cost factors.
2. Read or skim some of the more valuable information sources you find.
3. From this list, compile a bibliography of sources that can be used as legacy documents or secondary research for writing the report.
4. Share your findings with others to see what other references you might have not considered.

CONVENTIONS AND STYLISTICS

The use of conventions can contribute to the usability and accessibility of a document. They can help readers find information more rapidly and use the document more effectively. Many conventions are based on organizational practices, including prescriptive guidelines on style and usage. Conventions can be communicated both formally and informally in organizations. Formally, they can be packaged as written professional style guides and technical document templates. Informally, they can include tacit, or unwritten, knowledge that you learn on-the-job after working for some time in an organization. For example, there may be alternate choices for paper and binding of printing reports, which are not documented in a style guide but which are known in an organization to be acceptable substitutes.

Conventions, both formal and informal, influence the organization, stylistics, and content of genres and specific technical document types. In particular, conventions that are specific to a particular field, organization, or audience can influence changes in how document types are formatted, written, organized, and constructed. For example, organizations might include different sections or provide organizational templates for teams to use as guidelines for writing certain types of reports. Depending on the intended audience and readership for each type of report, the report might include different levels of description and detail. Internal readers, employees, and managers in an organization might have different information needs than external readers, such as potential customers or the general public. As another example, proprietary information, which would be appropriate for internal audiences, is not for the general public or competitors. Other related and equally important issues to consider conventions include the use of professional style guides, document templates, version control, naming conventions, and localization/translation issues.

Professional Style Guides and Style Sheets

You have probably used a style guide, such as the MLA and APA style guides, before for an introductory writing course or perhaps in a job you have held. **Style guides** are essential when writing and editing technical documents. On a smaller scale, writers and editors often create style sheets for specific documents to help them record and remember decisions about how to spell, punctuate, capitalize, and even format content in a particular document. They document the choices made when writing, formatting, and producing good technical documents, which may vary depending on audience, organization, and product.

Style guides can be written for general use, or they can be organizationally specific. Their main goal is to provide consistency across technical documents that individuals in organizations or professions produce, despite the range of authors, contributors, and content sources. They provide directives on how technical documents should be organized, designed, and written. These directives represent conventions specific to a discipline or an organization. They may specify fonts, colors, graphics, typefaces, and organizational patterns or templates. Typically, they include examples of documents to help writers model their work. Figure 4.3 is an example of an organizational style guide's table of contents, which depicts a wide range of stylistic choices and illustrates how detailed organizational style guides can be.

Similarly, style sheets are useful for smaller projects. Style sheets are particularly useful when collaborating with others because they allow collaborators to maintain consistency as they produce different sections, which are then combined into a whole document. Creating an electronic style sheet in a shared location, such as a GoogleDoc, allows collaborators to add to the style sheet as they make decisions and to consult when questions arise. Figure 4.4 is a sample style sheet used to edit an organization's ornithological (research on birds) proposals.

Contents

Chapter		Page
	About This Manual	v
	GPO's Online Initiatives	ix
1.	Advice to Authors and Editors	1
2.	General Instructions	7
3.	Capitalization Rules	27
4.	Capitalization Examples	43
5.	Spelling	79
6.	Compounding Rules	95
7.	Compounding Examples	109
8.	Punctuation	193
9.	Abbreviations and Letter Symbols	221
	Standard word abbreviations	238
	Standard letter symbols for units of measure	247
	Standard Latin abbreviations	251
	Information technology acronyms and initialisms	255
10.	Signs and Symbols	259
11.	Italic	265
12.	Numerals	269
13.	Tabular Work	281
14.	Leaderwork	299
15.	Footnotes, Indexes, Contents, and Outlines	303
16.	Datelines, Addresses, and Signatures	309
17.	Useful Tables	321
	U.S. Presidents and Vice Presidents	321
	Most Populous U.S. Cities by State	322
	Principal Foreign Countries	325
	Demonyms: Names of Nationalities	332
	Currency	334
	Metric and U.S. Measures	339
	Common Measures and Their Metric Equivalents	340
	Measurement Conversion	341
18.	Geologic Terms and Geographic Divisions	343
19.	Congressional Record	371
	Congressional Record Index	406
20.	Reports and Hearings	417
	Index	433

Figure 4.3. The first page of the 2008 U.S. Government's Printing Office Style Guide illustrates the types of content that detailed style guides contain.

Style Sheet for Ornithology Proposal

Bullets & Numbering
- In keeping with APA, introduce bullets with a colon. Follow each bullet with a semicolon and end the last bullet with a period.
- Lowercase the first letter of the bullet, unless it constitutes a complete sentence.

Figures & Tables
- In keeping with APA, refer to all figures and tables in-text as

    (See Figure 1.)

- For each figure or table, include
    Figure/Table X. Descriptive Title. Description/Caption.

- Headings in tables are bold, arial 12; text within the table is arial 10.

Spelling
ornithologist

Kejimkujik

Assume spelling of authors' names are correct.

benthic macro invertebrates

geographic information systems (GIS)

Capitalization
- When seen together, capitalize both: Kejimkujik Park
- When only 'park' appears, though referring to Kejimkujik Park, don't capitalize.
- Capitalize important words in titles, headings, and subheadings.

Punctuation
Use comma before "and" in series of three or more.

Use colons to introduce lists.

Use commas between author and date for sources.

Use semicolons between multiple sources.

Measurements
Hectare (ha) – distance of study plots. Ex: 20-ha or 35-ha

Figure 4.4. Shorter style sheets help writers and editors maintain a common style when collaborating or editing.

Style guides are often used as writing guides when documents are developed and tested. For novice writers, they are valuable to ensure consistency in stylistics, organization, and conventions of their discipline and workplace. For experienced writers, they are ideal to have as an off-the-shelf resource to ensure the finer details of each specific document type are addressed.

EXERCISE 4.3
The World of Professional Style Guides

Conduct an Internet search to identify the style guide most commonly used in your field. You may locate the style guide by visiting the website of a professional organization or reviewing the style guidelines of key journals in your field. After identifying the name of the style guide, locate a copy either online or in your institution's library, and make a copy of the manual's Table of Contents. Does it contain sample documents? What kind? For what other conventions does it provide guidance? Summarize its contents. Bring your copy of the Table of Contents to class, and be prepared to discuss and compare your findings to others' findings in your class.

Tasks to be completed:

1. Identify a style guide used in your field.
2. Locate a copy of the guide.
3. Make a copy of the Table of Contents and analyze it.
4. Summarize your findings.
5. Bring a copy of the Table of Contents and your findings to class with your for discussion.

Document Templates

Templates serve as structural organizational patterns that help writers follow specific guidelines with regard to content, layout, and consistency when writing specific kinds of technical reports. They are often included as a supplement to many style guides. When single-sourcing, or reusing, existing documents, often parts of their structure and organization are used as templates for new documents that are written. Templates can be content outlines that indicate to writers what content should be included in each section and how to organize it, so it is consistent with organizational guidelines. They can also provide specific patterns for stylistics, such as layout, use of fonts, graphics, colors, labels, and so forth. Templates help novice writers learn the conventions of a specific technical document type or genre. They also help reinforce consistency across multiple reports of the same type, such as with annual or periodic reports. While they can be somewhat prescriptive, the advantages of being stylistically and organizationally consistent can be important in maintaining quality and accuracy in technical reports. Figure 4.5 provides a sample organizational template for a progress report.

Templates provide a starting point for writers in terms of the organization, stylistics, and general conventions for document types. Determining how to modify or adapt templates for the writing task depends on project variables, such as scope and audience. Additionally, there may be other factors unique to the subject or discipline that affect the content itself, for example, safety, regulatory, legal, or other related issues. Template

Elsa Productions, Inc.
Weekly Progress Report

To: [Recipient Name]
From: [Your Name]
Subject: [Project/client name]
Week: [Day of month, weekdays covered, year]

Introduction

[Paragraph 1: Background on project; reuse information from project description in proposal]

Tasks completed

[Paragraph 2: Describe progress/list tasks completed this week; use list if multiple tasks have been completed]

Task 1.

Task 2.

Obstacles encountered

[Paragraph 3: Describe obstacles encountered and discuss steps taken to overcome obstacles; use list if multiple obstacles have been countered.]

Obstacle 1.
Obstacle 2.

Tasks to be completed

[Paragraph 4: Describe upcoming tasks that you will complete next week/list tasks you will complete next; use list if multiple tasks will be completed]

Next Task 1.
Next Task 2.

Conclusion

[Paragraph 5: State whether you are on schedule and when you expect to complete all tasks for this project. Provide contact information for questions.]

Figure 4.5. Templates assist writers by outlining recommend content and organization in genres.

changes may also depend on other localized factors with an organization, such as expectations of managers and company policies or regulations.

While templates are beneficial in many workplace writing situations, they can be detrimental if used uncritically. Many word-processing programs include templates for memos, letters, and resumes. Electronic presentation software offers users many design templates for slides. While these templates may be useful starting points, you should remember that while templates promote consistency, they do not demonstrate creativity. If your document needs to stand out from others, such as during a job search or a conference presentation, and if your organization does not require design compliance, then you should consider modifying templates to make them more appropriate for your particular communication task.

EXERCISE 4.4

Word-Processing Templates

Using any word-processing software that you have, identify the genres that are common available as templates. What kinds of placeholders do the templates include? How are templates for the same genre similar and different? What advantages and disadvantages do you think accompany use of these templates? Be prepared to discuss your answers.

Tasks to be completed:

1. Open your word-processing software.
2. Click on File>New
3. Make a list of 10 or more templates available within the software program or online.
4. Answer the following questions:
    a. How are templates for the same genre similar and different?
    b. What advantages and disadvantages do you think accompany use of these templates?
5. Bring your answers to class and be prepared to discuss.

Version Control

Version control is essential when you are authoring documents with a group or over time. Simply put, version control conventions allow you to recognize the revision sequence of a document, from oldest to newest version. Without version control, you may encounter problems in these situations:

- When collaborative authoring, where multiple authors work on a single document.
- When multiple versions of the same document may be archived or kept for specific purposes, and you need to know what the current version is.
- When older versions may be saved for archival purposes, or as backups.
- When software and networking resources permit file and folder sharing.
- When archiving and researching older versions.

- When single-sourcing content, or reusing and repurposing content.
- When documents are frequently updated (including online and multiple versions of the same document).
- When consistency and professionalism are highly important.

Naming Conventions

Naming conventions are a form of standardization, which provides descriptive information about each document (or metadata). This standardization is particularly helpful when working on a team where multiple members contribute to documents and store them in a centralized location, such as a network folder, for access, retrieval, and editing. It is also useful when multiple people contribute to writing and developing a single document and can be valuable to new team members or to others you may pass your work to when transitioning to a new project or job. When working with multiple document and file types, you should be able to quickly identify, locate, and access the correct document or file without having to waste time asking for assistance. Naming conventions are like creating a shorthand code for each document or file type, which can be learned and easily interpreted by others.

Naming conventions also provide benefits that positively impact a number of project quality metrics. They help maintain consistency across multiple documents, shared files, and folders, which is beneficial when working on a team where multiple authors, editors, and reviewers are using the same resources and documents. Naming conventions provide valuable metadata for documents, making it easier to search through files and folders in locating specific documents. They also can improve findability of documents and information. When the rules of naming conventions are clearly known, the file name itself can be a useful source to determine things like document type, author, date, and other useful details just from looking at the name of the file, without having to actually open and search through individual documents for that information. As such, they aid in archival research, retrieval, and other related research tasks. And ideally, they are an important component of standardization and formal or informal conventions within an organization.

Establishing consistent naming conventions is important for several important reasons. First, many individuals in the company often access organizational intranets, where project documents are stored, so naming conventions can help others locate documents more easily. Second, others may inherit your files or work, and these documents may be useful legacy documents for those individuals. Third, it helps in the transition of projects to other teams or even to clients. The ultimate goals of using naming conventions are to ensure maximum access, reduce possible errors, and miscommunication.

EXERCISE 4.5

Naming Conventions

A team working on a documentation project uses a single folder on the company's intranet to deposit all of their team documents. The types of documents include progress reports, memoranda, process descriptions, quality assurance spreadsheets, and meeting minutes. The problem is that there is no consistency in how documents are named or labeled, making it difficult for anyone but the original author to locate documents quickly without asking for assistance. To address this problem, you have been given the task of researching a better method of naming files. Conduct an Internet search and read two to three articles on improving file naming conventions. After reading about how to improve file names, create a short list of steps that everyone in your group can follow to improve your file naming conventions. Be prepared to share your recommendations in class.

Tasks to be completed:

1. Conduct an Internet search using the terms "file naming conventions" or "improving file naming conventions."
2. Read two or three articles that can help you improve your group's naming conventions.
3. Make a list of recommended changes or guidelines.
4. Bring your list to class and be prepared to explain your guidelines.

Localization and Translation

Other important factors to consider when adapting specific document types within a genre relate to the context of their use with respect to audience demographics, particularly localization and translation issues. Some documents may have a geographically and culturally diverse range of users, so it is important to consider these cultural factors in writing style, use of idioms, and terminology. Differences in languages may also exist among a wide range of users and may require translation of a document into different languages. There may also be local factors that require the need for slightly different versions. Localization and translation may also affect overall marketing or distribution strategies based on demographic factors. Research and consider these factors in writing and adapting specific document types and genres.

Figure 4.6. Some documents may have a geographically dispersed users, so technical communicators should consider these audiences when creating documents.

> **EXERCISE 4.6**
>
> ### Localizing for a Specific Country or Culture
>
> Using the U.S. Central Intelligence Agency's World Factbook (https://www.cia.gov/library/publications/the-world-factbook/), choose a country to research. Read about that country and its culture, and create a summary of what you learn. Make a list of recommendations for localing a document for that country or culture based on your findings.
>
> **Tasks to be completed:**
>
> 1. Visit the World Factbook.
> 2. Select a country or culture and read about it.
> 3. Write a summary of your findings.
> 4. Recommend a list of suggestions for localing documents for that country or culture.

Copyright and Intellectual Property Issues

When working with legacy documents, published sources, or other secondary research materials, consider copyright and intellectual property issues, particularly when using that information in writing technical documents of any genre. Document authors and the organizations they represent have an ethical responsibility to provide appropriate citation and attribution to original authors of published works. Even though future versions may be edited and new content added, it is important to provide citation to original authors. Online and electronically published materials have complicated the issues of citation, permission, and fair use. When in doubt regarding issues of ownership, copyright, citation, and permission, it is always best to ask the owner first rather than use the content and risk possible legal consequences.

As a result of these factors, you should consider a wide range of issues as you plan to integrate legacy content into writing technical documents. Often, you are writing on behalf of an organization or workgroup, rather than as an individual, so it is especially important to follow organizational conventions and standards in writing technical documents. It is also important to understand the difference between single-sourcing and citation. Single-sourcing is content reuse and typically applies previously written material by an organization, which is copied, edited, or reused in new documents.

Figure 4.7. Because copyrighted material is protected, technical communicators need to seek permission before using it.

Citation typically involves published content that is not owned by the organization or individual and requires proper citing or permissions for use.

Many technical documents may have an instructional component or function, but they are still subject to different rules with regard to citation and fair use. For online and print content alike, citation rules still apply for all copyrighted material. This rule is particularly important when using legacy documents, which require citation for use in newer technical documents. It is also important to follow citation styles appropriate for specific genres and disciplines, which include APA, AMA, Chicago, and MLA, to name a few. Many professional style guides will recommend the use of specific styles and provide examples of their proper usage.

Another important issue to consider is acquiring permission for use of published materials. Typically, you will need to find contact information for an author, publisher, or organization to request use of their material. Fair use laws generally permit the use of 250 words from a single-source, with citation; however, it is important to consult your organization's legal team to determine appropriate use. Permissions for copyrighted material must be obtained, often through a written form and, in some cases, a fee. Permissions generally apply to documents that are published and circulated outside an organization and particularly for products with a price. When acquiring permissions, you will need to provide copy for the grantor to review, including a discussion of its use and related documents. When considering use of copyrighted material, consider backups since there is no guarantee you will be able to get permissions.

EXERCISE 4.7
Research Rules for Acquiring Permissions

Your team is responsible for writing a white paper on Internet use among college-age students in the past year or two. The paper should include relevant and useful information, graphics, and statistics with appropriate citations and acquired permissions. Your task is to conduct online research to find useful information graphics for the report and specific information about the guidelines or permissions required for their use.

Tasks to be completed:

1. Research statistical data on Internet use among college-age students by conducting a series of online searches.
2. Locate information graphics online that could be used in the report, including the guidelines for their use and/or permissions for use.
3. Write a list of sources you will use for the paper, and, for each one, a short description of the guidelines for their use or how to acquire permissions.
4. Discuss the variations in permissions requirements with others to identify what trends exist.

Other options are available when you are unable to acquire permissions for use of content. Clearinghouses of content, including graphics, templates, code, and text are available online, which offer subscription fees to use their content libraries. In some cases, you can find content libraries online that are free to use, but they often have limited inventories. Sometimes creating your own original content is the best option when resources are available to do so, to avoid additional time and cost factors.

DEVELOPING A DOCUMENT OR PROJECT PLAN

After determining what kind of technical document you should create, the next step is to produce a document or project plan. Document and project plans draw on many chapters you will read in this book. Although you may not be familiar with the terms "document plan" or "project plan," you have certainly worked through the processes of completing both. As introduced in the previous chapter, a **document plan** is a general guide for writing or completing a communication product. Shorter documents require a document plan while a longer project plan details more complex, detailed, and time-consuming tasks. These longer project plans are often called "specifications" or "specs."

Document and project plans are similar to roadmaps. They provide directions to achieve the project's goal or purpose. If you are working alone on a document or project, then you are personally responsible for all planning, but, if you are working with a team, the team leader and more experienced team members will likely take the lead in mapping the steps necessary to complete a project. Whoever is the lead on a team project, everyone is expected to contribute.

As the roadmap for a document or an entire project, the plan provides a blueprint and outlines the boundaries or project scope. It allows you or your team to articulate what you know in a single document and includes the following information:

- Task analysis.
- User profiles and use scenarios.
- Resources allocation.
- Team assignments.

Setting the parameters of a document or project before you begin serves many useful purposes:

- You can manage multiple projects and allocate resources more effectively when you have detailed plans prior to beginning each project.
- In team projects, you can move more agilely toward completion because team members know their assigned tasks, and they are aware of what successful completion requires of them.
- When you are faced with changes (expected or unexpected), you can adjust the plan to accommodate changes or explain to your team, manager, or client why such adjustments are untenable.
- When you are working with a client, establishing the boundaries for the project helps to prevent "project or feature creep," a situation in which requirements can snowball and project expand without the necessary resources to complete them.
- Your plan can help your team processes mature as you monitor its effectiveness over the life of the project.

While these benefits are helpful, it is worthwhile to remember that any preliminary plan is likely to be incomplete. As you begin the project, the scope and the requirements may become clearer, or you may obtain new information about the needs of the client or audience with whom you are communicating. Agile communicators realize that planning, like other forms of communication, can require them to revisit and revise. For this reason, some modification of the original document or project plan is likely high.

Historically, when document and projects are plan-driven, the preliminary planning stage is highly detailed and the resulting planning document includes all components. These planning documents attempt to predict all possible changes and obstacles then account for them. During implementation, detailed plans, such as these, do not frequently or easily allow digressions during development. Digressions lead away from the plan and into unknown and unpredictable results. Agile approaches tend to have more streamlined planning documentation and, consequently, more modifications and updates during the plan implementation. Visually speaking, the plan-driven approach is more linear, moving step-by-step from project beginning to end whereas the agile approach is more circular, oscillating, and looping through phases of planning and development again and again. Whichever approach you take, this section discusses key components that you should consider when planning a communication document or project.

Document and Project Plan Components

As discussed earlier in this chapter, communication products vary significantly in organizations. For this reason, your plans for these communications can be simple document plans, such as a quick content outline of an impromptu progress report, or complex project plans that include hundreds of pages of product description and specifications that take months to create. Depending on the complexity of your document or project, you may use all of the following components or just a few in your plan.

Overview, Outcomes, and Deliverables

Your document plan should include a project title, problem or goal statement, and an identification of the project deliverable(s). The plan typically begins with a discussion of the communication need or problem that led to the task, which was discussed in Chapter 3. Analyzing the communication need helps you to frame the objectives or goals as well as describe briefly the outcomes (or deliverables) of the project. When read by a manager or client, this section of the plan assures the reader that you understand your task, have a clear objective for completing it, and will conclude the project with an acceptable deliverable.

Audience and User Analysis

Your document plan should next include an analysis of your audience, which includes readers, clients, or users, and their distinguishing characteristics. Another second component of document and project plans is an analysis of the audience, users, or intended readers of the final document or project deliverable. This section may simply highlight reader characteristics, or it can include detailed user profiles and use scenarios, which are also discussed in detail in Chapter 3. When this section is well written, your readers know for whom the final deliverable is written. As you write the user analysis section, remember that document and project deliverables may have multiple audiences, who must all be addressed. For example, if the final deliverable for a project is a set of instructions for a consumer product, the instructions must not only be safe and usable for consumers but also pass the inspection of corporate lawyers, who oversee organizational liability. Analyzing the needs and requirements of each audience can be challenging, but recognizing these various needs early in the process helps you or your team to address each audience in the final deliverable.

Tasks and Milestones

After your audience or user analysis, this section of your document plan includes a discussion of tasks to be completed and your schedule for completing them. Chapter 3 also describes communication task analysis in detail. You may find that reiterating the objectives is a good way to begin this section. Expand each objective with an explanation of the tasks or steps required to accomplish each objective, and describe the final deliverable or outcome. What genre will you produce as your final deliverable, and what kinds of guidelines or conventions must you consider in order to create it?

As you expand these objectives into tasks, you should consider whether the tasks require research and, if so, what kind. Reviewing the kinds of research discussed in Chapter 5 can help you to determine what methods to use if research is required. You should also consider how you will model information in your product and what visual components you will include. How will you differentiate headings visually, and what kinds of headers and footers will you use? Will the final deliverable include information graphics? If so, what kind?

Your description should include a discussion of the scope of the final deliverable and its physical details. For written communications, this discussion should include estimated page length, outline of contents, and physical characteristics, such as length, page layout and dimensions, style guide, and publication plans. Will a printing and binding completed in-house or at a print shop? Will the copy be black-and-white or color? Will print documents be bound or unbound?

Reporting preliminary style and formatting decisions is also a key to describing the assignment. Before completing the project plan, make preliminary formatting and style decisions and make all parts of the document consistent in design to guide your writing. For example, you should decide what fonts to use in the document for text and headings; what size graphics and illustrations to incorporate; where captions will be placed; and where page numbers appear. Page design decisions, such as margin size and paragraphing style, are also important to consider and record. As discussed in this chapter, you might begin to draft a preliminary style sheet for the project or designate a specific style guide to help with these decisions. Another strategy is for your team to follow the guidelines used in legacy documents (similar documents that have been written previously in the organization). Whatever guide you choose, be sure to keep a running list of style decisions, sometimes called a style sheet, to guide writers as they draft their assignments.

After you have delineated the objectives, steps and requirements for the assignment, incorporate the objectives and steps into a timeline or schedule for completion, including milestones for success. If the assignment requires a team approach, account for each team member's time and assignments. You can use a table or Gantt chart to illustrate your schedule and timeline. Draw from the information you gained in Chapter 8 on visual information to write this section of the plan. As a whole, this section describes your methods for completing the assignment and sets important milestones that help you gauge your progress.

Resource Allocation

This section includes descriptions of personnel assigned to the project and their roles, materials or resources needed, and a budget. While some readers will pay close attention to your entire plan, this section will be of considerable interest to corporate management and accountants because this section estimates the costs of the projects. It takes into account the expenses created when one or more employees complete the project, new or additional equipment is required, and deadlines are missed. In an earlier chapter, you read about the process of allocating resources in more detail; the outcomes of that process are incorporated into the document or project plan described in this section. Resources may also be required, as discussed in this chapter, for permissions of content that you do not produce yourself. In addition to incorporating the budget figures and estimates, you will also need to explain briefly what the overall expenses are as well as depicting them in table or chart.

Request for Approval

When you are working on a complex project, you will likely need to submit your plan for approval. Sometimes this approval is given informally through team consensus, but at other times, approval requires signatures from management to move forward. Whatever the situation, prepare your document plan as your organizational conventions require and get sign-offs to ensure that your plan has the necessary support and backing needed to succeed. Signatures and contact information are usually placed at the beginning or end of the document plan.

Putting the Plan Together

For example, Figure 4.8 is a short document plan for a professional resume. Depending on the scope of your document or project plan, the plan itself can vary greatly in length and format. If your organization has legacy plans that you can review, these documents should provide you with the greatest assistance in designing the plan. If not, then you will need to consider who will read the plan and how it will be used. If the plan is for your use only, you may simply create a file with jotted notes that you can use as you complete your work. If the plan will have more formal readers, then you might create a more formal report that contains headings and graphics and that can be distributed electronically to others for their review. For plans that teams will follow, a file shared on an intranet or file-sharing site, such as GoogleDocs, might serve your purposes. A shared file will allow you and team members to add and edit information as your plan evolves. Whatever form your plan takes, it should probably address all of the following questions. You can use the checklist that follows Figure 4.8 to determine if your plan is complete:

Professional Résumé Document Work Plan

Overview of outcomes: The purpose of my résumé is to get a job as technical writer. It needs to address every requirement or skill the company is seeking. I need to stand out from the crowd because I just earned my degree and I already have two years internship experience.

Analysis of audience: The managers who will read my résumé will review it with a critical eye for grammar, design, and content. They will check their job requirements against my education and experience to see how well I meet their needs. They will not consider me if my résumé has spelling or grammar errors. The jobs I want are asking for someone who can write clearly, use technologies (like Word and Adobe InDesign), and edit. Managers will want to know that I have completed projects and created documents like this ones they produce. They will also want to know about how well I collaborate with others and how well I can conduct research to gather content. They will want me to show them my skills by mentioning projects I've completed in coursework and internships. They will want to know about my experience writing grants for Big Brothers Big Sisters and Jefferson County.

Methods and milestones: Here are a few ideas I have about how to create a strong résumé.

- List documents I've produced in my classes
- List documents I've produced at my internships
- List skills I've used to produce these documents like researching on the Internet, interviewing, and formatting documents
- List technologies I know like InDesign, Word, and Excel
- Research résumé examples to make sure my résumé design and format are competitive
- Figure out how to organize all of these lists in résumé content

I should probably keep my résumé to one-page in length. I need to have it ready for evaluation by September 28th, and I need a PERFECT revision in time for the Career Fair in mid-October.

Resource Allocations: I plan to draft résumé in a two-hour block I've set aside on September 20th. I will need my laptop and Microsoft Word to create my draft. I also need to find my old résumé from the Career Center to see if I can use it as a starting place. I will need printer paper for reviewing my drafts. I need to see if my brother has résumé paper left over from his job search. I can use that paper or get some résumé paper for my final draft.

Figure 4.8. This is an example of a document plan for a professional resume.

The Document Plan

1. Have you analyzed your audience and included user profiles and/or use scenarios in the document plan?
2. Does your document plan include an assignment purpose statement and objective(s) for reaching this purpose?
3. Does it include specifications and requirements for the final deliverable?
4. Does it include methods and milestones for completing the assignment?
5. Does your plan include visual aids that illustrate your resource allocation?
6. If it will be distributed to others, is your plan free from grammatical and mechanical errors?
7. If it will be distributed to others, have you included advance organizers in your plan to assist your readers?
8. Have you evaluated your plan for completeness and accuracy?

Chapter Summary

Technical communication products vary widely and are typically characterized by specific genres, or categories of documents. Genres help define organizational patterns based on the document's overall purpose and are used and recognized across disciplines and workplaces. Each genre is comprised of various document types that fit specific audiences, purposes, or contexts. Within each document type, smaller variations in design, content, style, and organization exist based on organizational and other constraints.

Legacy documents (or legacy content) are also important to the initial stages of writing technical documents, and involves researching existing sources that can help write new documents. They provide an informed foundation, including relevant background information, for writing technical documents. They can also serve as models for writing style, organization, and consistency.

Document conventions exist in many forms, including formal (written) and informal (tacit knowledge). These can include professional style guides, document templates, and other unwritten forms of knowledge within an organization. Conventions help maintain consistency in content organization and stylistics, and contribute to technical document quality, usability, and accessibility. When using content from existing sources, it is also important to consider copyright and intellectual property considerations, such as citation, fair use, and acquiring permissions.

After determining your communication product and considering its forms and formats, your final step is to create a document or project plan. Such a plan provides a working outline of content, genre, format, and style as well as organizational considerations, such as resource allocation and timelines. The format of such plans will vary, depending on their purpose and the scope of the project, but developing a plan early can help you and your team produce your communication efficiently and effectively.

Chapter Assignments

The exercises in this section ask you to apply what you have learned in this chapter as well as explore how this knowledge applies to and connects with other information in the textbook.

1. From Table 4.1, select a specific genre of technical documents. Interview a technical writer, subject matter expert, or other professional about the different technical document types within that genre. Ask how the genre and specific technical document types are used within their organization and how they contribute to them (i.e., as reader, editor, subject matter expert, approver, etc.). Also ask what other kinds of technical document types they typically write most often and any specific guidelines for writing them.

2. Locate a technical report written and recently published by a local organization or company. Scan the document looking for references to other documents, including any footnotes or works cited list at the end of the report. Contact the organization and inquire about what other kinds of information is typically used as legacy content to produce similar reports. Inquire about the process of developing new reports, including what style guides, conventions, and other decisions are part of the writing process. Also ask about any important lessons learned or best practices they would offer to new writers. Share your findings with your class.

3. Locate a professional style guide for a specific discipline. Read through its table of contents and skim any sections that specifically address writing style and conventions. Make note of some of the general guidelines to share with others. Which of these seem to be discipline specific, or unique to a specific profession? Discuss with your classmates how writing style and conventions are similar and different between different disciplines.

4. Research the subject of "fair use" by performing an online search. Read on the history of fair use and its relationship to copyright and intellectual property issues. How does fair use differ in educational vs. organizational or workplace products? How has electronic content and the Internet affected the ways in which fair use is determined?

5. Visit *klariti.com* tips + tools: *Smart Business Tips for Smart People*, a Dublin, Ireland, based blog and commercial site (http://www.klariti.com). In addition to blogging ideas for better business writing, the site also sells templates for business writing. Two articles on klariti.com tips + tools: provide discussions of document plans: the document planning checklist (http://www.klariti.com/technical-writing/Document-Planning-Checklist.shtml) and the business action plan template (http://www.klariti.com/action-plan-template/): the Business Action Plan. Compare these document plans to those described in this chapter. How and why are they similar and different to the chapter's recommendations?

6. Businessballs.com is a website developed and run by Alan Chapman, in Leicester, England. This website has multiple resources for project planning business projects. In the project management section of the website, you will find a section called "Project Management Tools," which describes four different visuals that are useful for project plans: brainstorming, fishbone diagrams, project critical path analysis (flow diagram or chart), and Gantt charts (http://www.businessballs.com/project.htm#project-management-tools). Read about these different tools and differentiate between them: when and where are they most effectively used in project plans?

7. Working with one or two partners, plan a simple communication project and sketch a project plan. Possible project include sending a birthday greeting, asking for a day off from work to attend a wedding, making an appointment for a meeting with your college advisor, arranging for a group meeting in your instructor's office, or a simple project of your own. You have 10 minutes to plan the project (not to complete it). As you work, make a record of the steps in your planning process, and be ready answer the following questions:

    a. With whom are you planning to communicate and why?

    b. Does the recipient of your communication modify the actions you plan to take or decisions you make? What planning decisions did you make?

    c. What tasks have you planned to complete and in what order?

    d. How long do you estimate it will take you to complete the project?

    e. What will the project cost?

Report your answers to the class, as a whole. Remember the object of the exercise is not to *complete* the project, but to *plan* it. After the class has discussed and critiqued your plan, revise it and write up a one- to two-page project plan with your partner(s).

Figure Credits

Figure 4.1. © Olena Yakobchuk/Shutterstock.com

Figure 4.2. © Cristian Lungu/Shutterstock.com

Figure 4.3. U.S. Government Printing Office

Figure 4.4. Reprinted by permission of Dr. Laura Brandenburg

Figure 4.6. © Dragon Images/Shutterstock.com

Figure 4.7. © Trueffelpix/Shutterstock.com

Building Teams and Improving Processes

5

CHAPTER OVERVIEW

This chapter introduces you to the concepts of project management, process maturity, and successful teaming practices. After reading this chapter, you should be able to meet the following objectives:

- Explain why teaming is so important in the 21st century workplaces.
- Distinguish between different kinds of workplace teams and functional roles.
- Identify and implement strategies for effective teaming.
- Describe personal attributes that support effective teaming.
- Identify information technologies that support distributed teamwork.
- Describe and discuss project management and the process maturity model as they pertain to technical communication projects.
- Discuss the relationship between iterative work processes and maturity of those processes.
- Describe the three phases of process maturity.
- Propose specific strategies for working towards sustainable work practices, process improvement, and quality assurance.

Recent changes in workplace communication methods and tools underscore the importance of project management and sustainable work practices in virtually every industry today. Organizations have become increasingly globalized, with distributed work teams and responsibilities. In today's workplace, you will likely work on teams where individuals are located in different offices or cities and use a variety of electronic communication tools to work collaboratively. Electronic communication technologies, such as the Internet, social media tools, and cloud computing, have made it easier to collaborate more rapidly, with more sophisticated tools, and across wider geographic distances. Online networking and researching tools allow technical communicators to consult with a wider range of subject matter experts and information resources. As a result, the need for consistency, standardization, translation, accessibility, and reusability of content has placed additional demands on information resources and associated products. As such, formalizing project management activities, working practices, and processes can help address these needs and provide a structured working environment that an organization needs to be competitive and successful in today's global business market. This chapter focuses on team building, process maturity, and management.

Defining Team Roles

Another important aspect of project management is defining specific team roles, outlining the tasks and responsibilities for each role, and determining how each will function as part of the iterative process. As an important part of process planning, team roles and skills needed for a project should be clearly defined and documented in a project plan. While specific roles may vary widely depending on the type of product, resources available, and expertise of available staff, they often include roles specified in Table 5.1.

Project managers	Designers	Technical staff	Editors	Testers	Writers
track tasks, resources, and deliverables. They also manage team, communication, and content strategy.	oversee graphic design, page layout, and multimedia development.	oversee programming, coding, markup, network or systems administration.	revise and review content. They also oversee developmental writing.	conduct usability tests, including user and individual tests.	research, write, and develop content.

Table 5.1. Team Roles

Depending on the number of individuals available to comprise a team, multiple people may serve one role or function, or one person may serve multiple roles or functions. Often, technical communicators, as practitioners with multiple skill sets and specializations, serve in more than one role on a documentation project, such as project manager, writer, and editor. Depending on their skill sets, assigned roles for each team member may vary from project to project. Additionally, depending on the resources and skills available, new or more highly specialized roles may need to be defined. Figure 5.1 illustrates the many team roles possible in workplace communication projects.

In addition to these roles and tasks, project managers are also typically responsible for maintaining important documents that define and report on the overall project scope and goals. These documents include a project plan, project schedule, progress reports, memoranda, and the actual project deliverables. While a project manager may not have the individual responsibility for writing these documents, the manager often coordinates and collects information from continual communication and contribution from individual team members, and the project manager supervises their writing and development.

Another important part of successful project management is developing a sustainable **content strategy** for projects. Content strategy involves developing specific processes, practices, and methods of creating, structuring, producing, and reusing content effectively across platforms and teams (Rockley & Cooper, 2012). Often these project management responsibilities include the development of strategies for sharing knowledge and information resources across distributed teams, through a wider range of online publishing tools and platforms, including Wikis, Web sites, and social media applications (Dalkir, 2011). It is the project manager's responsibility to communicate this strategy to the team through the project plan to help keep the team on track.

Project management activities can also reflect the level of **process maturity**, or overall commitment to sustainable practices and their improvement, within an organization or team. As project documentation, assessment, quality tracking, scheduling, written process, and other such activities become more formalized and improved, the team or organization becomes more process mature. As a result, project management and the project manager have a significant impact on the overall organization's process maturity, as well as the success and quality of a particular project.

Figure 5.1. Work teams are comprised of different functional responsibilities such as project managers, designers, technical staff, editors, testers, writers, and others.

DISTRIBUTED WORKPLACES AND TEAMS

You might be surprised to learn that teaming—working with one or more coworkers, colleagues, or customers to accomplish a goal or complete a task—is consistently identified as one of the key skills necessary for success in the 21st century workplace. Why is teaming so important? Today's workplace has few jobs that require individuals to work completely alone. Almost everyone is connected to others, and these connections allow workers to share information, to develop solutions, and to implement plans collaboratively. Individual workers are not only connected to each other technologically through instant messaging and email, but they are also frequently joined into teams to complete complex tasks that require group problem-solving, such as planning, development, and review. It is not uncommon for new team configurations to be formed for almost every project. Depending on the needs of the particular project, team members may be located in adjacent cubicles or scattered across the globe.

> **EXERCISE 5.1**
>
> ## *Defining Project Roles for a Team*
>
> Your project team has been asked to develop a Web site for the local chapter of the Animal Humane Society. The Web site will include content about the local shelter, information about services and adoption, photos and videos, and a feedback form for site users with contact information for the shelter. For this task, you will identify the skills required for the tasks, survey the skills of your team, and write descriptions of roles and assign them to individual members of your team.
>
> **Tasks to be completed:**
>
> 1. Identify the skills required to develop the Web site project.
> 2. Survey individual team members to determine their skill sets, using the typical team roles list provided above as a guide.
> 3. Write descriptions of roles needed for the project. You may modify, combine, or create new roles, as needed.
> 4. Assign individual members to roles.
> 5. Discuss some of the decisions made in developing and assigning roles with other groups.

Within organizations, business practices like outsourcing (work completed by contract workers outside the home office) and offshoring (similar to outsourcing except that the contracted workers are generally located in another country) result in the creation of virtual teams, requiring individuals to work with others across time and space. Even workers located in the same geographic area are taking advantage of virtual teaming, completing their work by telecommuting from their home offices. Technologies, such as social media, groupware, and collaborative authoring applications, allow and support the work of these distributed teams.

Because teaming is such an important part of the 21st century workplace, the latter half of this chapter focuses on teamwork. Although you may sometimes work alone, your work will almost always require you to engage with others and to rely on these individuals for content, support, and other tasks you cannot complete yourself. For this reason, you should know how to work with different types of teams and how to perform varied teams activities. You should also recognize and know how to implement strategies for working in teams, including how to use technologies that can help you do this work. The chapter concludes with important considerations to help you work well with others. While most of the examples in this section refer to writing in teams, these guidelines are effective regardless of the kind of team project you find yourself engaged in, and they can help you to allocate your team's resources more effectively when scheduling and making assignments.

What are the Advantages and Disadvantages of Teaming?

Teams are useful for solving complex problems and completing complicated tasks, like writing documentation or proposals. Individuals working alone can often complete the same work that a team can, but working alone takes more time, focus, and commitment. Solutions that are individually completed can sometimes be myopic, or short-sighted, because individuals cannot take into account all the aspects necessary for successful problem resolution. In contrast, teams can tackle problems and find solutions by drawing upon these strengths:

- Multiple experiences and approaches for problem-solving or researching can lead to unique and innovative solutions.
- Team members typically have differing interactions with clients, users, or customers, so the team has a broader perspective and understanding of their target audience's needs.
- Shared decision-making allows solutions to be vetted and approved after being considered from many angles.
- Distributed work responsibilities draw upon the team's varied skills, allowing team members to focus on what they know best.
- Distributed work responsibilities also allow team members to multitask, potentially working on several projects at once.
- Diverse feedback derived from team members' skills, training, and experiences increases possibilities for overcoming obstacles and arriving at successful solutions.
- When successful, working in teams can be socially satisfying, improving morale and building a sense of community within workplaces.

Of course, not all team projects are successful. Among the reasons for team failure, inadequate team-building and project management are most often the culprits. When teams are inadequately built and managed, they may suffer from a lack of focus; that is, team members do not know why they are on the team, what the project goals are, or what they should contribute. Lack of focus can also result in **project creep** (when the project gets larger and larger because the goals are unclear) and **wheel spinning** (when teams spend too much time planning and re-planning without gaining traction or accomplishing their goals). Conflict among team members often accompanies these problems, and disunity, dissatisfaction, and decreased morale may soon follow. All of these problems can result in a reduced sense of ownership and disjointed communications. This is why it is so important to understand the kinds of teams that occur in workplaces and know how to make them work.

EXERCISE 5.2

Thinking about Team Experiences

Recall team experiences you have already had at work or at school. Describe a good team experience and a bad one. What made the first experience a good one? What went wrong with the second? What new insights has this chapter given you for building good teams and improving bad ones?

Tasks to be completed:

1. Write a short description of two team experiences, one good and one bad.
2. Make a list of pros and cons for each experience.
3. Identify specific strategies or lessons from the chapter that align with your list of pros and cons.
4. Make a list of other lessons learned, looking back, that you would recommend to others or use in future team projects.

What Kinds of Teams are Commonly Found in Workplaces?

Teams are typically categorized by location of their members, their members' specialties, and team tasks. When teams are categorized by location, three types commonly occur:

- **Face-to-face teams**: These teams occur when all members are located in the same space, work approximately the same hours, and can meet at the same time and place. Before the internet allowed teams to meet technologically, almost all teams met face-to-face. Members who did not work or live locally, that is, within commuting distance of the same office, had to travel to participate in team meetings.

- **Virtual teams**: In virtual teams, at least one of the team members does not work within commuting distance of the home office and must participate in teamwork through technology. Virtual teams collaborate technologically using shared files and other resources and communicate using telephone, email, instant message, and conferencing applications. Sometimes, virtual teams are also called *distributed* teams because they are located, or distributed, in different locations geographically.

- **Hybrid teams**: Hybrid teams meet face-to-face occasionally but also rely on virtual teaming to conduct business. Individuals on these teams use technology to support their work, depending on their locations and their availability to meet in person.

Location is only one means of categorizing teams; teams are also formed according to members' specializations. When teams are categorized by specialization, two types are possible. **Functional teams** are made up of individuals with the similar training and background. These teams work together on common goals. Functional teams draw upon team members' common skills and knowledge to complete large projects quickly and efficiently. For example, groups of software developers may work in pairs or teams to program or test an application. In the same way, teams of writers may work together to write the software documentation or a grant proposal with all individuals contributing parts to the same document. While contract or outside workers are sometimes included in functional teams, they are generally hired because of their knowledge and experience with the specific task to be completed. Unlike functional teams that are similar in training and background, **cross-functional teams** are comprised of individuals with different backgrounds, skills, and training. Cross-functional teams draw upon the varied perspectives and strengths that individual team members bring to play within the group. A cross-functional team at a biomedical company might be comprised of individuals with backgrounds in management, nursing, engineering, marketing, and technical writing. Cross-functional teams may also include individuals from outside the organization, such as contractors, clients, customers, and consultants, who add valuable insights in accomplishing the team task. Cross-functional teams, unlike functional teams, are often temporarily formed. They are created to accomplish specific, targeted tasks; upon completion, they are dissolved. New teams then take their place, depending on the needs of the next project.

A third way to categorize teams is to consider their reasons for coming together for work, their work tasks or purposes. These two categories are known as **communities of practice** and **communities of inquiry**. Communities of practice (CoP) are comprised of individuals who have a common interest and who come together *to learn* more about that interest. They engage each other in discussions, tell stories, and share information with each other. CoPs are common online. For example, motorcycle enthusiasts form CoPs when they participate in online discussion forums, suggesting rides to other enthusiasts, learning how to work on their machines, and sharing information about useful products. Similarly in the workplace, a group of engineers might work together to research an aspect of a particular problem, or a group of teachers might form a community of practice to implement a new teaching strategy. In all their endeavors, CoPs focus on learning. They typically include a core group of individuals who are joined in varying degrees by others to help solve problems and activate learning, yet they are open to outsiders because new members frequently bring new knowledge to group discussions In contrast, Communities of inquiry (CoI) are created when individuals come together to solve a complex problem. Individuals join the community because they have specific skills and knowledge that will aid in problem-solving. Within a community of inquiry, all participants are encouraged to engage in questioning and discussing possible solutions to the complex problem. CoIs focus on problem-solving, and new members are rarely invited to join once the team is formed.

Figure 5.2. Teams that come together to complete a tasks are called communities of inquiry (CoI).

Understanding different categories of teams can help you to form workgroups that achieve your specific purpose. For example, if you need to solve a complex problem that requires knowledge across professions or disciplines, then you will likely form a CoI cross-functional team comprised of individuals with differing areas of expertise. On the other hand, if your organization has an information need that requires research, you might create a functional CoP comprised of individuals with some knowledge of the topic. Whatever configuration you choose, however, you will need to know how to work successfully as a team player and leader.

What Strategies do you need to be a Successful Team Player?

The strategies described in this section are organized chronologically from the beginning of the project to the end. Recognizing when these strategies come into play can help you to establish and check the well-being of your team. Using them will help you to complete teamwork successfully.

Getting Started

When teams form, it is important to understand the team's goals, acknowledge the different personalities and their contributions to the team, and build a strong support system for accomplishing team work.

Establishing a Personal Identity

Sometimes project managers, the individuals who form teams, are present at the first meeting to explain the team's assignments and composition. If a project manager is not present to introduce you, then you must introduce yourself by describing your abilities, training, and background. Take this opportunity to disclose your primary work functions and describe anything else you think you might be able to contribute to the team's work. Introductions from each team member will help you to understand how team members' talents fit together for this particular project and allow you to determine if you are working as a functional or cross-functional team.

Designating a Leader

When all members have introduced themselves, it is time for work to begin. Even though teams often have project managers, these supervisors may not actually work directly with the team. When a leader is not yet identified, the team's first task is to designate a leader, someone with teaming experience and a clear understanding of the problem or product that the team is producing. Your introductions typically help you to identify this person, but, if not, the team will need to weigh each person's strengths and afterward designate one person to lead.

Writing a Purpose Statement

With a designated leader identified, the team's next assignment is to write a brief purpose statement and objectives. Purpose statements outline the job the team must accomplish. Is the purpose of the team to solve or fix a problem, to create a document, to design a product, or to implement a plan? After answering this question, consider whether your team will be working as a CoP (community of practice seeking to learn or gain knowledge) or a CoI (community of inquiry seeking to solve a complex problem). Stating the team's purpose clearly from the beginning of the project, assures that each member understands the end game, the result that everyone is working toward. With this purpose in mind, team members are almost ready to develop a plan, outline, or list of steps necessary to complete the project.

Setting the Ground Rules

The final step before developing a project plan is to set some ground rules for team interactions. Every team encounters problems or experiences conflict eventually. In fact, constructive conflict is one of the reasons teams can be so effective; innovative ideas emerge from the clash of ideas and the creative input of diverse team members. Unfortunately, not all team conflict is constructive. That is why it is important to establish ground rules for behavior and decision-making early in the process. To begin this process, you must decide what to do when conflicts arise: How will the team handle disagreement? Is a procedure necessary for stating differences of opinion? When two or more individuals disagree about an action, who will arbitrate the differences? What if the disagreement gets personal? Thinking ahead about the kinds of conflict that can arise will prepare the team to continue to work positively and smoothly together.

Working as a Team

Projects generally require teams to meet frequently to complete the task and check progress. Even after individual assignments are made, team members rely on each other to report their progress and seek guidance when they encounter obstacles. Successful teams employ strategies to make sure their meetings are efficient and productive. The following suggestions are designed to help team members and leaders work productively in meetings.

General Etiquette Suggestions

These suggestions apply to everyone on the team, both members and leaders. They imply that team members should work to be ethical and considerate of others.

- **Be a good listener**. (Figure 5.3) Pay attention to what others' are saying in team meetings. Jot down notes to make sure you understand key points, and ask questions, if necessary. If you need to ask questions, wait until the speaker finishes.

- **Be courteous of others**. Being courteous takes many forms on a team, such as being aware of others' workspaces, especially when these spaces are shared or when you are working at a conference table. Keep your work organized and do not take up more space than necessary. Courtesy can also mean respecting your team members' privacy by not writing negatively about them on social networking spaces, like Twitter, Facebook, or LinkedIn. Courtesy also includes acknowledging others' contributions to the team and crediting others for their work. Finally, you are courteous when you respect others' time and do your own work. In other words, do not be a slacker.

Figure 5.3. Listening to each other is an important skill for teams.

- **Respect cultural differences**. Cultural differences, especially in teams that are geographically dispersed, can cause problems with team communication and trust-building. Cultural differences can become especially problematic when we stereotype, assuming we know someone based on a "type," a TV or movie character, or someone else with a similar background. To avoid these kinds of problems, take the time to learn about people from different cultures with whom you work, and be frank if you do not understand a team member's perspective on a problem. Being frank means initiating a conversation with the person and explaining what seems odd or unusual to you about your interactions. Avoid accusatory statements that place your misunderstanding on others; people respond better if they understand that you are having a problem with your ability to communicate and need help. Remembering the previous suggestion to be courteous, engage individuals who are culturally different from you and be respectful of new ways of seeing and doing work. If cultural differences get in the way of accomplishing your goals, work with your teammate to acknowledge the differences and then move on to more constructive conversation and work.

- **Respect disciplinary differences on cross-functional teams**. When individuals with different backgrounds, training, and skills come together, prejudices and biases can easily arise. Many times these prejudices and biases present themselves in the words we use; for example, team members from similar disciplines may use jargon, or professional language, that other team members do not understand. When members do not understand jargon or ask questions, they may be ridiculed as "dumb" or "less well educated." When jargon is used to gain power over others, it is belittling to those who do not understand it, and belittling others does not build strong teams. Power issues can also come into play when some members have more training or education than others and seek to gain advantage by exploiting these differences at the expense of others. Successful teams and their leaders recognize these games for what they are—obstacles to successful team interactions—and avoid them.

> ## EXERCISE 5.3
>
> ## *Thinking about Cultural Differences in Teams*
>
> Have you ever noted a cultural difference with someone else? Describe it. Did it affect your ability to communicate or work with that person? How so?
>
> **Tasks to be completed:**
>
> 1. Make a list of a few cultural differences you have encountered when working on teams.
> 2. Write a short description of each.
> 3. For each description, give examples of how each instance affected your ability to communicate with that person.

Teams rely on synergy, the idea that the whole is greater than its parts. Team members are selected for projects because of the strengths that they bring to the project, and members have individual responsibility to use those strengths to complete the project. In addition, team members have a responsibility to each other. The suggestions below describe some of the behaviors you can adopt to become a successful team player.

- **Be trustworthy**. One of the most important behaviors you can exhibit as a team member is trustworthiness. Within a team relationship, trustworthiness means that you are predictable and reliable: in simplest terms, you do what you say you will do. When you are given assignments, you complete them in a timely manner. When you receive email from a team member, you respond. When a team meeting is scheduled, you show up on time and prepared to work. When you have a deadline, you meet it or beat it. If team members are trustworthy, teams function more smoothly because members are responsible for and complete the work they are assigned to do.

- **Do not succumb to groupthink**. Groupthink occurs when team members conform to the same ideas without questioning their soundness. Groupthink hurts teams because it can lead to mediocrity and a lack of personal responsibility within the team. To avoid groupthink, speak up when you are in team meetings. Share your perspective. Remember that you were selected for the team because of the insights and talents you offer. Constructive conflict can lead to creative solutions, so do not be afraid to state your opinion, even if it differs from others. When you do disagree with others, however, be courteous, calm, and clear as you state your ideas.

- **Support and be supported**. When you feel isolated, reach out to the team members for support and help. At the same time, be willing to help others when they reach out to you.

What Strategies Do You Need to Lead a Team?

As a team leader, your role is to organize and support your team's efforts, keeping the project moving forward while, at the same time, checking your progress along the way. Below are a few suggestions that can help you with this work.

Recordkeeping

Running a smooth team meeting is easy if you plan your time together using an agenda, a list of items to guide the team discussion. Using an agenda keeps the discussion focused and productive. Some agendas include the amount of time the leader plans to spend on each topic, but other agendas are less structured, such as a simple emailed list of items that the meeting will cover. The key to a successful agenda is to send it by email before the meeting and ask the group to review it to be sure you have covered all the important topics. When you have the member's feedback, organize the agenda so that important information is discussed first. Less important information can be tabled for later meetings, if discussion runs long. Equally important are meeting minutes. As the team leader you may keep the minutes or designate another member to write them. Like agendas, meeting minutes can be very detailed or very simple. Ideally, meeting minutes capture key decisions and record actions to be taken, agreements made, or assignments given or completed.

Distribute Agendas and Minutes

Use the communication technologies available to your team to distribute your team agendas, minutes, and other agreements as quickly as possible. To stay on top of their assignments, team members not only need to know what is expected of them but also to report how well they are accomplishing their tasks. Minutes and agendas are useful for documenting decisions and making new assignments, but they are also important for tracking attendance and progress. These documents are discussed in detail in a later chapter.

Keep in Touch with the Team but Do not Micromanage

A common team problem occurs when team members feel isolated, especially when teams are working virtually. When team members feel isolated or disconnected from others, their productivity may decrease and they accomplish less. Informing team members that you will check with them periodically establishes a connection and an expectation, which can help keep team members on track and productive. Be careful, however, not to hover or micromanage. Your role as leader is not to manage or oversee others' work but to support them as they do it. Let your team know you are available to help with obstacles or problems that arise, but, most importantly, let them do their work.

What Technologies Promote Teaming?

A final consideration when forming teams is how your team will use technology. Teaming in the 21st century workplaces relies on many technologies to get teamwork completed. The information in this section briefly introduces you to some of the technologies that assist teamwork. In this brief section, we discuss technologies that promote synchronous and asynchronous meetings.

Synchronous Meetings

Synchronous meetings are real-time meetings. They allow active and immediate interactions between team members. Meeting synchronously, however, can be challenging when team members live and work in differing time zones. For examples, 1:00 pm in the United States' Central Daylight Time zone is 4:00 am in Seoul, Korea. Late morning and early afternoon synchronous meetings will require sacrifices of time and sleep in situations like this.

Figure 5.4. When some members are located in the same office but others are distributed elsewhere, teams need to employ technologies to connect them.

If your team members are distributed (not located in the same office), then you will need to access technology that will connect all the members of the group. The simplest technology is likely telephone services that allow you to connect one or more team members. Internet technologies can also provide such service. Depending on your organization's budget, many internet applications allow you to see and hear others synchronously, including Skype, Adobe Connect, and Go2Meeting. Most of these applications also allow you chat on an SMS backchannel, use a whiteboard to take notes or brainstorm, or open a video channel to distributed members of the team.

Asynchronous Meetings

When groups are not able to meet in real-time because of time or budget constraints, meeting asynchronously is an option. Asynchronous communication occurs outside the office at any time from anyplace. To share information asynchronously, consider these options:

- Telephone messaging and instant messaging allow you to exchange short, quick messages or ask questions
- Email exchanges support longer conversations or are useful for exchanging written drafts
- Collaborative workspaces like wikis and Google Docs support co-authoring tasks and allow uploading of completed drafts
- Intranet shared drives and cloud computing support co-authoring and uploading completed drafts. (If you use a shared drive or cloud, be sure to develop naming conventions for files, so you can distinguish between them and their versions.)
- Wikis allow you to track changes easily and efficiently by identifying authors' contributions, noting changes made, and archiving dates of change and previous versions. They also allow you to backtrack to see previous versions of the same document.
- Word processing and publishing applications like Microsoft Word and Adobe Acrobat can help you to review, annotate, change, and track changes in documents.

> ### EXERCISE 5.4
>
> ### *Using Technologies to Collaborate*
>
> Have you ever used audio or teleconferencing software to collaborate to others? Which ones? How well did it work? Describe your experiences.
>
> After you have described your previous experiences, choose a partner and use a free online communication tool, such as Google Hangouts, Google Docs, or Blackboard's integrated meeting application. What challenges did you encounter as you used the technology? What are the advantages and disadvantages of such technologies?
>
> **Tasks to be completed:**
>
> 1. Make a list of audio or teleconferencing software you have used in communicating or collaborating with others on team projects.
> 2. Write a sentence or two for each describing your overall experiences.
> 3. Select a free online communication tool and practice using it with another individual.
> 4. Identify specific advantages and disadvantages of the tool.

TEAM PROCESS IMPROVEMENT

Every team has practices and processes that can be improved upon. Effective project management is also based on improvement of both the team and its processes. Effective business practices can also contribute to ethical business practices. Think of **process maturity** as a method of evaluating or measuring the overall effectiveness of an organization or team, and setting goals towards improvement. The process maturity model helps evaluate a team's effectiveness in terms of its structure, sustainability, usability, and innovation. Collectively these factors describe characteristics of the team's managers, workers, work processes and practices, standards, and customer focus. And when project managers and teams work towards improving these aspects, it contributes to higher levels of process maturity. This section discusses practices and strategies that contribute to process improvement, or maturity.

Structure

A team's structure is defined by its organized formal procedures and processes. For example, a team with effective structure explicitly discusses how to organize content into deliverables such as manuals, tutorials, technical reports, and Web sites. As noted in Chapter 2, this discussion is called information modeling, that is, discussing how information can be organized for different purposes and audiences. Information modeling requires the team to think systematically, and systematic thinking reflects greater research and superior organization in higher levels of process maturity. In addition to knowing how to organize content effectively, more mature teams also use set templates to ensure consistency and organization in their technical products and documents. Structure also includes the organization of the project, by creating consistent standards, documenting and formalizing processes and roles, and using planning tools to track various project metrics, such as time, cost, and resource allocation.

Sustainability

Sustainability means learning from the past and planning for the future. Teams with process maturity think about the success and longevity of processes and practices. Specifically, they conduct reviews as they complete tasks and projects, document what they have learned from these activities, and use this knowledge to determine what practices and activities are worth repeating, improving, or eliminating. Teams with sustainable practices also create and test prototypes and develop and use set procedures throughout the lifecycle of a project, and potentially in future projects. Successful sustainability also involves regular assessment activities such as evaluating quality metrics of a project; that is, teams know how much time, money, and resources a project requires. They use this knowledge to plan for future projects. Sustainability and product stability tend to be implemented in mid- and higher levels of process maturity.

Usability

Usability involves formal and informal testing the actual use of a product within a specific working context, or against a set of heuristics or standards to ensure they conform to user needs and functioning specifications. These tests and heuristics typically involve actual users with the goal of collecting feedback to inform revisions and future iterations of a product. The goal of usability is to improve the accessibility, readability, and ease of use of a product or process.

As process maturity increases, so does the focus on the customer and usability. Robert Johnson (1998) characterizes three different approaches to designing technical products, with ties to software development practices that identify the level of involving the customer, or user, in the overall process, which include the following:

- **System-centered approach**. Developers create products without considering specific user needs and expectations. They create features, structures, and systems based on their own mental models and unique understanding of a product at the developer's level of knowledge.
- **User-friendly approach**. Developers create products with some data and feedback from what is known about users and their preferences. Some attention is given to product design that attempts to appeal to some of the user expectations and information needs. While the actual product may seem more system-centered in nature, a user-friendly product may add design features, performance tips, or other minor additions to help the user understand or use the product more easily.
- **User-centered approach**. Developers involve users throughout the entire process of product development, including the collection of user feedback during planning stages, user testing and feedback during design and development of drafts and prototypes, and comprehensive usability testing towards production and delivery. A commitment to monitoring user feedback after product deployment is typical, through the use of forums, surveys, focus groups, and emails.

There is also a relationship between process maturity and these different approaches. System-centered approaches that tend to discount user feedback are typical in lower process maturity levels. User-friendly approaches consider some user feedback and expectations reflected in mid-level process maturity. User-centered approaches involve users throughout the project development process and consider users' input as potential sources of innovation. User-centered approaches are more typical in higher levels of process maturity.

> ### EXERCISE 5.5
> ### *Innovating your own Writing Process*
>
> Think about your own writing process and habits when writing a longer report for a class or in your current job. If you had to write a short set of instructions that describes the process, what steps would you include? For example, do you make notes or outlines before starting? Do you write a few sentences for each section or work it all out in your head before you write the final product? Do you divide up the writing by section, number of words, pages, or some other method? Once you have written your process down into steps, make a list of improvements to your process that could help you be more efficient in your writing process.
>
> **Tasks to be completed:**
>
> 1. Write a list of numbered steps, or instructions, which describes your typical process for writing longer reports or papers.
> 2. Make a list of improvements to your process.
> 3. Revise your instructions by integrating the list of improvements.

Innovation

Innovation is all about improving, upgrading, and making products and processes better. It involves a commitment to process improvement and the integration of new practices and approaches. Organizations and teams committed to innovation will actively seek out feedback from workers, customers, and peer organizations on how to continually improve their own operations and processes. Project evaluation, as illustrated in Figure 5.5, is often an important part of innovation by collecting lessons learned from past projects, teams, and customers and by using these lessons to improve the process or future iterations of the project. Innovation strives towards overall improvement of the product by documenting improvements in processes, practices, quality and usability.

Figure 5.5. Evaluating projects as they end builds team knowledge and improves team maturity performance in future projects.

Process Maturity Levels

Process maturity levels can also vary within a single organization, down to the team or individual level, depending on a variety of factors. For example, an organization may function at mid-level process maturity, with repeated and sustainable work processes and procedures, while an individual team in that same organization may exist at a higher level in terms of its ability to innovate practices and incorporate user-centered design practices.

The Information Process Maturity Model (IPMM) describes how organizations and teams can improve and assess their process maturity in terms of successful elements and shortcomings (Hackos, 2007). In this model, Hackos characterizes six levels of process maturity which include oblivious, ad hoc, rudimentary, organized and repeatable, managed and sustainable, and optimizing (Hackos, 2007). Another way to characterize maturity is by ranking them low, mid, and high. Several key themes are present throughout the process maturity model, which suggest an incremental process from low to moderate to higher levels of process maturity (see Figure 5.6).

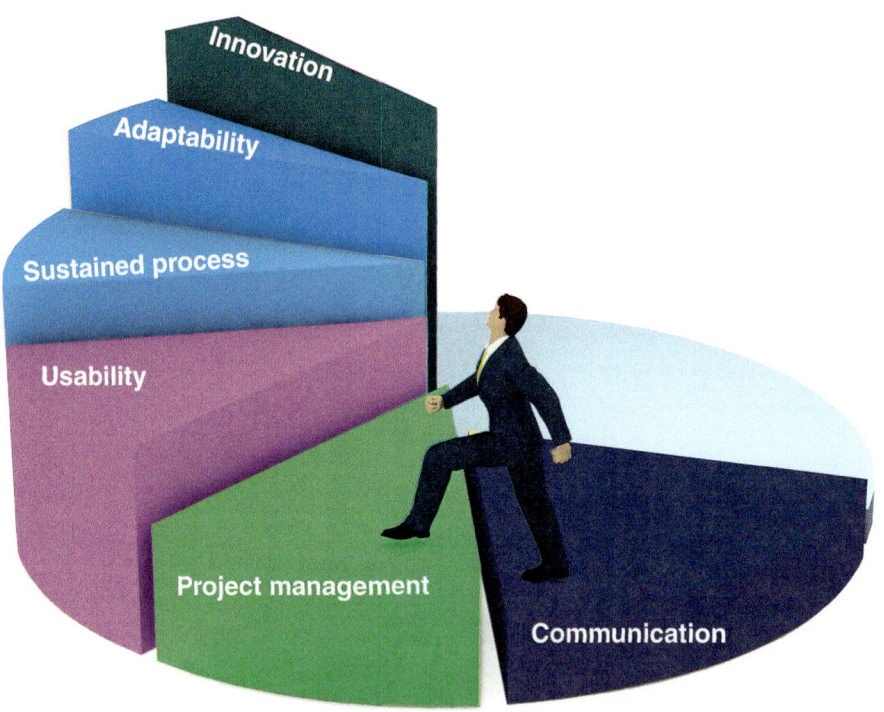

Figure 5.6. The incremental process of process maturity begins with communication and moves progressively towards higher levels of maturity, which include adaptability and innovation.

Low Level Maturity

Lower levels are often are characteristic of new project or ones where there are unstructured or semi-structured processes that dictate how to perform tasks. The lower levels of process maturity are characterized by an almost ad hoc approach to project and task completion. While low maturity processes typically offer a great deal of flexibility in accomplishing and assigning tasks, the lack of structure often causes problems with consistency, communication, and possibly project quality assurance and usability. This level may require several highly experienced and highly technically competent staff members who are capable of handling unforeseen dependencies and challenges throughout a project's development. Below are the characteristics, results, and needs of teams with low level maturity.

Low Level Maturity

Characteristics

- Team has limited or no structural processes for accomplishing projects or tasks.
- Lessons learned and assessment are not tracked; problems and poor quality are repeated.
- Team focus is on getting product out the door rather than the customer's needs.
- Team has limited or no commitment to usability testing or user-centered design practices.
- Team has high level of flexibility in accomplishing goals and tasks.

Results

- No repeatable processes
- Team coordination and communication problems
- Repeated mistakes, increased error reporting
- Increased problem reporting and need for technical support
- More revisions and higher costs for products

Needs

- Increased awareness of customers and their needs
- Documented processes and procedures to ensure compliance and consistency
- Project management
- Formalized metrics and assessment
- Organized structure for documents
- Prototyping and user testing
- Established and consistent standards and practices

Moderate Level Maturity

Moderate-level maturity levels often indicate the presence of repeatable and documented processes, a commitment to usability, some degree of assessment and tracking, and defined team roles and structure. It often relies on a certain level of experience with projects and teams. Despite these factors, sometimes mid-level maturity processes stagnate, where a procedure is followed blindly, without considering potential dependencies it creates or ways to improve those processes. Teams develop and implement a process and repeat it, but this environment may be challenging to individual contributors who tend to think outside the box and want to innovate processes and practices.

Moderate Level Maturity

Characteristics

- Repeatable and documented processes are used.
- Project management activities and reports are used.
- Quality and lessons learned are tracked and considered.
- Customer needs are considered to make products more user-friendly.
- Some formalized usability testing is conducted.

Results

- Repeated processes not continually updated and improved
- Some repeated mistakes
- Focus on completing projects and tasks per specs
- Processes for the sake of processes are placed ahead of improvement
- Resistance to change
- Barriers to innovation
- Process stagnation

Needs

- Willingness to change and adapt
- Focus on improving existing standards and processes
- Communication mechanisms for collecting feedback and ideas
- Implementation plans for lessons learned
- In-depth quality metric and assessment analytics

High Level Maturity

High levels of process maturity are all about building on previous successes. Higher levels of process maturity embrace innovation and process improvement throughout, encouraging new approaches and changes to existing roles, processes, and practices. While potentially inspiring for teams, without a clear vision and some degree of self-motivation and buy-in from team members, it can be difficult to manage changing standards and practices. As a result, less experienced team members may need additional mentoring or supervision to acclimate to such a rapidly changing work environment.

Each level has its own unique characteristics as well as relative advantages and disadvantages. Often, what the next level up has in terms of characteristics can be seen as goals for lower level organizations in improving their own process maturity. Process maturity is also a function of project management, sustainable practices, quality assurance, user integration, and commitment to innovation and improvement of practices. Process maturity is not a static value. It must be continually assessed since changing factors, including staff, resources, management, technologies, and business goals, can all affect an organization's maturity level in different ways.

High Level Maturity

Characteristics

- Processes are repeated and the team continues its commitment to improvement.
- Corporate culture includes innovation and outlets to collect and test feasibility of new ideas.
- The team sustains project management activities and is self-directed.
- The team uses formalized assessment methods and quality metrics.
- Customers are involved or the focus in all aspects of project.
- User-centered design practices integrate users throughout the entire project lifecycle.

Results

- Reduced error reporting and costs
- Commitment to sustained improvement
- Change-based environment
- Higher performance work teams and self-motivated individuals
- Revision for the sake of revision

Needs

- Consistent training of new staff to keep up with standards and practices
- Multiple levels of communication
- Higher levels of employee buy-in
- Formalized change management

Process Maturity Assessment

Process maturity assessment should be an integral part of project management because it can help evaluate current processes and practices, which provide project managers and teams with valuable information that can be used to set goals towards improvement and innovation. The same heuristics which help define process maturity, from the previous section, can also be used to evaluate process maturity. Table 5.2 is a matrix that provides a heuristic assessment of a team's process maturity. Teams can use this matrix to check their maturity level as overall low (L), moderate (M), or high (H).

In terms of structure, maturity assessment involves evaluating the extent and formality of project management activities, structure authoring practices, information modeling practices, and documented standards. Sustainability examines the use of formal reviews, prototypes, documented procedures, and quality metrics in project management. Usability evaluates the extent to which user-centered practices, customer focus, and formal usability tests are implemented. And finally, innovation examines the frequency of updated practices, feedback from customers and team members, and formalized methods of improving processes in the organization.

In addition to this list of heuristics, other localized aspects can also contribute to process maturity levels of organizations and teams. These aspects might include project or organization specific guidelines, experience levels of staff, or other problems. Aspects like

Category	Heuristic	L	M	H
Structure				
Project management	Project tasks, milestones, schedule, and resources are monitored, documented, and tracked.			
Structured authoring	Consistent software tools are used, documents are stored in centralized accessible locations, and global templates and stylesheets are used.			
Information modeling	Content is organized into coherent structures, such as outlines, sitemaps, topic architectures, and templates.			
Standards	Documented practices and standards are maintained, distributed, and actively used by team members.			
Sustainability				
Formalized reviews	Multiple reviews (copyediting, subject matter expert, design, etc.) are scheduled for each project.			
Prototypes	Working drafts and prototypes of technical documents are created and revised based on reviews and feedback.			
Documented procedures	Specific procedures for developing project plans, progress reports, reviews, production tasks, and assessment are documented and followed.			
Quality metrics	Consistent and specific metrics are used to track various aspects of the project including quality, cost, time, dependencies, etc.			
Usability				
User-centered design	A focus on users is integrated throughout the project lifecycle.			
Customer focus	Customers are queried and working contexts examined in testing and revising products.			
Usability testing	Formal testing of products and features is conducted throughout the development and design phases.			
Innovation				
Updated practices	Documented work practices are maintained and updated regularly.			
Feedback	Input from customers and employees is encouraged, gathered, and used to update and improve business operations.			
Process improvement	Documented processes are evaluated and improved to maximize quality, efficiency, and satisfaction.			

Table 5.2. Using this process maturity assessment matrix, each heuristic can be rated L (low), M (moderate), or H (high) in terms of individual process maturity or integration and averaged by category to determine overall level of process maturity.

these should factor into any assessment tool. They can fall within the existing categories or suggest additional categories to assess process maturity. Whether using this tool, a modified version, or other one, process maturity assessment can also help organizations identify potential problems areas for improvement related to project management. When process maturity assessment becomes a regular practice of an organization or team, it serves as a value-added activity to improve the level of project management and working processes.

> ### EXERCISE 5.6
> #### *Assessing the Process Maturity of your Workplace*
>
> Assess either your current or former workplace's level of process maturity using the process maturity assessment matrix provided in Table 5.2. If you have not participated in a work team, then consider a group experience you have had in school. Think about how processes, practices, and rules were learned and communicated to workers or students. How were reviews conducted or workers assessed or evaluated in terms of the documents or tasks they performed? Also, consider the ways in which customer suggestions or needs and a commitment to improvement were addressed. Write a short description (500 words) of your assessment, including specific tasks, processes, and practices.
>
> **Tasks to be completed:**
>
> 1. Select either your current or former workplace to assess.
> 2. Make a list of how the structure, sustainability, usability, and innovation were handled in the workplace.
> 3. Use Figure 5.1 as your assessment tool and fill out each section.
> 4. Report your findings by writing a short description of your assessment (500 words).

STRATEGIES FOR IMPROVING TEAM PROCESSES AND VALUE ADDED

As process maturity increases in teams and organizations, it is more likely they will focus on improving products and processes. Iterative work processes, or processes that often involve revisiting and sometimes revising previous practices, and process maturity are also closely related. Reviewing and revisiting completed tasks can have a positive impact on product quality and therefore contribute to greater process maturity. Lower maturity teams would typically complete a task and move on to the next one with limited revision or review. Higher maturity teams would have formalized, sustainable processes that are continually reviewed and improved.

An important part of process mature iterative work practices includes specific quality assurance activities. Some of these activities, mentioned in the previous section, include formal reviews, customer focus, assessment methods, and tracking project metrics. For example, formalized review processes involving subject matter experts (SMEs) are one way of helping improve quality of a product. With competent reviewers in place, a project has the potential to improve quality through continued levels of review, which occur both formally and informally in an iterative working process. User feedback and customer focus are important for planning, development, testing, and continual evaluation of the project.

Project assessment is essential throughout development to ensure that quality levels are maintained and errors are reduced. These improvements can be achieved through identifying and tracking metrics related to quality, such as accuracy, completion, functionality, and resources. A sustained commitment to quality must be maintained in such reviews, such as formalizing the review process, documenting it, and assessing it using tested heuristics.

Achieving sustainable quality and improving processes are the main goals towards becoming a more process mature organization or team. As mentioned earlier in the chapter, process maturity is a function of structure, sustainability, usability, and innovation, which are key assessment factors. Some specific strategies for improving process maturity in a team or organization include the following:

- Implement formal project management activities and a sustainable content strategy.
- Follow user-centered design practices throughout the project lifecycle.
- Integrate methods of assessment and evaluation into work processes.
- Document and review processes to keep them improving, repeatable, consistent, and sustainable.
- Conduct mid- and post- project review meetings on project status.
- Create an atmosphere that encourages team feedback.
- Identify and maintain a list of subject matter expert (SME) reviewers.
- Distribute and update a list of generalizable lessons learned.
- Formalize usability testing throughout the development cycle.
- Create working project prototypes for development and testing.

While this short list offers some suggestions, other strategies that are specific to the organization or project should be considered as well. Some strategies may emerge from lessons learned or from post-project meetings and should be documented and added to the list. Identifying success factors and dependencies can also help organizations pinpoint areas that could use improvement, which can translate into strategies for success.

Impacts on Business Operations and Return on Investment

In a project management context, quality assurance and process maturity impact the bottom line or return on investment, in terms of the product and resources, including cost, time, and value added. Tangible benefits include savings in cost, time, resources, and error reports. Higher levels of project maturity contribute to return on investment by helping improve processes and business operations. Resources spent on additional planning, testing, and quality tracking return benefits by saving time and costs in project development, revisions, and production.

Intangible benefits contribute to return on investment for businesses, but they may not be directly attributable to quantitative metrics. These intangible benefits include customer satisfaction, business reputation, working environment, job satisfaction, and social capital, or the value added. Social capital includes three dimensions, including structural (information networking resources), relational (trust and trustworthiness), and cognitive (collective common knowledge or shared code) that encompasses the collective cultural and organizational value of information products, not directly attributable to revenue or profit (Baehr & Alex-Brown, 2010). Process mature organizations can also build social capital through the information networks and their information sharing capabilities, including social media tools, such as blogs and wikis to collect and share knowledge, best practices, ideas for innovation, and lessons learned.

> ### EXERCISE 5.7
> ### *Understanding the Value of Social Capital*
>
> Interview a workplace professional to learn more about what social capital resources exist in their organization. Using the three social capital dimensions, structural (information networking resources), relational (trust and trustworthiness), and cognitive (collective common knowledge or shared code), ask questions that focus on each area. For the structural dimension, ask what information networking resources exist in their workplace and how valuable each resource is. For the relational dimension, ask how trust and trustworthiness are earned, established, and recognized in their workplace. And for the cognitive dimension, ask how collective common knowledge is created or shared, and what tools or media are used to share knowledge.
>
> **Tasks to be completed:**
>
> 1. Select a workplace professional for a short interview.
> 2. Using the three social capital dimensions and suggestions above, write a short list of questions, considering each dimension.
> 3. Conduct your interview and record your findings.
> 4. Report and compare your findings with others, or to experiences you have had in professional workplaces.

Chapter Summary

Project management involves supervising a project and the process from planning through production, and includes a wide range of roles, such as communication, quality assurance, planning, resource management, and technical oversight. These roles come with a wide range of tasks that document the scope, procedures, practices, reporting functions, and project deliverables. Project management applies to all projects regardless of the size of a team, which can be an individual or an entire organization, and involves the development and supervision of various documents, tracking metrics, and diverse work teams.

The options for teaming and engaging in the 21st century work models are diverse and multiple. Technology further supports this work and provides technical communicators with many means for approaching and accomplishing work. To be successful, it is important to understand how professionals in your field view their work. As a new employee, you should ask about work processes, note how teams are created and why, and use your communication skills to effectively work within these teams. Finally, this chapter provided you with guidelines for participating and leading teams within your next workplace.

Project management and process maturity share an important relationship, which can be characterized in terms of an organization or team's structure, ability to create sustainable processes, user-centered practices, and ability to innovate. Process maturity involves assessing organizations and teams in terms of these factors with the ultimate goal of improving practices, processes, and quality. Process maturity also suggests the importance of iterative work practices, which underscore the need for continual improvement and revision across the project lifecycle.

Teams and organizations can improve their process maturity and effectiveness by implementing several quality assurance activities and strategies, such as integrating user-centered design practices, conducting assessment methods to track quality, documenting processes, adding formalized reviews, and maintaining lessons learned. These activities can also have positive impacts on return on investment and improve process maturity and project quality for an organization.

Chapter Assignments

The exercises in this section ask you to apply what you have learned in this chapter as well as explore how this knowledge applies to and connects with other information in the textbook.

1. Many movies focus on teams and team processes. Select and watch a movie of your own that features a team or choose on the following "Iron Will," "Remember the Titans," "Apollo 13," or "Oceans 11." Analyze and assess the teams in your movie by answering these questions:
   - What tasks or activities do team members complete?
   - How are these task or activities assigned?
   - How mature are the team's processes?
   - What improvements might these teams undertake to improve their process maturity levels?

2. Consider your class as a team, including your instructor. Take a few minutes for members to introduce themselves by major, leadership experiences, and interests. Then divide yourselves into teams for a collaborative writing assignment. First, divide into functional teams. Then divide into cross-functional teams. What challenges do you encounter when trying to form these teams?

3. Watch an episode of a television show that involves teamwork. Any kind of television show is acceptable; you may choose a cartoon, a comedy, a drama, a game show, a documentary, or reality TV. (If you do not have a television, use the internet to find an episode.) Describe the teamwork you see on the show. Is the team you observe successful? If they are, what makes them successful? If they are not, why do they fail? Apply what you have learned about teams in this chapter to what you see in this episode. How might the teamwork be improved? Write a short report, no more than one typed page, describing your television research on teamwork and be ready to share your findings in class. (For guidance writing your report, review Chapter 26.)

4. Team up with someone in your class who is interested in pursuing a similar career. Working together, visit the Occupational Outlook Handbook <http://www.bls.gov/oco/> and look up the profession that you are both interested in. Do individuals in this profession work on team? How, when, and where? Prepare a short two-minute collaborative oral report on your findings. Use what you know about successful teaming to accomplish this task. Be prepared to talk about how your team accomplished its assignment.

5. Identify a list of five tasks or activities that would help a workplace become more process mature, focusing on improving their existing procedures and practices.
6. Your manager has asked you to justify the list of tasks from the previous exercise in terms of return on investment (ROI) for the organization. Write a short memo (500 words) making an argument for implementing your suggestions, focusing on return on investment (ROI) factors mentioned in the chapter. List any additional tangible and intangible benefits you discover, as well.
7. List ten specific best practices that characterize your work processes for a project. Then make a list of five practices that characterize your challenges or problematic behaviors that sometimes impede your work.

Figure Credits

Figure 5.1. © Batshevs/Shutterstock.com

Figure 5.2. © OPOLJA/Shutterstock.com

Figure 5.3. © StockLite/Shutterstock.com

Figure 5.4. © Syda Productions/Shutterstock.com

Figure 5.5. © Mila Supinskaya/Shutterstock.com

Figure 5.6. © Michael D Brown/Shutterstock.com

Researching Content

CHAPTER OVERVIEW

This chapter introduces you to technical communication research. It explains why research is a critical skill that technical communicators need to answer workplace questions and to solve workplace problems. After reading this chapter, you should be able to complete these objectives:

- State research goals as either problems to be solved or questions to be answered.
- Identify a variety of research methods that technical communicators use.
- Apply these methods to conduct workplace research.
- Explain your research process.
- Describe your research responsibilities.
- Use conventional means to document your research.

You have, no doubt, encountered research in your academic career. You probably have conducted science experiments, researched controversial topics, and written lab reports or persuasive research papers. While these forms of research are common in academic settings, workplace research is more practical and employs a variety of methods.

Figure 6.1. Workplace research improves organizations' abilities to adapt to rapid changes and trends.

What drives workplace research? As discussed in the Chapter 1, 21st century workplaces often encounter rapid and unexpected change. To adapt, organizations and their employees need to know how to act or respond to these changes. Research requires that communicators identify what they already know and what they need to know or learn to respond to workplace change, needs, or problems. According to Kim Sydow Campbell (1999), three situations drive most of the research that technical communicators conduct:

- Others have faced similar problems, and you want to know how they have solved them.
- Others have faced similar problems, but you cannot identify out how they solved them. Therefore, you must find an answer on your own.

- As far as you can tell, no one has faced a similar problem or, if they have, they have not shared their solutions. You must find an answer on your own (536).

In the first situation, the technical communicator conducts research to find the published answer. In the second and third situations, the technical communicator, alone or with others, conducts research to find answers. In all three situations, good research practice begins with developing a problem statement and then a research question. Without a clear statement or question that guides your research, you cannot begin to target possible answers or solutions.

FORMULATING PROBLEM STATEMENTS AND RESEARCH QUESTIONS

In an earlier chapter, you learned about the importance of articulating problem statements and objectives to guide your project planning. Conducting sound research requires you to use similar skills. To begin the research process, the first step is to determine *why* you need to conduct research. To find the *why*, you may have to backtrack somewhat by considering some preliminary questions in order to contextualize the research that needs to be completed.

> - What is the problem or need that the research must resolve?
> - Why is this problem or need important to your organization? Does it affect the organizational bottom line, your customers, or clients?
> - What is the magnitude of this problem? That is, how big or important is it to your organization, your customers, or your clients?
> - What do you or your organization already know about the problem or need?
> - What more do you need to learn?
> - What are the real-world considerations or constraints that will affect the viability of any answer or solution you discover (financial limitations, expertise, legal/regulatory restrictions, other designs, development processes)?

Below are two scenarios that illustrate how these questions guide you through this initial research phase. In brackets, the contextualizing question is highlighted:

> **Scenario #1: Intermittent internet service**
>
> Our company's server connectivity is being disrupted by intermittent internet outages. [the problem or need] During work hours, we are often unable to connect to our e-commerce Web site where customers order products, and it appears that our customers are unable to connect to the Web site to place orders. [how the problem affects our customers and our bottom line] Our online sales are down 10%. [the magnitude of the problem] We need to know how to eliminate these disruptions, so both we and our customers can access the e-commerce Web site. [what we need to know] We know that our current service provider is inexpensive but apparently unreliable. This provider was a good choice when we started our business [what we already know]. We need to find out if we can get more reliable, improved service from our current provider, but, if not, we need to find a new provider with more reliable service offered within our current budget. [what we need to learn or discover; what real-world constraints we must consider]

> **Scenario #2: Problems with proposal writers**
>
> Our non-profit organization relies heavily on external funding to provide after-school math tutoring for underprivileged children. Currently, we rely on volunteers to write grants and compete for funding **[what we already know]**. While our volunteers do the best they can with limited resources and time, the grant proposals they produce often require more administrative time to edit than produce **[the problem or need]**. We are concerned that we are wasting our time and our volunteers' time by asking them to draft our proposals **[how the problem affects our volunteers, our employees and our bottom line]**. We need to find out how to improve the efficiency of our volunteers' efforts, or we need to find another means of producing proposals **[what we need to know]** because without successful grant-making, our organization will fail **[the magnitude of the problem; real-world constraints]**.

If these problem statements remind you of the planning processes recommended in earlier chapters, then you are on the right track. Researching is a type of project. Like other projects, assessing your knowledge, needs, and constraints is the opening move that will guide you as you complete your research. Problem statements describe the problem or need you are addressing, contextualize it, and limit your research to the information that will help you to address these concerns.

> **Scenario #1: Intermittent internet service**
>
> **What we need to know:** *We need to know how to eliminate these disruptions, so both we and our customers can access the e-commerce Web site.*
>
> **Scenario 1 research questions:**
>
> 1. **Are our declining online sales related to provider outages?** [We are assuming declining sales are related. This question will allow us to determine if these problems are actually related because, if they are not, then we do not need to worry about internet outages. If they are, then we have found the root cause of our problems.]
> 2. **If so, what can our company do to eliminate its internet connectivity issues?** [If we determine that declining sales are caused by internet connectivity issues, then we need to fix this problem. But how? To get the answer, we need to ask two secondary questions.]
>   a. **Can our current provider improve its service, with or without an increase in charges?** [First, we seek information from our current provider.]
>   b. **If not, can we identify a different service that provides more reliable, improved service within our current budget?** [Then we identify other possible providers, which will give us comparable information on services, charges, and reliability.]

> **Scenario #2: Proposal problems**
>
> **What we need to know:** *We need to find out how to improve the efficiency of our volunteers' efforts, or we need to find another means of producing proposals.*
>
> **Scenario 2 research questions:**
>
> 1. Why do administrators spend so much time editing grants written by volunteers? [This question allows us to find out more specifically about the problems we need to address.] In discovering the answer to this question, we might identify several possible sub-questions, such as the following:
>   a. How long does it take to edit drafts?
>   b. What kinds of problems are administrators editing or correcting in volunteers' grant drafts?
>   c. How frequently do administrators have to edit drafts?
>   d. What problems or challenges do they encounter when they edit?
>   e. What kinds of changes would they like to see in the grant-writing process?
> 2. What problems are volunteers experiencing when they write grants? [This question allows us to find out more specifically about the problems we need to address.] In discovering the answer to this question, we might identify several possible sub-questions, such as the following:
>   a. What kinds of training are volunteers receiving?
>   b. What kinds of proposals are they writing?
>   c. What problems or challenges do they encounter when they write?
>   d. What kinds of changes would they like to see in the grant-writing process?
> 3. Based on what we learn from administrators and volunteers, how can we improve our proposal writing process to reduce redundant efforts?

After you have written your problem statement, then you are ready to develop your research questions. Research questions serve as guides to direct where and how you will conduct your research. They are pivotal to successful practical research because they arise from the problem statement you have already written, and they help you to determine what methods you should employ to conduct your research in the future. Although your research questions arise directly from your problem statement, you will often discover that your questions can lead you in many directions. Your job is to decide which direction is most efficient and optimal for getting the answers you need. In the paragraphs below, you will see how problem statements generate research questions and how these questions need to be honed to get the answer you need quickly and precisely.

To begin, identify the information that you need to discover in each scenario. (For each of the scenarios, we have copied this statement from the problem statement and italicized it.)

CHOOSING RESEARCH METHODS

After you have created your detailed problem statement and written your research questions, you are ready to identify **research methods**. As the introduction to this chapter notes, you will need to discover if someone else has answered comparable questions before or if you need to conduct original research to find an answer. In either case, what you are doing is research.

Depending on your discipline, research methods are classified in different ways, and you already know about many of these methods. You have already conducted experiments in science classes, participated in surveys online, and seen or read interviews in blogs, articles, and documentaries. You have seen statistics used to prove claims, and you may even know how to run statistical tests. These methods are all viable approaches to research, and many of them are used in workplace communication research. To categorize these methods, this chapter relies on two commonly defined types of research: primary and secondary research.

- **Primary research** includes methods that allow you to seek new knowledge that has not already been published or is not readily available. This is research that you conduct by yourself or with others.
- **Secondary research** is based in scholarship. When you use secondary research, you are looking for answers in publications, answers that others have found and published.

Like most work technical communicators do, both primary and secondary research may require you to work in cycles, moving between these two categories. For example, you might start your research with secondary research by doing a search of existing literature. After you complete your search, you decide that there is nothing published that answers your questions. In this case, you might conduct in-person interviews with clients to get the answers you need. After conducting the client interviews, you analyze the interviews and begin to write up your findings. At this point, you realize you need follow-up information from your clients. Instead of meeting face-to-face again, you send your clients a brief email with a follow-up question, and they reply to you by email. Finally, as you complete the report, you discover that your findings are similar to ones you read earlier in a trade journal. This discovery leads you back to the literature, where you find the article and cite it in your report. Although your process may not be this complex, it will likely be iterative; you will cycle through primary and secondary methods as you focus in on what you need to know and what you need to report. For this reason, you should not value one form of research over the other. Both have their purposes and are equally important to understand.

EXERCISE 6.1

Practice Writing Problem Statements and Research Questions

Working with a peer, brainstorm a possible communication research scenario you might face in your future workplaces, or, if you are currently employed, identify a research scenario in your current position. For example, you might need to learn more about technology, a human resource, or budgetary problems or concerns. Imagine or identify a scenario that would require you to do research, and write a problem statement. After you have written your problem statement, generate two or three research questions that could guide your research. Be prepared to share your research scenario with the class and to discuss the questions you have generated to guide your research.

Tasks to be completed:

1. Working with a partner, identify a workplace problem that requires research.
2. Describe in a problem statement.
3. Generate two or three research questions that could lead to an answer or solution to the problem.
4. Prepare to share and discuss your answers with the class.

Primary Research

Think of primary research as research that is *firsthand*, that you personally conduct. It is original research that is intended to discover answers to a new and specific problem. Primary research involves finding answers that are not already published elsewhere and cannot be answered simply by reading a book, skimming a journal article, or searching the internet. It frequently involves working with other people in some way, such as asking them questions or watching them work. It may also include gathering data or information about their work habits or performance. This section on primary research focuses on three categories of research methods: asking other people questions, observing them, and collecting user data.

Figure 6.2. Interviews allow you to gather in-depth information directly from a subject matter expert.

Methods for Asking Questions

When you have a research problem or research question that can be answered by asking other people questions, you have three methodological options: conducting interviews with individuals, conducting focus groups with a small group of individuals, or fielding a survey or questionnaire to learn how many individuals will answer your questions. All of these methods are similar, which requires you to create a series of structured questions to guide your research, but they differ in scope:

Interviews. Interviews are useful when you need information from someone with specific or personal knowledge about a problem or need. For example, you might interview a specific client about a problem he is encountering with your product, or if you are proposing a new product, you might need to gather information about the product from an engineer or scientist developing it (we often call that person a **subject matter expert** or SME). Use an interview when you need in-depth specialized information from an individual or series of individuals whom you interview one at a time.

Focus groups. Like interviews, focus groups are based on a series of structured questions, but instead of asking individuals one at a time, you interview three to seven people at the same time to get a diversity of opinions. When you conduct a focus group, you moderate a discussion, seeking to draw out varied opinions from the individuals in the group. Focus groups are useful when you want to learn about how a group thinks about a product, such as a television show or Web site. Individuals in focus groups frequently build

Figure 6.3. Focus groups are useful when you want to solicit group opinions.

on one another's ideas. As a group, they can provide rich and deep perspectives on your questions. In this way, a focus group can be a powerful method for discovering differences and similarities in group opinions, but they can also be tricky. Individuals may be reluctant to express disagreement in front of others for personal, interpersonal, or cultural reasons, and they may engage in groupthink (conforming to the group opinion even if it contradicts their own). Use a focus group when you want to gather group opinions.

Surveys. Surveys (also called questionnaires) are designed to reach a large group of individuals. Surveys are most frequently used when you want to gather information from a large but specific subset of people. You can use surveys to ask questions about products or events. For example, from the population of all grocery shoppers, you may choose to survey only individuals who purchase organic produce to determine how much they are willing to spend on a product, such as organic Washington-grown cherries. Unlike interviews and

Figure 6.4. Surveys are designed to gather information from large groups of people.

focus groups, which give you textual (or qualitative) answers, surveys are able to provide you numerical (or quantitative) data as well. Surveys allow you to gather information about products, procedures, beliefs, and opinions across a broad spectrum of individuals. With good planning, you can even conduct statistical tests to reveal patterns and trends in this information. Using a survey application like Survey Monkey is a useful tool for developing online surveys. Such applications also provide you a variety of options for developing questions, delivering the survey, and analyzing results.

Developing a Protocol for Asking Questions

All three of these methods require you to think ahead about questions to ask, and all of these questions spring from your initial research questions. If a question does not relate directly to some aspect of your research questions, then you should seriously consider its necessity. To begin to develop these questions, you need to know about the kinds of questions that are possible. In simplest terms, questions can be classified as closed or open-ended. **Closed questions** are comparable to multiple-choice answers, of which the respondent chooses one. For example, this question about technology use is closed as is the question about age that follows:

> 1. *Which of the following technologies do you use most often to access your email?*
>   a. *Desktop computer*
>   b. *Laptop computer*
>   c. *Mobile phone*
>   d. *Tablet*
>   e. *Other*

> 2. *How old are you?*
>   a. *Under 21 years*
>   b. *21–29 years*
>   c. *30–39 years*
>   d. *40–49 years*
>   e. *50 years or older*

Because closed questions limit answer possibilities, they are easy to tabulate and analyze. If you are working with a large number of respondents, you can even use statistical packages to run further tests.

Open-ended questions are comparable to short answer or essay questions. They allow respondents to provide personal detailed responses. Unlike closed questions, open-ended questions can result in widely different answers from respondents, and they require you to perform more textual analysis of responses. Below are some examples of open-ended questions:

> 3. *You have told me that you stream videos on your laptop. What kinds of video do you stream?*
> 4. *When and where are you when you typically stream videos?*

Note that the final question—*When and where are you when you typically stream videos?*—could be written as a closed question dividing the question into two parts (When? and Where?) and by adding answer choices below each question. However, providing answer choices limits the number of possible answers and does not provide easily for circumstances that do not fit within the limited answer responses. In addition, you should think carefully about asking multi-part open questions because they can be problematic. Do you require answers to all parts? What if respondents answer only part of the question? How will you deal with incomplete answers? You will need to consider all these points as you develop your questions.

Most methods that use questions include both closed and open-ended questions. When you are deciding what kinds of questions to write, think about how limited you want responses to be. More limited responses are gained through closed questions while open-ended are much broader and diverse. Closed questions are easier and quicker to tabulate while open questions require more time to analyze their more detailed and individualized responses. Thinking critically about how people will respond to your questions can help you to get you the answers you need. At the same time, you will need to consider your project constraints, designing questions that can answered and analyzed within the time you have.

Another important consideration when designing questions is the types of information you can gain from your questions. "Survey questions," according to Goodman, Kuniasky, and Moed (2012), "come in a variety of flavors" (331). Below are some common categories that these scholars note are frequently used in surveys and questionnaires (331–332):

- **Characteristic questions** include both demographic and technological questions: Demographic questions ask about the respondents' personal information, such as gender, age, race, education, geographic location, and other vital information. You can use demographic questions to describe the individuals you interview, include in your focus group, or survey. Technological questions ask respondents about technology experiences and skills as well as attitudes about technologies.
- **Behavioral questions** ask about how people act, use or complete activities or products.
- **Attitudinal questions** ask respondents about their attitudes, feelings, opinions, preferences, and desires.

As you begin to develop your questions, consider the order of questions in your interview and organize the questions from easiest to answer to hardest. Asking easy questions first puts respondents at ease, and they will be better prepared to answer harder questions as you draw the questioning stage to a close.

After you have developed interview, focus group, or survey questions, you will need to generate a research plan (or protocol) for your study. Most protocols include three parts:

- **Introduction**: where you explain your research and discuss how or if you will protect your respondent's anonymity or confidentiality. (More on this topic later in the chapter.) In general, then, this section is useful for making the observer and the observed more comfortable with the question strategy.
- **A series of questions**: where you actually ask questions, usually ranging from characteristics to behavioral to attitudinal habits and beliefs.
- **Closing or wrap-up**: where you draw the observation to a close and remind the participant that you may follow-up with additional questions.

EXERCISE 6.2

Analyze a Survey

Find a survey online or in print. You might search magazines, product websites, or social media to locate a survey or questionnaire. After locating the survey, make or save a copy of it. Then analyze the copy to determine whether it uses closed or open-ended questions, or both. Then determine what categories of questions it includes: how many questions are characteristic, behavioral, or attitudinal? After analyzing the survey, bring the survey questions to class and be prepared to share your findings with your peers.

Tasks to be completed:

1. Find a survey an analyze it by answering the following questions:
    a. Does the survey use closed or open-ended questions, or both?
    b. What categories of questions does your survey include?
    c. How many questions are characteristic, behavioral, or attitudinal?
2. Bring your survey and research results to class to discuss.

Methods for Observing Others

Similar to question-asking methods, observation methods are multiple and varied, but they all share a common purpose: observation methods are best used when you can learn the answer to your research question by observing what you are doing or what other people are doing. In technical communication research, four frequently used methods are creative play, field observations, think-aloud protocols, and usability tests.

Creative play is a method technical communicators use in situations when they need to learn to do something, for example, when they are given a product or software application to document. This observational discovery method is informal and involves getting familiar with an activity or object. Because of its informal nature, this method is called many things: "fiddling around," "sandboxing," "goofing around," "serious play," "orienting," "test-driving," or "AHFA" (ad hoc fumbling around). What all of these terms suggest, however, is that

Figure 6.5. Creative play is a good method for learning about a procedure or product.

Figure 6.6. Observations allow you to watch how others work in natural or laboratory settings.

creative play is how many communicators first learn about activities and products they are describing or documenting. Playing with a product or roleplaying an activity can teach you how it works and how it does not. By itself, this method might not provide you with all the information you need to understand an object or activity, but it is an excellent way to start your research, familiarizing yourself with the product or activity and figuring out what else you need to know about it.

EXERCISE 6.3

The Power of Creative Play

To learn more about the power and benefits of creative play, read Sean Michael Morris, Pete Rorabaugh and Jesse Stommel's article, "Beyond Rigor" in e-journal *Hybrid Pedagogy*: http://www.hybridpedagogy.com/journal/beyond-rigor/

After you have reviewed the article, work in small groups to discuss the advantages and possible disadvantages of calling a research activity "creative play." Imagine a scenario in which a supervisor asks your team what you are doing, and you answer by telling the supervisor you are "playing" with a product to learn about it. How might the supervisor respond (both positively and negatively) to your answer? What might your team say to explain "creative play" as a valid form of research to the supervisor?

Tasks to be completed:

1. Read "Beyond Rigor."
2. Work in teams to respond to the "creative play" scenario described above.
3. Prepare to discuss your answers with the class.

Field observations are a method that allows you to observe others in a natural setting. Using this method, you spend time with someone you are observing in their office, in meetings, or in other settings where work or other activities are performed. During this observation, you may simply stand by and watch, taking notes as activities are performed, or you may talk with the individual, asking questions about what it is you are seeing. Field observations have many challenges: (1) the field setting is usually unknown and uncontrollable, so you may or may not get to see what you asked to see; (2) good observations require you to have a working relationship, at least, with the individual observed; (3) they require that you note not only what the person is doing but also to attend to environmental factors that may be influencing or affecting observed behavior; and (4) field observations also require careful note taking, which is discussed in a later section in this chapter.

Think-aloud protocols are useful when you need to discover how someone performs an activity and what they are *thinking* as they perform the activity. Think-aloud protocols require you to watch what others are doing and to listen carefully as the observed individual talks you through the process. Think-aloud protocols were developed to "get inside the observed person's head." They provide a way for the researcher to listen in as the person being observed performs the work. As you watch the person at work, your job is to record what you hear, to remind the observed person to talk aloud about what he or she is doing and thinking, and to delve into these actions with questions, if necessary. Use think-aloud protocols when you are trying to understand what a procedure entails, how participants feel as they perform the procedure, and how they *think* as they complete it.

Usability can be used for primary research data collection and as a method of assessment. This section discusses its function in collecting primary research information, while the assessment function is discussed in a later chapter. Usability, as a primary research method, allows you to gather data from actual users of a product or software application. Usability tests provide a means to test document content or product and to determine if this content is adequately accessible and effective for its target audience. You might think of usability testing as a more formal means of peer or expert review taken one step further: usability tests provide researchers with an opportunity to see how well users are able to access and understand content as well as how easily they can use the documents.

To perform usability tests, you will likely begin by creating user profiles and scenarios. These documents will help you to recruit the users to be tested according to specific standards and requirements you have set. You will also need to determine whether the test will be conducted in a natural setting (the workplace itself) or whether it must be completed within a usability lab. Both settings have benefits: a natural setting will be more comfortable and familiar to users while the lab setting may provide you with improved technology to collect data. The setting you choose depends on a variety of factors, including methods, formality, resources available, participants, and product for testing. Testing can be done at a single computer at a desk, or at a formal usability testing laboratory.

Figure 6.7. Card sorting using sticky notes is an easy method to learn about users' understanding and use of content and structure.

Some types of usability tests that you can conduct on technical documents, either print or online include the following:

- **Card sorting**—evaluating content relationships, organizational and structural issues, and/or navigation paths.
- **Heuristic evaluation**—evaluating using heuristics, which must be defined clearly and ahead of time.
- **Observation**—conducting interviews, field study, focus group, laboratory testing.
- **Prototyping**—testing specific features or functions of works in progress, including draft documents, such as sets of instructions, training modules, or Web sites.
- **Technical testing**—using the software or system to test screen resolution, functionality, formatting, and style sheets to norm the experience for typical users.
- **User research** (scenarios, profiles, cases)—developing profiles of user groups, tasks, workflows to assess needs, expertise, and expectations.

The general process for usability testing a product includes determining the testing goals, selecting a testing method, developing the testing materials, conducting the test, evaluating the test, and implementing and formulating changes to the product based on testing results. Specific variables of the testing parameters may need to be adjusted based on the type of test, subjects, topic, resources, or product being tested.

> ### EXERCISE 6.4
> ### *Observing Others and Taking Field Notes*
>
> To practice taking notes while observing, take a field trip to your favorite coffee shop, the dorm cafeteria, the library, or any other location where you can sit quietly and watch others for 10 minutes. Take out a sheet of paper and draw a line down the middle to divide it in half. Now take 10 minutes of two-column field notes. In the left column, record what you see; in the right column, record what you think about what you see. Bring your field notes to class to discuss the challenges of taking field notes.
>
> **Tasks to be completed:**
>
> 1. Identify a site to complete a 10-minute observation.
> 2. Create a two-column field note, by drawing a line down the middle to divide the sheet in half.
> 3. Observe what happens during the 10 minutes, noting what you observe in the left-hand column and what you think about what you see in the right-hand column.
> 4. Bring your field note to class to share with others and discuss. Questions you may want to consider are the following:
>   a. What challenges did you encounter as you observed and took notes?
>   b. What kinds of research questions could you answer with the notes you took?
>   c. Would the observation have been easier if you had started with a research question? Why or why not?

Developing a Protocol for Observing Others

Observation methods, like question-asking methods, require you to develop a protocol or plan for conducting research. Your protocol for an observational method will have a similar structure to question-asking protocols: you will introduce yourself and your research purpose, explain the research procedures, and answer questions. Then you will arrange the room to allow unobscured observation and note taking. When the room is ready, you are ready to observe the individual.

Two additional considerations for your note-taking protocol are making video and audio recordings and writing field notes. Whether you are observing in a lab or a workplace setting, recording the research procedures is a good way to assure that you do not miss anything that is said or done. Most mobile phones or tablets are now powerful enough to do this work for you. Depending on the detail and length of the observation, you may choose between audio and video recording. If you choose to record your procedures, then you will need to tell your respondent what you are doing and explain how or if you will protect respondent anonymity.

A low-tech method for recording observations is simply using a two-column field note. To create a two-column field note, you will need a paper and pencil/pen. Draw a line down the middle of the page. In the left-hand column, you record details about the setting, the activities you observe, the time activities take, the people you are observing, and anything else of importance or significance in the location. In the right-hand column, record your thoughts about these observations. You can take similar notes with a laptop computer or tablet, but you will not be able to use the two-column technique as easily; instead, you could write your observation in regular font followed by comments in bold, or you can use font color or highlighting to distinguish between the two types of observation notes.

Methods for Collecting User Data

User data analysis is a more technologically sophisticated way to research information about users of products, Web sites, and other services recorded digitally. While there are many kinds of user data analyses, they all depend on a computer-generated count of digital records. Such information is useful for usability, marketing, and retail. Goodman, Kuniavsky, and Moed (2012) identify four metrics that are commonly employed for web analysis:

- **Site-wide measures**, such as total number of pages viewed, types of browsers used to visit site, and content popularity;
- **Session-based measures**, such as average direction of session and first and last pages visited;
- **User-based measures**, such as frequency of visits and retention rate; and
- **Clickstream measures**, which can describe how a visitor travels from page to page in a Web site (461-3).

Other technologies can allow you to track users' eye movements as they view a webpage. Eye-tracking technology provides a means of mapping where users focus and what they do while there. When used in combination with other data collection methods, such as think aloud protocols, eye-tracking can verify that what users tells you they are looking at is actually what their eyes are looking at. These more sophisticated tools are useful, but they require you to have access to fairly detailed applications that track and record user data or access to an information technology specialist who can gather the data for you.

Secondary Research

As the introduction to this chapter suggests, secondary research is necessary when you think you can answer your research questions by consulting published sources. Published sources vary widely. They can be as simple to access as checking for files in the organizational intranet or as complicated as sifting through information tucked away in industry white papers and standards. The more educated you are about *what* kinds of information are available to answer your questions and *where* that information can be located, the easier your research will be. In many cases, just discovering where to look is the greatest challenge you will encounter in secondary research. This section offers you a few suggestions for identifying, locating, and vetting secondary sources.

Identifying and Locating Sources

Two general categories of resources for secondary research are internal documents and external resources. Internal resources are documents and artifacts that have been generated and housed within your organization's intranet storage system or even its filing cabinets. A few of these sources include the following:

In-house legacy documents. Legacy documents are historical records of your organization. That is, they are documents that were written in the past and archived in organizational filing cabinets or data storage locations. These documents can be useful because they provide you working templates and sometimes even content for comparable texts you are working on now. For example, you might discover a legacy proposal for a service that your organization has previously provided. This legacy proposal will likely have content that can be modeled and potentially updated in the new proposal you are drafting for a similar service. In-house legacy documents show you how communication has been done in the past. As a precaution with legacy documents, find out if the legacy document was successful before modeling it since modeling a poorly written document is never a good idea.

Single-sourced texts. Single-source technology allows technical communicators to create and tag boilerplate text that can be used and reused for a variety of purposes. Boilerplate text is text that can be reused in multiple places without changes. For example, a course description is boilerplate text. It appears online in the university catalog, in brief course descriptions each semester, and again in the course syllabus. In general, boilerplate text can be repurposed for new documents being created. If you are new to your organization, ask a veteran employee how to search the single-sourced text tags to find what you are looking for. If the single-source text is applicable to your current project, then ask about using it. Usually, as long as the text is created in-house, anyone can use it in appropriate situations.

White papers. White papers are informal research reports, circulated internally, although they may have broader distribution. White papers are also known as grey literature because they are neither formal research reports nor informal documents that meet scholarly research standards. Not traditional or official research reports, white papers typically serve marketing, descriptive, and informational functions within an organization. As such, they archive current thinking about a subject, object, or product. Unless your organization has a detailed index of white papers previously generated, finding a white paper that will help you may be very challenging. Online, you will find white papers used primarily to report product specifications and case studies. White papers can be useful as long as you recognize that although they may appear to be scientific reports, the research they report is not necessarily scientific; for this reason, it is important to evaluate the research carefully before citing, a process that is described later in this chapter.

Reports. In this category are all the other reports generated within your organization. By reviewing local knowledge located in reports, you may find the answer to your question, and, if not, you will easily be able to locate a knowledgeable person to access through a careful perusal of organizational reports. Reports can be formal or informal, long or short, and individually or collaboratively written. Internal reports are often excellent resources for discovering conventional reporting procedures within your organization.

External resources are documents and artifacts that someone outside of your organization has generated and made available to the public. These resources are likely the most familiar resources in this chapter because you have probably used them to complete many course assignments since middle school. External resources are published documents and artifacts that report formal and informal research, and they are typically indexed in and accessed through print-based and electronic databases. Below is a brief list of external resources you might use to conduct your research:

Print publications: Think of these resources as the traditional sites of research: books, academic and professional journals/organizations, and trade magazines. To find information in these resources, use your academic or public library indexes, which are available online.

Electronic publications: Many books, most academic and professional journals, and most trade magazines are available electronically. Like the print publications above, electronic publications are findable through academic and public libraries. To conduct searches for electronic publications, you can also use online search engines, such as Google Scholar (http://scholar.google.com). Additionally, many Web sites are excellent sites for research. For example, you might visit a company's Web site to learn about their organization before seeking employment there, or you might find scientific and government documents through the Web sites of specific agencies and organizations.

Discipline-specific regulations, standards, related documents, and artifacts. Often, research can be answered by consulting discipline-specific or professional regulations or standards. This information is frequently available online and sometimes through professional organizations in your field. As with other secondary resources, this information is often best discovered through the use of electronic search engines.

Evaluating and Authenticating your Secondary Sources

With so many secondary resources at your keyboarding fingertips, you might wonder how to be certain that your sources are authentic and credible. When evaluating and authenticating your sources, consider the author, the publication source, the use of citations, and the dates of publication. Below are a few questions that can guide your process.

Figure 6.8. Website domain names, such as .com, .edu, and .gov, provide clues about sites' credibility and authenticity.

With both print and electronic sources, a good start is to consider the authority and expertise of the author: who wrote the text? What are his or her professional credentials? On what authority or credentialing does the author base his or her expertise on the subject? If you check the author in an online database or in Google Scholar, do you find other articles, and are other researchers citing the author? If the source is credited to an author and you identify that he or she has adequate expertise and authority, then these are good signs that others consider the author a credible and authoritative source.

Next, consider the authority of the publication source: is the source a reputable scholarly journal, trade magazine, or blog? Is the source published by a reputable organization or publishing house, or is it self-published by the author? What is the purpose of the source—to advance knowledge about a subject or solely to make money for the author? Of course, some self-published books and industry-specific Web sites are authoritative; considering the author's reputation and reason for self-publishing will help you to make this determination. With Web sites, you should also examine at the domain name: if the URL (web address) ends in .edu or .gov, then you likely have a credible source. Other domain names are also possible: .com tells you that the source is a company and .org, an organization. Credible sources can be located in any of these domains, but it is your job to be sure their information is reliable, not just self-aggrandizing. Evaluate publication sources to determine if they are doing more than marketing a specific person or products.

> ### EXERCISE 6.5
> #### Evaluating Two Sources for Credibility
>
> Below are two web sites that discuss methods for vetting secondary sources for credibility. Visit each of these sources, and evaluate them. Which source is more authoritative? Which one is more credible? Be prepared to discuss your findings with your peers.
>
> - Lesson Four: Vetting Authors of Secondary Sources, *Researching Treasure Leads* (http://treasurehuntingresearch.com/research-lessons/lesson-4-vetting-authors-of-secondary-sources/)
> - Evaluating Sources of Information [a short tutorial], *The Purdue OWL* (https://owl.english.purdue.edu/owl/resource/553/1/)
>
> **Tasks to be completed:**
>
> 1. Visit both web sites listed above.
> 2. Evaluate and authenticate their content using the guidelines in this section
> 3. Compare and contrast the two websites and answer these questions:
>   a. Which source is more authoritative?
>   b. Which one is more credible?
> 4. Prepare to discuss your findings with the class.

A third consideration is the quality of the source's research. Quality, like the other considerations, can be recognized in different ways. For example, with scholarly articles and trade publications, the use of relevant citations and a list of references is a good sign the publication is credible. In a Web site, you might also consider the links out of the site: where do they take you, and what is the purpose of the links? Similarly, does the site have popup windows that promote products or services? What is their purpose? As with the publisher, the intent of these links and popups can tell you much about the quality of the content and its purpose.

Your final consideration should be the currency of the information. Is the publication dated? If so, is the information current? Does it appear that the Web site is maintained and kept current? The dates associated with the information can tell you whether it is in keeping with the best and most current practices.

While a single question may not allow you to evaluate and authenticate the quality of a source, using this series of questions can help you decide whether the information provided in the source is credible.

Benchmarking with Legacy Documents

As you conclude your secondary research, you should carefully analyze comparable documents (or legacy documents). Using rhetorical analysis, you can learn about the genre you are writing by looking at examples you have found in your organization or online. For example, you can note how the writers address audience, shape the organization of the genre, and make style choices. These kinds of analysis provide benchmarks for the document you will be creating. This comparative analysis can be done on the documents themselves, if you have access to print copies, or you can create lists or tables to compare and contrast content.

EXERCISE 6.6

Benchmarking Product Specifications

Product specifications (specs) provide technical details. This exercise requires you to identify a product that has specifications (for example, an electronic device, hardware, a part for a car or motorcycle, an appliance, or something else). After you've decided on your product, locate two manufacturers who produce comparable products and compare the specifications. Create a table, identifying the two products and their specs. After you create the table, write a brief description of what content typically appears in specs.

Tasks to be completed:

1. Identify a product with specifications in its description.
2. Find two comparable products from different manufacturers.
3. Compare the specifications of each product in a table.
4. Write a brief description after your comparison that describes typical content in a spec.

Aligning Research Questions and Methods

Before leaving the topic of research methods, recall how this chapter started. With any project, you begin by considering the problem or question you want to answer. You place it within a context with a problem statement. From this statement, you develop research questions, which then lead you to consider the research methods needed to answer the question. These steps are interrelated and may be iterative; that is, you may cycle through them multiple times before you finalize your work.

The relationship between problem statements, research questions, and research methods is symbiotic. In other words, every research question should relate directly to the scope of the problems statement. To ask questions that are unrelated to the problem statement creates a scoping problem with your research, and potentially creates additional work outside the boundaries of the problem you are trying to solve. In addition, each method you select should directly correspond to one or more research questions in your list. To select research methods not related to a specific question, again creates additional work which is unnecessary. Table 6.1 illustrates the close relationships, or alignment, between problem statements, research questions, and research methods. To illustrate how your problem statement leads to research questions, which then lead you to methods, Table 6.1 returns to the original scenarios that started this chapter.

RESEARCH REPORTING RESPONSIBILITIES

Throughout the research process, you will be asked to report your work in both written and oral formats. Later chapters in this textbook will provide you with specific guidelines for developing these reports. In this final section of the chapter, we focus on the reporting process, not on its formats or genres. Specifically, this section offers you ethical and professional guidelines for planning your research and writing your findings. These guidelines are less about the documents or presentations you will make and more about the responsibilities you undertake when you conduct research in workplace settings.

Responsibilities When Planning Research

Your first responsibility when conducting research is to be able to articulate or describe what you are researching and why. You can address this responsibility by developing a research plan. This plan will detail the research problem, questions, and procedures or protocols you will follow, including any sources you plan to consult, questions you plan to ask, and individuals you plan to observe. With your plan in hand, your next responsibility is to run a pilot test to see if your plan successfully gathers the information (data) you are seeking. A **pilot test** is a dry run or a rehearsal of your research protocols; for this test, you may use a peer or an actual client. The more authentic your pilot test audience, however, the better your results will be. If your pilot test is not successful, revise and repeat it. The pilot test is important because it can save you time and money, assuring you and your employers that your plan will accomplish its goals. Once you have a successful pilot and you are confident that your procedure is working, you are ready to recruit your participants.

With primary research, another important responsibility is to recruit participants for interviews, focus groups, and surveys appropriately. A **recruitment protocol** identifies criteria that you have for individuals whom you will ask to participate. To determine these criteria, consider your target audience: who are they? How old are they? What qualifications or experiences do they need to respond to your questions? What other criteria are important to assess? Developing recruitment criteria is especially important if you are gathering information on surveys and hoping to draw conclusions about a larger population of people. To illustrate, think about political polling during election seasons. Pollsters want to recruit specific kinds of people to answer questions about the popularity of their candidates. For example, a political poll might seek information about the political leanings of women under 30 who live in Iowa, who work inside the home, and who are raising one or more children. In choosing to interview or question a small number of these individuals, pollsters hope to be able to draw conclusions about all women who fit into this category. Carefully selecting criteria for participants allows you a greater ability to draw conclusions.

If you are engaging in primary research for an organization that receives federal funding, you also have a responsibility to protect individuals who participate in that research. At universities and other organizations, such as hospitals, that receive federal funding, committees oversee research to assure these protections. Vulnerable groups, such as children and individuals with illnesses require special protections. While these protections and procedures are too lengthy to discuss in detail, it is important to know about them and to learn them if they apply to your workplace. Talking to a senior colleague about research protections is a good way to learn if these requirements apply to you and the research you are conducting.

Scenario #1: Intermittent Internet service

Problem statement	Research questions	Research methods
Our company's server connectivity is being disrupted by intermittent internet disruptions. During work hours, we are often unable to connect to our e-commerce Web site where customers order products, and it appears that our customers are unable to connect to the Web site to place orders. Our online sales are down 10%. We need to know how to eliminate these disruptions, so both we and our customers can access the e-commerce Web site. We know that our current service provider is inexpensive but apparently unreliable. This provider was a good choice when we started our business. We need to find out if we can get more reliable, improved service from our current provider, but, if not, we need to find a new provider with more reliable service offered within our current budget.	Are our decreasing online sales related to provider outages? If so, what can our company do to eliminate its internet connectivity issues? Can our current provider improve its service, with or without an increase in charges? If not, can we find a different service that provides more reliable, improved service within our current budget?	Request Web site analytic data from our information technology team to identify outage frequencies and determine outage effects on sales. Gather information from our current service provider to obtain diagnosis of connectivity issues, to determine the providers' ability to correct or resolve problems, and to discuss additional charges necessary for improved service. If dissatisfied with answer from current provider, contact other service providers to obtain information about services and monthly service charges.

Scenario #2: Problems with proposal writers

Problem statement	Research questions	Research methods
Our non-profit organization relies heavily on external funding to provide after-school math tutoring for underprivileged children. Currently, we rely on volunteers to write grants and compete for funding. While our volunteers do the best they can with limited resources and time, the grant proposals they produce often require more administrative time to edit than produce. We are concerned that we are wasting our time and our volunteers' time by asking them to draft our proposals.	Why do administrators need to spend so much time editing grants written by volunteers? What problems are volunteers experiencing when they write grants? How can we improve our proposal writing process to reduce redundant efforts?	Interview administrative staff to identify grant-writing issues and to determine specific writing issues that need addressing. Observe administrative staff during grant-editing process to determine if other problems are present. Conduct a focus group with our three volunteer grant writers to determine specific writing issues that need addressing. Observe individual volunteer(s) during grant-editing process to determine if other problems are present. After problems are identified, conduct second round of interviews/focus group meetings to identify solutions.

Table 6.1. This table illustrates the relationship between problem statement, research questions, and research methods.

Responsibilities When Writing Findings

Researchers also have responsibilities when writing their findings, such as supporting claims and conclusions with evidence that demonstrates effective research skills. Claims stated with adequate support give the report findings credibility, providing evidence that you have considered your findings and carefully drawn conclusions to respond to the need or problem that initiated the work. Choose supporting documentation for your findings that you have carefully vetted, and beware of support that is biased or unsubstantiated with evidence. If your research revealed dangerous or harmful information, include this information in your report. Glossing over potentially troublesome findings is ethically questionable, and dismissing this information without consideration can lead to legal issues later. Similarly, when you visually represent your findings in charts and tables, create these visual representations ethically. Do not overemphasize positive findings and de-emphasize negative ones. At the same time, if you borrow images or text from a source, be sure to credit the source in your report, whether that source is in print or electronic format. For more on the ethics of visual representations, refer to Chapter 9. Finally, when writing your report, attend to the citation of others whose work you reference or borrow. Most professions have style guides that provide detailed guidance for citing others. For example, the *APA Publication Manual*, *The Chicago Manual of Style*, and the *Council of Biology Editors* are three frequently referenced style guides. These guides can provide you information on everything from referencing sources to formatting reports to abbreviating words. Refer to the style choice your organization prefers and cite sources accordingly.

As a final step in explaining how these responsibilities fit with other guidelines suggested in this chapter, this section concludes with Table 6.2, which illustrates these connections. Table 6.2 explores the close relationships between problem statements, research questions, methods, and reporting. As the other tables do, this one draws upon the two scenarios first introduced at the beginning of the chapter.

Scenario #1: Intermittent Internet service

Problem statement	Research questions	Research methods	Reporting responsibilities
Our company's server connectivity is being disrupted by intermittent internet disruptions. During work hours, we are often unable to connect to our e-commerce Web site where customers order products, and it appears that our customers are unable to connect to the Web site to place orders. Our online sales are down 10%. We need to know how to eliminate these disruptions, so both we and our customers can access the e-commerce Web site. We know that our current service provider is inexpensive but apparently unreliable. This provider was a good choice when we started our business. We need to find out if we can get more reliable, improved service from our current provider, but, if not, we need to find a new provider with more reliable service offered within our current budget.	Are our decreasing online sales related to provider outages? If so, what can our company do to eliminate its internet connectivity issues? Can our current provider improve its service, with or without an increase in charges? If not, can we find a different service that provides more reliable, improved service within our current budget?	Request Web site analytic data from our information technology team to identify outage frequencies and determine outage effects on sales. Gather information from our current service provider to obtain diagnosis of connectivity issues, to determine the providers' ability to correct or resolve problems, and to discuss additional charges necessary for improved service. If dissatisfied with answer from current provider, contact other service providers to obtain information about services and monthly service charges.	Illustrate the relationship between outages and sales. Create a table that compares and contrasts information from all service providers. Write a report that includes a recommended solution/action for resolving this problem.

Scenario #2: Problems with proposal writers

Problem statement	Research questions	Research methods	Reporting responsibilities
Our non-profit organization relies heavily on external funding to provide after-school math tutoring for underprivileged children. Currently, we rely on volunteers to write grants and compete for funding. While our volunteers do the best they can with limited resources and time, the grant proposals they produce often require more administrative time to edit than produce. We are concerned that we are wasting our time and our volunteers' time by asking them to draft our proposals.	Why do administrators need to spend so much time editing grants written by volunteers? What problems are volunteers experiencing when they write grants? How can we improve our proposal writing process to reduce redundant efforts?	Interview administrative staff to identify grant-writing issues and to determine specific writing issues that need addressing. Observe administrative staff during grant-editing process to determine if other problems are present. Conduct a focus group with our three volunteer grant writers to determine specific writing issues that need addressing. Observe individual volunteer(s) during grant-editing process to determine if other problems are present. After problems are identified, conduct second round of interviews/focus group meetings to identify solutions.	Compare responses from interviews and focus group to determine problems that staff and volunteers encounter. Identify any additional problems based on observation notes. Create questions for second round of interviews/focus groups based on initial findings. Based on second round of interviews/focus groups, make recommendations for grant-writing process improvements. Possible improvements include development of a style guide, development of boilerplate text, and development of library of successful grants to use as models.

Table 6.2. This table illustrates the relationship between problem statement, research questions, research methods, and documentation.

Chapter Summary

In this chapter, you have learned about researching in the workplace. This research typically arises from a change, a problem, or a need. The research process outlined in this chapter requires you to develop a research problem statement and then develop research questions. After refining these questions, researchers choose methods that specifically allow them to answer the questions. Using these methods, researchers seek answers and finally communicate these answers in written or oral reports. Throughout this process, researchers must be aware of their responsibilities as ethical communicators.

Chapter Assignments

The exercises in this section ask you to apply what you have learned in this chapter as well as explore how this knowledge applies to and connects with other information in the textbook.

1. The Purdue Online Writing Lab (OWL) includes a citation chart comparing citation style in three frequently used study guides: the Modern Language Association's (MLA) style manual, the American Psychology Association's (APA) style manual, and the Chicago Manual of Style (CMS). You can access this chart at this location: https://owl.english.purdue.edu/media/pdf/20110928111055_949.pdf. Conduct research to find another commonly used style guide and create another row for this chart explaining how the style guide you have found handles these citation forms.

2. Identify a problem on your campus that could be resolved by research. Create a table like Table 2 and fill in the columns: research problem statement, research questions, research methods, and reporting responsibilities.

3. Visit the Survey Monkey tutorial on Question Types (http://help.surveymonkey.com/articles/en_US/kb/Available-question-types-and-formatting-options). Create a series of questions for an interview. Then modify the questions to make them appropriate for a survey. Be prepared to explain how and why you modified the questions when your primary research method changed from interview to survey.

4. Conduct a brief review of the following Web sites that describe "bitcoin." You may find these sources to be very technical, but using the guidelines for evaluating and authenticating sources, you should be able to compare and contrast them. How would you describe each source? Which one or ones seem credible? Why? Which ones would you use in a formal or informal report? Why?

    a. "Bitcoin: A Peer-to-Peer Electronic Cash System," http://nakamotoinstitute.org/bitcoin/

    b. "Bitcoin," http://en.wikipedia.org/wiki/Bitcoin

    c. "Bitter to Better—How to Make Bitcoin a Better Currency," http://eprints.qut.edu.au/69169/1/Boyen_accepted_draft.pdf

5. Imagine that you are vegan and living in one of your university's dormitories. You have found that your food choices are limited, at best, in the dormitory cafeteria. As a member of the university's Vegans Unite organization, you would like to learn more about vegan food options around campus. Decide what research methods would help you to conduct this research and develop a detailed research protocol to conduct this research.

Figure Credits

Figure 6.1. © Rido/Shutterstock.com

Figure 6.2. © stockstudio/Shutterstock.com

Figure 6.3. © coka/Shutterstock.com

Figure 6.4. © jannoon028/Shutterstock.com

Figure 6.5. © William Perugini/Shutterstock.com

Figure 6.6. © CandyBox Images/Shutterstock.com

Figure 6.7. © wavebreakmedia/Shutterstock.com

Figure 6.8. © nasirkhan/Shutterstock.com

Writing Content, Technical Style, and Editing

CHAPTER OVERVIEW

This chapter focuses on authoring content for communication products. After reading this chapter, you should be able to meet the following objectives:

- Select the best words to use in your documents.
- Draft sentences that are effective and punctuated correctly.
- Combine sentences into paragraphs that are unified.
- Craft paragraphs that introduce and conclude your documents.
- Explain the differences between structured and unstructured authoring.
- Explain methods of editing and revising.

Historically, technical communicators were advised to write as clearly and concisely as possible. The theory behind this advice went something like this: technical communicators are responsible for gathering technical, often hard-to-understand information from subject matter experts (such as engineers and scientists), removing the technical terminology and jargon and replacing it with easier language so that less technical users of the information could understand it. Technical communicators were taught to use "windowpane" language, words and sentences that were so clear anyone could understand or "see" their meaning. This advice was based in two working assumptions about technical communication audiences: they were humans, and they were culturally similar to the technical communicators.

While the assumption that audiences are human may sound odd (of course, they are human, right?), humans are not the only readers of technical communication. Much of today's technical communication must also be machine-readable; that is, it must be written and tagged so that machines, directed by scripting language, can read it and use it to construct texts on the fly. Similarly, today's technical communication is often translated into multiple languages, and the original text must be created in a way that it can be efficiently, affordably, and accurately translated into another language.

Figure 7.1. Editors often use proofreading symbols when editing by hand.

For these reasons, we now have a broader, more complex awareness about how technical communicators use language in their workplaces, and the guidelines are not as clear as they once were. We know, for example, that technical communicators assess their audiences when they choose their words, and these audiences do not necessarily need or want simplified language. In these situations, technical communicators learn the specialized languages of science, technology, and engineering, to name a few, so they can communicate with others in these fields. In other situations, such as medical websites, technical communicators continue their traditional work, making technical concepts and practices easier for lay audiences to understand. They create content as well as edit it.

Writing situations, too, are not so easily defined; for example, writing for print and writing for digital Internet-based delivery require different knowledge, skills, and technologies. Complicating communication situations even more are new methods of authoring content, requiring technical communicators to consider not only whether human readers (possibly using different languages) can read and understand their products but also whether these products are machine-readable so the content can be used in multiple contexts and displayed by media in variable formats. These situations are just a few of the content development considerations discussed in this chapter.

Because it would be impossible to anticipate all situations in which technical communicators work, this chapter does not attempt to provide strict guidelines for writing or communicating with others. Instead, it offers you guidelines and an introduction to vocabulary. This information will assist you in developing and structuring content so that all readers, whether human or machine, can easily find, read, and understand communications you produce.

The first and longest section of the chapter provides you with guidelines for choosing words, stringing words into sentences, connecting sentences into paragraphs, and combining paragraphs into complete texts. It concludes by providing textual, visual, or computer-coded signposts to help readers assemble all of these parts into a readable document. In doing so, it offers you a specialized vocabulary for talking and thinking about your communication products, whether they are written or spoken, printed or digital. This vocabulary will be useful in situations where you are asked to author a communication product or to edit someone else's. It will also assist you if you are in other situations, such as writing for translation, which is increasingly common in today's marketplace, or writing collaboratively with others. The chapter concludes with suggestions for reviewing the content you generate as well as others' content.

A BRIEF INTRODUCTION TO CONTENT AUTHORING

Traditionally, people who created texts, such as novelists and essayists, were called authors. The words author and authors were used primarily as a noun to name such people. The word author may also be used as a verb, to author, to describe the action of creating or inventing technological texts, such as writing a computer code. The title of this chapter uses the term, **author**, in both senses—as a noun to describe people who create texts and as a verb to describe the act of creating text.

Authoring can also be used as an adjective to describe programs or applications that support the work of creating or inventing; we refer to these programs or applications as authoring tools. As these tools have developed, so have other terms coined to describe their work, for example, unstructured authoring and structured authoring.

Unstructured authoring is a term that describes how most people learn to create a document following more ad-hoc practices, such as with a computer; it describes the action of writing and formatting content or texts with a keyboard and word processing application. As the content is entered, the writer makes formatting decisions, such as when to emphasize content using boldface or what font to employ for headings and text. To move content to another document or to a different place in a document, the technical communicator uses the word processor's cut and paste function. Creating a new document with the same content often requires the content to be reformatted.

In contrast, **structured authoring** describes a more deliberate organizational process, including the action of writing content in discrete chunks and organizing them into information models or templates. This can be done using a variety of methods including the use of software tools, markup and scripting languages (such as HTML, XML, or CSS), or even content management systems (including blogs, wikis, text editors, and other Web site development tools).

An **information model** is an outline of content that illustrates the relationship between various content chunks in the document's structure. After content has been organized, information designers can integrate the use of links, tags, navigation toolbars, or other semantic markup to create a fully interactive document. An in-depth discussion of information models and these related activities will be discussed in the next two chapters.

Figure 7.2. Authors are traditionally defined as writers of novels and essays, but today the word has broader implications particularly to technical communicators.

Structured authoring has become increasingly important and an essential technical writing skill as a result of online and electronically published content. This chapter offers you suggestions and guidelines for choosing effective words, stringing those words into meaningful sentences, and composing sentences into unified and coherent paragraphs. These suggestions and guidelines are good rules of thumb, particularly for situations where you are developing content for printed or oral delivery. Content, today, is often delivered in other ways: it is downloaded and read on smartphones, tablets, laptop and desktop computers, and even televisions. In fact, if you think about it, you probably receive and process technical content on these digital devices more than any other way. To distinguish between structured and unstructured authoring, keep in mind their similarities and differences. Both types of content authoring require you to use good diction, effective sentence construction, and unified paragraphing.

Digital technical content delivery has presented new challenges in technical communication. For example, technical communicators (content developers) have to be able to create documents that are **flexible** (can be viewed and read easily on a variety of devices) and **dynamic** (can be updated frequently and easily). They also need to be able to develop content consistently within collaborative teams, and teams need that content to be reusable so that it can be delivered via a webpage but also pushed to and shared by consumers through social media, such as Twitter or Facebook. Structured authoring practices were developed to meet these practices.

Although you may be unfamiliar with structured content delivery as a term or process, you are probably very familiar with it in your everyday life. It is very commonly used for online product documentation, but it is also frequently used for online marketing. For example, if you have received marketing emails from a company or corporation, then you are familiar with the brief descriptions in those emails that link you to longer, more detailed descriptions on websites. Some of the information from the email appears on the website, but the website provides more details. If you have received photographs or video content through social media that leads you to professional content on a photo- or video-sharing website, then you have encountered structured authoring. If you have searched an online help site, then you have accessed content that has been structured to assist your search.

Figure 7.3. Digital techical content creation presents new challenges for technical communicators.

To become proficient in structured authoring, technical communicators need specialized skills with tools, as well as markup language (HTML or XML), and scripting languages (CSS for style and JavaScript or PHP for interactive elements). Markup languages are used to tag or label content, while scripting languages add visual styles, positioning, and interactive features. Figure 7.4 illustrates how a book entry in a library database might be marked up with XML so its parts can be presented as needed in various kinds of lists, ranging from a list of sources to complete citations to a product inventory list like you might see on online bookseller's website.

Structured authoring offers many benefits to organizations that employ digital content. As this example illustrates, it allows information to be written in discrete chunks of digital information that can be deployed when and where they are needed. It also separates formatting from the content, which allows information to be used and reused whenever and wherever needed. In this way, content can be customized for different audiences. When content is used or reused in different countries or cultures, it allows it to be localized to meet the needs of individuals in specific locations. You will find more detailed information on structured authoring in Chapter 8.

```
<mylibrary>
<book>
<book_title>JavaScript & AJAX for the Web</book_title>
<author>Negrino</author>
<isbn>0321430328</isbn>
<series>Visual QuickStart</series>
<edition>6</edition>
<pubdate>2007</pubdate>
</book>
<book>
<book_title>The Zen of CSS Design</book_title>
<author>Shea</author>
<isbn>0321303474</isbn>
<series/>
<edition>1</edition>
<pubdate>2005</pubdate>
</book>
</mylibrary>
```

Figure 7.4. This sample XML markup illustrates how book entries can be labeled or marked up for varied uses.

Differences between Unstructured and Structured Authoring

To illustrate the differences between unstructured authoring and structured authoring, consider a genre familiar to you, the résumé. When you create a résumé with a word processor, you type in the content. You then design and format the layout. You may add headings and format them for emphasis. In another section, you use a bulleted list. When you gain new experience or earn a new degree, you open the file and enter the new information directly into the old one, updating and modifying content as well as formatting as necessary. The word processor you use is your authoring tool or technology.

In contrast, when you use an electronic networking or job search application to create a resume, you enter content in structured database chunks. Figure 7.5 is a screen shot from Monster.com's résumé entry page.

Notice how the content is organized in discrete chunks of information that, in this case, are tagged and stored in a database. These chunks allow the content to be machine-read and modified as needed for one job application or another. As a user of the website, you can pick and choose what content to include. The choices you make generate a script that calls the content you have selected into a new résumé. The organization of the new résumé is structured because its parts are tagged and able to be called on demand, as needed.

While unstructured and structured authoring appear to be quite different—one seems written by and for human readers while the other seems initially to be written by and for machine or computer readers—both types of authoring are human-created systems that rely on hierarchies to work. Unstructured authoring relies first and foremost on a logic called **grammar**, a system of wordsmithing (the skills of putting words together to create content), and **style**, the rhetorical choices one makes to create readable documents. Structured authoring, similarly, relies on a hierarchal system of organizing, coding, tagging, and scripting, activities that are also designed to create content.

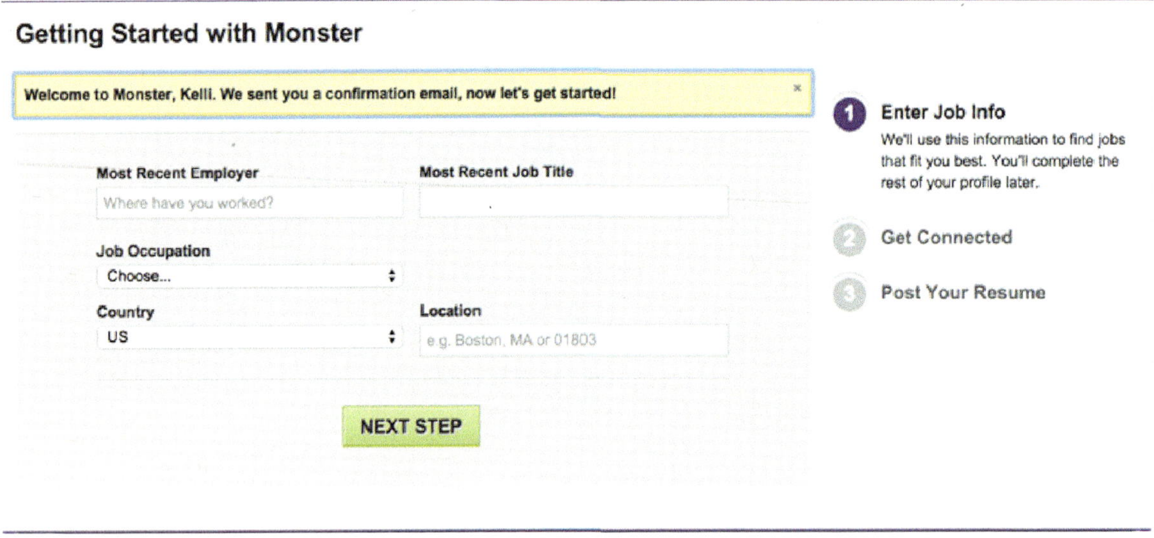

Figure 7.5. This employment entry page from Monster.com demonstrates how content can be structured and chunked into separate categories of tagged information.

WORDS, SENTENCES, PARAGRAPHS: THE BUILDING BLOCKS OF STYLE

The building blocks of any communication—whether unstructured or structured—are its words, sentences, and paragraphs. In this section, you will consider the choices you make when selecting words, crafting them into sentences, and combining these sentences into paragraphs. Additionally, as you make these choices, you must decide how to punctuate your communication. Together the choices you make when combining these components—words, sentences, paragraphs, and punctuation—determine the *style* of your communication.

Figure 7.6. The choices you make about words, sentences, paragraphs comprise your writing style.

Diction: Selecting the Right Words

The English word for "selecting the rights words for a particular audience and situation" is **diction**. To understand diction choices and their effects on style, you need to develop a vocabulary that helps you to describe and distinguish between words and their functions. This vocabulary can also help you to understand how word choices create various levels of diction, from informal slang expressions to highly formal academic prose. This vocabulary begins with recognizing words as parts of speech. Following an introduction to the parts of speech and parts of a sentence, this section discusses levels of diction, methods for improving your diction choices, common diction faults, and strategies for recognizing and correcting these faults.

The Functions of Words

At some point in your schooling, you have certainly encountered the parts of speech in language courses, but, like most college students, you may not remember much about them or the memories you have are not good ones. If you are planning to be a technical communicator, then this linguistic vocabulary will be essential for you to learn, and you should take a linguistic or style class to master it. It will help you to explain how and why you have written and edited documents the ways you have. If, however, you are planning another career, this vocabulary may be less important for you to learn. In either case, what you need to know now is that words are classified by their functions: as naming words (**nouns** and **pronouns**), actions words (**verbs**), modifying or qualifying words (**adjectives** and **adverbs**), and connecting words (**prepositions**, **conjunctions**). Understanding how words function can help you choose the best word for the sentence you are composing.

Levels of Diction

Another key consideration as you make diction choices is the level of diction of the communication. Recognizing these levels (sometimes called **registers**) will also help you to make good choices. Simply put, word choice in a document can be described as one of four levels, which are arranged from least formal to most formal: slang, colloquial, informal, formal.

Slang is the least formal level; think of slang as "street talk," words used commonly in speech among friends. New slang words are added daily, and they frequently rise and fall in popularity. Slang terms are often used to designate in-group vs. out-group membership; for this reason, many slang terms may be sexist or racist and, therefore, offensive to individuals who are being described. An example of slang from the 1970s is the term "AFA," meaning "A Friend Always" which is similar to the more current "BFF," "best friends forever." To find other examples of slang, visit the Urban Dictionary online (http://www.urbandictionary.com), where slang is defined as "the only reason UrbanDictionary.com exists." The Urban Dictionary identifies current and past slang words and defines these terms for individuals who do not recognize or know their meaning.

Using slang is acceptable among individuals who understand it; however, in professional communication, this level of diction rarely appears. When it does appear, it is usually inappropriate unless it is defined or used to explain. Here is an example of an appropriate use of slang from the National Institute on Drug Abuse:

> "MAB-CHMINACA, ADB-CHMINACA (sold as "Mojo," "Spice," "K2," and "Scooby Snax") resulted in over 150 hospital visits in Baton Rouge and Lafayette, LA in October, prompting the governor to ban the drug in that state" (http://www.drugabuse.gov/drugs-abuse/emerging-trends).

In this example, the words in all caps are the scientific names while the words in parenthesis and quotation marks are the slang names for this drug. Using slang in this sentence is appropriate because it provides readers with names users of the drug prefer.

Like slang, **colloquial diction** choices are also informal. The colloquial level is typically used in conversation, and it may even include slang. Colloquial expressions include contractions (for example, "you'll" instead of "you will" and "shouldn't" instead of "should not") and informal expressions ("to check out" instead of "to investigate" or to say "something doesn't add up" instead of "something is nonsensical"). In the professional communication, you may use colloquial expressions when writing email to or messaging a close colleague, but, in more formal documents, this level is best avoided. Colloquial diction can also be problematic if you are communicating with someone whose first language is not English because colloquial expressions are less easily understood by nonnative speakers.

Informal diction includes every day, common conversational language. Informal or standard diction choices are common in magazine or blog articles, emails, social media, texting, and even newscasts. You also likely use informal diction when addressing or writing to your professor or your supervisor. This level of diction is the baseline for professional communication. Most TED talks use informal diction, so everyone who hears them can understand their messages. Informal diction is mid-range on the diction register.

Formal diction is the highest range on the diction register. It includes words that are common among highly educated or specialized language users. Formal diction also includes **jargon**, technical or field-specific terminology. You might encounter formal diction in academic journal articles or a lecture on technical topic, such as a medical procedure. Unless you are member of one of these groups of specialized language users, you will probably not use formal diction very often; in fact, many technical communicators are employed to adapt formal diction into more commonly understood informal or standard language, which is more easily understood.

Table 7.1 illustrates how word choices change depending on their diction level. The words in each column reflect diction choices you might make depending your audience and situation. As this table demonstrates, the key to understanding these levels of diction is to remember the audience you are addressing and the situation. If you are talking to a friend, then slang or colloquial language may be appropriate; however, when you communicate in the workplace, that is, in a professional setting, your diction should rise to informal or formal level.

Level	Example 1	Example 2	Example 3
Slang	Wingman	Big-mouthed	Grok
Colloquial	Pal	Chatty	Catch on
Informal/Standard	Friend	Talkative	Understand
Formal	Colleague	Loquacious	Perceive

Table 7.1. Each examples illustrates how words with similar meanings represent different levels of diction.

EXERCISE 7.1

Levels of Diction

Discover other examples of diction levels to add to Table 7.1. Identify a slang term or phrase you know and then seek out other word or phrases you might choose if you were writing at the colloquial, informal, or formal levels of diction. Be sure to choose a term that you can discuss in class without offense to others.

Tasks to be completed:

1. Choose a slang word that can be shared in class
2. Work though the levels of diction to identify examples of colloquial, informal, and formal words for the slang word.

Other Word Choice Considerations

Recognizing the appropriate level of diction to use in professional communication is the first step in making good diction choices. These additional guidelines can assist you as you select words for the most impact in your documents. They are useful to remember whether your audience is comprised on people who speak English as a first language or who speak English as a foreign language.

Choose Words that are Grammatically Correct

Understanding how words work together in English to create sentences will help you to decide which word works best in any given situation. Using grammar appropriately in your sentences assures that your diction choices are **correct**. Correctness is an important key to making your communications understandable. A simple way to enact this guideline is to use nouns as nouns and verbs as verbs. For example, "sandwich" is a common English noun, but it can sometimes be used as a verb to mean "placing between two other things." Using "sandwich" as a verb may cause confusion for readers who do not use English as a first language. Another example is the word "weasel" when used as a verb as in "to weasel out", meaning "to avoid" or "to mislead." The verb's meaning arises from the behavior of the animal called a weasel, but readers who are unfamiliar with weasels may not understand what the verb means. Finally, this example illustrates how using a verb instead of noun can cause confusion: "The only interrupt designed into the system supported RF communication." (Instead of the verb "interrupt," the writer should have used the noun "interruption.") While these usages may be acceptable in some situations, using words in grammatically unusual or incorrect ways can confuse readers.

Use References Like Dictionaries and Thesauruses Carefully

Improving your vocabulary gives you more diction choices from which to select. To improve your vocabulary, you must read, but reading alone will not help you to increase your vocabulary. You must also use a dictionary to grasp the subtle differences between words. If you choose to use a thesaurus, a tool that can provide you with many potential synonyms, do not use it alone. Always use a thesaurus and a dictionary together to be certain that the word chosen is the best for the sentence's context and ultimately your intended meaning.

Know the Difference Between a Word's Denotation and Connotation

The **denotation** is a word's dictionary meaning while the **connotation** is the feeling, nuances, or attitudes that readers attach to the word. Because many words have similar meanings, choosing the right word requires you to know its connotation as well as its denotation. For example, if you writing a report about a weight loss experiment and describing the participants in the study, you might use the following words to describe individuals who weigh below the national average ("underweight," "scrawny," "thin," "malnourished," or "skeletal") or these words to describe individuals who are above the national average ("overweight," "fat," "heavy," "chunky," "obese"). As you can see, some of these words have an almost neutral meaning while others convey more positive or negative feelings. Choosing words with an appropriate connection is essential. The best word for your writing situation would need to take into account the communication's situation and purpose (a scientific report) and the connotations of the word you choose.

Choose Words that are as Concrete and Specific as Possible

Readers are more likely to get a clear picture of what you are describing if you use concrete specific words rather than abstract, general words. **Concrete** words are words that relate to the five senses whereas **abstract** words describe feelings or emotions. **General** words are summary terms while **specific** words are examples. If you must use general or abstract words, try to modify them or follow these words with specific examples to clarity what you mean. For example, if you are explaining how hot an oven should be in a recipe, you might write a "medium oven," and some readers would understand while others would not. Stating that the oven should be "preheated to 350 degrees" is specific and provides readers with exactly the heat setting needed. Or consider how easy it would be to find a car in a mall parking lot with these descriptions: "a car," "a red car" or "a red Jetta Sportwagen." The third description narrows the field considerably, doesn't it?

Prefer Expressive Words to Impressive Ones

Impressive formal word choices may strike your reader as pretentiousness in professional communications. To avoid pretentiousness, choose words that best express what you mean, and avoid using literary language in nonliterary writing. Unless you are communicating with an audience in a very formal situation, avoid using formal words when less formal ones will do. For example, use "fire" instead of "conflagration," "use" instead of "utilize," "count" instead of "enumerate." While using less formal expressive words may lower the reading level of your communication, it ensures that everyone who reads it will understand your meaning.

> ### EXERCISE 7.2
> ### *Practice Making Good Word Choices*
>
> Working in pairs, practice good word choices by writing sentences to describe each situation:
>
> 1. Imagine that you are writing a restaurant review for a new hamburger restaurant in your area. Think about connotations and denotations as you write three sentences that describe the restaurant's cheeseburger as irresistible, average, and inedible.
> 2. Translate the following sentences to make them more understandable:
>   a. Terminate the engine to prevent excessive heating.
>   b. He attempted to employ his expertise in securities to accrue a fortune.
>   c. Lubricate the chain with oil often.
>
> **Tasks to be completed:**
>
> 1. Working with a partner, choose a hamburger restaurant to review.
> 2. Collaboratively write one sentence to describe the restaurants' hamburgers as irresistible, average, and inedible, for a total of three sentences.
> 3. After you have completed this exercise, revise the three sentences in #2 above to make them easier to understand.

Syntax: Writing Effective Sentences

Just as choosing the right words helps you to write stylistically appropriate sentences, writing effective sentences also improves your communication's style. Sentence structure, also called **syntax**, refers to how sentences are arranged or organized. Effective sentences are complete and well punctuated. This section helps you to make choices that will improve the sentences you write.

All sentences have at least one main clause. A main clause must contain both a **subject** (noun or pronoun) and a simple **predicate** (a verb). Together the subject and predicate create a complete thought. A **main clause** is **independent**; it makes sense and can stand alone. In contrast, **subordinate clauses** are **dependent** on the main clause and cannot stand alone. They must be attached to a main clause can act, and they serve as nouns, adjectives, or adverbs to rename or describe something in the main clause. Like main clauses, subordinate clauses have subjects and predicates, but they usually start with a connecting word (a subordinating conjunction or a relative pronoun) that makes them dependent on the main clause. The following list of subordinating conjunctions and relative pronouns is not complete, but it will give you an idea of the kinds of words that frequently begin dependent clauses:

- Subordinating conjunctions—although, because, since, when, while, how, since, though
- Relative pronouns—that, which, who, whom, whose, whomever, whichever, whatever

A good dictionary will help you identify other examples of conjunctions and relative pronouns that create dependent clauses.

Common Arrangements of Main Clauses

The most common order for complete sentences or main clauses is subject + predicate, but this pattern can be changed or expanded depending on communication needs. What follows are the six most common arrangements of main clauses and examples of each:

> 1. **subject + verb**
>   *Alanna runs in two marathons each year.*
>
>   *John runs in only one.*
>
> 2. **subject + verb + direct object**
>   *Alanna runs marathons in Buffalo Springs Lake and in Austin every year.*
>
>   *Marathons test an athlete's physical and emotional stamina.*
>
> 3. **subject + verb + indirect object + direct object (Verbs that commonly take indirect objects include give, buy, teach, bring, tell, teach, and offer.)**
>   *Marathons give John an opportunity to test his stamina.*
>
>   *After marathons, local businesses offer runners breakfast items and other nourishment.*
>
> 4. **subject + verb + direct object + object complement**
>   *John find marathons challenging.*
>
>   *The news about the Buffalo Springs marathon made John and Alanna happy.*
>
>   *The marathoners elected Alanna their team leader.*
>
> 5. **subject + verb + predicate adjective (describes subject)**
>   *Marathons are challenging.*
>
>   *Running in marathons is emotionally and physically exhausting.*
>
> 6. **subject + verb + predicate nominative (renames subject)**
>   *John and Alanna are athletes.*
>
>   *Marathons were one of the first Olympic events.*

All of the sentences in the examples above are **simple sentences**, having only one main clauses. When sentences have two more main clauses but no subordinate clauses, they are classified as **compound sentences**. When they have two or more main clauses and at least one subordinate clauses, they are called **complex sentences**. Sentences with two or more main clauses and two or more subordinate clauses are called **compound-complex sentences**. Being able to recognize each of these types of sentence constructions can help you create better sentences as well as punctuate them more effectively.

EXERCISE 7.3

Sentence Choices and Audience

Compare the sentences in two comparable news stories written for two different audiences—one for adults (parents or teachers) and the other children (students). For example, you might visit one of the following websites that provides educational content for teachers, parents, and students:

- NASA.gov (http://www.nasa.gov/audience/forstudents/)
- Scholastic (http://Scholastic.com)
- Society for Science and the Public's Student Science page (https://student.societyforscience.org/sciencenews-students)
- Any major news outlet, such as Time, Newsweek, CNN, or FOX, that has a student section

As you examine the articles, note the following information:

- How many sentences are in each article?
- What is the average length of sentences in each article?
- What kinds of sentences (simple, compound, complex, compound-complex) are included in the article?

Finally, be ready to discuss with your classmates how audience might be affecting the kinds and complexity of sentences found in your two articles.

Tasks to be completed:

1. Find a news story reported on two different online news sources and written for different two different audiences.
2. Compare the articles' contents by noting the following:
   a. How many sentences are in each article?
   b. What is the average length of sentences in each article?
   c. What kinds of sentences (simple, compound, complex, compound-complex) are included in the article?
3. Bring your findings to class and discuss whether and how sentences changed in each article.

Punctuating Sentences

All sentences are required to have end punctuation. **End punctuation** helps readers to understand the function of the sentence: making a statement of fact, asking a question, commanding the reader to do something, or exclaiming. Each of these functions is a designated type of sentence, and each requires a different form of punctuation:

- *Declarative sentences* end in periods (.).
- *Interrogative sentences* end in question marks (?).
- *Imperative sentences* end with either a period or an exclamation point (. or !).
- *Exclamatory sentences* end with an exclamation point (!).

While end punctuation may seem straightforward, you may have problems with it if you forget your level of diction. For example, in emails, texts, and other messaging communications, end punctuation is less formal; individuals sometimes use multiple end marks (!?!) to indicate confusion, excitement, or indifference. More formal communications, however, should reflect the conventional use of end punctuation as described above.

Some sentences also require punctuation internally in addition to end punctuation. While there are many types of internal punctuation that you may use, two punctuation marks are essential to know: the comma and the semicolon. These two punctuation marks and their misuse cause more sentence faults that any other marks. The following guidelines will help you to understand common comma and semicolon guidelines.

Commas

These guidelines will help you to use commas effectively in sentences. Following each guideline is an example incorrectly punctuated without commas and correctly punctuated with commas.

1. ***Use a comma to join items in a series.*** *(Remember that items in a series must be similar or parallel. That is, join words with other words, phrases with other phrases, and clauses with other clauses. If you join dissimilar words, you create a parallelism fault.) Example without commas (incorrect): Our new business sells office supplies computers and other electronic equipment.*

   Example with commas (correct): Our new business sells office supplies, computers, and other electronic equipment.

2. ***Use a comma and a coordinating conjunction to join two independent clauses in a compound sentence.***
   Example without commas (incorrect): We offer students a 10% discount on all online electronic purchases and college students are our most loyal customers.

   Example with commas (correct): We offer students a 10% discount on all online electronic purchases, and college students are our most loyal customers.

3. ***Use a comma after an introductory phrase of three words or longer.***
   Example without commas (incorrect): In the computer market it is important to distinguish your product from your competitors'.

   Example with commas (correct): In the computer market, it is important to distinguish your product from your competitors'.

4. ***Use a comma after an introductory subordinate clause.***
   Example without commas (incorrect): When I shop for a computer I always compare prices using the Internet.

   Example with commas (correct): When I shop for a computer, I always compare prices using the Internet.

5. ***Use two commas to set off non-essential phrases and clauses in the middle of a sentence.***
   Example without commas (incorrect): Best Buy which has several locations in our college town and a strong online presence is our biggest competitor.

   Example with commas (correct): Best Buy, which has several locations in our college town and a strong online presence, is our biggest competitor.

6. ***Never separate the subject of the sentence from its verb/action with a single comma.***
   Example without commas (incorrect): College students are using mobile devices, such as mobile phones and tablets to take notes in their classes.

> 7. *Example with commas (correct): College students are using mobile devices, such as mobile phones and tablets, to take notes in their classes.* **Use commas to prevent misreading.**
> *Example without commas: Soon after starting our business has grown quarterly.*
>
> *Example with commas: Soon after starting, our business has grown quarterly.*

Semicolon

Semicolons separate main clauses that are closely related. Following each guideline is an example incorrectly punctuated without a semicolon and correctly punctuated with a semicolon.

> 1. **Use a semicolon to join two independent clauses in a compound sentence when the clauses are not linked by a coordinating conjunction.**
> *Example without semicolon (incorrect): Starks Business Supply and Staples are the two office supplies stores in our town Starks is locally owned while Staples is a franchise.*
>
> *Example with semicolon (correct): Starks Business Supply and Staples are the two office supplies stores in our town; Starks is locally owned while Staples is a franchise.*
>
> 2. **Use a semicolon to join independent clauses in a compound sentence when the clauses are linked with a conjunctive adverb, such as therefore, however, consequently.**
> *Example without semicolon (incorrect): Starks Business Supply offers the best service and equipment in our town, therefore, I shop there before searching online.*
>
> *Example with semicolon (correct): Starks Business Supply offers the best service and equipment in our town; therefore, I shop there before searching online.*
>
> 3. **Use a semicolon to separate compound sentences when one of the main clauses contains commas.**
> *Example without semicolon (incorrect): Whenever I can, I prefer to buy electronic equipment for our office locally because Starks Business Supply offers the best service and equipment in our town, I stop there first.*
>
> *Example with semicolon (correct): Whenever I can, I prefer to buy electronic equipment for our office locally because Starks Business Supply offers the best service and equipment in our town; I shop there before searching online.*

Sentence Faults

The end punctuation, comma, and semicolon guidelines in the previous section can help you to avoid sentence faults. While it is true that professional writers sometimes include sentence faults in their writing, they do so intentionally. You should be sure that your use or decision to include such faults in your writing is intentional as well. Recognizing the following sentence faults and knowing strategies for correcting them can help you improve your sentence structure:

1. **Fragment:** *A fragment is an incomplete sentence (lacks a subject or predicate/verb); although commonly used by professional writers, fragments that are unintentional can cause problems for readers. Fragments can be corrected in two ways: (1) adding the missing subject or predicate/verb, or (2) connecting the fragment to a nearby complete that it modifies or renames.*
2. **Comma splice.** *A comma splice is a faulty sentence in which two or more independent clauses are joined using a comma rather than a coordinating conjunction, a period, or a semicolon. Comma splices can be corrected by separating the main clauses with end punctuation, a comma and a coordinating conjunction, or a semicolon.*
3. **Fused or run-on sentences.** *A fused or run-on sentence is similar to a comma splice without the commas. It is a faulty sentence in which two independent clauses are placed together with no coordinating conjunction or punctuation. Like the commas splice, fused or run-on sentences can be corrected by separating the main clauses with end punctuation, a comma and a coordinating conjunction, or a semicolon.*

EXERCISE 7.4

The Importance of Punctuation

The selection below has been modified from an article on a U.S. government website Women's Health. All beginning of sentence capitalization, end punctuation, and internal punctuation have been removed. Working with a partner, revise this paragraph. Because you have punctuation choices, your revision may be different from other teams.

> each year on Thanksgiving which coincides with National Family Health History Day I encourage everyone to focus on the importance of family health history through the Office of the Surgeon General's Family Health History Initiative why is it important to discuss your family's health history diseases such as cancer, diabetes, and heart disease often run in families tracing the illnesses of your parents grandparents and other blood relatives can help your health care practitioner predict your risk for specific diseases and make vital screening and treatment decisions before any disease is evident with our online tool My Family Health Portrait you can gather together with your family and record your family health history. The tool is a great resource to use before going to medical appointments so you have your health history to discuss with your health care practitioner in addition the tool allows users to save their family history information to their own computer and share health history information with other family members before you start using this tool you will need to talk with your family members to collect details about their health histories we even have tips on starting the conversation for you and in about 20 minutes you can create a unique family health history portrait

When you have finished your revision, compare your work to the website (http://www.womenshealth.gov/blog/family-health-history-priceless-gift-you-and-your-family.html). If your choices are different, be ready to explain why you punctuated and capitalized the selection as you did.

Tasks to be completed:

1. Rewrite the paragraph above with correct sentence capitalization, end punctuation, and internal punctuation.
2. Compare your revision with others in your class. If you find differences, explain why. Decide which revision is best.

Constructing Sentences for Economy, Variety, and Emphasis

Three of the most common strategies for constructing sentences well are to improve sentence *economy* (make every word count), *variety* (vary your sentences length and structure), and *emphasis* (put important words in positions of power). This section of the chapter provides you with strategies for improving your sentence economy, variety, and emphasis.

Economy

Economy means using no needless words—getting the most mileage from the fewest number of words. Economy is almost always required in technical and professional communications, although it is not always a concern in creative writing when words may be added for aesthetic purposes (sound, rhythm, and/or visual interest) or other reasons. The guidelines that follow describe ways to improve the economy of your sentences. In the examples below, phrases are underlined and subordinate clauses are boxed.

1. **When possible, use adjectives, rather than prepositional phrases.**
   Original: The sponsor <u>of the contest</u> is offering the winner <u>of the contest</u> a prize <u>of grand proportion</u>. (Sentence length: 20 words; 3 prepositional phrases)

   Revised: The sponsor is offering the contest winner a hefty prize. (Sentence length: 10 words; 0 prepositional phrases)

   Original: As you can see <u>from the acknowledgements</u> <u>in this report</u>, we were contacted and coordinated <u>with many individuals</u> <u>in the design and development</u> <u>of this project</u>. (Sentence length: 26 words; 5 prepositional phrases)

   Revised: <u>As the report's acknowledgements</u> show, our team contacted and coordinated many individuals to design and develop this project. (Sentence length: 18 words; 1 prepositional phrase)

2. **Change who, which, and that (subordinate) clauses to adjectives.**
   Original: The signal strength indicator ⟦that is on the front panel of the receiver⟧ identifies the strength of the wireless connection. (Sentence length: 20 words; one subordinate clause with two prepositional phrases; one additional prepositional phrase)

   Revised: The signal strength indicator on the receiver's front panel identifies the wireless connection's strength. (Sentence length: 14 words; no subordinate clauses, one prepositional phrase.)

   Original: At the next meeting, your supervisor will recognize anyone ⟦who has a plan⟧ ⟦that is feasible⟧. (Sentence length: 16 words; one prepositional phrase, two subordinate clauses)

   Revised: At the next meeting, your supervisor will recognize anyone with a feasible plan. (Sentence length: 13 words; two prepositional phrases; no subordinate clauses)

3. **Choose strong, active verbs to reduce wordiness.**
   Original: Figure 2 <u>gives estimates</u> <u>of all</u> <u>of the sizes</u> <u>of the boards and boxes</u> ⟦that the boards will⟧ <u>ship in</u>. (Sentence length: 20 words; weak verb; three prepositional phrases; one subordinate clause)

   Revised: Figure 2 <u>estimates</u> boards' and their shipping boxes' sizes. (Sentence length: 9 words; strong verb; no prepositional phrases; no subordinate clauses)

> *Original:* If the temperature <u>is</u> below the desired <u>temperature of the aquarium system</u>, then the heater <u>is turned on</u>. (Sentence length: 18 words; 2 weak verbs; one subordinate clause with one prepositional phrase)
>
> *Revised:* If the aquarium system's temperature dips below 72 degrees, then the heater activates. (Sentence length: 13 words; no weak verbs, more specific temperature stated; one subordinate clause with one prepositional phrase)
>
> 4. **Eliminate "there are," "there were," "it is," and "it was" at the beginning of your sentences.** Exceptions: Use "there are" and "there is" constructions to shift a phrase toward the end of the sentence and thereby emphasize it. You can use this device at the beginning of a paragraph to introduce concepts that you will develop in sentences that follow.
>
> *Original:* <u>There were</u> a few decisions <u>that we made</u> <u>that had a definite impact on the outcome of our project</u>. (Sentence length: 19 words; "there were" start; weak verb; two subordinate clauses, one with two prepositional phrases)
>
> *Revised:* Two decisions impacted our project's outcome. (Sentence length: 6 words; strong verb, no subordinate clauses, no prepositional phrases.)
>
> *Original:* <u>It is thought</u> <u>that Visual Basic might have been a better way to go for the interactive map</u> graphics. (Sentence length: 20 words; "it is" start; one subordinate clause with one prepositional phrase)
>
> *Revised:* Using Visual Basic might have improved our interactive map graphics. (Sentence length: 10 words; strong verb; no subordinate clauses or prepositional phrases)

Variety

Sentence variety means that your sentences are different lengths. When you are writing for a general audience, remember that the more complex the information, the shorter the sentences. Why is this so? Shorter sentences are easier to read and understand. Varying the length of your sentences will also improve the rhythm of your communication and reduce the monotony created when sentences are all the same length. Short sentences create sudden emphasis. Longer sentences suggest a longer thought process or flow. Follow these suggestions to increase variety in your sentences.

1. **Count the words in your sentences and note their lengths.** Do you have a variety or does one length predominate? If necessary, shorten longer sentences and combine shorter ones to make them longer.

2. **Check the sentence structures you have used in your sentences.** Identify them as simple, compound, complex, or compound-complex. Do you tend to write simple, compound, complex, or compound-complex sentences? Does one sentence structure dominate? If so, combine some sentences to make them into more complex forms, or separate more complicated sentences into simple or compound ones. Revise your sentences to vary your patterns.

3. **Vary your sentence beginnings and endings to create variety.** To create variety, think about starting your sentences with prepositional phrases or subordinate clauses. If you frequently start your sentences with these constructions, then reorder your sentences to start with the subject and verb.

Emphasis

Each sentences has two power points—its beginning and its end. The most powerful position of the two is the end. For this reason, the most important information in the sentence should appear at the beginning or the end. Non-essential information, including interrupters and parenthetical comments, belong in the sentence's mid-section. The examples below illustrate how you can revise to improve sentence emphasis:

> Original: When removing toast slices, <u>be very careful</u> as the toaster's metal parts and the bread become very hot.
> Revised: <u>Be very careful</u> when removing toast slices because the toaster's metal parts and the bread become very hot.
> Original: The fact that she acknowledged the mistake <u>impressed me</u>.
> Revised: I was impressed that she acknowledged the mistake.
> Revised: She impressed me when she acknowledged the mistake.

As these examples illustrate, communicators must decide what is the most important idea in the sentence and then craft the sentence emphatically. Deciding what to emphasize then informs the content placement in the sentence.

Thinking about economy, variety, and emphasis will improve your sentence construction. These strategies also assist readers by reducing word count, increasing flow and rhythm, and placing key ideas in strong locations.

EXERCISE 7.5

Improving Your Sentence Construction

Look through your files and find a short piece (seven to ten sentences) you have written for this class or another. Analyze your sentence style in this piece for economy, variety, and emphasis. Answer these questions in your analysis:

1. How many sentences are in your piece?
2. How many words are in each sentence?
3. What is the average length of your sentences?

After you have examined sentence length, locate sentences that you could revise for better economy, variety, and emphasis. Revise. Bring the original and the revised pieces to class and be prepared to discuss your findings.

Tasks to be completed:

1. Locate a short writing sample from this class or another class you have taken.
2. Analyze the writing to determine the following:
   - How many sentences are in your piece?
   - How many words are in each sentence?
   - What is the average length of your sentences?
3. Based on what you find, evaluate your writing and revise for improvement.
4. Be prepared to show your changes and explain why you revised as you did.

Writing Paragraphs

A sentence collects words to express a complete thought. Paragraphs work similarly to collect sentences into a larger, more complex unit of meaning. Paragraphs are effective when all of the ideas in them function to convey meaning, when the ideas are related, when they are organized logically, and when they are clearly connected. These qualities are defined in more detail below.

Functional Paragraphs

Paragraph length will vary greatly from writer to writer and from document to document, depending on the document's purpose. Like sentences, paragraphs conveying complex or unfamiliar information should be shorter than paragraphs that convey simpler information. Most importantly, whatever length of your paragraph you choose, all of the ideas in it must be relevant and build toward a unified point.

Unified Paragraphs

The point of a paragraph, as you likely know, is stated as a topic sentence; topic sentences typically are stated at the paragraph's beginning or end. All of the other sentences in the paragraph must, in some way, relate to the topic sentence and to each other. If a sentence does not relate to the topic sentence or other sentence in the paragraph, delete it.

Developed Paragraphs

Adequately developed paragraphs are logically organized. How you organize your paragraph's content depends on the paragraph's function: are you trying to explain, to summarize, or to categorize content in your paragraph? Each of these functions, as well as others, have a specific organizational method that you should follow. Below is a list of possible developmental organizations you might follow:

- Classify information
- Compare or contrast
- Define and give examples
- Describe a person, place, or thing
- Describe a process
- Describe cause and/or effect
- Present facts
- Present or refute an argument or part of an argument
- Qualify, elaborate, or restate the main idea
- Summarize or analyze
- Tell a story

Coherent Paragraphs

When ideas are connected, they are coherent. Coherent paragraphs are not only organized logically, but their sentences are also connected with obvious organizational patterns and transitional words. Communicators have many organizational patterns to choose from: sentences can move from general to specific or, conversely, from specific to general.

Ideas can be also be organized by chronological, spatial, or climatic order. When using chronological order, you may chunk items into lists which are usually numbered 1., 2., 3., etc. When items in a list are not in any specific order, use bullets instead of numbers. Other common organizations include alternating order, question and answer, and numerical order. The organizational pattern you choose will depend on the content you are communicating.

Chunking

For electronic or online publications, such as Web sites, content chunks may be used instead of or alongside paragraphs. A **content chunk** is discrete block of textual, visual, and spatial content on a specific topic. A content chunk can be written using any of the paragraph types described above. In structured authoring, technical communicators write text that is strictly controlled and written in small discrete content chunks, such as "title," "description," "example." In content management systems, such as wikis, blogs and some Web sites, these chunks are tagged with keywords and stored in databases for retrieval, based on search results. Structured authoring requires technical communicators to think about online or electronic version of texts differently, not as complete documents but as units of meaning that can be constructed, deconstructed, and reconstructed as needed for specific communication situations.

Transitional Words and Phrases

Another strategy for connecting sentences is related to organizational patterns: the use of transitional words and phrases. For example, if you are describing an object in space, you might use words or phrases, such as "to the right," "in the back," "next to the...." Chronological and numerical order organizations call for numeric transitions like "first," "second," "third," or even numbered lists. For alternating order, "on the other hand" and "in contrast" cue readers to a change from one subject to the next. Incorporating these words and phrases into your sentences as you build your paragraph assists readers as they move from one sentence to the next. These words and phrases create cognitive bridges that build coherence.

Transitional words and phrases are not the only kinds of words that build coherence. You can also create connections by repeating key words, repeating key ideas, and substituting a pronoun for a noun. A final strategy for building coherence is to use a given/new order to construct your sentence. Using the given/new order, you begin your sentences with a given idea, that is, an idea that you have already addressed, explained, or introduced in some way. After introducing the sentence with given idea, you end your sentence with new information, ideas that your readers do not know or are less familiar with. Like these other strategies for building coherence, the given/new order provides the reader with something familiar (a word, a phrase, an idea) before moving to something new and unfamiliar. The familiar information thus sets a hook for the new information to hang on.

All of the transitional strategies are useful for creating coherence within a paragraph, but they can also be used to make entire documents coherent. You may use all of them to connect sentences to sentences within paragraphs, paragraphs to paragraphs within sections, and sections to sections within entire documents.

EXERCISE 7.6

Transitional Words and Phrases

Choose two of the organizational patterns listed below, and make a list of transitional words and phrases that are commonly used to connect sentences in paragraphs using these organizational patterns.

- Classify information
- Compare or contrast
- Define and give examples
- Describe a person, place, or thing
- Describe a process
- Describe cause and/or effect
- Present facts
- Present or refute an argument or part of an argument
- Qualify, elaborate, or restate the main idea
- Summarize or analyze
- Tell a story

Tasks to be completed:

1. Choose two common organizational patterns from the list above.
2. Make a list of transitional words for each pattern.
3. Prepare to share your list with the class.

EXERCISE 7.7

Using Effective Paragraphing Strategies

Visit the Wikitravel description of Bologna, a city in Germany (http://wikitravel.org/en/Bologna). This travel guide introduces potential visitors to the city, its attractions, and its history.

Read the Bologna travel guide and find at least five strategies the writer uses to make paragraphs functional, unified, developed, and coherent.

After you have identified the writer's strategies within paragraphs, examine the guide as a whole. What strategies does the writer use to make the complete guide functional, unified, developed, and coherent? That is, how does the writer connect all the paragraphs into a unified whole?

Tasks to be completed:

1. Locate the Bologna description online.
2. Identify at least five strategies the writer uses to create functional, unified, developed, and coherent paragraphs
3. Identify strategies the writer uses to make the entire descriptions functional, unified, developed, and coherent.

Putting it all together

Paragraphs serve specific functions in professional and technical communication. Depending on its location in the document, a paragraph can serve to introduce the content of the document, develop and elaborate that content, or conclude the content. While it is true that genres have differing requirements, almost all professional and technical communication have paragraphs that serve these functions. This section briefly describes how you can draft these types of paragraphs.

Figure 7.7. Paragraphs, depending on their location, serve different functions.

Introducing a Text

As you learned in an earlier chapter, professional and technical communications address specific readers or audiences for specific purposes. The purpose of introductory paragraphs is to set the stage and inform your readers of the purpose of the document. With their opening sentences, introductory paragraphs explain what you are doing—for example, providing information on a recommended purchase, responding to a call for proposals, requesting a refund on a defective product. Telling the reader immediately what and why you are writing provides the reader with an immediate understanding of the intention of your document, no guessing required.

These opening remarks may be very detailed or quite short. Shorter introductions may be only a sentence or two setting the stage. Longer opening paragraphs may provide background, describe a problem, or, in the case of communication across some cultures, set the stage by polite inquiry about the reader's health or with a brief inquiry about seasonal celebrations.

However long your opening, most introductions end with a **forecasting or mapping statement** that overviews the rest of the document's content. Forecasting statements are typically a brief list of major sections that follow. These statements may be one sentence long in short documents or they may expand to one or more paragraphs in longer reports with many major sections. The forecasting statement is important for a number of reasons: it gives readers a preview of the sections to follow, it sets expectations for the content to follow, and it provides readers with a clear organization of the contents. Having this content at the beginning of the document assists readers to read selectively and to easily find the contents they want to read first. In a sense, the forecasting statement is a navigational tool provided early in the document that helps readers to find the information they need quickly and efficiently.

Developing the Middle of the Text

The middle sections of professional communication develop and elaborate your content. These paragraphs should be well developed using conventional organizational patterns, such as comparison and contrast or description of a process, and they should be carefully ordered to reflect this organization (for example, spatial or chronological order). In addition to these considerations, you can help readers understand how your content is developed and elaborated by providing advance organizers. Advance organizers provide readers with textual and visual cues to the content that follows. Below are four of the most common advance organizers that help readers to understand the content you are providing:

- **Headings**: Headings can be used at the beginning of sections and subsections. They may be complete sentences, phrases, clauses, or simply words that preview the content of the section or subsection.
- **Topic sentences**: Topic sentences are typically located at the beginning of a paragraph. They introduce the main idea of the paragraph. Using a topic sentence helps you to keep all the ideas in your paragraph unified, and it provides readers with an overview of paragraph content.
- **Bulleted and numbered lists**. Lists indicate that the items are related. Bulleted lists are not necessary chronological; use bulleted lists when items are related but not necessary in any specific order. Numbered lists suggest an order (a specific number of items or a specific order from first to last for those items). Both list types require a sentence before the list items that tells readers what kind of list follows.
- **Other visual cues**. In addition to headings and lists, you may use other visual cues to orient readers. These cues include page numbers, headers, and footers. Like other advance organizers, these document elements tell readers where they are in the document and remind them of content they are reading or viewing. Chunking content into short readable bites is also an effective visual cue to assist readers with skimming when combined with other advance organizers.

Concluding the Text

Like introductions, conclusions may be very short or very long, depending on your document; interestingly, some short documents such as brief instructions may have almost no conclusion, simply ending with the last step. When conclusions appear in documents, however, they tend to serve these purposes: they restate the purpose of the document and request action from the reader; they draw conclusions about the research being reported (such as implications or findings); and they suggest next steps that the reader should take. Some concluding paragraphs provide a combination of these purposes.

These brief descriptions of the paragraphs that appear at the beginning, middle, and end of professional documents overview their purposes. Later chapters discuss methods of developing conclusion for different types of technical documents.

> **EXERCISE 7.8**
>
> ## *Identifying Paragraph Functions in a Section*
>
> The section of paragraphing introduced you to three specific types of paragraphs that typically appear at the beginning, middle, and end of professional documents. The paragraphs in this section were written to illustrate how these paragraph types work. Analyze the paragraphs in this section, and prepare to discuss how each paragraph in this section works. Specifically, be able to answer these questions:
>
> - How does each paragraph in this section function?
> - How is each paragraph organized and ordered?
> - What are the topic sentences in each paragraph?
> - What advance organizers cue readers to paragraph and section content?
>
> **Tasks to be completed:**
>
> 1. Reread this section.
> 2. As you read, identify how paragraphs function in it.
> 3. Describe how each paragraph is organized, and locate each paragraph's topic sentence.
> 4. Identify the advance organizers used to cue paragraph and section content.

REVIEWING AND EDITING YOUR OWN AND OTHERS' CONTENT

Reviewing your own work is often harder than reviewing the work of others, but, in both cases, good technical communicators are systematic when they review documents. Eventually you will develop your own system for reviewing documents, but, until then, this final section of the chapter will offer you a series of questions to guide your review. These questions, you may notice, summarize guidance provided in other parts of this textbook.

Editing includes two important tasks: assessment and revision. The **assessment** task involves using a set of clearly defined criteria to evaluate a document, which vary depending on the type of editing you need to use. For example, you may want to have your work assessed based on its content accuracy, completeness, appropriateness for the intended audience and purpose, or simply its grammatical and mechanical correctness. You may even want to develop a checklist or a list of questions in assessing a document to more clearly document your comments. You may even enlist different individuals to review your work, that is, a subject matter expert to check for content accuracy and completeness or a professional editor to evaluate writing style and grammar. The second task involves **revision**, including making use of the assessment your document receives from its review. This task also involves reading the review comments, making a list of revision tasks, and prioritizing those tasks in revising your document.

The next few sections describe the five rounds of editing, which can be seen as different kinds of assessments you can perform to assist with editing and revising documents. A good review of technical and professional content requires you to complete a number of review rounds. As you become more proficient in your review, you may be able to conduct some of these rounds simultaneously; but, as you learn to review, try to focus on specific concerns in each round. As you complete each round, take notes. At the end of the process, you should write up a report or meet with the author to make suggestions for improvement, or, if you are the author, developing effective strategies and tasks for revising.

Round One: General Background of the Document

To complete the first round, you will need to gather background information before you even begin to review the document. When you review your own work, this background can easily be gathered by returning to planning documents, including user profiles, use scenarios, and tasks analysis. If you are reviewing for others, ask to see their planning documents. If they do not use planning documents, then interview them briefly to generate quick guides to inform you of who will read the document, why they will read it, and for what purpose. Reviewing these plans will help you to evaluate whether the document meets those goals and, if not, how the document might be revised to meet them.

Questions to answer during this round include the following:

- ☐ Who is the document's audience? (How do you know?)
- ☐ What is the purpose of the document, or what is its intent?
- ☐ What is the reader or audience supposed to do with the information?
- ☐ What kind of document are you reviewing? What is its genre?
- ☐ What genre conventions will the reader expect the writer to include in the document?
- ☐ Was the document's author required to work under any specific constraints? What were they, and how did they affect document production?

Round Two: Genre Conventions and Content Organization

Readers will expect professional communications to meet their generic expectations. They will expect memos to look like memos and to be organized like memos they frequently reader. The same is true for other genres, such as reports, proposals, and progress reports. In the first round, you determined the genre called for in this communication situation. In this round, you briefly review the document to see if it complies with generic conventions. Later chapters will provide you with the various conventions associated with different genres. Compare the document you are reading to these conventions, and ask the following questions:

- ☐ Does the document conform to generic expectations?
  - ☐ If yes, how does it conform?
  - ☐ If no, how does it not conform?
    - ☐ Does the document need revisions better to conform?
      - ☐ If yes, what revisions do you suggest?
      - ☐ If no, why not?

- ☐ Does the document include expected content in its beginning section?
  - ☐ Does the beginning indicate what kind of document is being presented?
  - ☐ Does the beginning include a forecasting statement?
- ☐ Does the document include expected content in its middle section, and is this content well organized?
  - ☐ Does each section begin with an opening paragraph that forecasts section content?
  - ☐ Does each paragraph within a section flow logically from the forecasting statement?
  - ☐ Does each paragraph have a topic sentence?
  - ☐ Are sentences with paragraphs clearly organized and ordered?
  - ☐ Are paragraphs and sentences connected with effective transitional words, phrases, or clauses?
- ☐ Does the document include a clear conclusion?
  - ☐ Does the conclusion summarize the content or draw conclusions?
  - ☐ Does the conclusion include a call for action?
- ☐ If any of these answers to these questions are no, what recommendations do you have improvements or revisions?

Round Three: Design

If the document is unstructured and requires formatting, this round requires you to consider how the document looks and whether this design supports the reader's use and navigation of the document. To review the design, ask these questions:

- ☐ Does the document include advance organizers, such as page numbers, headers or footers, and headings?
- ☐ Does the document include visuals to support and elaborate on its written contents?
  - ☐ Are visuals properly labeled as tables or figures?
  - ☐ Are visuals captioned and titled?
  - ☐ Does the author clearly reference and explain these visuals in the text?

Round Four: Style

This round requires you to read for style, specifically checking for possible improvements in diction, syntax, and punctuation. If you are reviewing some else's document, you may want to familiarize yourself with common editing symbols. You can find many examples of these marks online, such as Merriam Webster Online (http://www.merriam-webster.com/mw/table/proofrea.htm). To review for style, ask these questions as you review the document:

> ☐ Has the author chosen words effectively? If not, where do you suggest changes? Why?
> ☐ Has the author crafted sentences effectively? If not, where do you suggest changes? Why?
> ☐ Has the author punctuated sentence effectively? If not, where do you suggest changes? Why?
> ☐ Does the text have other mechanical errors, such as misspellings? If not, where do you suggest changes? Why?

Round Five: Overall Effectiveness of the Document

In the fifth and final round, consider any notes you have written or marked in the previous four rounds and comment on the overall effectiveness of the document. Asking these questions can help you to think about the document as a whole:

> ☐ Is the document readable?
>   ☐ Do you understand what it is asking the audience/reader to do?
>   ☐ Are its parts coherent and unified?
>   ☐ Does everything in it make sense?
> ☐ Is the document usable?
>   ☐ Can you find the information you need quickly and easily?
>   ☐ Is it easy to navigate through the document?
> ☐ Is it persuasive?
>   ☐ Does it meet its objectives?
>   ☐ Do you know what you are expected to do after reading it?
> ☐ What has the author done particularly well in this document?
> ☐ What are the overall and most important revisions necessary to improve the document?

Completing the Review Assessment and Planning Revision Strategies

To conclude your review, you may either meet with the author to discuss improvements or send the author a marked copy with comments or an emailed report. Offer your critique positively, focusing first on what worked well in the draft and following with suggestions for improvement. Base your observations and recommendations on actual instances in the text, and be ready to explain where you encountered difficulties and think improvements are necessary. The more specific your critique, the more likely the author will know how to make changes. Finally, approach the review of others' work with generosity. Remember that writing is hard work, so hearing criticism of that work can be difficult. Acknowledge this challenge as you make suggestions for improvement.

Once the review has been completed, revision of the document is the next task. Depending on the kinds of reviews, as well as quality and quantity of review comments, the time and amount of work necessary to successfully revise your document may vary. Some suggestions for planning your revision strategy include the following:

- Read the review comments carefully.
- Take notes as you read.
- Prioritize comments, in terms of their importance.
- Make a list of specific tasks to complete.
- Note the kind of revision needed for each task, (i.e., content, design, style, grammar).
- Try not to take a defensive posture.

Taking time to plan you revision will help ensure a higher level of quality in your final product. It is important to identify and prioritize tasks, so you know which ones are absolutely necessary to complete, and which ones are simple suggestions to consider. And finally, remember to keep in mind the overall purpose of a review is to help you with revision, so that you can improve the quality of your document.

Chapter Summary

This chapter has focused on writing content in both structured and unstructured authoring environments. It has offered you a number of writing style guidelines for choosing words, crafting sentences, punctuating sentences, and creating paragraphs. It also addressed techniques for reviewing and editing your own and others' work, including five levels of editing technical documents. It also discusses how to complete an editorial review and strategies for approaching revision of your document. The guidelines in this chapter are essential to writing and developing content, whether your writing is structured or unstructured, or published in print or electronic venues.

Chapter Assignments

The exercises in this section ask you to apply what you have learned in this chapter as well as explore how this knowledge applies to and connects with other information in the textbook.

1. Develop a one-page review checklist, using the five rounds of review you read about in this chapter. Include important questions, criteria, and a description of how you will assess each round. If you use specific criteria to develop the checklist, write a clear definition of each criterion so readers will understand the scope of each one. If you use questions, make sure your questions are specific and provide space for plenty of written comments. Also, you may want to include a rating scale (1 to 10, letter grade, etc.) for each category, criterion, or question.
2. Find a brief one- to two-page document you've created for another class and review it. Identify its strengths and weaknesses. Then revise the document for improved writing style. Bring the revised document to class and be prepared to discuss the changes you have made.
3. The Internet has dozens of résumé builders. Search and find a free résumé builder online, enter your résumé's content into the building, and compare your unstructured résumé to the one the builder generates. How are they similar? How are they different? What are the advantages and disadvantages of each?

4. Read the document adapted from a university newsletter, and critique the writing using the review guidelines at the end of this chapter.

> ASK A SPECIALIST: HOW CAN I KEEP MY BIRD FEEDER SAFE?
>
> *Terry Messmer, Utah State University Extension wildlife specialist*
>
> *Adapted from* Utah State Today *(http://utahstatetoday.usu.edu/archives/february2003/02-07-03/newsreleases-02-07-03.cfm#3) February 7, 2003 News Releases (Released 2/6/03)*
>
> Feeding birds in the winter is both a humanitarian act and a way to bring birdwatching to your own backyard during the cold winter months. Poorly maintained bird feeding stations, however, may do more harm than good to the birds you are trying to help. It is important to be aware of the diseases that can be spread through bird feeders.
>
> According to the National Wildlife Health Center, five diseases can affect birds visiting feeders. They are salmonellosis, aspergillosis, avian pox, trichomonias, and mycopalmosis. All of these diseases can lead to death, either directly or indirectly, by making the bird more vulnerable to predators. Sick birds can easily be spotted. They appear less alert and less active. Their feathers look unkempt, and they are often reluctant to fly away.
>
> Consider these tips to lessen the chance of spreading diseases from your bird feeder.
> - **Give them space.** Avoid crowding at bird feeders by providing ample feeders.
> - **Clean up waste.** Keep the feeder area clear of droppings and waste food. A broom and shovel will work, but a wet and dry vacuum is great.
> - **Make feeders physically safe.** Use feeders with rounded corners. Feeders with sharp edges can cut a bird, leaving an opening where bacteria can enter and infect an otherwise healthy bird.
> - **Keep feeders clean.** Clean and disinfect feeders regularly. Use one part liquid chlorine bleach in nine parts of warm water. Make enough solution to immerse empty feeders completely for 2-3 minutes. Allow the feeder to air dry. This should be done at least once a month.
> - **Use clean food.** Discard food that is wet, smells musty, looks old or has fungus growing on it. Clean and disinfect storage containers or scoops used on unclean food.
> - **Prevent contamination.** Keep rodents and pets out of stored food. Rodents can carry and spread some bird diseases without being affected themselves.
> - **Spread the word.** Tell your bird feeding neighbors and friends about the risks. Since birds may use several feeders in a neighborhood, your feeder is only as safe as your neighbor's.
>
> Follow these precautions and both you and the birds will enjoy a wintertime of bird feeding. For more information, contact your local USU County Extension office or the National Wildlife Health Center, USGS, Biological Resources Division, 6006 Schroeder Road, Madison, WI 53711-6223.

Figure Credits

Figure 7.1. © Pixsooz/Shutterstock.com

Figure 7.2. © Monkey Business Images/Shutterstock.com

Figure 7.3. © Rawpixel.com/Shutterstock.com

Figure 7.5. http://my.monster.com/ImproveAccount/UpdateProfileEjc?landedFrom=BamWizard&fwr=true

Figure 7.6. © Ermolaev Alexander/Shutterstock.com

Figure 7.7. © Modella/Shutterstock.com

Developing Information and Instructional Content

8

CHAPTER OVERVIEW

This chapter introduces you to concepts, practices, and strategies for managing and structuring information applicable to various genres and technical documents. After reading this chapter, you should be able to meet the following objectives:

- Describe concepts, strategies, and practices related to managing content and information, including information modeling, single-sourcing methodologies, and developing meaningful metadata.
- Describe processes and practices for designing for instructional information products.
- Discuss learning styles, modalities, and theories and explain how they inform instructional design practices.
- Understand guidelines for sequencing, organizing, and developing navigation for instructional products.
- Develop basic information models for technical documents, including using benchmarking research to inform their development and create scalable information structures.
- Describe single-sourcing methods and their relationship to content management.
- Understand the importance of metadata, including tagging content, and their importance in establishing meaningful relationships, which can contribute to higher levels of findability and usability.

The work technical communicators do has shifted from writing and editing to a broader range of skills and talents, including the ability to manage content and information. Content management is usually a team effort, with varied practices that draw upon a wide range of skills. These skills support tasks as varied as information storing, organizing, retrieving, and sequencing. It also includes relating and reusing content in a variety of publication forms and media types. As a result of technical communicators' increasing and broadening responsibilities, it is important to understand fully the concepts and related practices in managing content and information.

A wide range of factors, particularly changes in technology and publication media, has expanded the scope of technical communicators' responsibilities and the methods used to manage content. First, online publications have become a dominant form of delivering information to customers and clients. Producing these online publications requires a more sophisticated set of technical skills and resources. Second, these publications include mixed media forms, such as video, audio, and interactive content. Third, the increasing demand for user-driven content has placed additional demands on how we organize, re-purpose, and restructure content in Web sites and other online publications and media. Fourth, the trend in reusable, or single-sourced content requires more sophisticated methods, including the development of navigation and search tools as well as delivery systems. Fifth, the evolution of desktop publishing software tools and content management systems have enabled more rapid solutions to building Web sites and databases that allow individuals and companies to drag-and-drop content into an existing system. These solutions provide easy-to-use templates and tools for structuring, searching, and navigating content more readily.

Regardless of whether the output media—print, electronic, or hybrid—technical communicators are more frequently using electronic tools to accomplish tasks. Finally, structured and collaborative authoring has added to complications when managing content. For structured authoring, markup and scripting languages must be learned or used to deliver online content; afford collaborative authoring in wikis, blogs, and other social media forms; and manage permissions, access, editing, and so forth.

One specific type of content that technical communicators frequently produce and manage is a wide range of instructional products including training courses, educational materials, presentations, instructions, procedures, and various forms of help documentation. You are probably familiar with these products if you use videos to learn how to complete a task or to view a walkthrough demonstration for a game challenge. Applications like YouTube and Web sites like EHow are populated with thousands of user-generated training materials. Similarly, subscription sites like Lynda.com are increasingly popular with students and professionals seeking to learn how to use new technologies for school and work. Instructional content can be published in a wide range of formats and media types and often is developed for very specific audiences and purposes. As a result, researching and understanding the user (or learner) is just as important as managing the content when creating instructional materials. The relationship between instructional design and user experience is very important to consider as it relates to user-centered design practices.

This chapter will introduce you to the concepts, practices, and strategies related to content management, including information modeling, findability, single-sourcing, and developing metadata. It will also address the instructional development process, including methods and practices in creating instructional documents.

CONTENT MANAGEMENT CONCEPTS AND PRACTICES

Content management and process maturity are closely related, in that systematic, planned content management practices typically lead to higher levels of process maturity. Successful **content management** involves developing standardized processes, procedures, and methods of tracking and reporting. Good content management practices include documenting the specific processes, strategies, and related practices in managing information through its creation, design, development, production, delivery, and archiving (Clark, 2008). (You may have heard of a related concept, **content management system,** which refers to a software system, or platform, that uses markup, metadata, templates, and database tools to manage information in a Web-based product, such as a wiki, blog, or Web site.)

Sustained content management processes, a tenet of middle and higher levels of process maturity, are vetted, tested, and reused. As such, content management involves more mature information planning, often relying on previous practices, document templates, spreadsheets, working processes, lessons learned, and other resources. It takes time to develop sustainable practices and information resources, so often content management improves as your experience working on projects or in teams increases.

Figure 8.1. Content management improves as your experience working on projects and on teams increases.

Another key process mature content management practice involves documenting two forms of knowledge: tacit and explicit. **Tacit knowledge** includes the unwritten or undocumented processes, practices, and general knowledge a work group or organization possesses. Examples may include known practices for formatting reports, knowledge about the order of writing sections of a report, performance tips, and other unwritten lore within an organization. **Explicit knowledge** is the documented (written) processes, practices, and other information within an organization. Explicit knowledge is located in workplace documentation, such as policy manuals, written procedures, technical descriptions, style guides, and document templates.

Other integral, process mature practices occur during early development: information modeling, single-sourcing, and developing metadata. **Information modeling** includes the tasks of developing structure, organization, templates, and patterns for technical documents. It involves considering **scalability**, developing information models and structures so they can be adapted, appended to, grow, develop, and managed. It may also involves **benchmarking**, researching what other information models of similar document types suggest about what typical audiences expect in terms of organization, style, and terminology.

Single-sourcing involves considering the reuse or repurposing of content, whether the method is copy and paste or dynamically driven. Like information modeling, it suggests a modular aspect of developing content, where individual paragraphs, images, chunks, sections, or other divisions can be repurposed or reused. Single-sourcing may include the reuse of previous versions of documents, which provide valuable background information in writing new technical documents.

Finally, **metadata** help explain relational aspects of content items within a given information model. Effective metadata also help in grouping and analyzing patterns within content. Using informative headers, navigation aids, tagging, and file naming are all examples of how documents incorporate metadata. The primary goal of metadata is to improve the findability and usability of content for both developers and users. One way this goal can be achieved is by developing written principles and practices in organizing content and labeling that will aid information use and location in searches.

Collectively, these aspects of developing and managing content are important information planning tools. First, they help establish structural patterns to ensure consistency, optimal organization, usability, accessibility, findability, and use. Second, they create and communicate meaningful relationship between sections or chunks of content in a technical document or information product, whether textual, visual, spatial, or hybrid. Third, they help reinforce conventions, whether they are organizational, discipline, or genre based. And finally, as information planning tools, these approaches can help identify potential problems with usability, structure, prior to the publication and delivery of a technical document or product. Each of these concepts will be now be discussed specifically in terms of their importance, methods, and practice.

INFORMATION MODELING AND STRUCTURE

Every technical document or information product requires the development of an organizational pattern or structure, often one that follows conventions appropriate for the genre, document type, discipline, and other project-specific factors. **Information modeling** is an important content management task that involves developing an organizational pattern and associated navigation aids for technical documents and information products. It is the process of developing "logical structures that help us find answers and complete tasks" within an information product (Rosenfeld & Morville, 2007). Ideally, a user-centered approach to developing information models also integrates users in the testing, development, and organization of content in a variety of ways. Related terms you may have encountered in previous studies or readings include information architecture, information structuring, and topic architectures.

Information models outline the standardized patterns, internal structure, information types, metadata, and overall strategy for developing content for individualized products (Rosenfeld & Morville call these high-level architecture blueprints, 2007). Simple information models include tables of contents, indices, outlines, site maps or any other organizational pattern which helps writers and users understand the structure of technical documents. More complex information models may be topic-based architectures that serve as content maps, identifying individualized topics, their information types, metadata, annotations, and relationships to other topics in a coherent structure.

Many large-scale Web sites have site maps, an information model type, which also serves a dual function—as structural model and interactive navigational guides. Breadcrumb links as well as design elements such as the use of repeated colors, graphics, and styles also support these two functions on Web sites. In printed reports, other elements communicate structure and help users navigate contents, such as tables of contents, headers, page numbers, footers, and lists.

In a previous chapter, you learned how structured authoring works; you can think of it as writing content for use (and reuse) in a database form or into a template. Content is broken into chunks that the technical communicator or content developer can assemble into pages or templates. When you break a communication into smaller components or elements, you are creating an information model. To illustrate how information modeling works, imagine that you are creating a directory of employees at your organization. Your job is to collect all employee names by division, their office locations, phone numbers, emails, and IM name. You will publish all of this information on your company intranet, but you also would like to list employees and their phone numbers on a contact page on your public Web site. All of this information will be updated annually but, if need be, more often. Figure 8.2 below illustrates how you might model the information for the directory.

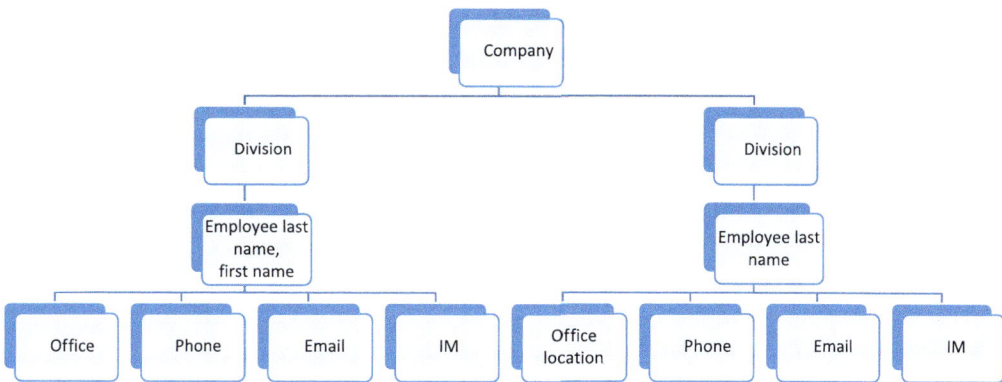

Figure 8.2. Information in a company directory is fairly simple to model. In this example, the company is divided into divisions. Within each division, its employees are listed.

Information modeling is a good content planning tool for any document, especially for longer or more complex information products. For shorter, less complex ones, a simple list or outline may suffice. For example, modeling the information is fairly simple with an example like a company directory. You may start anywhere in the model (such as employee names) and work up (from division to company name) or work down (specific office, phone, email, and IM content). Wherever you start, your end result will be a concept map or model of how the information will need to be gathered and tagged for easy retrieval into a variety of documents.

After you have visualized the information into a map or model, then you are ready to gather information from employees and tag it. The content of each element of the document can be entered by anyone, and the output is checked for consistency before it is formatted and displayed. For the intranet directory, all of the information could be included in an entry, but, on the contact page, only the employee's first name last name and phone number could be displayed on the page. The script used to create the web page controls how the information looks in each document. Because it can be used in multiple locations and for multiple purposes, structured writing is often called **single-sourcing**. When technical communicators use structuring writing to single-source, they write once but publish that content in many places.

Information models are typically stylistically and organizationally repetitive, organizing content in ways that are logical and appropriate to specific document types. Document genres, or specifically their templates, are also good examples of generic organizational patterns or information models for specific types of technical documents and reports. For example, an analytical report, which examines alternatives for a given problem or need, typically includes the following major sections: introduction, methodology, results, discussion, and conclusion. If you were to research different analytical reports on varied subjects, you might discover subtle variations in the organizational patterns, level of detail, and stylistics of each report. These variations account for the different ways the information modeling—that is, the organization of information—can vary depending on the topic, audience, company, purpose, or other factors.

Information models are essential to content management for a variety of reasons. They are a common content management and information development tool used widely in electronic documents, or those meant for online distribution. Information models provide structural consistency across various information type and products and are a way of documenting and enforcing organizational standards for technical documents and information products. They also serve as a roadmap or content plan for teams, so each individual follows a consistent set of organizational guidelines. Ideally, they integrate user preferences and expectations, as well as their need to know to maximize usability of technical documents. They should also consider the relational aspects of content and sections within a given technical document and use terminology familiar to users, to maximize their usefulness.

Developing Information Models

Developing information models is an important aspect of the planning process, assisting you as you define user needs, information types, consistent standards, relatedness of content units, and an overall guiding structure (and labeling scheme) for information products, such as Web sites (Hackos, 2007). Communicating the structure visually to users, although the content itself may not be highly visual, is a challenge, and it can be important to provide multiple views or diagrams that enable clients and users to access the information they need to complete work or make decisions (Rosenfeld & Morville, 2007). The process for developing an information model includes the following four tasks (see Figure 8.3):

1. **Research** information modeling conventions for the specific genre, such as looking at previous versions of the same document, existing references, organizational style guides, textbooks, or similar products. Also, research information related to the user's needs for information and expectations, including any feedback or metrics.
2. **Identify content** that will be used in the new document, such as topics, major sections, paragraphs, information graphics, and references.
3. **Create an information model or map** of the major sections or topics of the information product.
4. **Develop a prototype and test** the information model with sample users.

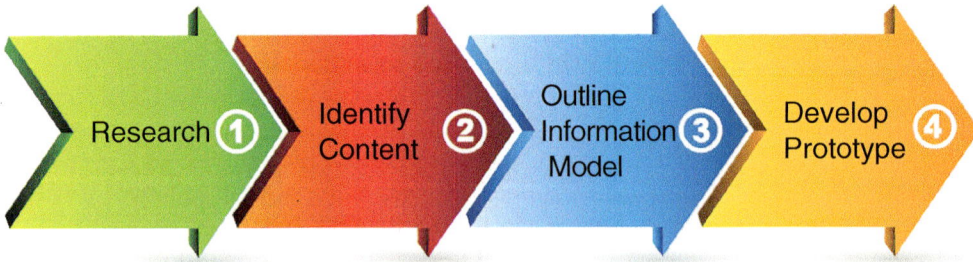

Figure 8.3. The process for developing an information model includes four tasks.

In the previous directory example, the first phase, researching, occurs when you consider what information needs to go into the model. You might ask others or look at older directories to see what information is included. You might even consider how printed phone books serve as directories or how other organizations use employee directories on their Web sites. The second phase, identifying content, occurs when you formalize or decide exactly what content you will gather. The third phase, modeling, occurs when you create a visual depiction (whether it is a drawing, an outline, or list). The final phase, prototyping and testing, occurs when you test your content to see if other members of your organization can find the information (phone number, office, etc.) of individuals listed in the directory. The rest of this section discusses two other practices you should consider as you develop your information model: **benchmarking** and **scaling**.

Benchmarking

Benchmarking is researching or learning about your competition, or, in some cases, previous versions of a particular technical document or product. It is also the focus of the first two tasks of the information modeling process. It will allow you to take advantage of best practices and conventions from similar products as well as gain insights about user expectations. For these reasons, benchmarking is particularly important in the research phase of information modeling. Benchmarking allows you to evaluate similar products to determine best practices and possible errors to avoid. It also allows you to examine patterns in organization, style, design, and content to replicate in future versions. It builds on user expectations from previously published genres and document types, and it helps you avoid replicating bad practices, errors, or less usable practices.

EXERCISE 8.1

Benchmarking Information Modeling Techniques

You have been assigned the task of creating a site map for a new online bookseller. To prepare yourself for the task, the first step is to research existing site maps on a handful of similar Web sites to learn more about the conventions and trends that are currently used by other book sellers. Locate three separate book selling Web sites online and examine their site maps. Make notes of their organizational patterns, design elements, and features that seem to be best practices. Compose a list of your findings, including a list of trends and differences among the three sites you examine.

Tasks to be completed:

1. Locate three booksellers online with site maps and examine each closely.
2. Make a list of consistent patterns of organizing content, design elements, and other features.
3. Prepare a spreadsheet or table with your findings.
4. Make a list of key similarities and differences among the samples.
5. Write a list of recommendations for creating a new site map, incorporating the best features you find in your research.

Scaling

Scaling is another key aspect of content management. Scalability, or designing information structures and content so the product can accommodate changes, involves the practice of considering and planning how new and updated content can be added to your model after initial publication. In terms of information modeling, you must consider how the organization and information model you are using can best accommodate additional content or reordering. You might consider the necessity of including blank pages or templates, which can be added when new content becomes available. You should also determine where new content will likely be added as part of your planning and assessment tasks. In terms of single-sourcing, it involves considering how content, including document templates, can be developed and reused as an information product, such as a Web site, evolves. Scaling will require you complete some or all of these tasks:

- Developing templates or forms that can be reused, filled in, like worksheets, and added easily to an existing information structure.
- Developing writing style or content guides for adding content within an existing information product, so it conforms to appropriate guidelines.
- Planning future drafts of information models and what they might look like as new content is added to the product.
- Developing strategies and best practices for scalability that can be reused for other information products.

CONTENT REUSE AND SINGLE SOURCING

Within an information product, or perhaps from one document to others, it may be necessary to reuse or repurpose content for a variety of purposes and information needs. For example, a technical product description may be reused in marketing literature, brochures, presentations, technical reports, or other documents. After developing a basic information model, your next content management step is to determine what new content will need to be written and what existing content can be reused and edited to be included in the new document. The latter is the task involved in determining how to single-source content. **Single-sourcing**, or **content reuse**, is an important part of content management since a majority of online publications involves delivering similar content in a variety of media forms and contexts and for various purposes and audiences. The notion of "write once, reuse many times," has become a tenet of online publication and writing. However, a single reuse strategy may not be appropriate for every purpose or audience. Some information repetition is necessary for consistency, while in other contexts, it may require minor revision in terms of detail, style, organization, etc., for different audiences, purposes, and contexts.

Figure 8.4. Technical communication content can be reused and repurposed in a variety of documents.

For example, a company may reuse, word for word, a product description in a wide range of advertising and sales materials; however, the description may need to be altered or adapted for international audiences. A legal disclaimer may be appropriate for reuse on a Web site or terms of service agreement, but it would not necessarily be reused on brochures or flyers. Content reuse potentially saves time and resources by avoiding repeating writing tasks. However, improper reuse strategies can create potential problems if content reuse does not involve appropriate revision or repurposing for each new context in which it is used.

Content Reuse

Content reuse can be accomplished in a variety of different levels of revision, based on information needs, audience, purpose, functionality, and other concerns. Ann Rockley (2001) defines single-sourcing methods in terms of four distinct levels or reuse, including the following:

- Level 1: Identical content, multiple media;
- Level 2: Static customized content;
- Level 3: Dynamic customized content; and
- Level 4: Electronic Performance Support Systems (EPSS).

Due to changes in content management systems and processes, there are significant overlaps and similarities between these phases. As a result, current strategies reflect content reuse for (1) identical content and multiple media, (2) static content for multiple media and users, and (3) customized and personalized content, each of which are discussed below.

Identical Content, Multiple Media

This level is the most basic method of single sourcing content, including mostly copying or cutting and pasting content with minimal or no editing. As a result, it is appropriate to use as a method when an exact or precise description and/or information sequence is required. In this category are written processes, which must be followed in terms of specific details and in a specific order. It might also include the use of technical definitions or standards, which must also be exact. Other examples are reusable descriptions of products or services, and data displays, such as charts, photos, and graphs, which require little to no modification for them to be appropriate for all users and potential uses.

- General cut and paste approach.
- Minimal editing.
- Appropriate for content that requires little modification, or that should be reused in its exact form, or closely resembling it.
- Examples include legal disclaimers, policy or product specifications, and definitions.

Static Content with Multiple Media and Users

This level of single sourcing content includes most non-interactive forms of content that may have a wider range of purposes or contexts in which it is reused. It includes reuse of content that may require minor to moderate levels of editing to be appropriate for reuse in a new document or context. While the content may need to be edited to some extent, it may require little customization or modification after its reuse. Examples include technical descriptions, results reports, memoranda, or instructional documents that may be rewritten for a different user, purpose, or context. Project documentation can also contain information that can be reused with slight modification. For example, some content, such a problem statement developed for a proposal, may be reused with only slight modification in the proposal, progress or status reports, electronic slide shows, product video demonstrations, and final research or completion reports.

- Non-interactive forms of content, which might include a broader range of purposes, users, and media types.
- May require minor to moderate levels of editing.
- Appropriate for content that may be edited and reused, with little customization.
- Examples include edited technical descriptions or instructional documents for different uses or users.

Customized and Personalized Content

This level characterizes typical functionality of content management systems on the market today, such as blogs, wikis, and other customizable Web-enabled platforms. While some customization is handled by the individual writers in creating content, the system handles the bulk of the work in terms of delivering it based on user input and interaction. For example, when users of an information Web site perform key word searches, the system generates a list of possible related topics based on those specific parameters, customizing the results for each user search. In more advanced content management systems, there may be functions that suggest content to users based on search histories, purchases, or other actions. Such systems are commonly used in applications and Web sites, such as Amazon, the Apple Store, and Netflix. The challenging tasks for writers of this content are that they must populate the database with topics and appropriate metadata tags, or keywords, so the system knows which content topics to display based on user search parameters. In order to determine how to rewrite the content, it may be necessary to conduct user research or develop user profiles to inform decisions and tasks.

- Interactive systems where users make selections or searches.
- May require precise writing and editing to ensure maximum reusability across a wide range of users and uses.
- Appropriate for all types of content, particularly material that can be used in a wide variety of contexts and uses.
- Examples include content topics in wikis, blogs, and Web sites, as well as user-driven keyword search results.

Guidelines for Single Sourcing Content

When determining both content and level of single-sourcing, you should consider several important guidelines for effective content reuse. First, select the appropriate level of content reuse depending on user needs, purpose, context, and other organizational factors. A cut-and-paste approach may not always be the best solution, particularly when writing documents for different, and potentially competing audiences because these audiences may have different needs and expectations. Second, consider a user's need to know when reusing or repurposing information. In other words, reuse only what is necessary and adapt it according to the user's information needs. Third, reuse and repurpose only what information is necessary to accomplish the intended use of the document or information product. Eliminate redundancies, unless they are absolutely necessary. And finally, edit and rewrite reusable content so it is appropriate for the new audience, purpose, and context, to avoid errors or potential miscommunication.

The process for single sourcing content includes four important tasks:

1. Make a list of content topics, sections, pages, and other items that will be single-sourced, including their format, location, and relevance.
2. For each item, identify the appropriate method, or level, of single-sourcing.
3. Determine the location in the information model where the content will be used.
4. Identify and complete the necessary writing, editing, and design tasks are needed to reuse the content.

Figures 8.5 and 8.6 map two sample information models. Figure 8.5 is a trip proposal that was written to request permission to travel. Figure 8.6 is the trip report that was written after the travel. Note the similar information in both maps—for example, the need for proposed trip, benefits, requested budget information. Some, but not all, of the information in the trip proposal is reused in the trip report. Additionally, some of the reused content can be copied and pasted directly from one document to the next while other reused content must be edited slightly before reuse. For example, the proposal will be written in present or future tense ("I request permission to travel…"), but the trip report, which is written after the trip, is written in past tense ("I requested permission to travel…")

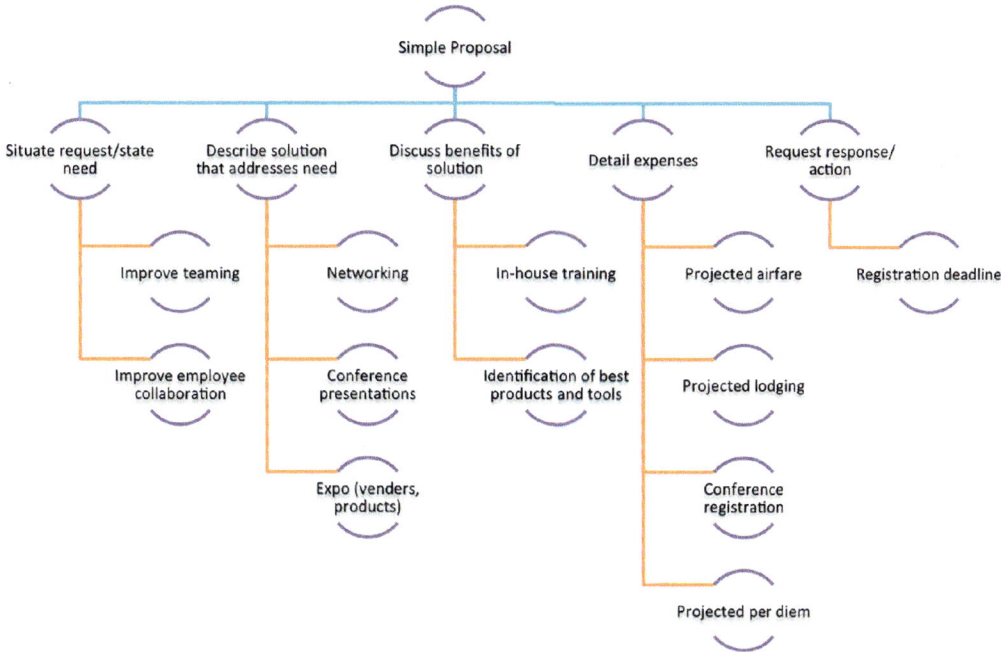

Figure 8.5. This information model identifies the content of a trip proposal, written to request permission and funding to travel.

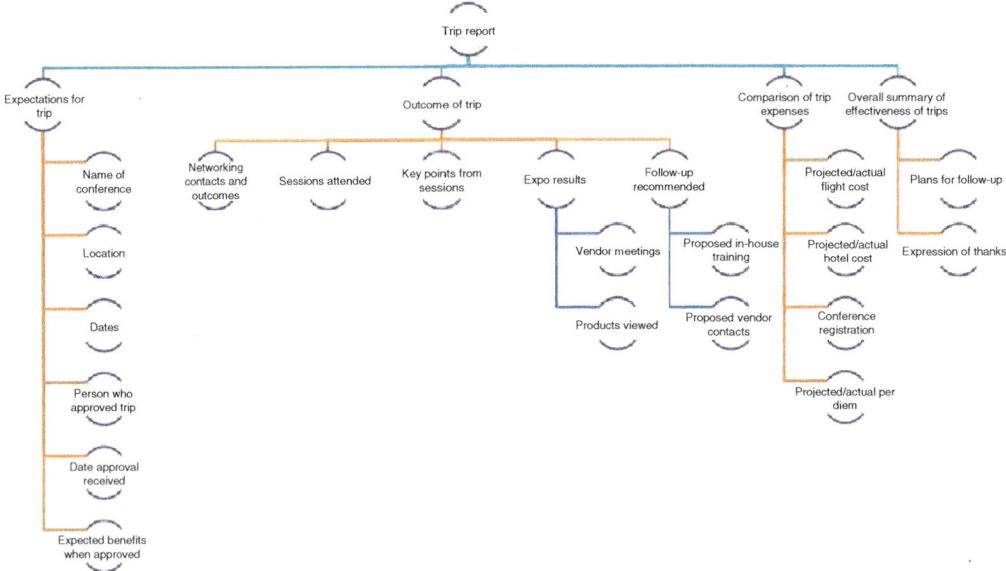

Figure 8.6. This information model outlines a trip report, written after the requested trip has been taken. Note how some information from the trip proposal is reused in the trip report.

DEVELOPING MEANINGFUL METADATA FOR YOUR DOCUMENTS

Metadata, put simply, is information about data, or descriptive details about information resources, such as reports, topics, and other forms of content. In some cases, metadata might be **keywords**, or anticipated search terms, that you include with a topic or article you have written. Another example might be the use of naming conventions for documents, which was discussed in another chapter. Part of the task of creating metadata is identifying tacit knowledge associated with the content, finding a method of organizing that tacit knowledge, and translating that knowledge into keywords that others will associate with the content. Metadata might not be used for all products or in the same ways, but when working with large volumes of content, such as databases, content management systems, document repositories, and the like, it can be a powerful and useful tool for developers and users alike.

Developing metadata for an information product, particularly in online publications, is important for a variety of reasons. First, it provides valuable descriptive details about content within an information product. These details might take the form of naming conventions for files, descriptive keywords for topics, or other details about the author, date, document type, all of which might be useful information. Secondly, it aids in the findability of information within a given product, making it easier to quickly locate information about documents. **Findability** is the degree to which information is easy to locate using common searching and browsing tools and methods (Morville, 2005). For example, a descriptive file name may make it easier for a user to locate a particular file in a folder that contains dozens of document. Adding tags or keywords to documents might also make it easier to use search tools to locate content related to a specific term or phrase and to increase the chance of finding that information more quickly and accurately. Third, metadata can aid in the writing and development process, by helping to organize, structure, and identify content using consistent standards, enabling it to be found and uses more efficiently. As such, it can also aids developers in their classification and organization tasks. The rest of this section discusses these strategies for creating metadata.

> ### EXERCISE 8.2
>
> ### *Evaluating the Findability of the E-Server Technical Communication Library*
>
> You have been asked to research a list of studies or published papers on the subject of the findability of Web site content, for an organizational context. Towards this goal, you have been asked to use the E-Server Technical Communication Library (http://tc.eserver.org) to compile a list of published materials on the subject. Using a series of keyword searches, locate relevant resources and make a short list of 5–10 you find. Make notes of any problems you encounter finding the resources.
>
> **Tasks to be completed:**
>
> 1. Search the E-Server Technical Communication Library site at http://tc.eserver.org using a series of key word searches for published materials on the subject of the findability of Web site content in an organizational or workplace context.
> 2. Make a list of 5–10 relevant resources on the topic that you find.
> 3. Make note of any specific problems related to the usability or accessibility of resources, or any findability problems in locating the resources.
> 4. Compose a list of your findings and problems, along with some possible workarounds or solutions.
> 5. Discuss any potential improvements to the site that would aid findability of information.

Descriptive Titles and Headings

One very basic way to create meaningful metadata for documents is to use descriptive titles and headings for every document, section, and content item within a technical information product. Titles and headings are often used to index documents or pages within a database or even in online publications. As a result, it is important to select terms which are consistent and familiar with your topic, discipline, and intended users. Doing so will enable users to more easily navigate, comprehend, and find content more quickly and easily.

File Naming Conventions

File naming conventions are a form of descriptive metadata, which serves as a code for understanding details about files or documents within a given information product. As you learned in another chapter, naming conventions are often a part of organizational style guides, and they can help individuals locate and collaborate with others in writing technical documents as part of a team.

Naming conventions provide valuable metadata for documents, making it easier to search through files and folders in locating specific documents. They also can improve findability of documents and information. When the rules of naming conventions are clearly known, the file name itself can be a useful source of determine things like document type, author, date, and other useful details just from looking at the name of the file, without having to actually open and search through individual documents for that information.

Keywords and Tagging

Keywords and tagging are descriptive forms of metadata that involves the classification of content into meaningful categories, using descriptive keywords. It relies on familiar and consistent terminology, and can act as a controlled vocabulary of sorts. In Web sites and other content management systems, it can serve as an alternate method of navigation or grouping, such as in the use of tag clouds. It involves grouping related information resources and content based on similarity of topic or concept. To accommodate a user-centered approach, it should include some form of user testing or vetting. There are different approaches in determining the best method of developing keywords and tags, which include making decisions based on the content itself, the intended users, or in some cases, a mix of both.

Folksonomies vs. Taxonomies

Two approaches to creating meaningful tags and metadata for complex information products include folksonomy, a user-driven approach, and a taxonomy, a content-driven approach. These approaches underscore two important aspects of content management products: the user and the content.

Folksonomies rely on user preference and consensus to serve as the guiding mental model for developing a list of topics in a knowledge base. Smith (2008) defines it as a bottom-up classification strategy that emerges from user-generated content and preferences, including content tagging. Content tagging allows users to "create their own classifications" adding descriptive keywords (or tags) to their contributions and creating links to other content (Governor et al., 2009, p. 58). Some challenges to this approach include potential inconsistent uses of terminology, metadata, and editing, when tagging content, which can create usability and findability problems. While this approach has a strong user-centered aspect, it relies more heavily on user preferences rather than specific standards, practices, or trends within the content of the information product.

Taxonomies focus on the content assets, and, in some cases, a small group of subject matter experts, to drive decisions made in organizing and tagging content. Decisions might be based on a number of factors including existing content patterns, metadata, content volume, trackbacks, links, and other factors. In some content management systems and wikis, taxonomies are often auto-generated, which can create potential usability and findability problems, since they are based on system-generated metadata, without human input. This context sensitivity problem still exists within many automated systems like wikis and blogs. A taxonomy approach also differs from the folksonomy in that it may not incorporate specific user preferences in organizing content, but rather, it relies on the system to generate metadata.

Hybrid approaches are more commonly used in mature information products, involving a combination or mix of user-driven, content-driven, and project constraints. This hybridity allows for maximum flexibility in terms of incorporating user feedback and content trends to make decisions in shaping an information product and its metadata. As a result, developing keywords or tags for content may involve a different process or approach, depending on the type of product and method desired for a particular technical document.

> ### EXERCISE 8.3
>
> ### *Tagging the Technical Communication Body of Knowledge (TCBOK)*
>
> You have been tasked with creating a set of tags for a topic within the Technical Communication Body of Knowledge (TCBOK) wiki. Search for the site online and browse the selection of topics in the site. Select a topic or article of your choice and read the article. Make note of the topic's placement within the information structure of the site. View the Tagging Cloud for the site and from its list of tags, select a few appropriate tags for your topic. Then, add a few new tags, not found in the cloud, which may be appropriate.
>
> **Tasks to be completed:**
>
> 1. Explore the Technical Communication Body of Knowledge (TCBOK) wiki site.
> 2. Select and thoroughly read a topic of your choice.
> 3. Make note of your topic's location within the information structure, especially pages above it in the structure.
> 4. Using the Tagging Cloud on the site, select a few tags that would be appropriate for your topic.
> 5. Add a few new tags to your list, appropriate for the topic.
> 6. Share and discuss your findings with others, including your rationale for selecting tags on your list.

REUSABILITY AND USABILITY CONSIDERATIONS

When making decisions on what content will be reused and at what level it should be revised, reusability and usability are important considerations. Lower levels of single-sourcing typically indicate the need for precise, static content, a specific order or organization that must be maintained for consistency, or situations where precision, repetition, or exact wording is needed for a particular purpose or product. Higher levels of single-sourcing typically indicate that content must be more dynamic, or reusable in a wider range of contexts and information types, with greater variability and flexibility in the organization and order of content, and an increasing need for metadata, to ensure proper context sensitivity, user needs, and findability of content.

Another important part of single-sourcing, or reusability of content, is connected to usability. When you reuse content, the users, purpose, and context of use likely change. Rockley (2001) suggests the importance of reusability, or single-sourcing, of content, into repurposed topics and chunks in different configurations and for different purposes. An extension of reusability is present in mobile design for tablet and mobile computing devices, as the mobile visual world continues to converge with the conventional desktop world. A related aspect, **adaptive content** is, ideally, free of format, compatible on any device, and scalable and filterable to the environment in which it is presented or delivered (Rockley & Cooper, 2012). We see examples of how content adapts differently based on the device used, in the use of visual iconography, display resolution, simplified interfaces, and the move towards platform-independent technologies, such as HTML5. Reusability also suggests the importance of repetition, which allows for knowledge transfer from one system or information product to another.

EXERCISE 8.4

Determining Content Reuse Strategies for a Product Description

Locate a product description or product specification information brochure online for a camera, computer, television, cell phone, or other electronic device. Read the document, paying particular attention to how content is organized, including use of headers, sections, and information topics. Determine which chunks and sections should be reused in the following new products: (1) a one-page advertisement appropriate for a magazine; (2) a one-page technical description appropriate for professionals or experts, rather than general users. Make a list of the content chunks or topics you would use in each of the two products and the order in which they would appear. Sketch a layout of your two new deliverables.

Tasks to be completed:

1. Locate a product specification sheet for an electronics product online.
2. Read and make note of the organization, content topics, and other distinguishing characteristics.
3. Develop a list and order of topics to be reused for a one-page magazine advertisement.
4. Develop a second list and order of topics to be reused for a one-page technical description for professionals and experts.
5. Draw a sketch of the layout of both product.
6. Discuss your single-sourcing methods for each product with others.

Usability Testing

Usability testing is an important, process mature, quality assurance activity in writing and development technical information products and documentation. It involves evaluating products using specific metrics and methods to ensure they meet the needs and expectations of users, as well as the required specifications and functions for the product as envisioned by the designers. Usability testing is an important part of user-centered design because it involves testing a product for the intended users and often testing by a representative sample of the actual users. It can function as a structural and functional editorial review of information products by testing the organization and use of the product. Additionally, usability testing is important to instructional design and user experience to ensure those products successfully meet their objectives and functions for the intended users.

Figure 8.7. Usability testing with actual users reveals their needs and expectations.

Usability metrics, also known as heuristics, are specific criteria used in analyzing and evaluating an information product. Each heuristic or criterion should be specifically defined, in terms of how it should be measured, including examples to aid evaluators. Heuristics can come from a pre-defined set of criteria or be specifically designed and developed for the type of test or product. Some examples include Nielsen's (1995) set of 10 usability heuristics found at http://www.nngroup.com/articles/ten-usability-heuristics/ which apply to the design of user interfaces, including Web sites. Morville (2005) stresses the importance of information findability as an additional principle of evaluating the usability of content. Findability suggests that content can be designed and structured in such a way that when users search for information, that semantics built into the system help them more easily perform those tasks. Usability testing focused on task performance can help determine how successful information findability is within a given instructional product. Additionally, some of the user experience design principles and factors mentioned in the previous section might be good potential metrics to use in evaluating and testing an instructional product.

EXERCISE 8.5

Evaluate a Web Site Design Using Heuristics

Select a Web site and use a set of Web usability heuristics to evaluate its effectiveness. You can use Jacob Nielsen's 10 usability heuristics found at http://www.nngroup.com/articles/ten-usability-heuristics/ or research online to find a different set of heuristics to use in your analysis. Make a list of each heuristics, its definition, and rate each in terms of how the site is compliant or non-compliant. Then, identify specific changes that would need to be made to the Web site for it to be in full compliance with the set of heuristics you used.

Tasks to be completed:

1. Select a Web site to use for your analysis.
2. Select a set of Web usability heuristics by researching online.
3. Make a list of each heuristic and a short definition.
4. Evaluate the Web site using each heuristic, making note of compliance or non-compliance, with examples.
5. Identify specific changes you would need to make to the Web site for it to be fully compliant with the set of Web usability heuristics you used.

Accessibility Testing

Accessibility involves following guidelines to ensure a consistent user experience across a broad user base, regardless of an individual's abilities or limitations. While it may be difficult or costly, it ensures all users, regardless of their limitations, can have equal access to content and services provided by an organization. While not specifically mandated, accessibility guidelines exist to help developers ensure a consistent user experience. Accessibility applies to all types of documents, particularly those with public audiences and online publications. Accessibility is an important component of usability focusing on the main goal of developing documents and products so they meet user needs and working contexts. Accessibility issues include sensory or physical impairments or limitations in hearing, sight, touch, or perception. They can also include technological limitations, which involve accessing content as most users do. Some accessibility technologies include software screen readers, which provide audio versions of textual content, or screen magnification tools that enlarge or enhance visual imagery.

Content accessibility has become increasingly important, in particular, with online publications. Regulatory guidelines exist that dictate rules for creating accessible online content, much of which applies to visual communication products. These include the U.S. Government Section 508 accessibility guidelines and the World Wide Web Consortium's Web Content Accessibility Guidelines. These guidelines were primarily developed for online content accessibility, but they also can be applied more broadly to other types of technical information products. Specific issues addressed by accessibility guidelines include the use of color or visual information to communicate meaning, using descriptive headers for tables, and including alternate descriptors, or text tags, for interactive and graphic content. Two online tools available to test the accessibility of online publications, including Web sites include the Web Accessibility Evaluation Tool, http://wave.webaim.org and the Section 508 Compliance Checker Tool, http://www.508checker.com.

EXERCISE 8.6

Using a Low Vision Simulator to Think about Accessibility

Visit WebAim's Low-Vision Simulator (http://webaim.org/simulations/lowvision-sim.htm) and interact with the different examples provided there. As you interact with the content, make notes on what you learn. Write a short description on how web design can help or hinder individuals' access to information online. Prepare to discuss your findings with the class.

Tasks to be completed:

1. Visit the low-vision simulator.
2. Take notes as you interact with the simulator content.
3. Write a paragraph describing what you learned about designing content for better accessibility.
4. Prepare to present your findings orally in class.

INFORMATION DEVELOPMENT FOR INSTRUCTIONAL PURPOSES

Instructional design draws from many information development concepts you learned, including information modeling, content reuse, and usability, but for a more specialized audience (learners) and purpose (to instruct). **Instructional design** involves selecting, organizing, and specifying learning experiences used to instruct, and **instructional development** refers to the implementation and creation of both print and electronic products, through careful execution of decisions made in instructional design, technology, and other resources (Horton, 2012).

Understanding users or learners as well as learning modalities and theories related to instructional design are essential to instructional design and development. Researching learner skills, aptitudes, and basic sensory abilities can help you better understand what kinds of activities and materials are best suited to the kinds of instructional products you create. In addition, you should consider ways in which learners appropriate, or use, those technologies in actual working settings, which can inform how you continue to support, deliver, and improve instructional products. For example, testing learner preferences and uses of a Web-based training course online might help you better understand how to customize and improve the experience for them. Making decisions on how to sequence and organize content topics is also essential to ensure an effective instructional product.

The instructional design process is a systematic process of tasks in five phases, which is used to create instructional materials and products. Lee & Owens (2004) advocate the **ADDIE** (Analysis, Design, Development, Implementation, Evaluation) process of instructional design, which includes five phases: analysis, design, development, implementation, and evaluation (see Figure 8.8). **Analysis** involves developing specifications of the instructional product including specifics on the learners, instructional goals, and desired outcomes. The **Design** phase involves developing instructional delivery methods, interface design, instructional outlines, media, content structure, and standards for instructional materials. The **Development** phase includes the actual product development, prototyping, and preliminary testing. The final two phases, **Implementation** and **Evaluation**, are often combined and include post-production, final testing and reviewing, and assessing the value and impact of the instructional product.

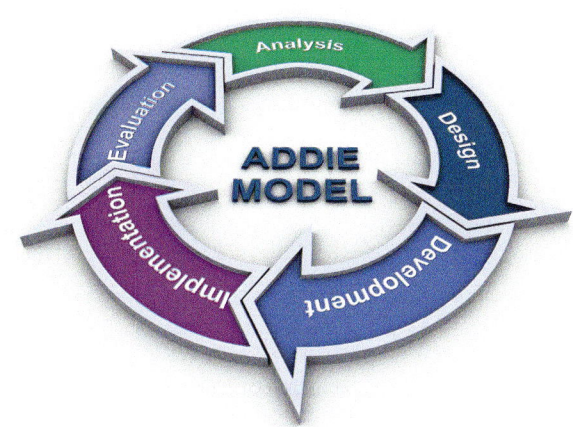

Figure 8.8. The ADDIE instructional design process includes five phases.

Analysis Phase

Understanding the learning modalities, instructional design approaches, technology factors, and guidelines for sequencing and organizing instructional content are all important tasks in the analysis phase. This phase also includes accommodating learner skills, prerequisite knowledge, demographics, and learning styles. From a content standpoint, it includes understanding how to properly organize, sequence, and structure information so that users can navigate, comprehend, and successfully use the product as intended. Designing instructional products that are usable and accessible, as quality assurance activities, helps ensure the user experience is effective and meets the required objectives of the instructional product.

An important part of designing instructional products is to define explicit **learning objectives**, or what learners are expected to gain in terms of knowledge, skills, and abilities. Writing clear learning objectives includes three important components: prerequisite knowledge, learning objectives, and a desired outcome (see Figure 8.9). These learning objectives are similar to the task objectives you wrote in Chapter 3. First, they should identify the knowledge learners are expected to have prior to starting the lesson. Second, the learning objectives should identify what learners will gain in terms of skills and/or complete in terms of tasks. Third, they should describe the desired outcomes of the learning experience, in terms of the actual behaviors, attitudes, or skills. There should also be an alignment between the learning objectives and the content of the instructional product. In other words, the product should include the content, including level of detail, which will allow learners to successfully meet the learning objectives.

> Prerequisite knowledge + learning objectives = desired outcome

Figure 8.9. Effective learning objectives has three components.

The learning objective itself will have three parts: a stem, a verb, and an outcome. The stem describes the activity (What activity are learners completing—reading a paragraph, watching a video, completing an exercise?). The verb describes the measurable action learners will demonstrate (What will learners do—analyze, describe, draw, and summarize?). The outcome describes the product or deliverable that will result (What is the end product—a report, an effectively punctuated sentence, a cake, an oil change on a car?) The example below illustrates a simple learning objective for this section of our chapter.

> *After reading this chapter, learners will be able to identify the five ADDIE phases of instructional design.*

An important part of instructional design analysis phase involves focusing on the learner (or user) of the instructional content. Learning objectives are focused on instructional content as much as they are the actual learner. In a previous chapter, you were introduced to the concept of user-centered design, where developers involve users throughout the entire process of product development, including the collection of user feedback during planning stages; user testing and feedback during design and development of drafts and prototypes; and comprehensive usability testing towards production and delivery. User research is an important part of instructional design, which might involve collecting information on users, or developing user profiles or scenarios to better analyze and understand their preferences and information needs.

EXERCISE 8.7
Practice Writing Learning Objectives

Visit a Web site with online tutorials, such as YouTube, EHow, or IFixIt. Many of these tutorials have implied, but unstated learning objectives. Working with a partner, choose two tutorials you would like to view or read. After choosing the tutorials, work separately to write at least one learning objective for each tutorial. Compare your learning objectives with your partner. Discuss differences and similarities, and revise, if necessary. Be prepared to share your learning objectives with the class.

Tasks to be completed:

1. Working with a partner, identify two tutorials you would like to read or watch online.
2. Working individually, watch or read both tutorials and write at least one learning objective for each tutorial.
3. Compare and contrast your tutorial learning outcomes with your partner.
4. Discuss similarities and differences and identify your best objectives.
5. Prepare to share your tutorials and objectives in class.

Learning Styles and Theories

After developing learning objectives, the next step in the analysis phase it to consider learning styles and theories. Learning styles and theories are important because they can account for differences in user aptitudes, skills, abilities, and preferences. Learners typically have multiple modalities in which they excel, making understanding their individualized learning profile a more complex task. When designing instructional documents, you should consider a broad range of learning styles to maximize effectiveness of your materials and to accommodate the widest range of users possible. This section introduces you to four specific types, including learning modalities (visual, auditory, and kinesthetic), multiple intelligences (linguistic, spatial (visual), logical-mathematical, bodily-kinesthetic, musical, interpersonal, and intrapersonal), adult learning theories, and related technology theories. How you choose to apply what you know about different learning styles in your technical documents will vary depending on the particular situation, users, product, and standards which apply to your project; however, some specific guidelines will be offered in this section to help you make those decisions.

EXERCISE 8.8

Evaluating Your Basic Learning Style

Perform an online search for a learning styles inventory test using the keywords "kinesthetic auditory visual test." Look for a shorter test that is not longer than 20 questions. Complete the test and evaluate your results. Which style is your primary learning style, or do you have multiple ones? Make a list of traits for you style and compare them to your peers. Discuss how these traits might inform your design of instructional materials for that style.

Tasks to be completed:

1. Locate a learning style inventory test online using the keywords "kinesthetic auditory visual test."
2. Complete the test and examine your results.
3. Make a list of traits for your primary or dominant learning style.
4. Discuss how these traits might inform the development of specific features of instructional materials to accommodate that style.
5. Discuss your findings with your peers.

Learning Modalities

Lee and Owens (2004) identify four approaches to learning, which incorporate four user sensory perception modes: visual, auditory, olfactory, and tactile. Effective learning occurs when more than one sense is engaged by the learning environment (Lee & Owens, 2004). Three of these modalities are widely addressed within instructional design research include auditory, kinesthetic (or tactile), and visual (see Figure 8.10). Learning modality tests are available that can determine the styles that each learner possesses as their dominant style. Learners typically have a primary (or dominant) learning style, which is the mode in which they learn new material most effectively. In addition, learners may have one or more secondary learning styles, which are almost as strong as the primary style. And finally, in some cases, a learner may have multiple primary styles.

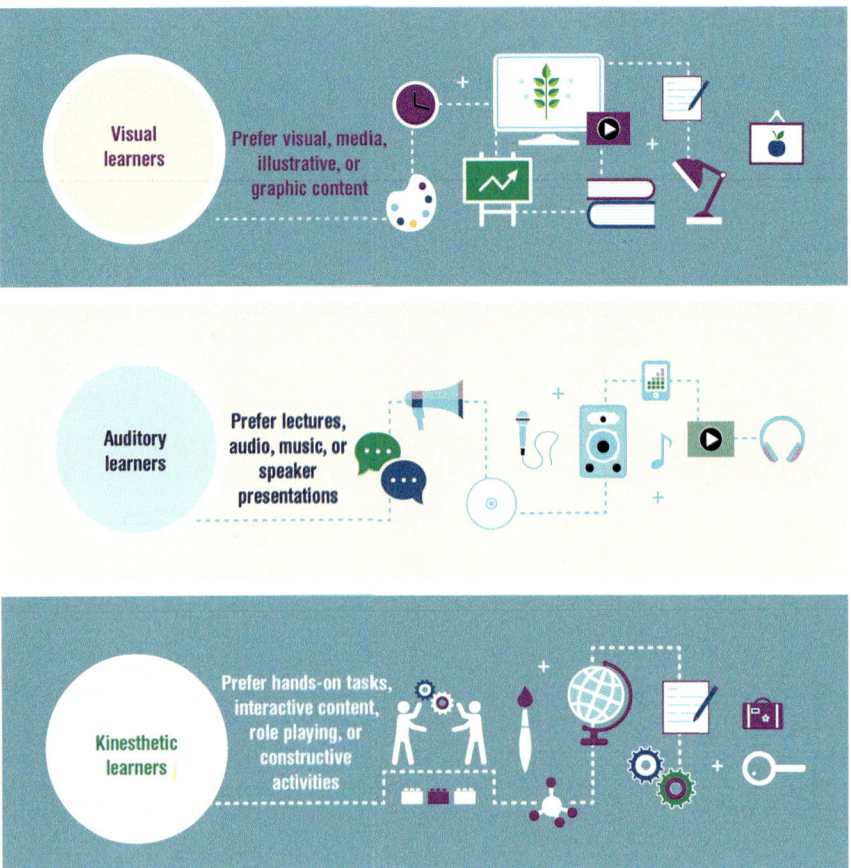

Figure 8.10. The three primary learning modalities are visual, auditory, and kinesthetic.

Multiple Intelligences as Learning Styles

Gardner (2006) and his landmark work on multiple intelligences has been applied successfully to learning styles for adult learners in instructional design research. He defines intelligence broadly as the ability to process certain kinds of information, and he relates each type of intelligence as a mode humans used to solve problems, produce products, and achieve objectives (Gardner, 2006). The primary set of intelligences he identified include the following: linguistic, spatial (visual), logical-mathematical, bodily-kinesthetic, musical, interpersonal, and intrapersonal (see Figure 8.11). Later iterations of his work included other factors such as natural and spiritual intelligences. The original list of categories incorporates the three learner modalities from instructional design theory (visual, auditory, and kinesthetic), but it expands them to include social and linguistic skills that learners may have as dominant styles.

Linguistic
- Skills: Verbal and auditory.
- Learning modes: Reading, listening.

Spatial (visual)
- Skills: Visual and spatial thinking.
- Learning modes: Graphics, diagrams, drawings, models, and visual media.

Logical-mathematical
- Skills: Abstract, conceptual, and numerical.
- Learning modes: Patterns, puzzles, and discovery activities.

Bodily-kinesthetic
- Skills: Physical and tactile.
- Learning modes: Hands-on activities, physical tasks, and role play.

Musical
- Skills: Sound, rhythm, and music.
- Learning modes: Lyrical, rhythmic, or other audio media forms.

Interpersonal
- Skills: Social interaction with others.
- Learning modes: Discussion, group activities, and social media.

Intrapersonal
- Skills: Understanding of self.
- Learning modes: Independent study, creative expression.

Figure 8.11. Gardner's multiple intelligences.

From an instructional design standpoint, each intelligence refers to a specific aptitude or mode that a learner may favor, or possess as a strength. Gardner acknowledges that all humans have some capability in each of the intelligences, based on both biological and experiential differences, some of which are dominant styles that affect their unique learning styles.

There are several important guidelines to consider when incorporating various learning modalities into your instructional materials. First, all learners do not successfully master or learn material the same way. It is important to understand that learners have different skills and modes of learning, and often multiple intelligences. Second, you should incorporate a wide range of learning modes into your design, but only ones that are feasible, meet learning objectives, and are effective. In other words, do not try to force incorporating a mode that is not an effective way of presenting the material. Providing a range of materials, formats, and activities will engage a wider range of learners and improve overall instructional value. Third, it may be impossible to account for every style and preference, but providing a range of options will likely appeal to a broader range of learners. As such, offering learners choices to accommodate different skills and learning preferences is another useful guideline to consider. And finally, it is important to conduct some basic user research into your primary audience to determine what kinds of learning styles, preferences, or basic skills they have, which can help inform the decisions you make in developing instructional materials.

Adult Learning Theory

Whether you are writing a set of instructions, a process description, a procedure, a presentation, or other kinds of instructional materials, you are likely to be writing for adult learners in technical and professional contexts. In addition to specific learning styles, it is important to understand the unique preferences of adult learners, and the factors and techniques that best facilitate the ways adults learn new information. Adult learning theory suggests there are unique differences in the interaction of perception, cognition, and learning in the adult user experience. Although research suggests adult learners experience learning and immersion in similar ways as children, adults filter those through previous intellectual experiences, which guide their behaviors in learning new material (Lee & Owens, 2004). As a result, their user experience may be somewhat different in that adult learners expect relevance, or a perceived relationship between what is learned and real-world application of that knowledge. They prefer an active, involved role in learning, rather than passive absorption of knowledge. Because of differences in learning preferences and experiences, adult learners prefer independence and flexibility, or control over their environment. As a result, they may be less receptive to abstract, novel, tangential, idealized, or potentially irrelevant visuals, compared to other learners. Active learning styles may also be a positive contributing factor in visual comprehension, particularly online, due to the highly visual and interactive nature of those environments.

Lee and Owens (2004) identify four essential factors that characterize adult learner, including relevance of content, level of involvement, control over the learning, and non-traditional forms of learning. The first factor, **relevance of content**, refers to the notion that adult learners expect a direct relationship between what is learned and real-world application of that knowledge. Without such application, such information might be discounted as irrelevant, tangential, or not useful to the adult learner. The second factor is **level of involvement**. Adult learners prefer an active, involved role in learning, rather than passive absorption of knowledge. As a result, they may expect more application tasks or interaction to facilitate absorption of material.

EXERCISE 8.9

Using the Brigham Grid for Learning (BGfL) to Discover how Your Mind Works

Take the Brigham Grid for Learning quiz to discover how your multiple intelligences (http://www.bgfl.org/bgfl/custom/resources_ftp/client_ftp/ks3/ict/multiple_int/index.htm). Compare your results with others in your class. Discuss how different intelligences might affect users learn and, consequently, how technical communicators should design instructions to assist their learning. Write a paragraph or two summarizing what your group decides.

Tasks to be completed:

1. Visit the BGfL site and take the quiz.
2. Discuss your findings in a small group.
    a. Consider how different intelligences might affect learning.
    b. Consider how technical communicators might design instruction for different intelligences.
3. Write a paragraph or two summarizing your discussion conclusions.

The third factor, **control over the learning environment**, refers to the degree of manipulation and customization adult learner have in a tutorial. Because of differences in learning preferences and experiences, adult learners prefer independence and flexibility in how they learn or master material, and, as a result, they are more responsive to instructional materials with greater control. The fourth factor is that adult learners prefer **non-traditional forms of learning**. They often prefer individualized, self-paced instruction to accommodate the rate at which they master material in an instructional setting. As a result, providing greater options in how content can be accessed, navigated, and used are essential components to aid adult learning. Some examples of how these four factors can be addressed in a variety of instructional documents are provided in Figure 8.12.

Relevance
- Provide clearly stated objectives.
- Create an alignment between objectives and content.
- Include statements of value of the learning.
- Provide specific examples used in working contexts.

Involvement
- Develop tasks that allow learners to apply their knowledge.
- Include practice tasks, drills, or other activities.
- Create interactive models or activities that facilitate active learning.
- Include kinesthetic learning tasks, which engage learners in physical activities.

Control
- Provide multiple navigation tools, outlines, or alternatives.
- Provide exploratory options that allow users to control the sequence or order in which they read or use content.
- Allow users to customize their learning experience, in terms of format, sequencing, or pacing.

Non-Traditional Learning
- Add variety to the format, presentation, or order of content, particularly if benchmarking from previous materials.
- Include independent tasks that allow learners to work by themselves.
- Allow learners to vary the pace in which they read or use the material, such as including options to start, go back, go forward, or stop.

Figure 8.12. The four factors that characterize adult learning are presented here along with examples of their application.

Technology Considerations

All technological products have intended uses, which developers of those products expect. But what happens when users find different uses for technologies? There has always been a gap between the developer's intended uses and the user's actual uses of any technological product. Technological appropriation focuses on how people make use of technologies and tools for their own purposes. User appropriation of such technologies becomes part of the iterative development, helping to shape the future iterations of technological products (McLuhan, 1964). Technological accommodation theory takes the notion a step further, by examining the actual contexts and far-reaching impacts on users and their lives. This theory suggests another important (perhaps latent) feature of technological products—the uses and impacts beyond our level of awareness. As part of instructional design process, you should finally consider the ways in which learners interact with technologies that you might be using as part of your instructional products.

Design and Development Phases

The design and development phases are most closely related to the content management concepts that began this chapter. These phases include the important tasks of organizing and writing content appropriate for your instructional product. Within larger instructional products, such as training courses or online help systems, content is organized into topics. A topic is a self-contained unit of content, which typically addresses a specific learning objective or function, in scope (Horton, 2012). In a set of instructions, topics might include a list of materials, description of the assembly process, troubleshooting advice, and the set of specific steps for assembling a product. In an online training course, it might include how to use a formula to calculate interest payments on a new car, or how to install a software program on a computer.

From a content management standpoint, you should design and develop instructional content from a learner (or user) perspective, but there are also several other important considerations to address in organizing and writing content topics for instructional products. First, you should consider how the subject matter affects how content is modeled: that is, how it is organized or sequenced. Some subjects may require more linear, step-by-step organization of topics, where following a specific order of topics is essential. Second, pacing the material is also important to consider, including the level of detail. This pacing involves considering timing issues, such as how long learners should spend on particular topics or sections or how to divide up larger instructional products into smaller units to better facilitate learning. For example, writing a set of instructions requires one task per step to avoid misunderstanding.

Third, you should consider customization options. This customization might include options that allow learners to control the order, pacing, format, or style of content within an instructional product. For example, online training courses often include multiple methods of navigating, searching, or controlling content at their own pace. And finally, technology issues related to content are important to consider, particularly with online or electronic versions of instructional products. Technology issues might include the type of computer, browser, media players, and other software tools available to the learners or required for viewing and using instructional products. Collectively, all of these issues should be considered when making decisions about the sequencing and organizing of instructional content.

As discussed in previous sections, information models outline the standardized patterns and structure of content within an information product (Hackos, 2007; Rosenfeld & Morville, 2007). They also help to explain relationships between individual content sections or chunks within a technical document. Information models are often incorporated into instructional documents and presented visually as site maps, interactive help, indices, tables of contents, numbered or bulleted lists, lesson plans, and navigation tools. As such, they can serve as information visualization products, which help users better comprehend the structure, relatedness, and organization of content in an information product. Four sequencing options for instructional products include linear, hierarchical, exploratory, and randomized (see Figure 8.13). For content that is complex or has multiple functions, more complex products, multiple sequencing options, or even customized sequencing structures may be necessary.

Linear
Follows a specific order, step-by-step. Useful when a rigid process must be followed in a specified order.

Hierarchical
Branched sequencing, where topics are organized into an outline from general topics to specific topics. Useful in products that have multiple major sections, units, or topics.

Exploratory
Customized sequencing, which can be hierarchical, but allows learners to navigate or search content, and interact with it following any pattern they choose. Useful for products that are for all kinds of learners, experienced and novice.

Randomized
System generated order of topics, where content is randomly presented. Useful for testing materials where varying the order of questions or topics is necessary.

Figure 8.13. Instructional products can organized, or ordered, in different sequences.

EXERCISE 8.10

Evaluate Instructional Materials Using Adult Learning Factors

Using a set of instructions, evaluate their effectiveness for adult learners. You might select a set of instructions for assembling a product, for completing a process for registration, or for purchasing a product or service. Make sure to select a set of instructions written for an adult audience. If it is feasible, test the instructions by completing them yourself, making notes of your experiences. Using the four factors of adult learning theory, including relevance, involvement, control, and non-traditional learning, assess the strengths and weaknesses of the instructions. Identify specific changes or additions you would make to the set of instructions to ensure they more successfully incorporate the four adult learning factors. Rewrite or edit the instructions incorporating your suggested changes and additions.

Tasks to be completed:

1. Locate a set of instructions for adult learners, such as instructions for assembling a product, or completing a process.
2. If possible, complete the instructions and make notes of strengths, problems, or challenges encountered.
3. Using the four factors of adult learning (relevance, involvement, control, and non-traditional learning), evaluate the instructions in terms of their strengths and weaknesses.
4. Make a list of additions or changes to the instructions, which would improve their usability in terms of adult learning theory factors.
5. Rewrite or edit the instructions incorporating the suggested additions and changes.

Implementation and Evaluation

The final two phases of instructional design includes implementation and evaluation, where you test and evaluate the overall user experience of the instructional product. In an instructional design context, particularly when interactive or online materials are used, user experience design (or information experience design) is also an important and related concept. **User experience design (UX)** involves the development of content (and features) that affect the overall experience for the user, which can affect their actions, behaviors, and perceptions (Unger & Chandler, 2009). It also includes the various visual, aural, and haptic (or touch-based) devices that comprise the user experience.

User experience design has strong connections to information design theory, particularly in terms of instructional products. As a result, you should consider information design principles in designing interactive content because they involve an understanding of user behaviors, such as perception, cognition, and experience. UX involves thinking about how users will perceive, process (cognitive effort), and act upon information in the instructional product. Hackos (2007) discusses the importance of design patterns for developing information within complex systems, which are informed by an organized hierarchy that is understood by users within a given context. While not specifically addressing information design, this approach suggests the importance of using related design concepts, such as consistency and grouping to create content patterns (whether visual, textual, spatial, or some hybrid combination) that maximizes usability. Garrett (2011) includes information design, information architecture, interaction design, and sensory design, among others, in his model depicting the various levels of user experience design.

Figure 8.14. These principles of universal design are key to evaluation of the instructional product.

User experience also involves comprehending the alignment, or relationship, between elements grouped to ensure they all contribute to the effectiveness of the whole product. Universal design, with its roots in the accessibility movement, is an inclusive design approach that aims to maximize usability in physical and virtual environments, with minimal need for adaptation (Steinfeld & Maisel, 2012). As such, user experience suggests a strong usability context and involves a variety of factors, including the maximum number of useful features, the technological feasibility, and user expectations and preferences with regard to the product. (See Figure 8.14.) While there may be similarities in how users or learner perceive and process information, the modes in which that information is presented affects their ability to understand, make meaning, and learn effectively from instructional products.

Challenges and Assumptions

Some challenges in addressing user experience design factors in instructional products involve a misperception of the medium, technological capabilities, and the user. The first assumption is that we expect the same user experience in electronic environments across all media forms. Differences in our mobile devices, computer operating systems, and Web pages we visit suggest that our experiences using these different tools will vary widely. For example, the sequence to print a document may differ if you are using a Mac, PC, tablet, or smartphone. As a result, the kinds of navigation tools, visual presentation, and content may create a different experience depending on which device or tool you are using. This challenge requires users to think and behave differently in different environments. The second problem is the assumption that content management systems or templates require no modification for them to be successful. For example, if you use an online content management system to create a blog or a wiki, you will likely need (and want) to modify the default page layouts, styles, colors, navigation links, and other features, to fit the overall users, purpose, and context.

Lack of process maturity, skills, resources, or other training may account for the approach—once out of the box, no assembly or modification required. The third assumption is that every user preference should be accommodated in order to achieve a high degree of usability. Designers have access to developer-level knowledge of the product and its context, that when factored with user feedback, may suggest impossible or improbable solutions. Conversely, attempting to integrate some user preferences into your product may simply be technologically or rhetorically unfeasible. A related technology problem is **feature creep**—where information products (and subsequently their interfaces) increase the number of features or functions in each new version, which, from a cognitive standpoint, has a potentially negative impact on users. The final problematic assumption is that usability is the ultimate deciding and determining factor in successful information design. New and novel interfaces and features, such as those in recent mobile and tablet computing interfaces, can sometimes be successful, if designed well, and underpinned by tested information development and design theories.

Chapter Summary

Managing content and information encompasses a broad range of concepts, practices, and strategies for technical communicators. Content management involves creating, developing, and producing content through the lifecycle of a project, including the tasks of information modeling, single-sourcing content, and developing meaningful metadata for technical documents and information products. An important part of content and project management is to develop a content strategy: developing specific processes, practices, and methods of creating, structuring, producing, and reusing content effectively in an information product.

Information modeling involves developing coherent structures for content, which serves as an organizational template for developing information products. The process involves researching information models, anticipating user expectations, identifying content assets, and developing and testing the information structure. It also involves a complex understanding of the relational aspects of individual content items and often, performing benchmarking research to inform its development, which relies on user expectations from similar products and genres. Information models for evolving products must also be scalable, or structured in ways that can more easily accommodate new content or changes to the information product. Scalability is particularly important to online publications, such as Web sites, wikis, and other content management systems.

Single-sourcing, or content reuse, has become an increasingly important part of content management, particularly in online publications and technical document development. Reuse and repurposing content for a variety of users, purposes, contexts, and media types is important to every workplace. Content reuse includes different levels, or approaches, including cut-and-paste, static content reuse, and dynamic content reuse.

Developing meaningful metadata includes selecting methods of writing descriptive titles and headers, developing standardized naming conventions for files, and selecting appropriate keywords and tags for content that may be indexed or searched. Metadata provides valuable descriptive details about content assets, improves findability, and aids in the writing and development process, by helping to organize, structure, and identify content using consistent standards.

Usability and access are also particularly important content management considerations. Users must be able to access the content you are generating. Access can be broadly defined as ways users find, navigate, and use information, but it also determines whether users with different abilities and learning styles can find and use your information products. Usability and access work together to create usability experiences, which is an important determinant in how well users receive and use your content.

Designing and developing instructional products involves understanding instructional design theories, models, learners, technology factors, and methods for sequencing and organizing content. The process involves five phases, including analysis, design, development, implementation, and evaluation. Important theories and factors related to learning include learning modalities (auditory, kinesthetic, and visual), multiple intelligences, and adult learning theory. It is also important to consider related technology theories and issues, such as how users appropriate and accommodate various technologies. Sequencing and organizing content involves making important decisions on the arrangement of topics in an instructional product, including information modeling, semantics, and use of navigation systems and aids.

Chapter Assignments

The exercises in this section ask you to apply what you have learned in this chapter as well as explore how this knowledge applies to and connects with other information in the textbook.

1. Select a large company's Web site that has a site map comprising its structure at several levels. Evaluate the headings used for the top three or four levels of the information. What patterns or conventions do you see at work in how the information is organized? Does the organization seem to favor or suggest a specific user group, function, or purpose, and if so, which ones? Based on the organization of the site map, are there areas that you would edit or change to optimize its effectiveness? Make a list of specific changes, or if possible, sketch out a revised site map and share your findings.

2. Using the E-Server Technical Communication Library site at http://tc.eserver.org, locate an article in technical communication on a topic of interest. Read the abstract and skim the article making a list of possible tags for the selection, appropriate as search terms. After making your list, revise it to ensure the terms selected are consistent with others used in the field.

3. Locate two separate feasibility studies on any topic online. Compare the two in terms of how each organizes information into individual sections. Sketch an outline or information model of each and make note of the similarities and differences in terms of both major content sections and overall organizational patterns.

4. Locate two versions of an annual report issued by a company for two different years. Skim both reports making note of the content and organization of the documents. Compare both reports and identify what content is single-sourced from the older version to the newer one. Identify the level of single-sourcing used. Discuss your findings, in terms of the effectiveness and single-sourcing methods used.

5. Research online to find a few sample tests that can be used to assess learning styles. Compare and contrast the different types of tests you find, by taking each short test and evaluating the strengths and weaknesses of each test. What guidelines are offered that you could use to develop instructional materials for each learning style? Which ones would you want to use in developing training materials or instructions?

6. Using Gardner's list of multiple intelligences in the chapter, assess your own skills and determine which of the intelligences are your strengths. Then, conduct some online research to find a short test for Gardner's multiple intelligences, and take the test. Compare your initial assumptions to the results of the test. Identify the kinds of learning activities associated with your dominant intelligences.

7. You have been given the task of creating a Web site version of a technical document. Using a printed version of a technical report, create a site map that would be used in the Web site. Examine the navigation aids within the document to get started. Then, decide how you would need to reorganize the document for it to be an effective Web site version. Consider how you would link sections together using hyperlinks, or what additional content you would want to add to the Web site version, to make it more interactive and usable. Discuss your proposed changes and additions with peers.

Figure Credits

Figure 8.1. © Zurijeta/Shutterstock.com

Figure 8.2. © Kendall Hunt Publishing Company

Figure 8.3. © phipatbig/Shutterstock.com

Figure 8.4. © Rawpixel.com/Shutterstock.com

Figure 8.5. © Kendall Hunt Publishing Company

Figure 8.6. © Kendall Hunt Publishing Company

Figure 8.7. © Lucky Business/Shutterstock.com

Figure 8.8. © asirkhan/Shutterstock.com

Figure 8.10. © Batshevs/Shutterstock.com

Figure 8.13. © vstock24/Shutterstock.com

Designing Visual Information

CHAPTER OVERVIEW

This chapter introduces you to theories, concepts, and practices in designing visual communication products used in various genres and technical documents. After reading this chapter, you should be able to meet the following objectives:

- Describe theories, principles, and conventions of visual communication design, including perception, cognition, experiential design, and color composition theory.
- Discuss the importance of accessibility standards and aesthetic considerations in developing visual information.
- Discuss the importance and function of information graphics, their types, and guidelines for using them in technical documents.
- Discuss the use and development methods for electronic stylesheets, design templates, and visual identities.

In the 21st century, information design is defined broadly, including the design of textual content, graphic elements, spatial layouts, and interactive experiences. Factors that have affected this definition include advances in technology, standards, processes, and content delivery. Our content has become more intelligent and information development processes have become increasingly adaptive, complex, and interactive; and these changes have impacted the visual design of information products. Intelligent content is structurally rich, semantically categorized (identified and tagged), making it discoverable (findable), reusable, reconfigurable, and adaptable (Rockley & Cooper, 2012). It is highly visual, spatial, semantic, modular, customizable (personalized), mobile, accessible (from both accessibility standards and technological standpoints), and usable (searchable, navigable). Ideally for users, content should be delivered as instantaneous, entertaining, useful, and even perhaps novel; and as a result, we expect more, visually, from our content.

Figure 9.1. The design process includes a wide range of design variables, including color theory.

Changes in the technologies and practices have in turn, affected the design of visual information. A wide range of design variables, which have emerged from these tools and practices, yields an increasingly complex and iterative design process.

The design process itself includes a wide range of design variables: color theory, iconography, imagery, branding, typography, spatial layout, interactivity, and aesthetics. In formation design processes often involve the separation of presentation and content in the development cycle, followed by a re-integration of these elements in the final product (Clark, 2008). Practices in information development such as information modeling, usability and reusability, semantics, and user experience create complex design challenges for technical communicators. For example, adaptive and reusable content is reconfigured based on user selection and input, which creates customized information that users must process through visual perception, cognition, and unique experiences. To put these changes into a context with which you are familiar, think of your experiences as an online shopper. When you are interested in purchasing a product, you can type search terms into a browser search function or go directly to the online store where you plan to make the purchase. In either case, your search terms will return customized personal options that respond to the parameters of your search. Other shoppers using the same browser or online shop search function might see an entirely different set of purchase of options, depending on what they are purchasing and what terms they use. In these cases, the content will be customized for the shopper, but the visual design of information returned will be the same.

Visual information includes a wide range of products, including developing graphics, charts, tables, illustrations, page layouts, and even entire visual themes or identities that comprise an important part of technical documents. Information graphics, simple and complex, incorporate data as supporting evidence, instructional material, or procedural illustration. These include bar charts, pie charts, tables, line graphs, and other data displays. Other types include graphics that communicate realism, illustrative detail, or a specific brand, theme, or identity. These include photographs, sketches, illustrations, or other artistic creations. Another type of visual information used in technical documents includes stylesheets, which document specific stylistic conventions, to ensure consistency across a technical information product. These can be printed standards used in developing documents or electronic stylesheets for online publications.

Figure 9.2. Technical communicators consider each design element to determine its function and usefulness.

Templates are another type of visual information, which reinforce structural and organizational consistency of design of a technical information product. These include forms, worksheets, interface layouts, or other organizational models, which allow writers single-source organizational patterns for documents and other forms of content. And finally, visual identity guidelines document stylistic, graphic, and organizational conventions that apply to entire products or product families. These are typically developer-only documents that document all standards and conventions used in stylesheets, templates, and other aspects of technical documents.

Several theoretical approaches, studied and documented in research, apply when making visual design choices, such as the study of visual perception, cognition, and experiential learning theories. However, the ubiquity of standardized templates often compromises the effectiveness of information design, sometimes ignoring the fundamentals of these underlying theories. Content designers may simply lack the technical knowledge, resources, or deeper understanding of design theory. They may not know how it might apply differently when approaching information design tasks. Albers (2009) suggests effective information design involves more than following prescriptive rules and templates; instead, he recommends a critical understanding and application of theoretical approaches and rules of design. From a visual standpoint, technical communicators who work as information designers must consider each graphic element and decide if it is conveying a level of information that extends, augments, or enhances the information presented and, if so, how it contributes to the overall user experience. In essence, visual content has its own language, or unique configuration, which involves how users perceive, process, and filter information through their own experiences and learning styles. Helping users understand that language is an important task in developing effective visual communication products.

EXERCISE 9.1

Identifying Visual Design Elements

This text chapter includes many examples of design elements. Quickly count and identify the visual information types used in this chapter. Enter that information into a spreadsheet and create an graphic that displays this information visually.

Tasks to be completed:
1. Make a list of all the visual information types used in this chapter.
2. Count the number of each type.
3. Enter the names and totals of each type in an spreadsheet.
4. Create an graphic that presents this information visually.

This chapter will introduce you to related visual information design theories and approaches, including perception theory, cognitive theory, experiential design, and color theory, as well as the importance of accessibility and aesthetic considerations. It will also discuss methods of developing various types of visual information graphics. And finally, it will discuss developing page-level designs, including stylesheets, templates, and visual identity guidelines for technical information products.

VISUAL DESIGN THEORIES

Research and practice in information design has been largely centered on three related questions:

- How do users perceive visual content?
- How do they process and make meaning from it?
- How do they experience or learn from it?

These approaches can be summarized as perceptual, cognitive, and experiential. In both simple and complex visual environments, users share common mental patterns, attributes and expectations informed by these basic psychological processes, despite the differences in their actual information needs (Raskin, 2000). Visual signals or triggers communicate through signs that incite action, sometimes based on recognition more than interpretation. For this reason, you need to understand the importance of what users see (or perceive), how they make meaning, and how they learn from this meaning. The connections between these behaviors are the underpinnings of many theories of visual design. An understanding of these basic underlying design theories and conventions is important in designing effective visual communication products. This section summarizes three theoretical information design approaches and discusses their relevance to developing visual information.

Perceptual Theory

Understanding perceptual theory will help you to understand what people think when viewing or interpreting visual content. Visual interpretation is the reasoning used to make meaning—our inferences are formed from clues through observation, from perception of elements in the visual field, and through the medium through which it is perceived (Arnheim, 1969; Barry, 1997; Moriarty, 2005). Visual perception has been studied in a wide range of fields, including art history, psychology, and technical communication.

For example, Gestalt theory, an applied psychological approach, explains the range of perceptual tasks users' exhibit in perceiving the whole, or whole effect, within a given visual medium. Rudolf Arnheim (1969) based his visual thinking principles on Gestalt theory, within art history and information design contexts, equating visual perception with the act of visual thinking. When we encounter visual information, we try ascertain its characteristics, placement, and distinguishing features based on our sensory perception. For example, in the act of visual thinking, users switch between figure and ground in examining objects in their visual field, regardless of media type. The process of discerning content and context within visual environments, such as Web sites, are conceptually separated, where the focus shifts continually between foreground and background (Johnson-Sheehan & Baehr, 2001).

Figure 9.3 provides a visual summary of key Gestalt theories of perception—proximity, similarity, closure, continuation, and figure/ground—that frequently are employed in visual design.

Figure 9.3. This figure demonstrates how key Gestalt theories are employed in visual design.

Cognitive Theory

Cognitive theory explains how individuals' brains process information. There is a close link between the perceptual and cognitive acts users experience when processing visual stimuli, but, in effect, one often triggers the other. Cognitive learning involves processing and using information, through rehearsal, chunking, and other classification and structured learning behaviors (Richey et al., 2011). While cognitive learning sounds very complicated, if you think about your own learning preferences, this theory is easy to understand: for example, do your prefer to learn new information by reading, viewing images, or both? To answer this question, think about how you prefer to receive directions. Do you prefer directions that are written or presented as an image or map to guide you? Or you might consider how you like to read: Do you prefer long, text-heavy paragraphs, or short skimmable lists that convey similar information? These questions illustrate how you prefer to process information. Your users will have their own preferences, and their preferences may vary from yours and from one another. Understanding cognitive theory can help you to accommodate these preferences when you plan and design information products.

Cognitive theory also suggests most individuals like to know in advance of reading what content is included in a document. For this reason, many documents include summaries at their beginning as well as tables of contents, site maps, and introductions that outline what is to follow. Content such as summaries, tables of content, and site maps provide a framework for what is to follow and gives readers cognitive clues about what lies ahead. This framework creates a mental model that assists readers as they progress through the content.

In this way, perception and cognition are related. There is iterative interplay between what users sense or perceive, how they process this information, and how they respond or react to the information. This interplay is why cognitive theory is an important design consideration. Cognitive design involves how users perceive the information environment in terms of structural elements, such as navigation schemes on websites and visual cues, such as headings, in print documents. Albers (2009) describes the cognitive process of interpreting design through structural patterns of information that users see. These patterns help users interpret highly complex information.

Designs that are unfamiliar or overly complicated create cognitive problems, or **cognitive overload**, for users. Such designs affect users' comprehension; users are less successful understanding information when it is presented with complicated structural patterns than when they are given information with easier and more familiar patterns (Albers, 2009). Figure 9.4 provides a simple illustration of cognitive load. It demonstrates how cognitive load can impact decision-making. In the upper example, the user wants to make search for a product on a website, locate it, and purchase it; however, when website designs include multiple images that are hard to see or recognize, unclearly marked menu items, or navigation schemes that take users away from their purchases, users become frustrated and may forego the purchase altogether. In other words, the more choices users have, the higher their cognitive load. When users have too many choices, the load becomes higher and harder to bear as the lower example on 9.4 shows. Understanding cognitive load can help you to simplify your designs, making them consistent and easy to learn.

To avoid users experiencing cognitive overload, designers need to establish clear patterns in their documents—whether they are print or electronic. These patterns, used consistently, assist users as they read or view information in these documents. Similarly, Colborne (2010) argues that the more features added to an information product, the less likely it is that users will perceive them as valuable. Applied simply, a few features done well, or repeated, may be inherently more successful than several done adequately, in terms of cognitive effect and perceived usefulness for the user. Another approach, proposed for the design of scientific visuals, involves classification into a taxonomy, which can serve as a model to dictate when and how to use specific and familiar visuals (Desnoyers, 2011). Using familiar and simple visual patterns consistently can create cognitive alignment between the visual rhetoric and the user's mental models, also resulting in reduced cognitive effort. From a user perspective, then, consistency becomes an important factor in the process of cognition.

Experiential Design Theory

Effective visual design integrates perception, cognition, and rhetorical concepts. From a perceptual standpoint, users actively seek out visual objects, solve problems, attempt to identify and comprehend context to make sense of the information environment. Cognitively, they engage and desire to make meaning, understand structure, contribute (narrative and dialogic engagement), acquire feedback, and make decisions. Users then filter this information to guide their interactions and reactions to visual information and learn from it. Richey, Klein, and Tracey (2011) quote Mayer's definition of learning as a "relatively permanent change in a person's knowledge or behavior due to experience". Experience, then, is a driving force that supports and promotes learning. Experiential design theory, therefore, informs visual design as a way to promote and sustain user learning and knowledge.

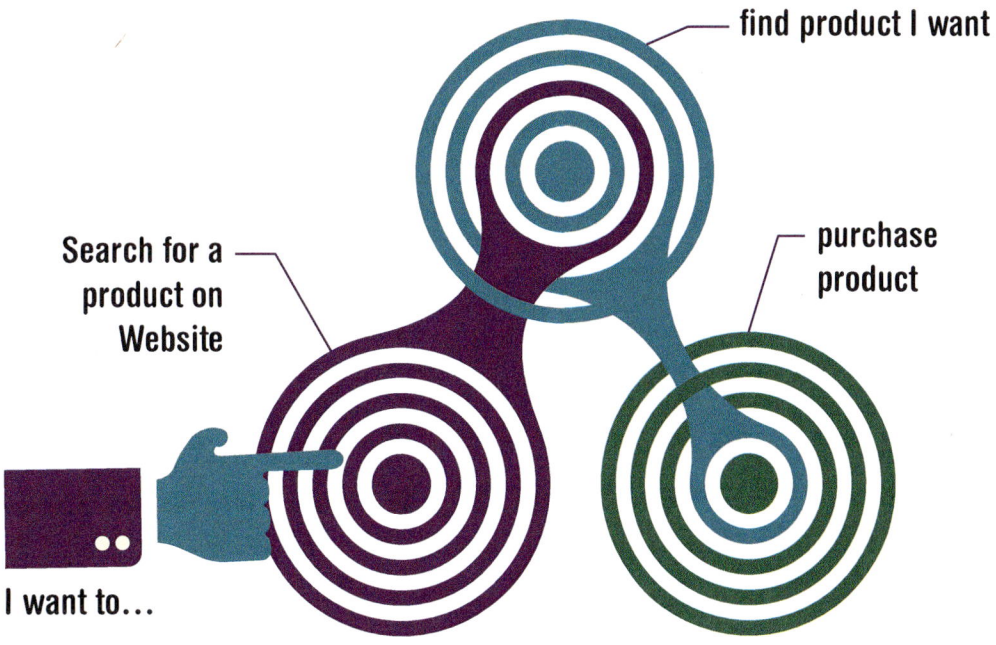
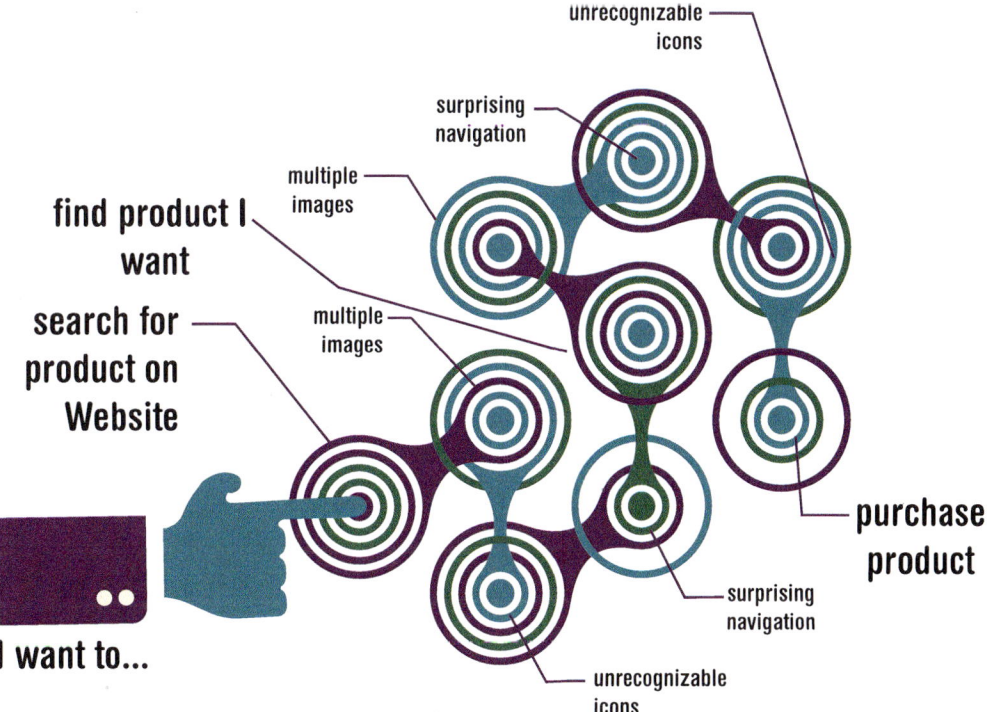

Figure 9.4. The upper example demonstrates a simple and easy cognitive process of searching, finding, and purchasing a product. The lower example demonstrates how cognitive overload can complicate that process and make purchasing a challenge.

Experiential design theory explains how users actually experience information and visual design—that is, how they learn and then act when engaging with an information product. Kolb's cycle of experiential learning provides a good model of a typical learning process works. First, users encounter or experience something new. Next, they reflect on this experience, attempting to place it within a familiar context; then they come to a conclusion about what they have learned. Finally, they experiment with this new knowledge to see how they can apply and transfer it. This cycle of learning repeats with each new encounter. Figure 9.5 illustrates Kolb's Cycle of Learning.

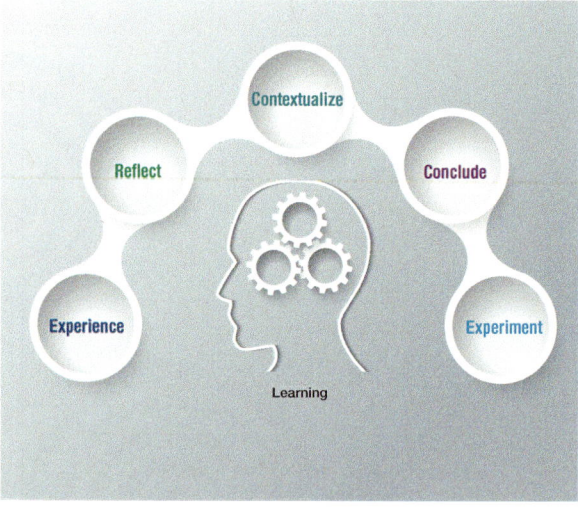

Figure 9.5. Kolb's Cycle of Learning provides a model of five different stages in the learning process.

Experiential learning theory expands the cycle of learning to explain what happens when users' prior interactive experiences cause them to override, differently filter, or alter their responses to visual stimuli. For example, prior experience can change how users navigate Web sites, deciding what to click, avoid, or follow (Baehr, 2002). This is one example of how experiences can influence users' perception and/or cognition of what they see.

Experiential learning theory also suggests that, when users encounter interactive content that is highly visual, it becomes crucial from an accessibility standpoint to provide alternate forms and tools to assist users with specific physical, mental, or perceptual limitations. These users experience information differently. For them, the experience must be accessible in different forms so they can have equivalent, or translatable, experiences. The ultimate goal is to ensure the precise meaning or situational experience is not lost for individuals who access information differently. Experiential design theory provides guidance as technical communicators consider what their users know, what they expect from visual design, and how visual designs promote and support users' experiences of new information.

Color Composition Theory

One of the most basic aspects of design is working with color. Color can be used to communicate meaning, tone, theme, mood, relation, and distinction in technical documents. We perceive differences in color and associate meaning based on them. Our experiences contribute to our collective understanding of the use of color in designs. As a result, color composition theory is an integral component visual information design. Color composition theory refers to the use of color patterns, schemas, values, and combinations to create specific thematic effects (Golbeck, 2005). **Subtractive color** mixes shades of red, blue, and yellow, common in print-based designs. Subtractive color mixes are often labeled as CMYK, which refers to the four inks used: cyan, magenta, yellow, and key (black). **Additive color** (often labeled as RGB) mixes shades of red, green, and blue, which are most often used in computer-based designs. Figure 9.6 illustrates how each of the mixes produces different colors.

Figure 9.6. This figure compares RGB and CMYK color mixes.

Also, in digital publications, hexadecimal values for colors are used, which are composed of six characters (A–F and 0–9); for example, solid white is #FFFFFF while solid black is #000000. The advantage of using hexadecimal values is that most graphic design software programs allow the use of the same values. Named color values or predefined color names which correspond to selected hexadecimal colors (red, blue, lime, magenta, etc.) can also be used to specific colors in digital designs. For more information on digital color use, there are several online color tools and resources available that you can locate online, similar to Figure 9.7.

Some other color composition terms which correspond to different values of individual colors include hue, saturation, tint, and shade. **Hue** refers to the quality or value of a specific color, such as the distinct individual colors shown on the color wheel. **Saturation** is the intensity or vividness of a color, from dull to bright. **Tints** are lighter values of a specific color while shades are darker values of a specific color. Figure 9.8 illustrates hue, saturation, and tint.

Figure 9.7. Charts like this one assist designers in identifying RGB colors and their corresponding hexadecimal values.

Color Schemas

Schemas refer to specific combinations of colors used to produce a specific tone, aesthetic, or desired effect. When using specific color schemes, carefully consider contrast issues when overlapping text, images, and backgrounds, to avoid visual clarity problems. Figure 9.9 describes different types of color schemas while Figure 9.10 provides examples of color palettes, or specific color sets.

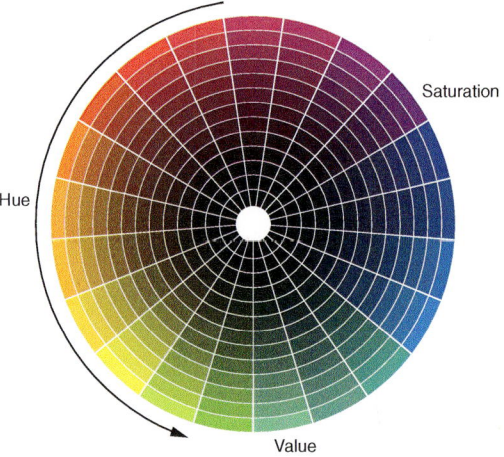

Figure 9.8. Hue, value, and saturation are key color composition terms illustrated in this figure.

While everyone may not be particularly skillful in picking color palettes for designs, a wide variety of color theory resources and tools are available online, which allow you to select individual colors and schemes and provide suggested palettes for design work. Often, designs will incorporate neutral colors (greys, browns, blacks, greys, and whites) to accent, or in place of, other vivid color palette selections.

Monochromatic. One color that can vary in tints, shades, and saturation.
Complementary. Pairs of colors found opposite of each other on the color wheel (i.e., blue and orange, yellow, and violet).
Analogous. Any set of three to five consecutive colors on the color wheel, which tend to provide more minimal contrast in designs.
Temperature. Use of warm (yellow, orange, red) or cool (green, blue, violet) colors to create a mood, tone or feeling in designs.
Harmonious. Selection of colors (dyads, triads, tetrads, etc.) equally spaced apart on the color wheel, usually work well in creating more contrast.

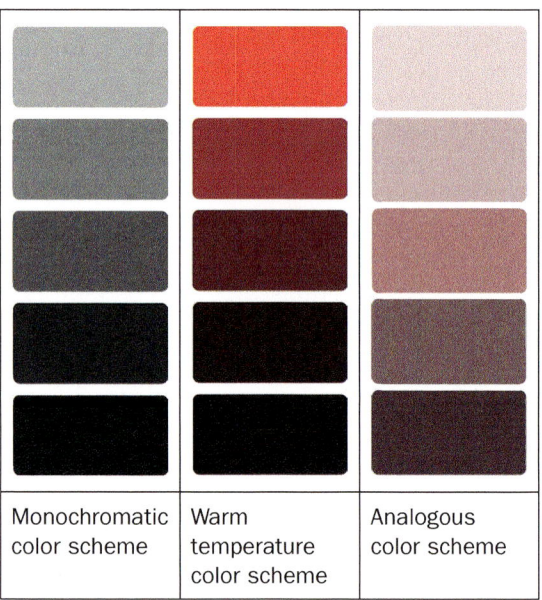

Figure 9.9. Color schema refer to specific combinations. Five common schema are defined here.

Monochromatic color scheme	Warm temperature color scheme	Analogous color scheme

Figure 9.10. Color schemes are common sets of colors that designers use.

> ### EXERCISE 9.2
>
> ### *Researching Color Scheme References and Tools Online*
>
> In preparation for redesigning marketing materials for a company brochure, you have been given the task of creating a series of color palettes (or swatches) that could be used in the overall design of the materials. Working with a company logo of your choice, identify specific colors used in the logo design. Then, using a series of online keyword searches, locate and experiment with some color scheme pickers or references. Using some of the colors you identified from the logo, enter these values into the color scheme tool and generate three different color palettes for consideration. Write a short description for each palette, explaining the overall scheme, theme, and tone of each and present your findings.
>
> **Tasks to be completed:**
>
> 1. Locate a company logo to use for the project. (Pick one with a few distinct colors, if possible).
> 2. Make a list of specific colors used in the logo. You can identify these colors visually or by using an image design software program that has an eyedropper tool that can be used to pick or identify color values.
> 3. Locate online color scheme tools by searching for "color scheme picker" and other relevant search terms using an online search portal of your choice.
> 4. Experiment with a few tools to determine which one you would like to use.
> 5. Using one of the tools, enter some of the color values from your list of logo colors.
> 6. Develop three distinct color palettes (or swatches) that you would consider using in the redesign of the marketing materials.
> 7. Write a short description of each palette and present your findings.

DESIGN PRINCIPLES

Design principles are based broadly in design theories and provide suggested guidance for designing visual information. They help information designers consider the complex interplay between different visual characteristics of images, pages, and documents when developing visual information. These elements may include the important relationships between individual visual styles and elements. Used together, they communicate concepts or other important information to users. These principles assist technical communicators to create more effective design elements. The following four principles are based in the design theories discussed in this chapter, which relate to user perception, cognition, and experiences with regard to visual information.

- **Consistency**—repeatedly using styles to suggest similarity or continuation in relationship between design elements and styles; related to user expectation, they learn and see patterns in documents.
- **Contrast**—using high or low contrast to suggest separation or blending of figure and ground elements in designing visual information; indicates relatedness or distinctiveness between elements.
- **Grouping**—positioning elements to suggest relation or desperate relation between elements, including the use of negative space, borders, shading, and other styles; related to balance, symmetry; suggests form or function, conceptual.

- **Unity**—creating a cohesive whole of design elements, including color, shape, position, theme, and styles; unity addresses the perceptual and cognitive whole effect on the user.

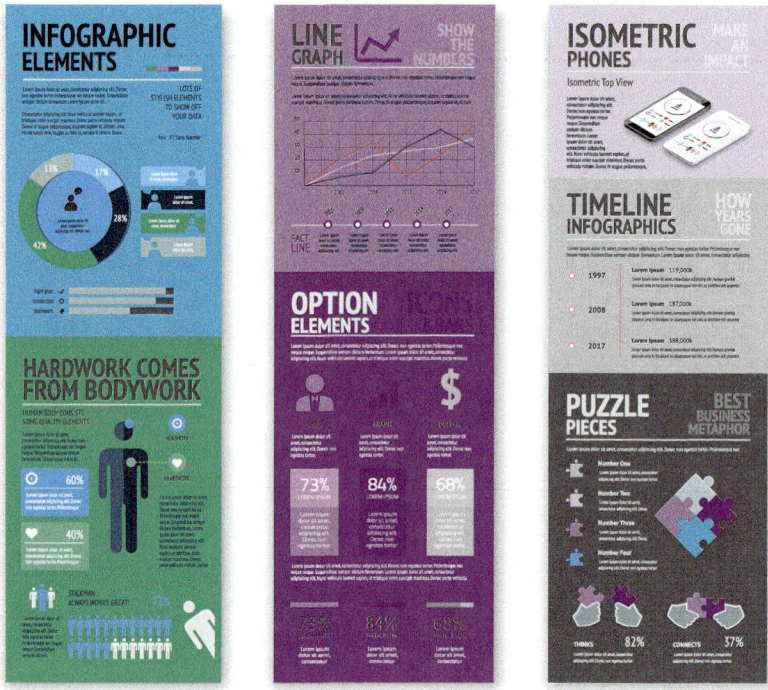

Figure 9.11. These infographics exemplify four basic design principles: consistency, contrast, grouping, and unit.

In Figure 9.11, consistency is demonstrated in the use of font faces and placement of headings at the top of each minigraphic. Contrast is shown using color and shading, in particular in the third column where colors used in the foreground and background enhance readability. Grouping is illustrated in a variety of ways, including the use of color blocking in each column, and also in the placement of icons and shapes near corresponding textual descriptions (as in the black Puzzle Pieces minigraphic). Finally, unity is demonstrated in use of column sizes, spacing, and use of visual images in each individual minigraphic that unifies the design of the entire illustration.

In addition, two other important factors to consider when applying design principles to your information products include accessibility and aesthetic considerations, which can help in making specific design choices and result in more effective and professional design products.

Accessibility Considerations

As discussed in previous chapters, accessibility has become increasingly important, in particular, with online publications and other online content. Its importance extends to information design. Regulatory guidelines dictate rules for creating accessible online content, much of which applies to visual information products. These guidelines include the U.S.

Government Section 508 accessibility guidelines and the World Wide Web Consortium's Web Content Accessibility Guidelines. While these guidelines were primarily developed for online content accessibility, they also can be applied more broadly to other types of technical information products. The only mandated regulation with regard to accessibility is the use of publicly accessible information on a U.S. Government Web site, but remember that these guidelines also apply to any organization that receives federal funds. Otherwise, accessibility guidelines and their implementation are only required at the discretion of the organization in which you work. Whether these guidelines regulate your information product or not, you should consider whether you want your information to be accessible to all users or just a few. The more accessible your content, the more broader your audience will be.

Several important accessibility guidelines pertain to color, alternative graphics, labeling, and accommodating assistive technologies. With regard to design, any use of color to communicate meaning must accommodate limitations in color perception. For example, if a topographic map used colors to denote different temperature zones or elevations, a designer might render the map using higher contrasting colors, hatch patterns, shading, or other descriptors. In general, to accommodate users with visual impairments, providing alternate content is essential to ensure they have access to the same information. Writing descriptions or providing large-format versions of visual content for assistive technologies, such as screen readers and magnification tools, are other alternatives. Also, it may be necessary to use descriptive headers, captions, and labels where appropriate for content presented as tables, charts, graphs, or in other visual formats. For more information on accessibility guidelines, see the U.S. Government Section 508 Web site at http://www.section508.gov or the World Wide Web Consortium Web Site at http://www.w3.org.

EXERCISE 9.3

Researching Accessibility Guidelines Related to Information Design

To learn more about how accessibility guidelines apply to the development of visual information, research the two sets of standards available for designing online publications. Select either the U.S. Government Section 508 Web site at http://www.section508.gov or the World Wide Web Consortium Web Site at http://www.w3.org. Search for the accessibility guidelines on either site and make a list of specifications that would apply for designing visual information. Consider how each item you list would affect the development of an analytical report and an informational Web site. Make a list of design conventions or rules you would follow in developing each of the two products.

Tasks to be completed:

1. Select a set of accessibility guidelines from either the U. S. Government Section 508 Web site at http://www.section508.gov or the World Wide Web Consortium Web Site at http://www.w3.org.
2. Search for the accessibility guidelines on either site and read them.
3. Make a list of each item that would apply to the design of visual information.
4. Identify the kinds of visual information included in both an analytical report and an informational Web site.
5. Make a list of design conventions or rules you would need to consider in developing visual information for both of these products.
6. Share your findings with others by developing an informal presentation.

Aesthetic Considerations

Another critical, yet difficult, characteristic of design involves aesthetics, or personal preferences about what makes a design attractive or beautiful. Different audiences may also have differing aesthetic preferences that may need to be addressed in editing and revising information design products. Aesthetics are highly subjective and can be difficult to ascertain, because they are often tacit, personal, and even cultural preferences. They can be highly individualized or specialized based on the expectations of specific groups of users. They also may be based on experiences with other designs, documents, or content. When making decision about color, you should also consider cultural associations with color. Users from cultures different from yours may associate different meanings with colors. For example, in many Eastern countries, brides wear red, representing happiness while, in Western countries, brides typically wear white, representing purity. The color yellow can mean cowardice to Americans while it means courage to Japanese. Even in the same culture, colors can have conflicting meanings. For example, Americans associate red with love but also with anger. Given the complexity of color associations, color is an extremely important consideration for any kind of visual design. To address this concern, you may need to include managers, production editors, team leads, or others responsible for reviewing, editing, developing, or producing the product you are designing.

As a visual designer, you might account for aesthetic considerations through user research, feedback, or even use cases or profiles to determine trends in aesthetic preferences and expectations. This work may involve copious data collection, but it still may be unsuccessful in accounting for every user and preference. For online or interactive content, offering personalization options for design, including color schemes and layouts, can permit users to select their own design themes. Also, providing multiple design options for users to choose from could be another method of attempting to address some aesthetic preferences with regard to design. Conducting product research or benchmarking research to collect information on standards, consistent practices, or other design techniques that are characteristic of specific products or media may be helpful techniques. Ultimately, the decision on how to handle aesthetic preference will fall on the designer, organizational standards, and selected user feedback.

DEVELOPING VISUAL INFORMATION GRAPHICS

Information graphics are an essential part of technical documents and serve a variety of functions. Technical documents often incorporate the use of information graphics as data displays, visual evidence, or as thematic or decorative elements. As **data displays**, they can show relational aspects between data sets, statistical information, volume quantities, parts in relation to the whole, frequency, area, location, descriptive details, or other patterns or distinguishing characteristics. As **visual evidence**, information graphics can show photo-realism, drawings, illustrations, figures, cross-sections, or other important details. As **thematic or decorative elements**, information graphics can include clip art or other visual elements that contribute to a specific graphic theme, tone, brand, or identity.

Information graphics also serve as an important supplement to technical documents. They help make arguments, support decisions, illustrate trends, or act as supporting evidence using visual means. Graphics help visual learners better understand the textual content by breaking up text-heavy documents. They also help establish a relational aspect between textual and visual content that aids comprehension or understanding. Finally, they can provide thematic or unifying design elements for technical documents. Figure 9.12 illustrates different kinds of information graphics.

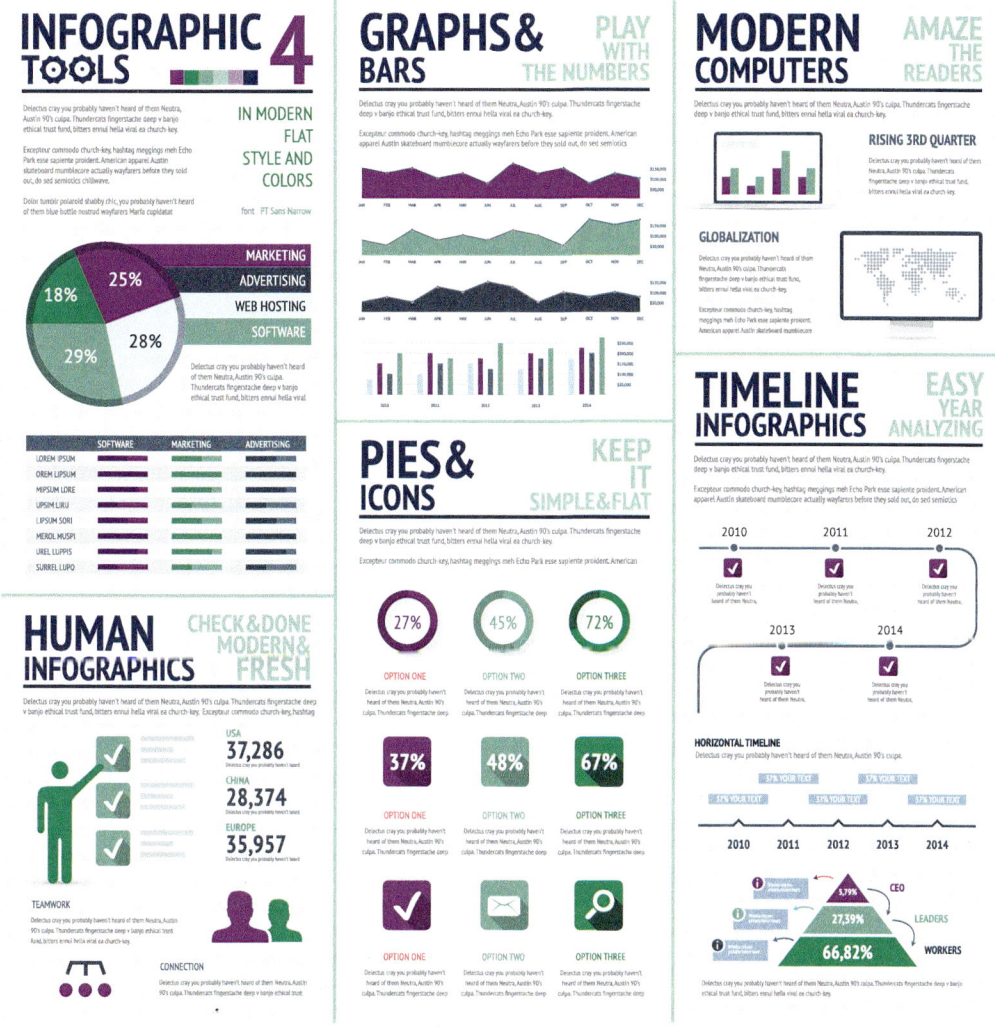

Figure 9.12. Complex infographic depicting sample pie chart, table, pictograph, bar and area graphs, and timeline.

Creating Information Graphics from Raw Data

In preparation for creating information graphics for your technical documents, do some preparatory and planning work. First, make sure you have the data you need available and organized in some fashion, such as a table or columns. Second, check and verify the data for accuracy and correctness to eliminate any possible errors. Third, decide what information you want to show with your graphics, considering the appropriate graphic type and what you want to emphasize (each of these are discussed below). And finally, decide what software programs or tools you are going to use to develop your information graphics.

Tables

Tables show individual values for multiple data sets, organizing data into rows and columns. They are organized in a logical pattern, such as numerically, alphabetically, categorically, etc. Headings or significant cells can be highlighted for added emphasis.

Graphs

Graphs include a wide range of information graphic types, including bar, line, pie, scatter, and others. They are generally used to show trends or relationships between data sets. Line graphics show individual data points and trends over time. Bar graphs show volume quantities or trends. Pie graphs show parts in relation to the whole, or percentages. Scatter graphs show relations between clusters of points, or anomalies.

Charts

Charts are used to illustrate processes or functions. An example is a flow chart, which shows organizational, processes, relationships between individuals, functions, or tasks.

Complex

Complex information graphics are often customized to fit specific purposes, information needs, or in some cases, combine multiple graphics into a single display. Graphic data mashup displays incorporate multiple sources of data and graphic types and combine them into a single presentation or image. Some examples can be found using an online search from the Center for Graphic Facilitation Web site (http://graphicfacilitation.blogs.com) or tool like Piktochart (http://piktochart.com/).

Photographs and Illustrations

Photos show realistic details, where the importance of resolution, color depth, and clarity are essential to communicate information. Graphic illustrations show details, which are not necessarily photo-realistic, but appear in sketch, draft, or cross-section form. They typically are used to illustrate concepts, processes, or working sketches. Samples are shown in Figure 9.13.

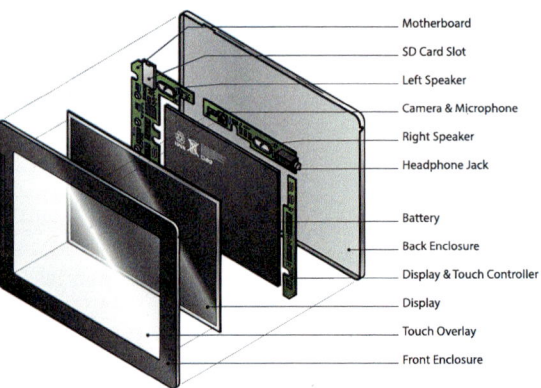

Figure 9.13. The tablet in this figure is depicted as a photograph, a simple illustration, and an exploded diagram.

Integrating Information Graphics into Technical Documents

You may use a variety of methods to incorporate graphic elements into your documents, including placement, captioning and labeling, and cross-referencing. Throughout this chapter, and others, you probably have noted that each image has a caption: a figure or table number followed by a title and description. This section provides further information on how to integrate graphics successfully into your technical documents.

Graphic Placement

Graphics should be placed within the margins of the document, in most cases. They should conform to style guidelines, consistent with other like types throughout the document. They are typically placed in-text or between text, and after their reference in the text. Larger graphics placed on pages of their own. In technical reports, sections typically should not end with a graphic.

Captioning and Labeling

Information graphics should be captioned, unless thematic or decorative elements. Labels typically include the words "table" or "figure." Use legends to illustrate differences in individual data sets. Consistent labeling schemes should be used throughout the document for each graphic. These schemes are typically numerical, sometimes by chapter and element number. Graphics should have a short descriptive title, and, optionally, they may include a short description, typically from one to a few sentences long. Also, be sure to include proper citation, author name and year in parenthesis, parallel citation in the works cited or references section, and, if necessary, signed (and/or paid) permissions for use.

Referencing and Citing

Information graphics should be referenced in the text, prior to their placement, in most cases, unless they are thematic or decorative elements. If not explicitly discussed in narrative, a reference and appropriate label are required elements. Also, appropriate citation, including author last name or document title, and year, are necessary, along with any signed or paid permissions fee for use.

Rendering Graphics

When rendering, or generating, information graphics, it is also important to consider different image file formats (.gif, .jpg, and .png) and their unique characteristics, such as color depth, compression rates, animation, and transparency properties. For information graphics used in online publications, screen resolution (number of pixels per square inch) is important to consider as well, when determining image type, size and quality. Table 9.1 illustrates the relationships between file format and their unique characteristics.

File format	Color depth	Compression	Animation	Transparency
.gif	256 colors	Low	Yes	One color
.jpg	Full color	Variable	No	No transparency
.png	Full color	High	No	Both multicolor and semi-transparency

Table 9.1. Three commonly used image file formats are shown here with their distinguishing characteristics.

Additional Guidelines

In addition, consider these important strategies when incorporating graphics into your technical documents. First, all visual content should have a purpose in the document. Creating graphics for the sake of filling space or including information the audience does not need is usually not the best practice. Second, visual content should enrich or complement textual content, not simply repeat it. The reverse is also true: textual descriptions should not simply repeat what the visual depicts. Descriptions should point out what you want the user to see, but they should not completely describe the graphic. Third, visuals should reflect consistency in the design standards set by the stylesheet, template or visual identity of the product. Follow conventions appropriate to the information product, its audience, purpose, and constraints. More information on stylesheets, templates, and product identities is provided in the next section. Fourth, developers should consider unity in the overall visual design of graphics, including their integration into the document. Allow other existing design theories and principles to inform your design practices. Finally, many software programs and tools are available to create information graphics and have templates or wizards to help you design and develop them. When using these tools, consider two factors: customization (everyone uses them, do not make yours look like the rest) and editing (make stylistic and design changes appropriate for conventions and principles).

EXERCISE 9.4

Information Graphic Analysis

Research information graphics online that depict average household Internet use. These graphics might depict user statistics such as average speed, bandwidth, user demographics, tasks, programs, times, etc. Select either a single graphic, or a single page of multiple graphics, which could use improvement. Evaluate the use of design principles, conventions, colors, and strategies used to develop the graphic(s). Make a list of specific strengths and criticisms of the graphic(s). Identify specific changes you would make to improve the overall graphic(s) quality and presentation.

Tasks to be completed:

1. Conduct online research and locate information graphics that depict statistical data on household Internet usage.
2. Select a single graphic, or single page of multiple graphics, which could use improvement in their display and/or design.
3. Evaluate the graphic(s) in terms of their use of design principles, conventions, colors, and strategies.
4. List strengths and weaknesses.
5. Identify specific recommendations and changes to improve the effectiveness of the graphic(s).

DEVELOPING DESIGN STYLE SHEETS, TEMPLATES, AND VISUAL IDENTITIES

Design conventions are prescriptive rules and guidelines based on user expectation, practices, standards, and/or rules. Often these rules are incorporated into stylesheets and design templates (Baehr, 2007).

Stylesheets

Stylesheets provide a list of consistent conventions and standards to follow for a specific technical document or product family. They include specifications on the uses of color, images, styles, and layout, which dictate the distinguishing characteristics of textual, visual, and spatial elements of technical documents. Typically, they are a single document, seen only by the development team. They are used in producing consistent styles in a document. Stylesheets can be applied globally to all documents in a collection or locally to an individual line, page, or single document. Some electronic stylesheet languages such as Cascading Style Sheets (CSS) can be used as well as other Web development tools available to assist in creating online stylesheets.

Templates

Templates are organizational patterns or layouts of individual pages, documents, or interfaces. Templates are used to help create and design consistent document formats, which help users' comprehension and usability of documents. Templates can be as simple as forms, outlines, worksheets, or even blank documents, which are formatted consistently to a specific set of stylesheet standards. You are probably familiar with templates for résumés and memorandums, which are commonly available in word-processing software.

Layouts and Visual Identities

Designing an interface layout involves the selection, arrangement and interactive nature of the elements that comprise the screen layout of Web pages for users. The interface creates a coherent whole from its unique visual, spatial, and graphic characteristics (Baehr, 2007). Interface work has progressed into a more modular layout, primarily due to the use of content management systems, personalized content, information modeling theory, and also scripting languages such as Cascading Style Sheets (CSS).

Figure 9.14. This set of images illustrates how corporate identities evolve from a unified set of styles, graphics, and layouts.

Like interface designs, visual identities are complex sets of visuals. (See Figure 9.14.) Visual identities are used to create a unified visual theme for a technical document or information product through consistent styles, graphics, and layouts. In a corporate context, visual identities help to brand a company and its products. Visual identities include information such as the colors, images, styles, layouts, and other specific guidelines for all media types, which comprise the visual identity for the company, organization, or entity. The Logodesignlove Web site (http://www.logodesignlove.com/brand-identity-style-guides) provides a lengthy list of sample style guides from around the world. Included in these style guides are all of the visual identity elements listed in Table 9.2 as well as other design elements. To see examples, visit the site to explore how brands created their unique identities through these visual elements.

Element	Examples
Color	Color schemes, color palettes
Images	Specific graphics, file formats, sizes
Styles	Headings, margins, fonts, text decoration
Layout	Spacing, page layouts or grids

Table 9.2. Visual Identity Elements and Examples.

EXERCISE 9.5
Creating a Visual Identity

You have been assigned the task of designing a new visual identity for the annual report for a company. Your job is to locate the most recent copy of a report and research any visual identity guidelines available. Then, your task is to create an updated visual identify, with specific conventions on use of colors, images, styles, and layouts. Include items listed for each of the four categories listed below, in addition to any others you wish to add.

Color: primary and secondary color palettes, color schemes
Images: logos, thematic graphics, or other images used, sizes and formats, resolutions
Styles: font faces, font sizes, colors, for all heading levels, including standard text
Layout: spacing, margins, justification, indentation, grid layouts

Write a short document that provides a name, short description, and specifics for each of these four categories. Include visual examples for each, as appropriate.

Tasks to be completed:

1. Locate an annual report for a company, using keyword searching on the Internet, or other method.
2. If possible, locate information on the visual identity guidelines for the document, or a general list for the company. Alternately, you could research other documents or Web sites the company has and look for trends in the design elements used.
3. Create an updated visual identity for the company's report, using your knowledge of design principles, conventions, and any online tools, such as color pickers.
4. Write a short document for the new visual identity, including the name, short description, and specifics for each of the four categories, with supporting examples.

Chapter Summary

Developing effective visual communication products requires and understanding of the underlying theories, conventions, and practices related to visual design. Design involves creating meaningful visual content for the purpose of displaying data, illustrating, creating templates, and visual identities for technical documents and their respective organizations.

Design theories help inform the specific design principles and conventions used in creating visual information. Informed by these theories, design principles include unity, consistency, grouping, and contrast. Design conventions vary widely, but they are more prescriptive or specific guidelines for using individual style elements and spacing rules. Equally important considerations include color theory, accessibility issues, and aesthetics. Collectively, these design aspects can help technical communicators design and create effective visual information products.

Stylesheets provide a list of consistent conventions and standards to follow for a specific technical document or product family. They include specifications on the uses of color, images, styles, and layout, which dictate the distinguishing characteristics of textual, visual, and spatial elements of technical documents. Templates and interface designs are organizational patterns or layouts of individual pages, documents, or interfaces. They are used to help create and design consistent document formats, which help users' comprehension and usability of documents. Visual identities help establish branding for documents, and encompass all aspects of design for a technical document or product and include all the details and aspects of a design from the individual graphic level to the page level to the document level and even to the product family. They include specifications on the specific colors, image characteristics, styles, layouts, and other specific guidelines for all media types, which comprise the visual identity for the company, organization, or entity.

Without an understanding of the theories, principles, and practices of designing effective visual communication products, the standardized templates, tools, processes, and structures we use in content design creation are only marginally successful and useful in technical documents and information products. Therefore, effective visual information design requires an understanding of the underlying theories, conventions, and practices, as well as knowledge of the specific document you are developing.

Chapter Assignments

The exercises in this section ask you to apply what you have learned in this chapter as well as explore how this knowledge applies to and connects with other information in the textbook.

1. Locate a company Web site online and examine its documentation paying particular attention to the design aspects. Make a list of the consistent styles, design conventions, color schemes, and other design elements that comprise the visual identity of the company. Evaluate the company's visual identity in terms of its use of design principles and overall effectiveness. Identify any improvements or changes that might improve the company's design presence.

2. What are your design preferences as both a user and creator of original visual content? Browse the Internet for examples of design work that best illustrates your own design aesthetic. Also, consider work you have created on your own. Make a list of specific styles, color schemes, layouts, and other characteristics that represent your own preferences when designing pages, documents, and other forms of visual content. If you had to challenge yourself to work outside of these styles, what specific changes would you make to stretch yourself creatively? Make a list and share your findings with others.

3. After reading the section on visual information graphics in this chapter, perform an online search for 'graphic data mashups'. Select an example of one and analyze its effectiveness in terms of design principles, selection of graphic types, color palette, and overall usefulness in conveying its information. Make a list of strengths and improvements for the graphic, and then, redesign any piece of it based on your suggestions.

Figure Credits

Figure 9.1. © everything possible/Shutterstock.com

Figure 9.2. © Rawpixel/Shutterstock.com

Figure 9.3. © Bobbijo Harrison

Figure 9.4. Image © Shutterstock, Inc.

Figure 9.5. Images © Shutterstock, Inc. Modified by the authors.

Figure 9.6. © Claudiu Mihai Badea/Shutterstock.com

Figure 9.7. © Vector Department/Shutterstock.com

Figure 9.8. © Ola-ola/Shutterstock.com

Figure 9.10. Images © Shutterstock, Inc.

Figure 9.11. © MPFphotography/Shutterstock.com

Figure 9.12. © MPFphotography/Shutterstock.com

Figure 9.13. Images © Shutterstock, Inc.

Figure 9.14. © AD Hunter/Shutterstock.com

Corresponding

10

CHAPTER OVERVIEW

This chapter introduces you to common forms of professional correspondence. After reading this chapter, you should be able to meet the following objectives:

- Distinguish between personal and professional correspondence.
- Identify the two most common purposes for professional correspondence.
- Describe common structural features of professional correspondence.
- Identify and write different kinds of request and response to request correspondence.
- Choose an appropriate correspondence format.
- Explain the affordances and constraints of print and electronic correspondence.

The term "correspondence" has been used to describe communication between individuals through hand-written or printed letters since the 16th century. Originally, the term meant "to communicate with" and, more specifically, "to communicate with letters." In modern usage, we still associate correspondence with hand-written or printed communication between individuals. Correspondence used in organizations includes **letters** to correspond with individuals outside the organization, **memorandums** (or **memos**) to correspond with others inside the organization, and electronic messages, such as **email** and **texts**, to communicate both inside and outside the organization. Printed letters and memos are still frequently used for official communications, such as records of business transactions, decisions, commendations, and disciplinary actions; however, electronic messages are also sometimes being used for these purposes now. Individuals and organizations store and keep these important communications for legal and historical documentation of both immediate and long-term importance.

Figure 10.1. Although less common today than electronic correspondence, print correspondence is still used for most official documents, such as contracts and commendations.

Correspondence has had an important role in organizational communication for centuries. Today, corresponding with printed letters and memos has a quaint, almost old-fashioned feel. This change in attitude has directly resulted from the ubiquity, convenience, and speed of electronic (or digital) correspondence. Postal delivery, even express mail, takes 24 or more hours to reach a recipient whereas electronic documents, such as faxes, text messages, and emails, are delivered almost instantaneously. In addition to slower delivery times, both letters and memorandums require production, storage, and monetary resources (paper, ink, printers, stamps, filing cabinets, and human resources to file and then find files when needed) that electronic communications do not. Electronic correspondence requires little more than a device (phone, tablet, or computer) and a connection to the Internet. Although electronic resources can be costly, devices provide us with instant connectivity whether we are using them for personal or professional correspondence. Corresponding with others has never been easier than it is today: electronic correspondence technologies allow us tell others in writing where we are, what we are doing, and who is with us. Electronic messages, however, have not completely replaced print correspondence. When time is not so important, corresponding with printed mailed letters is still common. This printed correspondence may be official documents, such as a letter of acceptance to a college or university, or important notices, such as an increase in your credit card interest rate or an automotive recall notice. You may also receive letters soliciting your support in your mailbox as well as formal and informal invitations to community and social events.

EXERCISE 10.1

Everyday Correspondence

Use this exercise to identify the kinds of correspondence you receive on a daily basis:

1. As you collect your postal mail over the next two days, keep track of the kinds of printed letters you receive: How many letters have you received? What kinds of letters have you received? Who sent you the letters? What kinds of actions do these letters ask you to take?
2. Over the same period of time, track the kinds of email you receive: How many emails have you received? What kinds of emails have you received? Who sent you the emails? What kinds of actions do these emails ask you to take?

Compare the two kinds of correspondence: what conclusions can you draw about the frequency and type of correspondence you receive on a daily basis? What else did you learn by conducting this survey of everyday correspondence?

Tasks to be completed:

Over two days, collect and record the following:

1. Number and kinds of printed letters you receive in the mail. Note who sends them and what actions they ask you to take.
2. Number and kinds of email you receive in the mail. Note who sends them and what actions they ask you to take.
3. Compare your results and draw conclusions about the uses of printed and electronic correspondence you receive. Prepare to discuss your findings in class.

This chapter describes correspondence types that are still fairly common in the workplace, whether they are delivered in print and electronic media: good news, bad news, thank you notes, recommendations, and transmittal letters. It also includes a short section on printed letter and memo layouts. The final section of the chapter, however, focuses on electronic correspondence—emails and text messages, primarily—which, in most organizations, have supplanted the need for print communications.

Figure 10.2. Mobile devices make electronic correspondence available from almost anywhere.

Electronic correspondence can be challenging to write because novice workplace communicators have extensive knowledge of using these technologies for personal communication but less knowledge of how their use changes in professional settings. The chapter concludes with a brief discussion of advantages and disadvantages that accompany electronic correspondence.

WRITING AND CRITIQUING PROFESSIONAL CORRESPONDENCE

Whether the message arrives by print or electronic means, most professional correspondence is designed for one of two purposes: to request the reader do something or to respond to a request. Within these two categories are many variations, depending on the action requested. In fact, sometimes these messages are almost hidden from the reader. You might, for example, receive a letter in the mail informing you about a new restaurant or yard service with a coupon attached. The content of the message may look informative, but its purpose is an indirect request and invitation to learn more. Although the content of these messages can vary widely, almost all correspondence has a common structure: an introduction, a middle section, and a conclusion. Each of these parts has a common function:

- Introductions provide context for the correspondence. They introduce the writer, politely seek the goodwill of the reader, and state the purpose or reason for the contact.
- Middle sections provide explanation for the contact.
- Conclusions maintain goodwill, restate the purpose, and offer information for further contact.

If you understand the two basic purposes that drive correspondence and the common structure, you can successfully write a print or electronic document that achieves either goal.

Writing a Request

Writers use correspondence to communicate many kinds of requests or actions. When you want a job, you write to request an interview. When you have a complaint about a product or service, you ask for a replacement, a refund, or some other consideration. When you want someone to support a cause you believe in, you describe your cause and ask others to give their support, time, or money to further it. You might also use correspondence to ask for support for others, such as when you write recommendations for people or products. All of these requests require you to be persuasive, to explain the purpose of your request, and to provide reasons why action is necessary or desirable. While each type of request will vary in content, the general content of a letter of request is fairly simple:

- In the introduction, open with a few sentences of background explaining why you are writing: *Who are you? Why have you written this person in particular, and what do you want him or her to do?* Even if your request is challenging, seek the favor of your reader from the start. As you write these opening sentences, remember that everyone responds more positively to goodwill than to anger or animosity. Follow your goodwill opening with a statement of purpose, your reason for writing. Specifically, include a sentence or two that states your request: *What action are you requesting?*

- In the middle of the message, detail the request specifically and explain the reasoning behind it: *What do you want the reader to do? Why should the reader take this action? What reasons do you have for requesting this action?* In this section, highlight the reasons that are the most persuasive and organize these reasons for the greatest impact.

- The closing section of the request is often called a "Call to Action" because it ends the request message and directs the reader to take the requested action. Additionally, when you write the final paragraph, you should return to the goodwill expressed in the opening paragraphs by thanking the reader for considering your request. The conclusion should reiterate what you want, discuss benefits or outcomes that will result if the reader takes the action, and include your contact information, in case the person needs further information.

The simplicity of the request content outline, however, hides the difficulty that can be involved in writing a request. Many challenges reside within this easy outline. Here are just a few examples that illustrate how difficult requests can be:

- **Complaints, Claims, and Adjustments**. You might write a complaint to make a claim about a damaged product or to seek an adjustment for an overcharge or mischarge. Whatever the case, satisfied people do not write complaint letters. The challenge with complaints is managing your dissatisfaction with the person or product. To meet this challenge, start by gaining the goodwill of readers so they will be predisposed to help you. An angry or demeaning introduction will turn off your readers and lessen your chances of success. A detailed description of the problem that resulted in your complaint can also be convincing. Do your research before you write, and provide as much description as possible outlining the problem and action you want to resolve it. Use logic, not anger, to convince your reader that action is necessary.

- **Recall Notices**. Recall notices are challenging because they require you to admit that your product is problematic and to convince the reader to take an action to repair or replace the product. Recalls must clearly detail the product (e.g., make and model), describe the potential problem, identify the part or parts that require repair or replacement, and warn the reader of potential consequences if action is not taken. Readers need to be able to understand why the recall is necessary, what needs to be done, and when and how to take action. Because product recalls typically involve human safety, the federal government has regulations for how recalls are written and delivered to consumers. Knowing federal regulations and abiding by them is essential when writing recall notices.

- **Recommendations.** Unlike complaints and recall notices, recommendations are more positive in nature. When you recommend a person or review a product, you are telling others that they should take your word about someone or something. You are encouraging them to purchase a product, accept a student to their program, or award a scholarship. To convince someone to take this action, you must not only convince them that the person or produce is excellent, but also you must convince them that you are reliable and trustworthy. Including information in the opening paragraphs that establishes your credibility is essential to success in this type of request.

EXERCISE 10.2

Invite the Governor to an Event

Many United States governors' offices use a similar form to allow their constituents to invite them to an event. This form requires constituents to provide information to their governor's office to help the office determine if the governor will be able to attend. Using a search engine and the terms "invite the governor to your event," locate one of these forms and visit it.

As you review the form, analyze how the required information fulfills the requirements for a good request message. Where is the background information for the request? Which parts of the form provide good reasons for why the governor should attend? What kinds of reasons does the governor's office prioritize? Why? What information is used for contact purposes? What kind of attachment would be best to include with the form?

Tasks to be completed:

1. Use a search engine and the terms "invite the governor to your event" to locate a form.
2. Review the form and answer these questions:
   a. Where is the background information for the request?
   b. Which parts of the form provide good reasons for why the governor should attend?
   c. What kinds of reasons does the governor's office prioritize? Why?
   d. What information is used for contact purposes?
   e. What kind of attachment would be best to include as an attachment to the form?
3. Bring your findings to class to discuss how the form's contents fulfill the requirements for a letter of request.

Critiquing a Request Message

If you are struggling to find the right tone and organization for your request message, you can find examples of standard formats and templates for requests on the Internet using search terms such as "letter of request," "job cover letter," and "complaint letter." You can even find examples of consumer complaint letters and a complaint wizard on the United States Government's Web site that will walk you through the complaint-writing process (http://www.usa.gov/topics/consumer/complaint/complaint-letter.shtml). While forms and wizards are helpful for gathering information for your request, you will need to know how to modify examples for your particular communication purpose and need. If you are writing at work, you will likely find that your organization has developed its own conventions, formats, and recommended organizations for requests. Ask a peer or supervisor if examples of past request are available.

Because there is no set form for every situation that requires you to write a request, you need to be able to find your own examples and critique their effectiveness. You can start your search on the internet or on your workplace intranet. Wherever your search begins, you will need a strategy for critiquing the effectiveness of letters of request examples that you locate.

Evaluating a Request
The following checklist will help you to evaluate the effectiveness of request correspondence you find or create:

1. Evaluate the introduction
   - ☐ Does the writer introduce himself or herself in the introduction?
   - ☐ Does the introduction state the request?
   - ☐ Does the introduction provide background for the request?
2. Evaluate the request detail and reasons for the request
   - ☐ Does the writer provide explanation and detail for the request?
   - ☐ Does the writer explain why the requested action is necessary or needed?
   - ☐ Are the reasons in the explanation convincing?
   - ☐ Are they prioritized and organized effectively?
3. Evaluate the conclusion
   - ☐ Does the conclusion seek the goodwill of the reader?
   - ☐ Does the conclusion reiterate the requested action?
   - ☐ Does the conclusion state benefits or outcomes of the action?
   - ☐ Does the conclusion include contact information for the writer?

> ## EXERCISE 10.3
>
> ### Critiquing Letters of Request
>
> Using the internet, find two or three examples of written requests. To locate these examples, use search terms such as "letter of request," "consumer complaint letter," "product recall letter," "recommendation letter," or "product review." Bookmark the location of these examples or save a copy for later reference. Using the checklist for evaluating a request, determine how effective each example is. Prepare to share and discuss your examples with your class.
>
> **Tasks to be completed:**
>
> 1. Locate written requests online using the above search terms.
> 2. Bookmark the location of two or three examples.
> 3. Use the checklist for evaluating a request to determine the effectiveness of each request.
> 4. Prepare to discuss your evaluation in class.

Writing a Response to a Request

If requesting action is a frequent purpose of correspondence, then responding to requests is equally as important. The challenge of writing a response is recognizing what kind of response is appropriate.

Some response correspondence relays information about a decision to act. When you are asked to do something, you typically react positively or negatively. That is, you decide either to act or not to act. Whatever your decision, you need to be able to relay your decision in a way that is courteous and professional. Correspondence that does the work of responding to action requests is typically called "good news" or "bad news" responses.

Figure 10.3. Requesting action and responding to requests are two frequent purposes of correspondence.

Other correspondence responds to a request for information. These requests can range broadly from requests for job applicants to requests for proposals to provide a service. To respond to these requests, you will need to create specific document, such as a résumé or a proposal. To submit that document, you will also need a cover letter, which is more formally called a letter of transmittal. Cover letters accompany other, usually longer, documents and provide information about the additional contents.

A third category of response comes at the end of a communication exchange: this category is the final message of appreciation, or thank you note. Messages of appreciation or thanks are useful for creating and maintaining relationships with individuals in your personal and professional networks. All of these types of response messages are described in more detail in this section.

Good News Responses

When you respond positively to a request, you are saying "Yes, I'll act as you request." To begin, you will start a good news response with a quick introduction of yourself and your purpose for writing. This opening move provides context for the reader. Then you may move directly to stating the news. Following the direct statement of the good news, you should describe exactly what you have agreed to do and, if necessary, discuss any conditions that will limit your ability to act. These kinds of responses are usually short, unless the conditions are extensive.

To illustrate how good news responses work, think about the complaint requests described in the previous section. Imagine that you have received a complaint about an overcharge on an online purchase. The writer of the complaint includes a copy of the purchase receipt and a credit card statement showing that the product was double-charged. You investigate the complaint and discover that the person was double-charged, so you respond with a good news message. Your message opens with your positive findings. You follow this opening with a detailed explanation of actions you will take to correct the problem, and you close with another statement of goodwill, thanking the person for their business and offering to answer further questions about the claim. It is that simple.

Similarly, think about the letter you received when you were accepted in your university. That, too, was a good news response. It probably started with an announcement that you had been accepted and a statement that welcomed you to the university. What followed was a detailed explanation of the conditions of your acceptance and a list of actions to take if you plan to accept the invitation. After explaining next steps, the letter likely closed with another goodwill statement, encouraging you to join others in the entering class.

Bad News Responses

Good news responses are relatively easy to write; unfortunately, you cannot respond positively to all requests. Sometimes you must say "no." In these situations, you need to know how to give someone a bad news message. Writing a bad news response is tricky because you have to disappoint your reader while, at the same time, maintaining goodwill.

As you have probably noticed with other correspondence suggestions, the key to a bad news response is the opening paragraph, in which you gain the goodwill of the person with whom you are corresponding but without directly stating the bad news. As you did with the good news response, start this message with context-setting information. Tell the reader who you are. Follow this introductory information with an indirect buffer statement related to the request. One strategy for this buffering statement is to start the letter with a description of the initial request; this description provides the reader with context for the message. Another strategy is to make a personal connection, thanking the person for the request or, more specifically, for some underlying idea behind the request, such as product loyalty.

Moving to the second paragraph, begin by explaining why you cannot fulfill the request; explain what is preventing you from a positive response. In stating your reasons, be as detailed as possible. After you have outlined your reasons for rejecting the request, state the bad news. Using this order—reasoning or explanation then negative response—adds another buffer before the bad news.

In the end, try to regain goodwill. You may conclude the bad news response with a consolation of some kind, a small token of appreciation. For example, if you are responding to a product request, you might offer a coupon or free service to maintain good relations. Even if you are unable to offer a token of appreciation, be generous and thank the person for contacting you.

Bad news responses are common when a requested service cannot be provided, such as a repair or replacement of a flawed product. They are also common in job searches and in other situations where everyone cannot be selected. The key to writing a bad news message is to recognize that the message you are delivering is a negative one so it should be buffered in its delivery.

Cover Letters

Cover letters, or more formally, letters of transmittal, respond to requests for information. They are used extensively in professional communication. They are usually short formally written letters that provide context for the longer documents they accompany. The two most common letters of transmittal are cover letters for résumés and formal reports, but they can also be used with contracts, financial records, requests for insurance documentation, and many other kinds of information requests.

Résumé Cover Letters. Jobseekers use résumé cover letters to introduce themselves to employers and to explain why they are a good fit for the job being advertised. When writing a cover letter for employment, you are requesting an interview and, if that goes well, a job. Professional résumé cover letters are usually one to two pages long. In this short letter, you must find a way to highlight how your experiences and education have made you an excellent job candidate. Your experiences and education become your reasons, but listing reasons will not get you a job. The best cover letters are organized into a narrative that illustrates how your education and experiences have prepared you for the job. You have to create an impression of yourself as the person who best "fits" the ideal candidate description—all within a page or two. Solving this puzzle is a major challenge, but using the job description can help you prioritize your reasons and showcase your experiences and education. Using keywords from the job description within your request is also a good strategy for success. Like letters of request, résumé cover letters often end with a statement of goodwill and a call to action, requesting an interview and providing contact information to make that arrangement.

Formal Report Cover Letters. Cover letters are also used with formal reports. These letters identify and introduce the longer documents accompanying them. They are addressed to the person or organization requesting the information, and they describe the contents of the longer document. Their introductions provide context by explaining what request for information they are responding to. Their middle sections provide a short summary of the contents of the report, and they may identify individuals who were responsible for the development of the longer document. Like résumé cover letters, report cover letters conclude with a statement of goodwill and a request for acceptance of the report. The final sentences provide the writer's contact information.

Messages of Appreciation or Thanks

These responses are appropriate when someone has considered a request you have made or given you an opportunity. They also may conclude a series of communications. A simple note of thanks or appreciation is gesture of goodwill that lets others know much you appreciate their time and efforts. These messages are appropriately written to show appreciation for an interview, to commend employees for good work, and to thank others for responding to your requests (whether these requests are fulfilled or not). Responding to requests with messages of appreciation or thanks demonstrate your courtesy and professionalism. These messages leave their recipients with positive impressions about your and your work.

Depending on how well you know the person you are writing, messages of appreciation can range widely in tone from informal to very formal. They are frequently short, only a few sentences, and they are often handwritten on stationary and mailed to their recipients. When writing a message of appreciation, begin by stating your thanks for the opportunity or response you have received. Follow this initial statement with a more detailed explanation of why you are grateful for this response. In a sense, this explanation explains reasons why you are grateful. If you would like to keep the communication channel open after you send this message, make a reference to some future connection you would like to make. End the message with final statement of gratitude.

Messages of appreciation are particularly important after job interviews. They can be written on a note card or emailed. However you send them, you will find that taking the time to thank interviewers for their time reminds them of your interview and leaves them with a more positive impression of your time together.

Evaluating a Response to a Request

Examples of response messages are also widely available on the Internet. Using search terms, such as "good news letter," "bad news letter," "cover letter," "letter of transmittal," "thank you note," and "note of appreciation," you can locate dozens of examples of these kinds of correspondence. At work, you may also find that your organization has standard messages to reply positively or negatively to a request. Wherever you find these examples, here are a few questions that can help you evaluate the effectiveness of a response to a request.

Evaluating a Response to a Request Checklist
The following checklist will help you to evaluate the effectiveness of request correspondence you find or create:

1. Evaluate the introduction
   - ☐ Does the writer introduce himself or herself?
   - ☐ Does the writer provide context for the response?
   - ☐ Does the writer establish goodwill with the reader quickly?
   - ☐ Does the writer explain the purpose of the correspondence? Or, in the case of a bad news response, does the writer buffer the bad news?
2. Evaluate explanation of the response
   - ☐ Does the writer provide explanation and reason for the response?
   - ☐ Are the reasons in the explanation convincing?
   - ☐ Are they prioritized and organized effectively?
3. Evaluate the conclusion
   - ☐ Does the conclusion seek the goodwill of the reader?
   - ☐ Does the conclusion include contact information for the writer?

> ### EXERCISE 10.4
>
> ### *Evaluating Responses to Request*
>
> Using the internet, find two or three examples of written requests. To locate these examples, use search terms such as "good news letter," "bad news letter," "cover letter," "letter of transmittal," "thank you message," and "note of appreciation." Bookmark the location of these examples or save a copy for later reference. Using the checklist for evaluating a request, determine how effective each example is. Prepare to share and discuss your examples with your class.
>
> **Tasks to be completed:**
>
> 1. Locate written responses to requests online using the above search terms.
> 2. Bookmark the location of two or three examples.
> 3. Use the checklist for evaluating a request to determine the effectiveness of each request.
> 4. Prepare to discuss your evaluation in class.

FORMATTING CORRESPONDENCE

If your organization has specific style guidelines for printed letters and memos, you should use them, but if not, this section provides you with guidelines on conventional letter and memo layout and formats.

Letter Layout

Formal letters have one-inch to one-and-a-half inch margins. The most common spacing for letters is single space. (Differences in spacing are described in the list below.) For ease of spacing, set your paragraph line spacing to single spacing. To insure easy readability, use 11- to 12-point font in formal letters.

Letters have seven typical parts, which are listed and defined below:

1. **Return Address**: The return address is your address. You may include your name in the return address, if you wish. Double space between the last line of your return address and the date.
2. **Date**: Double space before and after the date your correspondence will be sent.
3. **Inside Address**: This is the recipient's name and address.
4. **Salutation or Greeting**: In this part, you address the reader with "Dear," a personal title (Mr., Ms., Dr.), and the person's last name. In formal letters, a colon follows the salutation (:). Double space after the salutation.
5. **Body**: This is the content of your letter. You should single space paragraphs, but double space between paragraphs.
6. **Closing**: The closing is a goodwill ending, such as "Sincerely," or "With regards,". Notice that a comma follows the closing. Quadruple space after the closing.

7. **Signature**: Handwrite or digitally sign your name after the closing in the blank space created by the quadruple space after the closing. Type your name below your signature.

In addition, to these seven parts, some formal letters (such as cover letters) also contain two additional parts after the signature. These parts indicate that you have enclosed additional information and that you have provided copies of the letter to others. To indicate you have enclosures, double space after your signature and type "Enc:" and the names of the enclosed documents. To indicate additional copies, double space after your signature or the enclosure line; type "CC:"; and list the individuals to whom you sent copies.

Letters have two common formats or layouts: block and modified block. In **block format**, all lines of the letter are aligned on the left. In **modified block format**, the return address, the closing, and the signature are aligned on the right, but the other parts are left-aligned. See Figures 10.4 and 10.5 for examples.

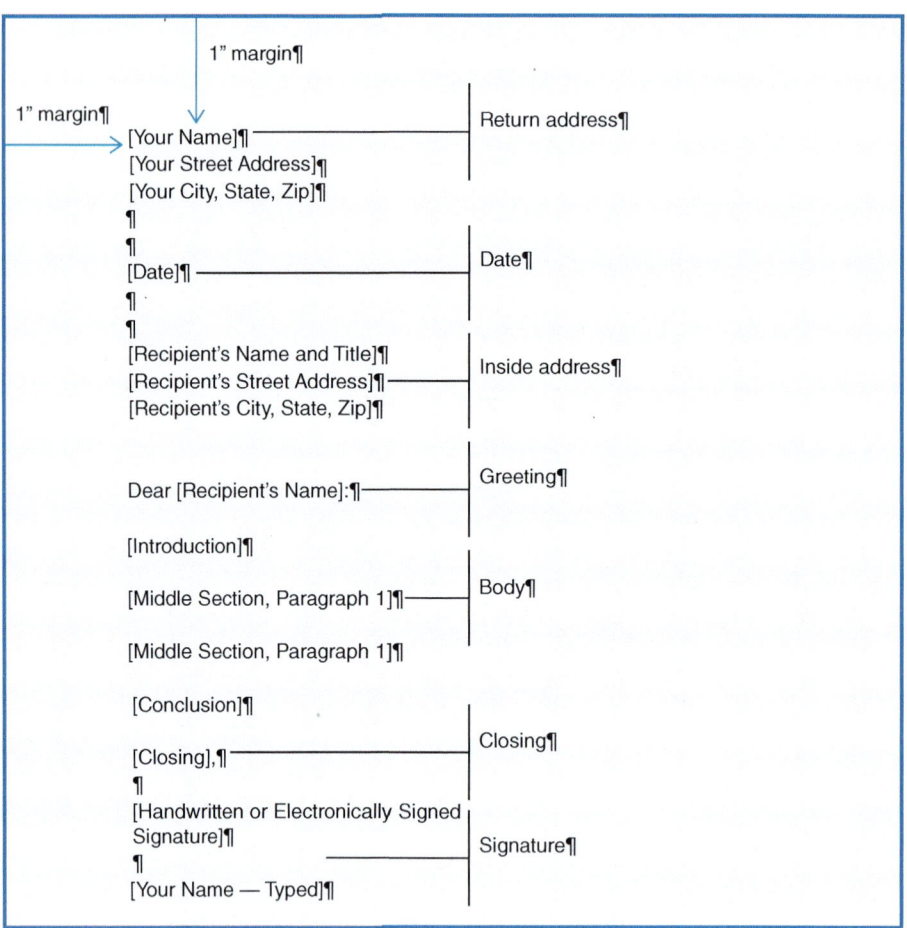

Figure 10.4. In block letter format, all content is left-justified.

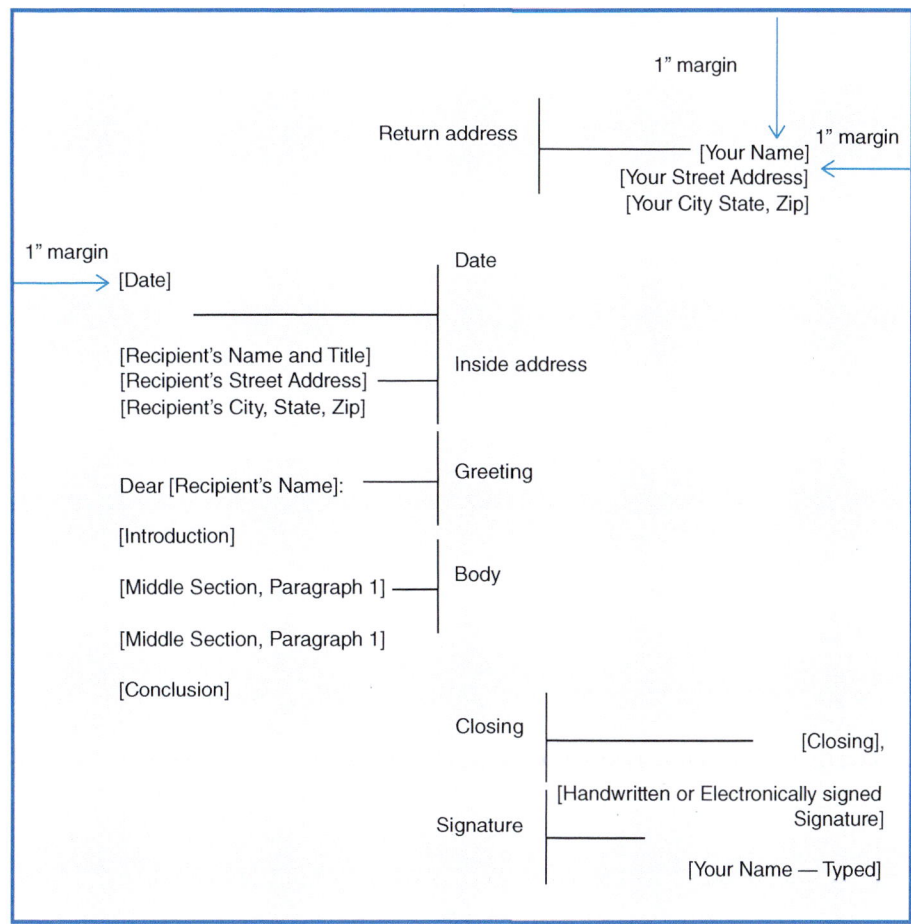

Figure 10.5. In modified block letter format, the return address is indented to the right, the letter itself is left-justified, and the closing and signature are indented to the right.

Most organizations have their own letterhead stationery and guidelines for writing and printing professional correspondence, which may include both formatting and style considerations. When organizational guidelines are not available, you may find pre-packaged letter templates in word-processing programs, like Microsoft Office, Pages, and OpenOffice, helpful. These templates are customizable and allow you to add and subtract components as you like. Because these templates are easy to use and customizable, let your communication purpose and objectives guide the content you place in the letter, not the template itself. If you decide to use a template, remember that the template is available to everyone who owns a particular software package, so your letter will look like everyone else's letter. While that may be an advantage in some cases, a more customized appearance will make your letter stand out from others.

Formatting Printed Memos

While letters are typically used for external communication to others outside of your organization, printed memos are internal office correspondence. They are used for announcements and notifications, permanent record commendations and recommendations, and other in-house communication. Like letterhead stationery, organizations often have standardized logos or images included on printed memos.

Memos are headed with specific information, according to organizational conventions. Usually, these headings include the following, but the order of the headings may vary widely from organization to organization:

The **date** refers to the day the communication is written or sent, "**To**:" is followed with a list of recipients, "**From**:" is the writer's or writers' names, and "**Re**:" is the subject line. Also, like letters and emails, memos are signed but often informally; the writer or writers initial their names after the "From:" line.

Use of memos for internal office correspondence has decreased in recent years. The financial and environmental costs associated with distributing printed memos have caused many organizations to shift internal communications to email or intranet (internal organizational networks or websites). Additionally, organizations with geographically distributed offices can connect with employees faster and more easily electronically than with printed memos. For these reasons, much of the information that was once distributed through memos has transitioned to electronic communications, such as email messages, which have been designed to communicate essentially the same information in their headings as memos do. If you are required to write a memo for print distribution, with a few modifications like the signature requirement, you can use the guidelines for email in the next section.

MEMO

UNIVERSITY PARKING AND TRANSPORTATION SERVICES

To: Vincent Martin
From: University Parking and Transportation Services
Date: August 15, 2016
Re: R05 Construction

This week you may have noticed a construction fence went up in preparation of construction on the new Plant Science Building expansion and renovation. The construction area occupies the easternmost aisle of Lot R05 where you are assigned to park. Ample parking should remain in the rest of R05 for the duration of the project. If you have any questions or concerns, please contact us at (806) 777-PARK or visit our website.

Figure 10.6. This memorandum's heading has typical four-part content: Date:, To:, From:, and Re:.

> ### EXERCISE 10.5
>
> ### *Modifying Word Processing Letter and Memo Templates*
>
> Explore your word processing software's correspondence templates or visit your software's Web site. What letter and memo templates are available for your use? Do the templates include conventional parts of letters and memos? What other content and visual elements are included in the template? What elements in the templates are modifiable?
>
> Open one of these templates, and see what you can modify in the templates. Try to change the order of information, remove images, and adjust the size and weight of font, or move the information from one section to another. How easy is modifying a template? What obstacles did you encounter as you tried to modify the template?
>
> In small groups, discuss the advantages and disadvantages of using letter and memo templates to write.
>
> **Tasks to be completed:**
>
> 1. Find one or two examples of correspondence templates in your word processing software or on the website for your word processing software.
> 2. What kinds of correspondence templates are available?
> 3. What conventional content is labeled on the template?
> 4. What other elements—textual or visual—are included in the template?
> 5. Can you modify the template? If so, what obstacles did you encounter when doing so?
> 6. In small groups, discuss your findings and the advantages and disadvantages of correspondence templates.

WRITING ELECTRONIC CORRESPONDENCE

Almost everyone has used email and other electronic correspondence, such as texts, by the time they enter college. These messages arrive on devices that we carry with us or that we access in our work spaces. We use them to tell others where we are, what we are doing, and where we are going. Electronic correspondence works in similar ways in the workplace, but it is important to recognize that professional etiquette for electronic correspondence use varies from personal use. This section of the chapter will help you to understand these differences.

Writing email has become the standard means of internal and external organizational communication. The organization you work for will likely have policies regarding email use, sometimes limiting your use of email to business purposes and restricting your professional communication to an assigned email account that supervisors monitor for appropriate use. As with any communication within a specific organization, you should check with your supervisor about email requirements and policies. When policies are not available, the following guidelines can help you write effective and readable emails:

1. **Identify your email's purpose immediately with a specific subject line.** The subject line helps the reader determine whether the email is important or not, and it helps with filing and retrieval of the email.

2. **Begin your email with your reason for writing.** Like a topic sentence in an essay or a heading in a report, the first sentence in your email should let the reader know immediately why are writing. Providing this information immediately saves the reader's time and gets to the point. If you are responding to an earlier email, then reference it in your response.

3. **Limit your message's content.** Whenever possible, limit your email's purpose and subject to one topic. When you include more than one question or topic in your emails, your readers may neglect to answer a question or overlook it. When you have multiple topics or requests, include each one in a separate email. Limiting your message's content also allows for easier filing and retrieval later.

4. **Keep email messages brief, if possible, and segment the message into readable chunks.** Reading on a screen is more challenging for some readers, so segmenting your message into short, readable chunks assists readers to grasp your questions and statements. When your message is long or more detailed, signal your reader to the length with a sentence in the opening paragraph. More importantly, do not ramble. Your readers have limited time and will appreciate messages that quickly come to their points.

5. **Use advance organizers and white space to assist reading.** Use white space between paragraphs to make reading easier. Email messages are typically single-spaced, like letters and memos. Using white space between paragraphs singles a change to the reader. Headings and lists are as useful in emails as they are in letters, memos, and reports.

6. **Take time to revise.** Proofread your message carefully. If the message is important, read the message aloud to check your wording, grammar, and punctuation. Always use the spell-checker, and review and revise your punctuation and sentence structure before sending an email. As with any other form of written or spoken communication, readers will make judgments about you based on your understanding of basic writing conventions. These judgments may affect whether the reader decides to respond to you or not. To see how the received email looks and reads, email a copy to yourself before you send it to the actual recipient.

7. **Close all emails with a signature.** Most email applications allow you to create a personal signature that is included in every message. Include your name and contact information in your signature. If you are writing to someone who does not know you, sign your emails with your complete name.

In addition to considering these guidelines when you correspond with email, you should also consider potential problems that arise with this kind of correspondence:

- **Electronic Correspondence is Never Private.** Never assume that email correspondence is private, and avoid sending any private information through email. You should always assume that anything you write is permanent, public, distributable, and printable. What you write can and often will be shared with others. For this reason, you should never include anything in an email that you would not want a large audience to read.

- **Protect your Privacy and your Reputation.** Remember that email correspondence, like other communication assignments you complete, can affect your personal reputation as well as your organization's reputation positively or negatively. Make certain that what you write reflects the impression you want to make.

- **Avoid Unprofessional Negativity**. Because emails are most often sent to individuals who are separated from us, writers can feel free to be harsh, unkind, or hateful, in the guise of "honesty." Early writers about the internet called this kind of behavior "flaming" because the writer was emotionally hot and the reader metaphorically was burned by the message. To avoid flaming, do not write anything about or to a person that you would not say to that person's face.

- **Avoid Hasty Replies**. Related to the last two points, never send an email when you are feeling strong emotions, especially anger. As a general rule of thumb, you can write the email when you are feeling strongly, but you should save it and delay sending it until you have a cooler head and can look at the text more objectively. Haste when hitting the "send" button creates a much higher chance of harm than good.

EXERCISE 10.6

Things You May not Know about Email

The International Center for Integrative Systems hosts a Web site called The Email Lab (http://theemaillab.org/email-lab.asp). Visit The Email Lab. There you will find pages describing its history (http://theemaillab.org/history-of-email.asp) and offering tips for professional use (http://blog.theemaillab.org/). After reviewing the contents of The Email Lab, what have you learned about email and its use that you did not know before? How has the practice of email grown from practices of other forms of communication? What factors affect successful professional use of email? How are professional and personal emails different from one another?

Tasks to be completed:

1. Visit the International Center for Integrative System's Email Lab.
2. Review the contents of the Email Lab.
3. Answer these questions and prepare to discuss:

    a. What have you learned about email and its use that you did not know before?
    b. How has the practice of email grown from practices of other forms of communication?
    c. What factors affect successful professional use of email?
    d. How are professional and personal emails different from one another?

WRITING SOCIALLY MEDIATED COMMUNICATION

Socially mediated communication includes many common communication technologies that you use everyday: from texting, instant messaging, and distribution lists. You will learn more about these socially mediated technologies in a later chapter.

With the advent of mobile devices, texting has become a commonplace, quick correspondence channel. Also called SMS (short message service), some devices and applications limit texts to 140 characters. Even with capabilities for longer text messages, text messages remain brief and concise, and they often include abbreviations, acronyms, and emoticons to shorten messages but convey meaning. Not everyone, however, will understand texting shorthand, so avoid using it if your reader may not understand it. Texts are most commonly used in the workplace for person-to-person communication, but they are also becoming more popular as marketing tools.

Instant messaging (IM), like texting, is a common way to communicate instantaneously with others through a computer application. While you may be familiar with IM-ing in your personal life, it is very likely that you will use IM even more at work. Many workplace intranets allow employees to communicate through IM. It can be a quicker method for a short conversation to occur than emailing or telephoning, and employees can engage in multiple conversations at the same time. At some workplaces, IM's are also used to send new flashes, alert employees of appointment arrivals, and send meeting reminders.

Along with email, distributed lists (listservs) are popular means of corresponding, both personally and professionally. A listserv is a mechanism for distributing and exchanging email with a group of like-minded individuals. Beginning in the late 1980's, lists were first generated by placing multiple email addresses in the To: line. As group sizes increased, so too did viral attacks and the use of spam filters to reduce infections from unwanted emails. Emailing large distributed lists eventually became less viable. As a result, dedicated list management tools or software like LyrisList Manager became more popular. They have allowed individuals to type a single group name into their To: line and conduct extensive conversation through correspondence.

While list management tools are still used today, they are being replaced with social media like Slack, Twitter, and Facebook, which now have features that allow the same kind of targeted distribution to identified readers or friends. What all of these technologies have done is create a means for receiving professional and personal news and information, engaging in both short and extended conversations with individuals with similar interests over time and distances, and networking. You will find more information about social media and its uses in professional communication in a later chapter.

Guidelines for writing electronic correspondence

With all electronic correspondence, these guidelines will help you to present yourself and your messages professionally:

Figure 10.7. Texts and instant messages are commonly used for instantaneous workplace communication.

- **Gauge your voice** to the appropriate register or formality for the correspondence. Business letters are more formally written than memos. Emails to professional distributed lists are more formal than social media posts. In fact, notes on social media sites, like Twitter and Facebook, are often the most informal of all. Think about how these different levels of formality can maintain your professional reputation but also seem appropriate within the message itself.

- **Invite discussion**. On listservs and in emails, you can engage discussion with questions or concerns and ask for help. Successful messages often invite others to share experiences and stories of their own. When others respond to you, reply promptly. Nothing kills a conversation faster than extended silences.
- **Encourage reading**. Organize your emails and other electronic posts into readable chunks with plenty of white space to help with screen reading.
- **When appropriate, incorporate media, other than text, into your posts**. Social media posts are delivered on the internet, and, therefore, have the advantage of access to video, audio, and graphics. Take advantage of these affordances.
- **Use keywords and tags** in posts that allow them. Indexing your posts in this way helps readers to decide whether to read or not, and it improves findability when the posts are archived over time.
- **Consider the future**. Because electronic correspondence is archived, your posts may be available for decades, if not forever. What you post now can impact impressions of you in twenty years. This includes information you post in personal texts, email messages, and social network posts.
- **Remember your audience**. Although you may intend for a few friends or colleagues to read an electronic message, you are no longer in control of the message after you press "send" or "post." Because they are public, easily distributed, and stored on other servers and computers, the message can take on a life of its own. Think about the viral videos you have seen or accounts of poor texting choices. Avoid distributing any information that would harm your reputation now or later.
- **Protect your privacy and proprietary information**. For reasons already discussed, your privacy and your organization's proprietary information can easily be disclosed and distributed in electronic messages. Using discretion and thinking carefully about what you write in correspondence is the first line in protecting private information.

Chapter Summary

Corresponding is one of the most common activities performed in the workplace. Sometimes this work is written for print delivery but, more frequently, this work is conducted for electronic delivery. Everyday workers answer dozens of emails, requesting information, and responding to requests for information. Knowing the difference between these print and electronic correspondence is important, but, even more important, is knowing the difference between personal and professional correspondence. The final sections in this chapter provided you with guidance on the transition from personal electronic correspondence and professional. The exercises at the end of the chapter will help you understand more about how to correspond and how to make the transition from personal to professional correspondence.

Chapter Assignments

The exercises in this section ask you to apply what you have learned in this chapter as well as explore how this knowledge applies to and connects with other information in the textbook.

1. When you think about the differences between personal and professional correspondence, what do think the greatest challenges will be for you when you take your first (or next) job in a professional workplace?

2. Using the two examples you gathered in the "Everyday Correspondence" activity, answer the following questions:
   a. Into which of the two categories do the examples fall: requesting information or responding to a request? Explain how you know.
   b. Are the two examples organized with an introduction, middle section, and conclusion? If so, what kinds of information are in each section? If not, how are they different?
   c. Do you find variations on common request and response to request organizational patterns in your examples? If so, how are they different?

3. The three email messages below were sent by two students. The same student wrote Examples 1a and 1b sent them within 5 minutes on a Monday afternoon at approximately 4:45 p.m. A different student wrote Example 2, which arrived on a Tuesday at 3:35 p.m. Compare and contrast Examples 1 and 2. Which one(s) communicate their request most effectively? Why?

Example 1a

> Subject: One question about English majors
> Hi, my name's Julie. I'm an English major taking the writing path. Currently I'm in an English 2000 class, and we have been assigned to find out what types of writing we will be doing within our major. I went all over the English Department asking people and kept getting referred to someone else, finally leading to you. I was told that you're over my emphasis for my major and that you would best know what type of writing a Writing major would include. I imagine that as a Writing major my education will include many types of writing, but if I could just get a reply with the specific kinds that would be incredibly helpful. Be it proposals, essays, memos, research papers, poetry, fiction, nonfiction, creative, personal, more or less. I would more than appreciate your help. It doesn't have to be much, it could be a list or maybe just a 2 line reply, whatever applies. Thank you for your time and help!!

Example 1b

> Subject: deadline....sorry!
> I forgot to mention that if I could get a reply today I would appreciate it so much!!! I was planning on talking to you in person, but since you weren't in your office I was told to email you instead, so I hope that's okay. It can be short, it's nothing much. Sorry for the short notice and inconvenience!! Thanks again!

Example 2

> Subject: <missing>
> Professor,
> Hello, my name is Marsha Addison. Dr. Jones, my academic advisor, told me you would be a good person for me to talk to about possible careers available to technical communication majors. I am exploring different options right now, and she strongly recommended this major to me. Is there a time this week that I can meet with or talk to you about the Technical Writing program?
> Thank you,
> Marsha

4. Conduct an internet search for "text messaging workplace policies" or "text messaging policies." Why do many workplaces now include these employee policies? What kinds of behavior do these policies cover? Do you agree or disagree with these policies? Why?

5. Complete this exercise to learn more about workplace correspondence and to practice using some of the technologies that workplace writers use to correspond:

   a. Contact two or three of your friends who have recently gained employment after graduation. Ask them how people correspond with each other in their workplace.

   b. Write a description of your findings in your word-processor.

   c. Create a print version of your findings and submit it to your instructor. Before you create your version, ask yourself: What kind of correspondence genre will work best for print submission? Once you have made your choice, write it and submit it.

   d. Create an electronic version of your findings, and submit it to your instructor. Before you create your version, ask yourself: What kind of correspondence genre will work best for electronic submission? Once you've made your choice, write it and submit it.

   e. Be prepared to discuss your reasons for each version in class.

Figure Credits

Figure 10.1. © Dragon Images/Shutterstock.com

Figure 10.2. © KieferPix/Shutterstock.com

Figure 10.3. © Bacho/Shutterstock.com

Figure 10.4. © Kendall Hunt Publishing Company

Figure 10.5. © Kendall Hunt Publishing Company

Figure 10.7. © Odua Images/Shutterstock.com

Reporting Status and Progress

11

CHAPTER OVERVIEW

This chapter will introduce you to two kinds of short reports that are typically used to document single instances or events, such as meetings, or to document status on ongoing projects. After reading this chapter, you should be able to complete the following objectives:

- Identify and describe different types of instance and status reports.
- State the various audiences, purposes, and frequencies of these reports to distinguish them.
- Create a variety of instance and status reports

Instance and status reports are an essential component of daily business and workplace writing. Employers and employees use these reports to plan their work, to report progress on this work, to update that progress as work continues, and sometimes to document final results. They may be used at beginning, middle, or end of a project. Status reports may be created and delivered multiple times within a single project at specific intervals, or they may be created and written at specific milestones within the project. While instance and status reports vary in purpose, audience, and frequency, most are typically short and designed to be written and read quickly. Status reports that cover longer periods of time, such as quarterly and annual reports, can be much longer.

INSTANCE REPORTS

Instance reports function to document a specific occurrence of an event or interaction, such as a trip or a meeting. Some instance reports may be as short as a sentence or several pages long, depending on the length of the interaction. These reports can be created before the event to establish a plan for the interaction or created after the fact to mark milestones achieved or forthcoming. Just as their lengths may vary, so do their audiences, purposes, and frequencies. This section describes and provides examples of the following instance reports: trip reports, expense (or travel) reports, and meeting agendas and minutes.

Figure 11.1. Meeting minutes provide important records of decisions and actions needed.

Trip Reports

Trip reports, like expense reports, which are described in the next section, document the results of travel. The trip report is a narrative that describes the work activities in which you engaged while traveling. The report should provide the reader, probably your supervisor and perhaps the organizational accountant, with a detailed account of where you went on your trip, when you left, and when you returned. It should then provide details about your activities. These activities are usually organized chronologically by date and time. Activities might include meetings with clients, time spent on meals and entertainment with clients, attendance at meetings or conference presentations, and other kinds of activities in which you engaged. Although your organization may have specific formats for writing trip reports, the following organization and content is common in most trip reports.

As you review Figure 11.2 on the following page, a sample trip report, note that the format of these reports may vary from organization to organization, but the content is generally stable.

Introduction

In a short introductory paragraph, provide the following information:

- State the location(s) where you traveled
- State the overall dates of your travel
- Include your contact information, if you traveled alone. If you traveled with others, include their names and contact information.
- State the reason for your travel and identify the individual who approved your travel
- Explain why the travel was necessary or beneficial to your organization

Middle

Using chronological order and narrative structure, provide detailed explanations of the following items:

- What contacts did make and for what purposes?
- In what activities did you engage?
- How were these activities necessary or beneficial to your organization?
- If any of these activities require follow-up, explain what follow-up is necessary and why.

End

- Provide an overall summary of the trip and highlight your accomplishments in terms of advantages and benefits to your organization.
- Additionally, end the report with recommendations for follow-up actions.

Expense Reports

Like trip reports, expense reports are often used for reimbursement purposes for business expenses, including trips. When you travel or spend your own money on business meals and entertainment, your employer will ask you to file a detailed account of the money you spent, including an itemized list of items purchased and the business reasons or necessity for the trip or expense. In addition, you will need to state where you spent the funds and

TRIP REPORT

DATE: Oct 16, 2014
TO: Josephina Allen, Conference Logistics Manager
FROM: Viviana Rangel, Vender Contact Representative, ext. 2041
SUBJECT: Outdoor Sports Retailers Spring Market Planning Meeting Oct 14, 2014

This trip report describes my recent trip to the Outdoor Sports Retailers Spring Market planning meeting in Salt Lake City, Utah. I traveled from October 13-15, 2014, from our headquarters in Ft. Worth, Texas, to the meeting in Salt Lake City. The purpose of the meeting was to meet with other conference organizers to discuss how to schedule vendor space in the new convention center exhibit hall.

Activities

October 13: I left Fort Worth at 1:30 pm and traveled on Southwest Airlines to Salt Lake City, where I rented a car. I then traveled to the conference hotel and checked in.

October 14: I arrived at the Salt Lake Convention Center at 8:30 am and attended the meeting held in the Beehive room. In addition to me, the following Spring Market space committee members attended:

- Julye Fredlinson, Outdoor Retailers Association
- Allen Jameson, Cardinal Sports
- Valient Kora, Dick's Outdoors
- Mary Landis, Academy Sports
- Tye Smith, Outdoor Retailers Association

After brief introductions, Ms. Fredlinson began the discussion, which focused on two main topics: the introduction and use of the new exhibit space for vendors and vendor scheduling and logistics necessary for the upcoming Spring Market. We then toured the new ballroom exhibition space, and members of the committee addressed their general concerns. After this discussion, we broke into two groups, with each group addressing one item of concern. Each group hammered out the details necessary for their assigned item. By the end of the meeting at 4:30 pm, we had a working layout for vendor exhibit space in the new ballroom as well as a plan for notifying vendors and scheduling setup and breakdown of exhibits. The meeting concluded at 4:30, and I returned to my hotel where I had dinner and prepared to return home the following day.

October 15: I departed from the Salt Lake Airport at 7:30 am, landed at DFW at 10:30 pm, and returned to work at 1 pm.

Summary: Overall, the meeting was a success, and we now have a working plan for the exhibit hall. As soon as the Spring Market oversight committee approves our working space plan and schedule, we will be able to contact vendors and provide them with details for their exhibits' locations and schedule.

Figure 11.2. This sample trip report is written in memo format.

TRAVEL & ENTERTAINMENT REPORT

Date:
To:
From:
Re: Traveling Expense and Entertainment Record

Expenses

1. Travel Expenses
Airlines
Excess Baggage
Bus – Train
Cab and Limousine
Tips

2. Meals and Lodging
Hotel and Motel Name and City
Breakfast
Lunch
Dinner

3. Entertainment

Date	Item	Place	Amount	Business Purpose	Business Relationship

4. Other Expenses
Postage
Stationery & Printing

5. Car Expenses
Mileage:
    End
    Start
    Total
Parking fees, tolls

Note: Attached receipts for (1) ALL lodging and (2) any other expenses of $75.00 or more.

Requested REIMBURSEMENTS
Travel and transportation expenses:
Other reimbursements
TOTAL

Figure 11.3. This travel report is a modified version developed from one used by the U.S. Internal Revenue Service.

EXPENSE REPORT

DATE: October 16, 2014
TO: Josephina Allen, Conference Logistics Manager
FROM: Viviana Rangel, Vendor Contact Representative, ext. 2041
SUBJECT: Reimbursement for Outdoor Sports Retailers Spring Market Planning Meeting Oct 14, 2014

I incurred the following expenses on my trip to Salt Lake City to the Outdoor Retailers Spring Market Planning Meeting. Please let me know if you have any questions regarding my reimbursement request.

Expense	Amount
Southwest Airlines ticket—DFW to SLC	$693.47
Two nights lodging at the Salt Lake Marriott	$347.79
Meals (2.5 days @ $75 per day)	$187.50
Cab fares to and from DFW and SLC airports, including tips	$200.00
TOTAL REIMBURSEMENT REQUESTED	**$1,428.76**

Figure 11.4. This simple expense report is written in memo format and includes an expense table outlining amount of reimbursement requested.

the date of the expenses or travel. You may find that your organization has a specific form or format for reporting trips or expenses, or you may simply have to input data into an online form. Whatever the case, if you are working in the United States, most likely the report's content will include some or all of the following information required by the Internal Revenue Service (IRS). Figure 11.3 is an example of travel expense and entertainment record recommended by the IRS.

Depending on your travel and entertainment expenses, the content of your trip or entertainment report may be expanded or collapsed as appropriate. If you must create your own expense report, the simplest way to format this type of report is to use a table, dropping relevant information into the table as needed to document the expenses for which you request reimbursement. Figure 11.4 provides an illustration of a simple expense report submitted for the trip described in Figure 11.2.

In addition to discovering how your organization formats travel and entertainment reports, you will also need to know how it reimburses for meal expenses. Some organizations set limits on the amount of money allowed for meals; others set a **per diem** amount, which must cover daily meals and lodging expenses. Getting this information in advance of travel will help you to budget your expenses and remain within your organization's required limits. Figure 11.4 illustrates how you note *per diem* expenses on an expense report.

To learn more about the many formats and templates organizations require their employees to use when reporting on trips and expenses, complete Exercise 11.1.

> **EXERCISE 11.1**
>
> ## Exploring Different Trip and Expense Report Formats and Templates
>
> This exercise requires you to conduct an internet search to discover how varied these reports can be. Using your preferred internet browser, search using these terms: "business trip report templates," "business trip report examples," "business expense report templates," and "business expense report examples." Find at one example of a trip report and one of an expense report. How do these reports compare and contrast to the examples in this section? If you find differences, speculate on why these templates and examples differ.
>
> **Tasks to be completed:**
>
> 1. Conduct an internet search for business trip and expense reports using the search terms above.
> 2. Locate at least one example of each.
> 3. Compare and contrast them to the examples in this section.
> 4. Speculate on why templates and examples are similar or differ.
> 5. Bring your examples to class to discuss with your peers.

Meeting Agendas and Minutes

Two other common instance reports are closely related: meeting agendas and meeting minutes. Process-mature groups use agendas and minutes to track organizational or group progress in terms of decisions made, actions or work completed, and actions or work to be completed.

Figure 11.5. Meeting agendas provide advance notice of topics to be discussed and provide a clear order of discussion.

Meeting agendas are used to provide advance notice of the meeting's purpose to attendees and to establish a clear order for proceedings. Often, the meeting's leader sets the agenda before the meeting, distributes the proposed agenda in advance, and requests additional business items or changes to the agenda draft. After receiving feedback from attendees, the final agenda is set and distributed just prior to the meeting or at the meeting's start. In contrast, meeting minutes report what happened in the meeting. The group's secretary is responsible for taking minutes. Secretaries can be permanently designated, or the secretary's work may be rotated among group members at each meeting. Like meeting agendas, the minutes of the previous meeting are usually distributed to group members prior to an upcoming meeting.

Meeting Agendas

Meeting agendas typically look like simple outlines. They may be comprised of bulleted or numbered items. The first items on agendas are the call to order and, if the meeting is formal, a call for approval of minutes from the last meeting.

Outdoor Retailers Spring Market Planning Committee
Agenda for October 14, 2015

Business item	Assignment	Time Frame
Call to order and introductions	Julye	9:30 (30 min)
Discussion: new exhibit space and vendor logistics and scheduling	Committee	10:00 (60 min)
Exhibit hall tour	Julye	11:00 (60 min)
Discussion, cont.: new exhibit space and vendor logistics and scheduling	Julye	12:00 (30 min)
Lunch (provided)	Committee	12:30 (60 min)
Assignment to working groups and working group discussion	Julye	1:30 (60 min)
Coffee break	Committee	2:30 (15 minutes)
Continue working group discussions	Committee	2:45 (60 minutes)
Report working group decisions and assignments	Committee	3:45 (90 minutes)
Adjourn	Julye	5:15

Figure 11.6 This sample agenda identifies topics to be discussed, individual who will lead the discussion, and time set aside for the discussion.

EXERCISE 11.2
Minutes as Organizational Memory

This exercise requires you to find a series of minutes from an organization or committee. Working in teams of two or three, conduct an internet search of your university or an organization a member of your team belongs to and find a series of meeting minutes. (Consider using your university's search engine to locate many types of minutes. Use search terms, such as "monthly meeting minutes" or "committee meeting minutes.") Review two or three of these minutes and note specific actions taken or assignments made. After reviewing these minutes, do you have a good sense of what happened at the meeting? Why or why not? Did anything happen at the meeting that future members or leaders might need to know? Provide some examples. Would you recommend any changes to the way these minutes are written? What are they? Prepare to discuss your findings with other groups in your class.

Tasks to be completed:

1. Locate a set of meeting minutes and review them.
2. Evaluate how well the minutes are written using the questions above.
3. Identify information in the minutes that are important for organizational memory.
4. Prepare to present your findings to the class, including recommendations for improving the minutes you located.

Less formal agendas may simply list the items of business or items for discussion. In addition to listing items, agendas may include the amount of time designated for each item and the person responsible for leading the discussion of the item. Figure 11.6 provides a simple agenda for the meeting described in Figure 11.2.

Meeting Minutes

Meeting minutes are a record of group or committee work. Minutes are important because they record decisions and actions. As such, they document the growth of an organization and serve as institutional memory. They are also important because, as an organization matures, members of the organization change. New members must rely on the minutes—the archival records—of the organization to understand decisions that have been made in the past. In this way, meeting minutes create an historical record that can be referenced and consulted as an aid to making new decisions. Because they serve as an historical record, minutes should be concise and clear.

An excellent starting point when creating meeting minutes is the meeting agenda. Using the agenda as an outline for recording the minutes provides an easy structure. Meeting minutes typically include the following information:

Identifying information about the meeting
- Time, date, location of meeting
- Names of members who are present
- Names of member who are absent

A record of what happened in meeting
- Questions and resulting answers
- Motions and outcome of votes
- Actions completed prior to meeting
- Actions to be completed after the meeting

Time of adjournment

Remember that when you take minutes at a meeting what is most important to record is progress made, decisions made (or outcome of votes), and action items (tasks that need to be completed before the next meeting). Action items should also clearly designate who is responsible for completing them. You should not include a narrative of the conversation that occurred during the meeting, especially if that conversation was heated or included inflammatory statements. Nor should you include names of individuals, except to note who made motions, who seconded motions, who received assignments, and who is responsible for action items. Most importantly, as you write minutes for a meeting, remember that you are capturing a moment in time that needs to be remembered and referenced. Record the meeting with future readers and their needs in mind. Thinking about the needs of future readers will help you to decide what is important to record and what is not.

STATUS REPORTS

Status reports typically are written to document personal, project, or organizational progress and accomplishments. Status reports that are written at regular intervals are called **periodic reports** while status reports that document progress at specific project milestones are called **progress reports**. You may write both types of report from an individual or team perspective, depending on the type of project you are completing.

Periodic Reports

Periodic reports are written at daily, weekly, monthly, quarterly, and annual intervals. Common types of periodic reports are financial, sales, and activity reports. For example, you might be asked to create financial reports that document account balances, expenditures, cash flow (income and expenses), and changes in equity. Sales reports similarly may report sales calls, leads or customers contacted, productivity or sales totals, and other sales summaries. Some employers also require activity reports that document work accomplishments and assignments on daily, weekly, monthly, and annual intervals.

The format of these reports depends on report type and the information being reported. Formats may also vary from organization to organization. The report's purpose will also determine the medium and technology used to deliver it. For example, activity reports can be generated as a list of calendar appointments or work assignments that are sent as an email attachment to a supervisor. Financial reports may also be generated as a spreadsheet or graphic that is attached to an email. Simple reports can also be created through online forms that are submitted on a regular basis. More detailed reports, such as annual corporate reports, are printed, bound, and mailed to stakeholders. These lengthy reports can take months to create and deliver.

Because these reports vary so widely, depending on their purpose, audience, and reporting situation, it is difficult to specify content for them. However, you can learn what is expected in your periodic reports using good research skills. To gain insights on how to write periodic reports, use these approaches:

- Seek out legacy reports or previously written and published reports from your organization. Finding successful examples of periodic reports will help you to craft yours.

- Ask your supervisor or coworkers for examples of reports they have created. Because periodic reports are written on a regular basis, most experienced employees in your organization will be familiar with them.

- Finally, if you are writing a new form of report that has not been previously produced, then start with an internet search to see if you can locate examples or templates that can be customized to your particular reporting situation.

> ## EXERCISE 11.3
>
> ### *Investigating the Range of Periodic Reporting*
>
> This exercise asks you to investigate the different types of periodic reports written in workplaces. It requires you to go to a job search website and search using the phrase "periodic report." Set the search to any location and count the number of job ads that require periodic reporting. In addition, note the job titles and industries or corporations that require periodic reporting. Categorize these jobs by titles or industries. Write a short memo reporting your findings.
>
> **Tasks to be completed:**
>
> 1. Conduct an internet search at a popular job search website, such as Monster.com or Indeed.com.
>   - Use the phrase "periodic report" as your keyword search.
>   - Set the location to "any" or leave it blank.
> 2. Count the number of number of jobs listed that require employees to write periodic reports.
> 3. Analyze the jobs (up to the first 100 hits) to gather this data:
>   - If described, note the kinds of periodic reports required at these jobs.
>   - Note the job titles and categorize them. If you have over 100 jobs listed, work with the first 100.
>   - Note the types of organizations and industries that require periodic reporting in the first 100 hits.
> 4. Write a short memo reporting your findings.

Progress Reports

Progress reports are used in the workplace to gauge project-related work that has been completed, work that has not yet been completed, potential obstacles, plans to overcome these obstacles, and projected time to completion. Depending on the scope of the project, progress reports may vary in length: the broader the scope, the longer the report may be. They may report individual progress or team progress on the project. Most progress reports contain the following information:

- Identification of project and individuals reporting
- Identification and background of project
- Identification of individual or team reporting progress
- A list of tasks completed and discussion, if necessary
- A list of tasks yet to be completed and discussion, if necessary
- A discussion of obstacles encountered and plans to overcome these obstacles
- A projection of time to completion of project, including expected outcomes or action items

Figure 11.7 is a progress report for a workplace research project. This progress report would likely be sent as an email to supervisors.

PROGRESS REPORT

Date: February 15, 2016
To: J.D. Wilson
From: Annika Vonnegut
Re: Update on technical writer/support staff communications

Overall status
Two weeks ago you tasked me with evaluating the communication processes between our organization's technical writers who produce product documentation and the technical support staff who use it. My project is on schedule and will conclude on time. The rest of this progress report provides more details about work completed and work remaining.

Work Completed
I have conducted interviews with six interviews: four of eight technical support representatives and two of three technical writers in the documentation group. I have also collected samples documents and emails from interviewees. I have started analysis of the interviews and documents. I do not anticipate any significant obstacles in completing the interview or document analysis.

Work Remaining
I have scheduled the final five interviews, which will be completed in two weeks. I have not yet observed technical support representatives taking customer calls, but I plan to shadow two representatives in the next week. Although I do not anticipate that these observations will alter my analysis significantly, I think it is important to see representatives working with documentation.

Expected Outcomes
I do not expect any delays in my original projected completion date of April 2. On that date, I will provide you with a detailed analysis of the communication processes with recommendations for improvement.

Figure 11.7. This simple progress report is written in memo format with headings that allow readers to identify key content.

Chapter Summary

This chapter has introduced you to two types of short reports: instance reports and status reports. Its scope is not comprehensive because every workplace will have its own formats and content requirements. For this reason, this chapter's suggestions for content should be treated as recommendations, not templates. For this reason, when you are asked to create a new instance or status report in the workplace, your first task is to learn what information your readers need in the report. Then, if available, ask for models or examples that have been successful in the past, and consult legacy documents or organizational style guides. As with any technical and professional document, you need to know your audience, purpose, and situation in order to create an effective communication. Sound research and thoughtful planning are especially important when you are producing short reports such as these that can vary so dramatically from organization to organization.

Chapter Assignments

The exercises in this section ask you to apply what you have learned in this chapter as well as explore how this knowledge applies to and connects with other information in the textbook.

1. Imagine that you are a member of a two-person team that is researching printer solutions for Aladdin Technologies. Your teammate has drafted the progress report below to inform your supervisor of your progress. Critique the progress report below using the guidelines for content in this chapter. Identify important information that is included and excluded. Revise the progress note to improve it.

   > This email is to let you know how we are progressing on our project for Aladdin Technologies for our recommendation of printer remediation.
   >
   > Currently, Aladdin Technologies has a very un-organized print environment. Our project seeks to recommend the best way to bring their current print environment in line with industry standards. We are researching several tools that are free to Aladdin. These tools will allow Aladdin to streamline printing processes and to print from mobile devices that are currently deployed into the field.
   >
   > David and I have worked extremely well together on this project. We have both had some personal situations that we had to deal with during this time but we have been able to keep the lines of communication open so that we both know what the other is doing. Thus far we have conducted an inventory of all of the print queues and network attached print devices at Aladdin. There has also been research done on the mobile printing solution. A web based printer management utility has been identified and further research will be conducted on it. We should wrap up our research by the end of this week and begin compiling our information into the final report and presentation that will be ready Saturday May 12th.
   >
   > We have run into a couple of rough spots where David was out because his wife had a baby and I had a business trip that put me in a different time zone. We were able to work through these situations by emailing and texting each other. We work very well together and I am looking forward to presenting our report.
   >
   > As of today we are currently on time for a May 12th delivery of our report with an accompanying presentation.
   >
   > If you have any questions or concerns that were not addressed in this email, please feel free to contact me. My contact information is listed below in my signature.

2. Conduct an interview with someone in who works in the field you are interested in joining after graduation. The purpose of the interview is to learn about short reports that are required on his or her job. Make a list of the short reports and their descriptions. Would you classify them as instance reports or periodic reports? After completing your interview, write a short instance report informing your instructor of the research you conducted and your findings.

3. View one of the following video meetings that are designed to improve your minute-taking abilities. As you watch the meeting, take minutes.
   - Taking and writing effective minutes (http://youtu.be/3lMg2EERHj4); length: 6:58
   - Mock meeting for business minute taking (http://youtu.be/ItIpCy7o0L4); length: 6:41
   - First Strategy Review Meeting (http://youtu.be/RJAXQIAz9bk); length: 4:19
   - A video meeting of your choice, ranging from 4–6 minutes in length

Figure Credits

Figure 11.1. © Pressmaster/Shutterstock.com

Figure 11.5. © Pressmaster/Shutterstock.com

Instructing

12

CHAPTER OVERVIEW

This chapter introduces you to concepts, practices, and strategies for developing instructional documents, including written instructions, procedures, and learning materials. After reading this chapter, you should be able to meet the following objectives:

- Describe the specific concepts, practices, and methods for writing effective instructional documents.
- Discuss the importance of user research in developing instructional documents.
- Explain the process of developing instructional documents, including important planning, development, quality assurance, and publishing tasks.
- Distinguish between different types of instructional documents, including instructions, procedures, and learning materials.

Instructional documents are a specific genre that technical communicators produce. It has the purpose of informing, or educating, a specific audience on how to complete tasks, how to complete a process, or how to acquire new skills or knowledge. Whether you are developing content for learners using educational materials or for users following a set of instructions or procedures, the principles and guidelines in this chapter can assist you. Instructional documents also focus on one or more objectives that help users gain new knowledge, skills, or behaviors, or complete tasks. Specific document types include written instructions, procedures, and other kinds of learning materials. Whether you are assembling a product, following a process for registration, or attempting to learn a new skill from a video or a Web site, it is likely you will be using some kind of instructional document.

User research is particularly important in developing instructional documents because the documents themselves are designed for individuals to use or reuse in a variety of settings. User research can help you to understand what prior knowledge and skills that users must have to successfully use and benefit from

Figure 12.1. Observing users as they complete a instructions helps technical communicators understand where improvements and revisions are needed.

255

instructional documents. This research can also help you to understand the actual environment and context in which instructional documents are used, in order to write more effective instructions. User-centered design practices are also important when developing effective instructional documents since they involve the user in the entire process from the planning phase through evaluation of the product.

Instructional documents, whether they are a set of instructions, a process description, or learning materials, share similar characteristics. They all have a clear purpose statement and specific objectives or outcomes, so learners know what to expect in terms of scope and what they will gain from using the instructional document. They include appropriate background information, such as required skills, knowledge, materials, and settings in which the instructional document is used. Instructional documents rely heavily on succinct, precise, and clear use of language in terms of the writing style, and they should be written with familiar terminology. Instructional documents often incorporate visual information, such as graphics, symbols, photographs, diagrams, and drawings. In some cases, instructional documents may include mostly visual content, such as instructions for assembling furniture or other products with an international audience. Instructional documents also typically provide informational supplements to assist users, such as references, troubleshooting guides, list of frequently asked questions (FAQ), and performance tips. Supplements typically have some secondary purpose or need, which may be part of the project scope, or they can be derived from testing, user feedback, or previous iterations of instructional documents.

EXERCISE 12.1

Distinguishing Between Instructions, Procedures, and Learning Materials

Working in groups of three, conduct an Internet search to identify examples of instructions, procedures, and learning materials. Each team member should take on one term with one person searching with the keyword "instructions," the second member search with the keyword "procedures," and the third person search with any of the following terms: "worksheets," "handouts," "directions," or "exercises." After each team member has located one or more examples, compare your examples to see if you can determine the similarities in these examples as well as distinguishing features that differentiate them from one another. Be prepared to show your examples to the class and, if necessary, to question how easily it is to differentiate these terms.

Tasks to be completed:

1. Working in team of three, locate examples of instructions, procedures, and learning materials.
2. Compare and contrast your examples within your team and note similarities and differences.
3. Generate a list of questions you have about these similarities and differences.
4. Prepare to show your examples to the class and discuss any questions you may have.

As you prepare to develop instructional materials, you should know the distinctions between the individual document types when writing instructional documents. Written instructions and procedures are closely related. **Instructions** typically focus on a single objective, such as assembling a product or completing a task while **procedures** typically have multiple objectives to accomplish. **Learning materials** are more widely varied in terms of their formatting, including notes, worksheets, handouts, directions, exercises, and so forth. Their purpose is more focused on acquiring skills or knowledge because they are designed to educate learners by helping them complete specific learning objectives, apply knowledge, or demonstrate mastery of a specific subject.

This chapter will introduce you to the overall process and practices of writing instructional documents. It will describe specific differences and guidelines for the various instructional document types, including written instructions, procedures, and learning materials. The chapter will discuss the process and overall tasks in researching, writing, testing, and publishing instructional documents. It will also provide you with specific guidelines and examples that will enable you to write effective instructional documents. These guidelines and examples also draw on an earlier chapter that introduced you to the importance of instructional design principles, learning styles, and tool and media use for instructional documents. The end of this chapter will return to the activity you completed in Exercise 12.1 on the previous page. The chapter concludes with more specific information to help you differentiate between different kinds of instructional documents.

WRITING INSTRUCTIONAL DOCUMENTS

Writing instructional documents includes several tasks: researching, designing, writing, and testing. While many instructional documents will involve a similar process and set of tasks, they will also depend on the type of instructional document you are writing. For example, composing a tutorial on folding elaborately shaped dinner napkins might not have many health or safety issues that apply while a set of instructions on assembling a lawnmower will have more safety issues and concerns. Whether you are writing instructional documents to education or inform, remember that the process is iterative and that you may need to revisit or revise work from previous phases, based on issues that arise during researching, designing, writing, and testing phases.

Researching Tasks

Researching material for instructional documents includes learning more about your users, previous products, information resources, related standards, and any safety concerns. While these tasks can be performed in any order, they correspond to the analysis phase in the ADDIE process discussed in Chapter 8. It is important that you address each of them in your preliminary work, prior to writing instructional documents, as part of your planning process. For assistance with this preliminary work, consult previous chapters that address research methods and the ADDIE instructional design process. In particular, attend to the tasks described in the following paragraphs.

Research your Subject

Researching content on the subject matter of your instructional document is essential to writing documents that are comprehensive, complete, and accurate. Some information might be based on your expertise or gathered from other subject matter experts. Researching the latest information on some subjects is essential to providing up-to-date and accurate content for your instructional document. It is important to provide citations or to acquire permissions for using content from published sources.

Conduct or Collect User Research

Know your audience (or user): discover what they know, identify what they need to know, and gain insights about their expectations and preferences. You can start by asking these questions about your users and by conducting an audience analysis. Conducting user research is a user-centered practice and helps inform your choices about content, style, and development of instructional documents. You may want to even query, interview, survey, or collect information from users, including any feedback from experienced professionals.

Conduct Benchmarking Research

This step involves examining previous instructional products on the same, or similar topic, to determine best practices, ideas for improvement, or secondary research material that you might cite in your instructional document. Looking at other documents can provide some ideas about successful practices or features to add to your own instructional documents, or even potential errors or problems to avoid. You might also consult the use of templates, writing guides, or other examples of successful instructional documents to help you plan how to organize, write, and design your own documents.

Research Standards or Practices

Depending on the topic of your instructional document, you may need to find current information on specific standards. This research might include regulations, disciplinary conventions, organizational standards, or other guidelines, which apply to your topic. Following standards ensures compliance with legal, disciplinary, and organizational rules and policies. Subject matter experts and experienced professionals can be useful resources to help identify specific standards or practices that may apply.

Research Health and Safety Issues

As mentioned above, not every instructional topic will have health or safety concerns to address; others will have many. Safety messages usually are warnings or cautions, which help users avoid making potentially costly mistakes. Benchmark research or legacy content research will help you identify important safety concerns, so you can include them in your instructional document. Failing to include necessary health and safety information (when applicable) can result in possible injury and liability, so it is very important to research and include appropriate notes in your instructional document.

Figure 12.2. Images and icons like these convey safety warnings and cautions to users.

Identify Reusable Content

This research task is related to benchmarking research, where you might discover information you want to reuse (and cite or acquire permissions if necessary). You may also have gathered sources from other research, which can include textual content, graphics, or even templates. In addition, if you are revising an instructional document, a previous version might be valuable for content reuse. When working on new documents, you may rely on new content, and have little to reuse. However, when working on new versions of a document, there may be considerable content that may be used, with appropriate editing.

> ### EXERCISE 12.2
> ### *Depicting Health and Safety Concerns with Symbols*
>
> Quickly sketch symbols you have seen used in documents to indicate health or safety concerns. Try to identify at least five symbols that are commonly used. Compare your drawings to the "The International Language of ISO Symbols" booklet (available online at http://www.iso.org/iso/graphical-symbols_booklet.pdf). (Note the safety symbols begin on p. 15 of the booklet.) Did you sketch any symbols that are included in the booklet? Have you seen any of the symbols that appear in the booklet? Discuss your findings as well as the booklet images. Why do you think these symbols are internationally used, and why do you think symbols are an important way to convey health and safety information?
>
> **Tasks to be completed:**
>
> 1. Quickly sketch up to five safety symbols you know.
> 2. Compare your sketches to the ISO booklet.
> 3. Discuss your sketches and those in the ISO booklet to discover why health and safety symbols are important to include in instructional materials.

Develop an Organizational Structure for your Instructional Document

Planning an information model, or outline, of content in an instructional document is often based on conventions specific to the type of instructional document you are producing. Written procedures and instructions often follow a similar pattern, which includes introductory information, background, procedural steps, and supplemental content. The arrangement of content, however, may vary depending on other organizational or disciplinary conventions you may have to work with. Learning materials often follow a modified pattern, including introductory information, background, topics, and supplements. The organization of topics may vary depending on level of difficulty (from simple to complex), incrementally (building on previous topics), hierarchically (from general to specific), or have some customized organizational pattern. You can also find information helpful for planning design and layout through your other research activities, by examining similar instructional documents to help you make decisions on how to best organize information to maximize usability and effectiveness.

Plan Design, Layout, and Graphic Content

After deciding on an organizational pattern for your instructional document, you will want to consider its layout and design features. When conducting other research tasks, including benchmarking, previous versions of documents, or general knowledge research, pay attention to the use of formatting, styles, visual information, and graphic content. Visual graphics should complement the document, by providing illustrations, diagrams, cross-sections, or photos that help users perform tasks or understand concepts or processes more clearly.

Your benchmarking research can help you make decisions on the layout, formatting, and use of graphics in your instructional document. There are normally conventions or practices with regard to the use of visual information, which other documents will follow, so you might also find additional guidelines in standards you locate in your research.

> ### EXERCISE 12.3
> ### *Researching for Instructional Tasks*
>
> Find a set of instructions online that you might use. Using the research tasks listed above, evaluate the instructions to determine how effectively they are written. Make notes of any discrepancies or missing information. Complete this exercise by writing a short paragraph making recommendations for improvement.
>
> **Tasks to be completed:**
>
> 1. Find a set of instructions. You might explore websites like YouTube, WikiHow.com, or Instructables.com to find the instruction set you would like to analyze.
> 2. Evaluate based on the previous list of research tasks, and determine tasks.
> 3. Make note of discrepancies or missing information.
> 4. Write a paragraph recommending changes.

Writing and Designing Instructions

Writing tasks include introductory information (title, purpose statement, objectives), background information (prerequisites, materials, setting, conditions, time to complete, and warnings or cautions), procedural steps (specific numbered sequence of tasks), and supplemental content (references, troubleshooting, performance tips, and contact information). Design tasks include developing a stylesheet, layout, and any visual information that will be used in the instructional document. In the ADDIE process, this phase corresponds to the Development and Design stages.

When writing instructional documents, use clear, precise language to ensure the information in the document is accurate and to guarantee users will be able to perform the instructions correctly. Additionally, content must be accurate and sufficiently detailed, providing users exactly what they need to know to successfully use the document. When considering level of detail, you should provide only what users need to know, and avoid providing additional unnecessary details or description. Careful selection of details helps keep users from being distracted or confused by unnecessary complexity or detail, and focusing on a more concise writing style.

Consequently, you should balance the level of detail and level of conciseness. When using terminology, choose terms that are consistent with the overall topic, subject, or discipline. Careful term selection allows users to draw from previous knowledge, which can contribute to their understanding of the document. You should also consider incorporating visual information, such as graphics or illustrations, but only if they aid the process. While some graphic content might be thematic or decorative, focus on using visuals that contribute to overall usability, rather than distract users. Finally, edit your instructional documents precisely to avoid potential errors or problems with your document. Keep these writing guidelines in mind, when writing introductory information, background, steps, and supplemental content for your instructional documents. The guidelines that follow will help you write these sections of your instructional documents.

Introductory Information

The purpose of the introductory section is to identify the subject, scope, and overall objectives of the instructional document. This section is typically shorter and succinct in terms of its overall writing style and length. Provide a title and statement of purpose. A title should be succinct and clearly identify the topic of the instructional document. The title might also include keywords or terms that could be used to search for the document, particularly if it is published online. A purpose statement should also be succinct, and identify what task or outcome will result from completion. In addition, you should also identify what objective(s) will be accomplished, including a finished product, result, or skills or knowledge acquired. Learning objectives should briefly identify three elements as part of the instructional situation: prerequisite knowledge required; what skill, task, or knowledge will be gained or completed; and the desired (or ideal) outcome of the instructional document.

Introductory Information Tasks

1. Write a descriptive title, using relevant keywords or terms.
2. Write a clear statement of purpose using a single sentence.
3. Write one or more objectives that identify the desired outcome.

Background Information

Providing appropriate background information for your instructional document helps users understand the requirements, contexts, and constraints under which your document will be used. This section typically will include specific information on any prerequisites, conditions, time estimates, materials, settings, or any caution or warning notes. It also provides an overview of the setting and statement of the value or benefits that users will gain from using the instructional document. When writing background information for instructional documents, make sure to provide an appropriate level of detail and use precise language to ensure their usability and effectiveness.

Figure 12.3. Help users to understand instructional requirements by providing contextual information.

- **Provide a situational overview.** This should be a brief description of the intended setting, conditions, time to complete, and any cautionary notes or constraints under which the tasks can be performed. It should also include a statement of forecasting, that identifies the intended outcome.
- **Provide a discussion of prerequisites.** Discuss briefly the qualifications, skills, or knowledge that users must possess to successfully use the instructional document. You can also describe a typical user of the instructions, to help illustrate what is expected in terms of the successful user of the instructional document.
- **Provide a list of materials and resources.** Describe any materials or resources that users need to have in order to successfully complete tasks. This can be a bulleted list, identifying specific items required, including specific brands, quantities, or substitutes.
- **Provide a statement of value or outcomes.** This is often a good way of starting or ending the background information section of an instructional document. A statement of value often draws from the overall purpose or objectives but focuses on what benefit(s) or outcome(s) will be derived by the users by using the instructional document. For example, filling out a registration form for a product might have the value of providing free technical support.

Background Information Tasks

1. Write a brief overview, including details on the required setting, conditions, duration, and any important caution notes.
2. Write a short list or description of prerequisites, including specific skills or knowledge users are expected to have to complete the tasks.
3. List any materials or resources required to complete the instructions.
4. Write a short statement of value or outcomes that identifies the benefits or intended outcome.

Procedural Steps or Topics

This section is the main content of the instructional document, where step-by-step instruction is provided for instructional or procedural documents, or individual topics for learning materials. Precision, conciseness, and clarity are especially important in terms of writing style, to ensure users perform tasks successfully and/or are able to complete the learning objectives. Additionally, when using specific terminology, make sure it is consistent with the subject, discipline, and use throughout the document. And finally, avoid complicated explanations, if possible, or provide alternate forms of content, such as graphics or illustrations to aid comprehension.

- **Organize content logically.** This organization may include using numbering schemes, descriptive headers and subheads, bullet points, shading, or other methods that help users understand the organization of material. At this point, you can integrate your research on developing an organizational structure, from the planning phase, by using a pattern and labeling scheme that best suits the type of document you are producing. Pay particular attention to the order of steps, since some instructions or processes require users to follow a particular order. For other kinds of instructional documents, where a linear progression is not necessary, make notes of where steps can be repeated, or performed in any order.

- **Write only one task per step**. For instructions and procedures, restricting instructions to one task per step will help reduce misunderstanding or unnecessary complexity in the instructional document. Allowing users to focus on a single task for each step also contributes to good usability and error reduction in the process. It also will help users avoid missing a step, or only partially completing one before moving on to other steps.
- **Each topic should fulfill a specific learning objective**. For learning materials, this ensures there is alignment between learning objectives and the content in the instructional document. To assure alignment, revisit the learning objectives when writing topics to make sure the scope of your content is sufficient in detail to enable learners to successfully complete objectives. In this way, learning objectives can also be used to test the scope and completeness of your instructional content. And, in some cases, you may need to revise your learning objectives so they are in proper alignment with the content.

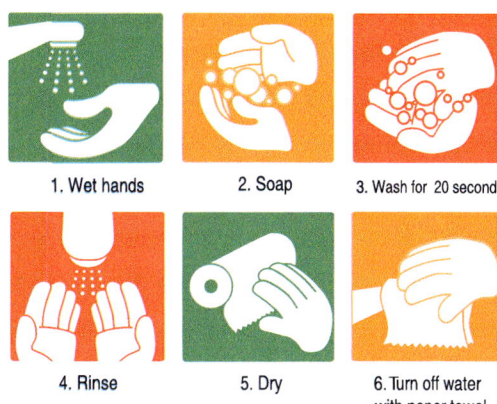

Figure 12.4. These simple instructions for handwashing are clearly organized and highly visual.

- **Include appropriate visual information or graphics**. To assist users as they complete steps, include illustrations, diagrams, photographs, or other media forms, which complement the written content and help users comprehend specific tasks, sequences, or concepts. Visuals should be clear, accurate, and appropriate for the subject, and not distract users from the task or material they are trying to complete. Graphical and other visual information might also include design elements that help enhance the readability and usability of the document, which you identify from your planning research on design, layout, and graphic content. For example, numbered lists help readers to comprehend the order of steps to be completed.
- **Include caution or warning notes**. If applicable, provide appropriate caution or warning notes, which might relate to health or safety concerns. Although you have likely identified these in the background information section, you should include them in this section as reminders. Be sure to place these notes by the steps or sections they correspond to so users can easily find them. These specific reminders will help ensure users will notice them prior to completing a specific step or part of the process. Also, be sure to include appropriate symbols or graphics to help users easily locate these important notes.

Procedural Steps Tasks

1. Organize steps or topics appropriately. This might include numbering or sequencing them in a specific order.
2. Write only one task per step (for instructions or procedures) and make sure each topic (for learning materials) fulfills a specific learning objective.
3. Include appropriate visual information or graphics, which are necessary to successful completion.
4. Write caution or warning notes to include with the topic or step to which they apply.

Supplemental Content

This final section provides any instructional supplements, references, troubleshooting, performance tips, or other notes that help enhance the instructional document, by adding content to help users perform the instructions successfully. Not all supplements are placed at the end of the document, but some can be placed throughout the document. For example, while you would expect references and contact information (for support or help) at the end of the document, performance tips, and troubleshooting advice can be place in the document, often near the step or section to which the pertain. Not all supplemental content is needed for instructional documents, so you can pick and choose which supplements you would like in your instructional document. Depending on the subject, standards, regulations, or other guidelines that apply to your instructional document, some supplements may be required (such as citations for copyrighted content) while others are optional. Supplements should provide a specific benefit to users of the instructional document; otherwise, they should be not included. Determine which of the following supplements are necessary, and only use the ones that are appropriate:

Figure 12.5. These icons caution users about potential health and safety issues.

- **Include references, works cited, or other resources**. When using material that is copyrighted or from other published sources, it is important to provide appropriate citations in the document and include a list of references or works cited. In some cases, you may have to pay for permissions for use of certain materials, or acquire signed permission for use. When providing a list of other resources, which can benefit users, you may also include a list of resources that users can research or explore on their own.

- **Include useful performance tips**. Performance tips can provide advice for completing tasks or steps, or provide alternate methods for users to accomplish the same task. These may also be short cuts or workarounds, which have been discovered by repeated use of the instructional product, which can help users master or complete tasks more quickly and efficiently. Performance tips are also typically placed next to the step or section to which they correspond, for ease of use.

- **Provide a list of frequently asked questions (FAQ) or troubleshooting notes**. These supplements provide self-help for users that may encounter problems with instructional documents, tasks, steps, or processes. They are typically based on the advice of experienced users or testers, or even consistent feedback from users. They may also be based on common or recurring problems or questions, and provide concrete answers that help aid performance or mastery.

- **Provide appropriate points of contact for assistance**. In some cases, instructional documents may require other resources, such as technical support, where users can ask specific questions or address concerns. If applicable, provide a brief description of contact information, such as names, addresses, emails, etc., for users to seek such assistance.

Supplemental Content Tasks

1. Include a list of references, works cited, or other resources, if available.
2. Write a list of performance tips, if applicable, to include in the document.
3. Write a list of frequently asked questions (FAQ) or troubleshooting advice, if applicable.
4. Write a list of any points of contact for assistance, questions, or support.

Testing and Reviewing Instructions

After you have written and designed your instructions, your next step includes comprehensive testing as well as content reviewing and editing of the instructional document. These tasks and the publishing tasks described in the next section correspond to ADDIE's implementation and evaluation stages. The first quality assurance task is to test documents to make sure they are accurate, well written, and can be completed successfully. Instructional documents should be tested with typical users and settings many a few times before publishing them. If possible, you can use existing standards or guidelines from your research as criteria (or heuristics) for evaluating the accuracy and completeness of the instructional document. For learning materials, you use learning objectives to evaluate content. When you complete testing and revision, you may need to retest the instructional document at least once to ensure you have addressed any concerns. You may also want to collect or incorporate user feedback or preferences.

Content editing is an essential task since precision, conciseness, and clarity are essential to the overall usability and success of the instructional document. As part of reviewing and editing, you may want to enlist subject matter experts, who are knowledgeable on the subject to provide suggested changes or edits. This step might also include submitting the document for a legal review (if applicable) to ensure health, safety, or other liabilities are addressed. And finally, you will want to perform a general writing and copyediting review.

In some cases, you might want to create a checklist of tasks to complete, prior to submission or publication of the instructional document. This checklist might include any final usability and accessibility checks and minor revisions, based on testing results. It might also include specific steps for distribution, delivery or publication, such as file formats, publication platforms, printing specifications, or uploading instructions. And finally, it may include a plan for collecting feedback or providing support.

INSTRUCTIONAL DOCUMENT TYPES

The instructional document types you will likely encounter fall into three categories: written instructions, procedures, and learning materials. Some important differences between these types involve their subject, purpose, ideal users, and overall objectives. **Written instructions** typically focus on completing a single objective, with multiple tasks, such as assembling a product. **Procedural documents** can incorporate one more objectives, and focus on a process or specific action or outcome. **Learning materials** specifically support learning objectives related to formal or informal training, such as courses, tutorials, or other instructional activities. In some cases, written instructions or procedures can function as supplemental learning materials, if they support a specific educational outcome or learning objective. Each type will be discussed to help you distinguish between the various kinds of documents and differences.

Instructions

Written instructions help users complete tasks, such as assemble products or complete a desired action. Instructions are generally shorter documents, and they are written clearly and concisely, to avoid errors in performing tasks. Instructions can be highly textual with detailed steps and descriptions or highly visual with information graphics that illustrate steps, tasks, materials, and finished products. Instructions typically include shorter tasks or are shorter versions of processes. They are completed in a short amount of time. Each step in instructions typically focuses on a single task for greater clarity and usability. They may be completed more than once, in some cases, and they can function as troubleshooting or reference guides, if saved after completing a task. Instructions for products are often included with many commercial or consumer products and are a valuable supplement for those products. They also will identify (or include) a list of specific materials, components, or other resources needed to successfully complete the task. The specific elements required for writing instructions include the following:

- Title (succinct description of task)
- Description (overview, purpose, objective, and outcome)
- List of materials (including tools or resources needed)
- Steps (individual tasks and actions)
- Caution and warning notes (placed near the step to which they apply)
- Resources and supplements (including support, troubleshooting, and references)

Exercise 12.4 provides you with opportunities to locate and critique instructional documents.

EXERCISE 12.4

Improving a Set of Instructions

Using a set of instructions for assembling a product, test the effectiveness of them by attempting to complete them. Pay particular attention to the use of graphics and other supplemental content, such as references, performance tips, troubleshooting advice, etc. Make note of any problems you encounter, as well as things you would change about the set of instructions. Write a set of performance tips for the instructions that you feel would assist users in comprehending or completing the instructions with greater ease. Identify at least 5–7 tips and note where you would add them in the instructions.

Tasks to be completed:

1. Locate a set of instructions for assembling a product, which you can test and complete.
2. Test the instructions by completing them.
3. Make notes of any problems or content you would change.
4. Write a set of 5–7 performance tips that would improve the usability of the instructions and help users.
5. Discuss your findings and improvements with others.

Procedures

Written procedures help users accomplish specific tasks or processes that are repeatable and reusable by a specific audience. They often involve performing a specific skill, action, or behavior that involves a process. Procedures typically follow a linear process, but, in some cases, may be more flexible in terms of their organization, depending on their purpose and intent. They are similar to instructions, but often describe a process that may include multiple objectives. Procedures can be used as assessment, diagnostic, evaluation, or testing tools. They can involve performing specific actions such as registration, purchasing, or maintenance (and repeated) tasks. Procedures are typically longer than instructions and may be more descriptive in terms of how each part must be completed. They may also include specific notes on critical tasks, which must be followed precisely, or cannot be reversed or undone, once completed. The specific elements included in writing procedures include the following:

- Title (succinct description of process)
- Description (overview, purpose, objectives, and outcomes)
- Prerequisites (list of materials, resources, skills, or prior knowledge)
- Procedural steps (list of tasks in order)
- Caution and warning notes (including critical tasks)
- Resources and supplements (including support, troubleshooting, and references.

Figure 12.6 illustrates a visual procedure for administering CPR on a victim in distress. The sample document in Figure 12.7 is adapted from the U.S. Bureau of Labor's Tornado Preparedness and Response web site. This excerpt provides an introduction explaining the need for preparation and includes information on planning for as well as developing procedures for a tornado while at work.

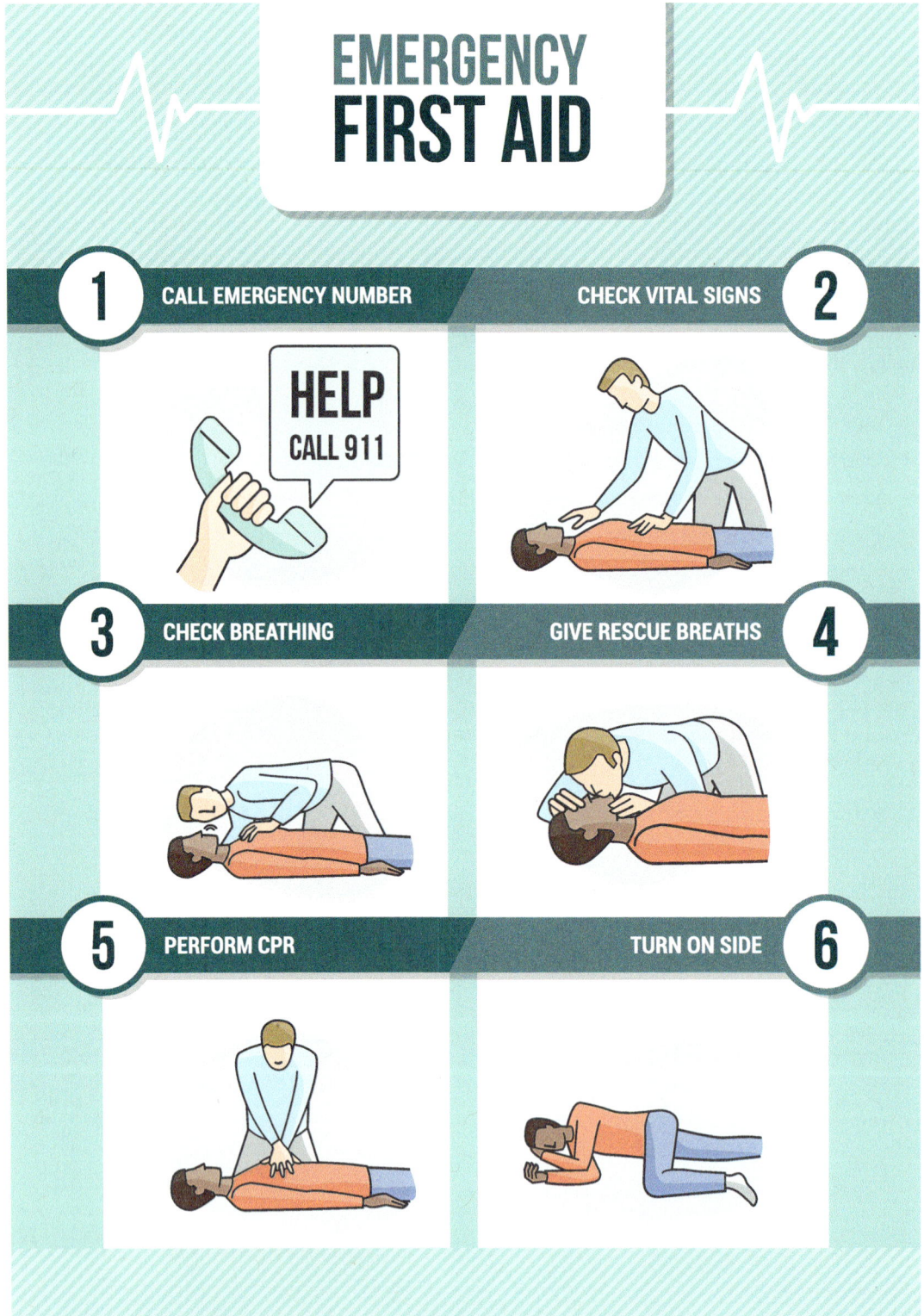

Figure 12.6. This procedure visually demonstrates how to conduct CPR.

Tornado Safety Preparedness

Preparedness involves a continuous process of planning, equipping, training and exercising. Planning for tornadoes requires identifying a place to take shelter, being familiar with and monitoring your community's warning system, and establishing procedures to account for individuals in the building. Employers may need to obtain additional equipment and/or resources (e.g. Emergency Supply Kits) identified in the plan. In addition, workers need to be trained and plans need to be practiced to ensure that personnel are familiar with what to do in the event of a tornado.

Planning

Identifying Shelter Locations

An underground area, such as a basement or storm cellar, provides the best protection from a tornado. If an underground shelter is unavailable, consider the following:

- Seek a small interior room or hallway on the lowest floor possible
- Stay away from doors, windows, and outside walls
- Stay in the center of the room, and avoid corners because they attract debris

Rooms constructed with reinforced concrete, brick or block with no windows and a heavy concrete floor or roof system overhead. Avoid auditoriums, cafeterias and gymnasiums that have flat, wide-span roofs.

Accountability Procedures

The following steps are recommended to help ensure the safety of personnel if a tornado occurs:

- Develop a system for knowing who is in the building in the event of an emergency
- Establish an alarm system to warn workers
  - Test systems frequently
  - Develop plans to communicate warnings to personnel with disabilities or who do not speak English
- Account for workers, visitors, and customers as they arrive in the shelter
  - Use a prepared roster or checklist
  - Take a head count
- Assign specific duties to workers in advance; create checklists for each specific responsibility. Designate and train workers alternates in case the assigned person is not there or is injured.

Figure 12.7. These procedures provide textual instructions for tornado preparedness.

> ### EXERCISE 12.5
>
> ### *Improving a Written Procedural Document*
>
> Using a procedural document, which asks you to perform a series of steps to complete a specific process, evaluate its effectiveness. Try to select a procedural document that you have completed, or need to complete, so you can test it as well. For example, you might select a procedure for registering for a course, conference, or Web site. Complete the process and make notes while you perform the procedure, identifying any problems you encounter. Make note of missing or incorrect information. Then, edit the procedure with any changes that would improve its use. Also, write a list of troubleshooting tips to help users with any potential problems they might encounter with successfully performing the procedure. Then, have another person retest your revised documents and evaluate the changes.
>
> **Tasks to be completed:**
>
> 1. Select a procedural document that you have completed before, or one you may need to use, and can complete in a short amount of time.
> 2. Complete the process.
> 3. Make note of any problems you encounter, including any missing or incorrect information.
> 4. Edit the procedural document, including any changes to improve its use.
> 5. Write a short list of troubleshooting tips for users that would help them with potential problems in completing the procedure.
> 6. Have another person retest your revised documents and report their results.

Learning Materials

Learning materials are instructional documents with educational or training purposes and can vary widely to include handouts, worksheets, tutorials, Web sites, audio, video, and even interactive documents. The process of developing learning materials follows a similar process involving planning (analysis & design) development, quality assurance and publication (implementation and evaluation), based on the ADDIE (analysis, design, development, implementation, evaluation model for instructional development (Lee & Owens, 2004). Analysis involves conducting user research (learning styles, technology, demographics, and prerequisite knowledge) and content research. Design involves writing clear learning objectives, designing information models for content (sequencing and organizing), and integrating semantics and navigation tools. Development includes the writing of topics and integrating guidelines and standards. Finally, the implementation and evaluation phases are often combined, including usability and accessibility testing to ensure compliance with stated learning objectives.

There are some key differences between learning materials and other types of instructional documents, such as written instructions and procedures. Their primary purpose is to help learners master a skill or gain new knowledge on a particular subject, with educational value or benefit. Often, learning materials are provided as primary or supplemental content for formal training, which can include classroom, online, or hybrid instruction. They can also include an assessment component that focuses on measuring the acquired skills, knowledge, behaviors, and impacts on business.

Learning materials are organized by topics. In an instructional context, a topic is a self-contained using of content that achieves or accomplishes a single learning objective (Horton, 2012). The sequencing and pacing of topics varies based on a wide range of factors, including the learners, subject, level of difficulty, and purpose. Some learning materials are designed to be self-paced, partially used, or accessed in any order, while others require learners to follow a specific order. The topic may require different organization of topics, from general to specific, easy to difficult, or some other pattern appropriate for the subject. The level of difficulty may also affect topic sequencing, which helps learners proceed at a specific pace or order. The purpose of the learning materials may affect sequencing, particularly if their function is to be a reference or a testing instrument to assess learners' skills. As mentioned, types of learning materials vary widely, depending on their function in an instructional context, a few of which are described below.

- **Handouts**. Handouts are instructional supplements used to support a specific course or tutorial. They are typically one page to a few pages long in length and focus on summarizing concepts, skills, or describing processes. As such, written instructions and processes can function as supplements, if they support a specific course or tutorial.
- **Tutorials**. A tutorial is typically a longer document, which functions as a short course on a specific subject. It can have one or more learning objectives and incorporate other learning materials as supplements. Many tutorials are Web-based, accessible through a Web browser, and integrate a wide range of activities, media, and interactive content for learners. Tutorials are typically asynchronous, in that they can be performed independent of a specific real-time class, and often at the learner's pace.
- **Activities**. Activities provide learners with tasks to help apply and practice the skills and knowledge they learn. These can be performed as part of a course or tutorial, or outside of the learning environment, by individuals or small groups. Activities include role playing, scavenger hunts, discovery tasks, independent research, and task-based scenarios, and assignments to name a few.
- **Media and Interactive content**. This learning content can include audio or video files, or even interactive applets or features as part of Web-based tutorials. They might include instructional videos, podcasts, calculators, games, puzzles, simulations, or other kinds of interactive content. They are often called learning objects, or self-contained content, which support a single learning objective. They also are typically electronic content, incorporated as part of Web sites or other kinds of electronically delivered documents.

The sample handout in Figure 12.8 provides students with instructions for writing a technical description. Note that the instructions include an introduction, a list of materials, the specific instructions for completing the task, and a series of questions to use to check completeness and accuracy of the task.

The Internet is populated with many examples of learning materials online. Most recent materials uploaded to the Internet take the form of audio or video instructions. Exercise 12.6 will allow you to explore the Internet for learning materials and examine their effectiveness.

Home Description Assignment

Technical descriptions are common in technical communication. The key to a good description is analyzing your audience's knowledge of the object, product, or mechanism and choosing descriptive language that will help your audience understand its design and use. In this particular assignment, you will be writing a technical description of your home layout. Your description should be specific enough that someone could draw your home after reading it. Your description must include at least three rooms, including major furnishings.

Materials: To complete this assignment, you will need paper, writing instrument, and good observational skills.

Steps for writing your home description

1. Familiarize yourself with the details of the layout at least three rooms in your home.
2. Record details, such as number, size, position, and layout of rooms.
3. Note where furniture, electronics, and appliances are located.
4. Using text only (no pictures or photographs), describe your home in enough detail that someone could draw your home based on your description.
5. As you write your description, organize it so readers can easy visualize the space. For example, you might describe rooms and objects from big to small, from general to specific, and so on. Techniques that describe your object in space are also helpful to readers; for example, you might organize your description clockwise or counterclockwise, right to left, or top to bottom.
6. Include details that will help your reader visual your home layout.
    a. Note: If you describe your home too generally, your partner may have problems understanding the room layout ("Enter the apartment through the door. Moving forward on the right is a bedroom, where you will find a desk on the left and bed beside the desk.")
    b. Use concrete words and measurements, such as "My apartment is rectangular, 12 square feet wide and 15 square feet long," to improve your detailed description.
7. After you have written your description, use the follow questions to evaluate it for accuracy and completeness;
    a. Is the home layout description clearly defined?
        i. Does the home layout description discuss at least three rooms, their locations, and main furnishings?
        ii. Are the connections between rooms explained so they can be imagined or visualized easily?
        iii. Is the description missing any important details?
    b. Is the content well organized, and are paragraphs in good order?
    c. Does the content use concrete, specific details that help readers visual location and placement of rooms and furnishings?

Figure 12.8. This is learning materials example is an assignment description, requiring learners to describe their homes visually and textually.

> ### EXERCISE 12.6
>
> ### *Writing Learning Objectives for Learning Materials*
>
> Find a short online tutorial, which can be an instructional Web site, short course, or video tutorial on any subject as long as it does not include specific learning objectives or background information for learners. Complete the tutorial making note of what you learned, specific perquisites that would be helpful, and any other useful information. Write a set of 1–3 learning objectives appropriate for the tutorial. Also, write a short paragraph including what background information might be useful to learners, such as materials they need, prior skills, or other prerequisites. Have another person complete the tutorial alongside your list of learning objectives and background description. Collect their comments or suggestions to improve your list of objectives and background description.
>
> **Tasks to be completed:**
>
> 1. Find a short online tutorial, which can be an instructional Web site, short course, or instructional video.
> 2. Complete the tutorial.
> 3. Make note of skills learned, prerequisites needed, or other useful information for learners.
> 4. Write 1–3 learning objectives for the tutorial.
> 5. Write a short background description including information on prerequisites, materials, or other information learners would benefit from.
> 6. Have another person complete the tutorial with your learning objectives and background description as supplements.
> 7. Collect their comments and suggestions on improving your list of learning objectives and background description.

Chapter Summary

Instructional documents help users complete important tasks, processes, or to learn new skills, and they include various document types such as written instructions, procedures, and learning materials. Writing instructional documents involves many important researching, development (writing and design), quality assurance, and publishing tasks. Planning research includes collecting information on the topic, users, other products or versions, standards and practices, and health and safety issues. It also involves making decisions on how to reuse or cite research. Development includes writing and designing content, including introductory information, background, steps or topics, and supplemental content. Quality assurance tasks include testing to ensure the document meets usability standards and achieves the overall purpose and objectives of the instructional document. And finally, publishing includes final testing, revision, and other details related to the distribution and delivery of the instructional document.

Instructional document types you will likely encounter fall into three categories, including written instructions, procedures, and learning materials. It is important to understand the differences of each type so you will know which type is more appropriate to support your project objectives. Instructions are shorter documents, which focus on completing a single objective, with multiple tasks, such as assembling a product. Procedures can encompass one or more objectives, often follow a linear organization, and include specific tasks or processes that are repeatable and reusable by a specific audience. Learning materials support educational course, tutorials, or specific learning objectives, and help learners apply, practice, and gain new skills, knowledge, or abilities for learners in a specific setting.

Chapter Assignments

The exercises in this section ask you to apply what you have learned in this chapter as well as explore how this knowledge applies to and connects with other information in the textbook.

1. Conduct an online search for visual instructions for assembling a product. Select a set of instructions that is comprised of mostly (or only) visual graphics, with minimal use of numbers or words. Read through the instructions carefully, making notes of visual images that might be potentially confusing. Also, make note of visual images that are particularly useful. Make a list of characteristics of successful images, and using your recommendations (and those from the chapter) redesign one of the problematic visual images. Discuss your changes and improvements.

2. Select a set of written instructions that has limited or no visual information. Complete and test the instructions, making note of any problems encountered or potential improvements you would make. Rewrite the instructions using only visual images, numbers, and symbols. Test your set of visual instructions and evaluate their effectiveness compared to the original text version.

3. Select a set of instructions, which can be easily completed and tested in short amount of time. The topic can be assembling a product or completing a simple process. Complete the instructions and make note of problems or inaccuracies you find. Have another person compete the set of instructions and make notes of problems. Compare your results and identify specific changes you would make to improve any of the major sections, including introduction, background, steps, or supplemental materials.

4. Find a handout used as an educational supplement for a training course or seminar. If possible, also conduct basic research on the course it supports to find a basic description, list of objectives, and course topics. Evaluate the effectiveness of the handout and determine how successfully it meets a specific learning objective of the course. What improvements would you suggest in terms of its organization, design, layout, and content?

Figure Credits

Figure 12.1. © VGstockstudio/Shutterstock.com

Figure 12.2. © Dream_master/Shutterstock.com

Figure 12.3. © wavebreakmedia/Shutterstock.com

Figure 12.4. © piyapongrot/Shutterstock.com

Figure 12.5. © VeZ/Shutterstock.com

Figure 12.6. © elenabsl/Shutterstock.com

Figure 12.7. OSHA

Developing Web Sites and Electronic Content

13

CHAPTER OVERVIEW

This chapter introduces you to concepts, practices, and strategies when developing electronic documents, including Web sites, blogs, wikis, and other types of electronic content. It will also address the use of social media platforms and best practices. After reading this chapter, you should be able to meet the following objectives:

- Describe the process of developing Web sites and other electronic documents, including important planning, development, quality assurance, and publishing tasks.
- Explain the differences between different electronic document types, including content management systems, blogs, wikis, Web sites, and other forms of social media.
- Discuss the differences in how content in electronic documents is developed, designed, read, and used.
- Discuss related concepts and skills from information architecture, navigation design, user experience design, and information design.
- Recognize how related concepts and skills are used in developing electronic documents.

The development and publication of electronic content is ubiquitous; nearly everyone uses computers to develop, distribute, and access documents and their contents, including products and services. Some content you will seek out (known as **pull content**); other content can be delivered to you automatically (**push content**). Pull content includes active online searches, downloads, and other activities users engage in online to acquire information resources, including media. Push content typically requires some kind of subscription, profile, or account to receive regular content and updates. Push content examples include sales promotions from an online store or subscription updates to blogs, news feeds, tweets, or other social media content. Whether classified as pull or push content, electronic content is used for a wide range of purposes and genres, including informational, educational, decision making, and instructional.

Figure 13.1. Websites remain the primary genre of electronically published content.

Web sites are the main genre of electronically published content; other electronic content forms (apps, social media, and electronic document forms) typically contribute to an overall Web site presence. Web sites as a genre include various types such as blogs, wikis, and learning management systems (for online educational and training purposes), just to name a few. Other types of electronic forms include social media, graphics, multimedia, and a wide variety of electronic document formats, such as Microsoft Word DOC and Adobe PDF. These kinds of electronic documents are often included as supplements for larger Web sites.

Developing electronic documents draws upon a wide range of skills and abilities, whether they are possessed by an individual or spread out amongst an entire team working on a document. Electronic document development may require a higher degree of technical skill and knowledge, depending on the tools you use to create such documents, than print document development. Electronic documents require computer resources for creation and distribution, including Internet and Web server access for publishing. Knowledge of structured authoring, which involves organizing, linking, marking up, reusing, and styling content, is also necessary. Other tasks also may require some knowledge of specific software, platform, and languages (including markup, scripting, and programming languages). Additionally, electronic documents require extensive testing to ensure functionality across wide range of users and computer environment variables, including browsers, operating systems, and devices (mobile device, laptop computer, etc.).

Developers need not necessarily possess all the skills since sometimes they work with team members who possess specialized skills and roles, such as a graphic designer, programmer, usability tester, or subject matter expert. Specifically, individual skills include the following:

- **Project management experience.** The ability to manage multiple tasks required to produce electronic documents, such as Web sites.
- **Design skills.** Development of graphics and media, including interactive media.
- **Markup and scripting languages.** Knowledge of common markup and scripting languages used in producing electronic documents, whether you use software or hand-code.
- **Writing and editing.** Ability to write, adapt, and single-source content. Strong editors are usually good coders, due to their skill with spotting errors and precision with use of language.
- **Software program skills.** The ability to use various kinds of graphic, word processing, media, and Web development programs to produce electronic documents.
- **Research skills.** Particularly online research, where you might search for graphics, templates, media, or scripts to assist in development.
- **Usability testing.** Experience in testing electronic documents in actual settings and to ensure they deliver content that is accessible and usable.
- **Content development.** Ability to structure and create information models for content and devise organizational patterns, labeling schemes, and content semantics.
- **User experience.** Designing interactive content, such as forms, navigation tools, games, etc.
- **Subject matter experts** who have knowledge about the Web site under development.

The majority of electronic documents are found online, such as through Web sites, which host other electronic documents and links to social media tools. Writing for the different genres of electronic documents follows a similar, iterative process, but, depending on the specific type, format, delivery, users, functionality, and purposes, specific tasks and strategies may vary.

Elements of user experience are components of developing electronic documents. These include information architecture, navigation design, interaction design, interface design, and information design (including visual, textual, and spatial elements) (Garrett, 2011). Information architecture involves information modeling or organizing content into coherent structures with relational aspects. Navigation design includes developing tools that are used to search, browse, and use content. User experience (or interaction) design involves creating interactive sequences, such as forms, media, or other tools that allow users to interact with content. Finally, information design includes creating information graphics, styles, interface designs, and page layouts. You were introduced to these concepts in earlier chapters, which will help you better understand how these skills are used in developing electronic documents.

DEVELOPING ELECTRONIC DOCUMENTS

As mentioned before, developing electronic documents draws from a wide range of skills, including information design, information development, usability testing, content markup and scripting, project management, and information technology. The process of developing electronic documents includes important planning, development, quality assurance, and publishing tasks. These tasks describe how various skills are incorporated into developing electronic documents (see Figure 13.2). The process is often iterative, where work completed during one phase might impact, or influence, the development of previous work. For example, when designing a page layout for a Web site, it might be necessary to revisit how content is written, chunked, or organized in order for it to be displayed or presented effectively in the design. Each of these phases will be discussed in terms of the skills and tasks required for successful electronic document production.

Planning

The planning process includes many tasks. A large part of planning involves considering the use of technology, including software, coding, and other variables of the computer environment. It also involves understanding the unique aspects of users in terms of how they access, use, and read content electronically, or in an online environment. Project management is essential in this phase to help plan and coordinate the project scope, resources, tasks, and timeline for a project. The critical tasks for the planning phase of developing electronic documents include the following:

- **Identify** user groups, through user profiles, user research, and analysis.
- **Determine** scope requirements, including functionality, technology, and content requirements.
- **Develop** timeline, tasks, project guidelines, and goals.
- **Determine** lifecycle of the product: is it a one-time product or a product that requires continuing support and management?

The planning phase is all about establishing a consistent roadmap or plan for the work that lies ahead. Creating a planning document that outlines the specifics for these critical tasks can be a useful planning and development tool for the project, particularly when working on a team or group project, to ensure everyone follows the same specifications for the project. An earlier chapter introduced you to the concept of writing a project plan, which may be useful in documenting the scope of your electronic document project.

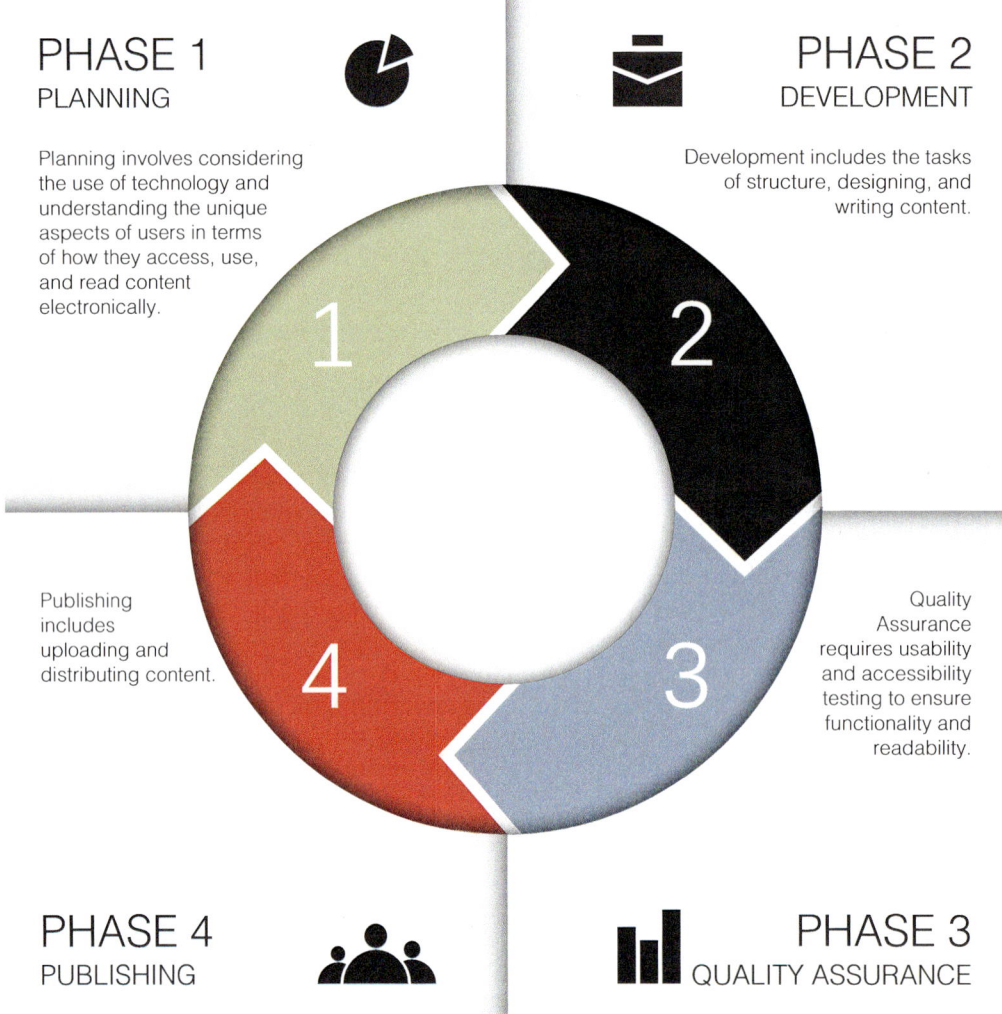

Figure 13.2. The process of developing electronic documents includes four phases.

Important Planning Factors to Consider

When planning an electronic document project, the following factors are important to consider:

How users access content, including what resources, aptitudes, and configurations are needed. User research can help reveal these details. Access is the first threshold for a Web site for users; if they cannot access, then usability and readability are not even factors to consider.

How users use content, including what tools users expect and rely on to access and successfully use content. Again, user research can be helpful in terms of the kinds of tools users expect. Usability is important because it measures user task performance and success rate in interacting with the site.

How users read content as well as their typical behaviors, perceptions, and thought processes. Users have different learning styles, but similar perceptual habits. Conducting research into the kinds of reader habits and behaviors is useful as well as conducting more localized tests on your own user groups.

What standards to use in similar documents. Benchmarking, researching other Web sites, and electronic document types can help determine user expectations to consider in developing similar information products.

What resources and technologies are available and which ones are the best to use. This planning task includes identifying the browsers, software, expertise, and budgetary resources available. It also includes determining which tools will contribute to the success of the product and helps maximize the best use of available resources.

Figure 13.3 illustrates effective design of content that accommodates how users access, read, and use content, through its familiar design and layout strategy, which resembles those found in popular magazines. The site also uses simple, familiar terminology, descriptive headers, and images designed to make reading information on a variety of space-related topics easy.

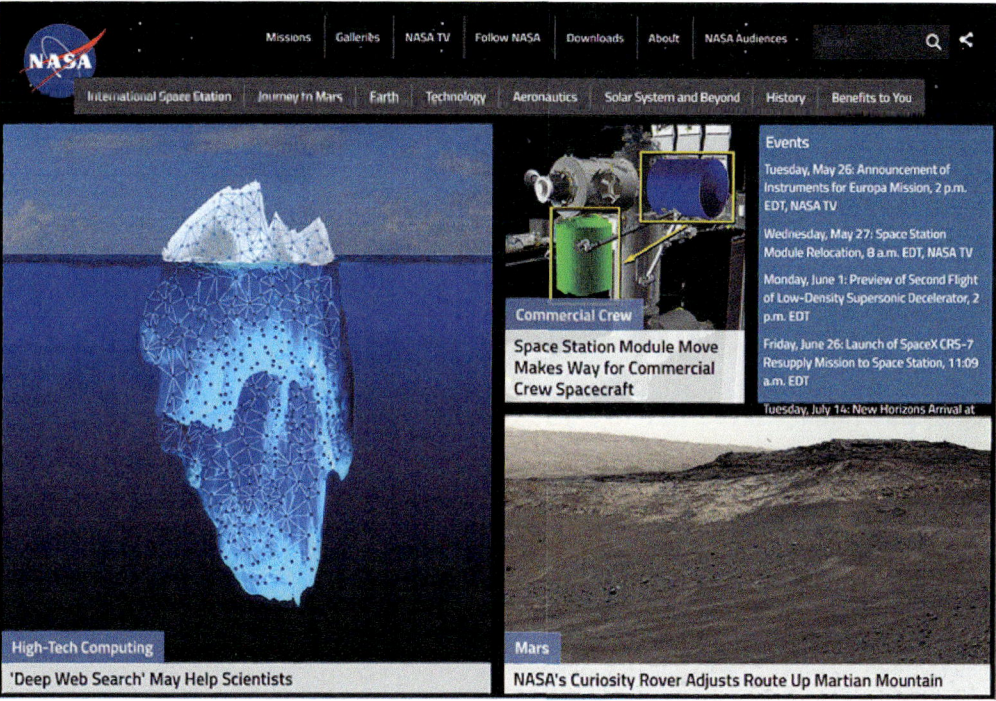

Figure 13.3. The National Aeronautics and Space Administration (NASA) Web site uses a familiar design and layout strategy to provide readers with cues for reading.

Development

The development process of creating electronic documents includes the important tasks of structuring, designing, and writing content. Work in this phase builds on the specifics identified in the previous phase, where the scope and specifications are identified in the project plan. Many of the aspects of user experience from above are major tasks in development, including information architecture, navigation design, information design, and interface/interaction design. The critical tasks of the development phase include the following:

- **Content development** (textual and graphic), including research and writing tasks.
- **Writing strategies** for developing content, including how to reuse or repurpose existing content.
- **Information model development** for organizing electronic document contents.
- **Design decisions**, such as styles and interface layouts for backgrounds, pages, forms, and supporting content.
- **Semantic and relational aspects** for content, such as how to link and tag content to maximize findability and accessibility of content within a document.
- **Supporting tool development**, including navigation tools, which enable users to search and browse content.
- **Interactive content development**, including forms, media, and customized scripts.
- **File formats determination** for graphics, documents, and other media.

These collective critical tasks involve the actual production work in creating the electronic document. Whether these tasks are accomplished by an individual or a team, work in this phase is the most demanding in terms of its required breadth and depth of technical skills. In team or group projects, these tasks may be divided up amongst individuals depending on their individual expertise and skill sets.

Important Development Factors to Consider

Before you develop your electronic document, you should consider these six factors that impact the content you will use and how you will use it:

What content assets are available and where to find them. This task is both research and planning oriented. Once you have inventoried all content assets, finding methods of organizing them and storing them for easy access by the team members will contribute to greater efficiency.

What to reuse and how to reuse it. This task requires you to determine single sourcing methods. Some content reuse can be automated, such as by a Content Management System, while, for other content, you may need to develop specific standards, such as writing and editing guidelines for reusable content.

What semantics to use. Determine what metadata to use, including labeling, linking, and tagging content. In some cases this task involves consulting any data you have on your typical users or even what terminology will be familiar to them. In some cases, you may want to test a labeling scheme with some typical users to ensure they grasp the meaning of semantic terms used.

How to optimally structure information that maximizes usability for the user and the system. In terms of users, finding optimal ways to organize content within an electronic document is essential. Information modeling strategies you have learned in earlier chapters will assist you. Remembering that computer systems as well as the user read content is key to optimization. What this insight suggests, is that when working within a particular software-authoring tool or content management system, knowing the limitations and customization options is important in helping determine what options are best (and feasible) for structuring information, and to maximize usability.

What structured authoring methods to use. Choose methods that best correspond to tools (and the platform) you have selected. This task requires you to consider specific markup and scripting languages, authoring tools, content standards, and procedures. In some cases, this may refer to the software program or content management system you are using, which often provides blank pages and templates for you to cut and paste your content into. Once entered into the system, you can then format appropriately.

What design styles and theme to use. This task includes the selection of colors, images, media, page layouts, and other visual, spatial, and graphic styles that will be used. Following a set of design principles and conventions can also be helpful in achieving this goal, which you read about in an earlier chapter.

What content standards should be followed. Content standards will help you to maximize accessibility, readability, and usability. This task is related to structured authoring. Developing a list of rules, styles, and standards for your document will help ensure consistency in quality throughout the project.

Figure 13.4 is a screenshot of a Web site developed and maintained by the National Oceanic and Atmospheric Administration. It successfully implements many of the development tasks required for Web pages, including a consistent use of visual images, styles, organized navigation tools and page layout, and well-written content.

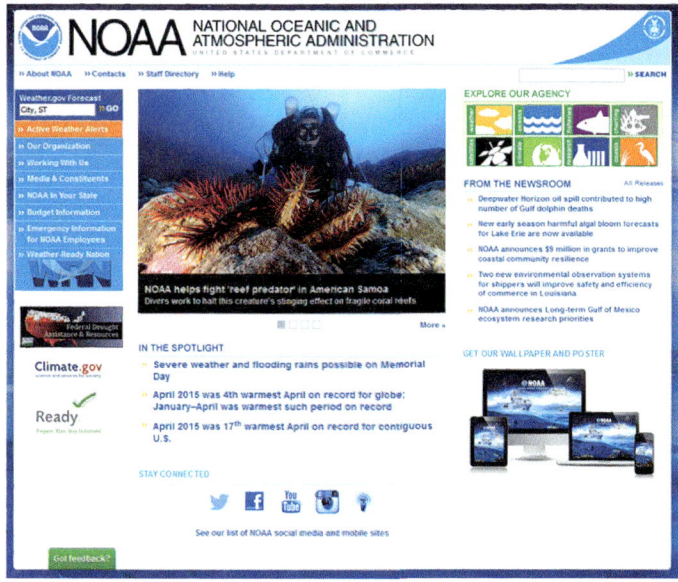

Figure 13.4. The National Oceanic and Atmosphere Administration website includes visual images, identifiable organization of content, navigation tools, and clear page layout.

Quality Assurance

The quality assurance phase involves usability and accessibility testing of electronic documents to ensure that they resolve any problems with functionality and readability and that they conform to user needs as best as possible. It involves testing electronic documents in various browsers or platforms. It also focuses on the goal of universal design, trying to create a user experience that accommodates the widest possible user base. You may find it helpful to test content, designs, tools, layouts, and usability of your electronic document throughout the development cycle to minimize errors and ensure a higher quality product. Quality assurance is something that ideally occurs throughout the development process, but, in particular, it becomes an important focus prior to publication. The critical tasks of the quality assurance phase include the following:

- **Conduct usability tests** to ensure functionality and readability.
- **Conduct accessibility tests** to ensure users with specific disabilities are accommodated.
- **Develop, prioritize, and complete list of development and production revisions** based on testing results.
- **Complete final editing and browser technical tests** to ensure readability and functionality, prior to publishing.

While the production work in the development phase may be ongoing, the quality assurance phase work often begins just after initial development, and it continues all the way up to the final phase, publishing. The quality assurance phase helps identify problems during electronic document development, which often requires revision of production work and prototypes based on findings from various quality assurance tests.

Important Quality Assurance Factors to Consider

Just as it is important to consider content factors before developing an electronic document, you must also consider the following quality assurance factors after the document is developed:

> **Usability testing heuristics and methods vary widely, so be selective.** Choose heuristics, methods, and criteria that will be most useful to test the product. User research, including tasks users will typically perform on the site, can help inform selection of testing criteria.
>
> **Accessibility includes a wide range of factors.** Among these factors are physical, cognitive, and technological limitations (including infrastructure). Ensure the maximum access for widest user base possible.
>
> **Quality assurance tasks must be scheduled and appropriate resources made available.** To ensure sufficient time to test, edit, and revise, set a schedule and stick to it. Completing quality assurance tasks in a timely manner reduces the potential for higher error reports, technical support requests, and other customer problems.

Figure 13.5 is a screenshot of the Section 508 Web site, which is designed to ensure accessibility on all government websites, including those Web sites managed of public universities. This Web site emphasizes the importance of user and accessibility testing to ensure Web site content confirms to applicable laws, policies, and best practices for users. In addition to being a useful reference for developers of Web sites, it also demonstrates effective organization of content by section and consistent layouts to help users find content on the site easily.

Figure 13.5. The Section508.gov Web site is designed to ensure accessibility and usability for all users.

Publishing

The publishing process involves uploading and distributing content, usually to a server or other online or electronic platform, or sending electronic documents to a group of specified users, such as through email or other electronic distribution system. Prior to publishing an electronic document, you should ensure it functions and displays properly in its intended medium, whether it is accessed online or through a software program or viewer. At this point in the process, the quality assurance phase overlaps one last time with the publishing phase. The critical tasks for the publishing phase include the following:

- **Finalize all documents, complete production checklist, and conduct final testing and revision.**
- **Upload or distribute the communication product, and complete a final test to ensure accessibility, usability, and readability.**
- **Determine and verify protocols** for electronic publication, including server or platform information, or marketing online to distribution lists or search engines.
- **Determine the process for collecting user feedback and troubleshooting problems**, if necessary.
- **Determine methods of support and continuing update and revision strategy** for the electronic document.

The publishing phase marks the completion of a specific version of an electronic document; however, most sites require continual updating and maintenance, cycling through the planning, development, quality assurance, and publishing tasks again and again. Additionally, changes or updates may need to be made depending on user feedback or problems encountered after publication.

EXERCISE 13.1

Web Site Publishing Protocols

Research two Internet Service Providers (ISP) and collect information on the protocols (or process) of uploading a small-scale Web site, for a small or local business. You should find out what kinds of software programs, available space, costs, and any other important technical details or requirements. You may find this information on the Web sites or by calling the technical support number from the ISPs you select. Create a comparison chart between the two providers, and make a list of pros and cons for each ISP. Then make a recommendation of which ISP would be the best choice with a supporting rationale.

Tasks to be completed:

1. Conduct online searches to find Internet Service Providers (ISPs) and select two that might be appropriate for hosting a small or local business.
2. Make a list of software programs, space available, cost, and other technical details or requirements associated with each ISP.
3. Create a comparison chart for the two ISPs and the data you collected.
4. Write a list of pros and cons for each ISP.
5. Write a short recommendation email that identifies which ISP would be the best choice, along with a supporting rationale and evidence.

Important Publishing Factors to Consider

Before you publish your electronic document, be sure to consider these factors:

> **Publishing has a strong focus on technology issues.** Publishing occurs at the end of the development cycle. This final task includes delivery, such as uploading or distributing the electronic content to its intended users.
>
> **Final technical and accessibility checks are essential.** These checks ensure proper functionality of the electronic document.
>
> **Determining methods of collecting feedback is necessary to learn how users are responding to your site.** This task includes deciding how to collect, analyze, and use the information in subsequent upgrades or versions.
>
> **Developing a separate schedule and scope of work for on-going projects will assist you as you maintain and manage the electronic document.** It may be necessary to update and manage electronic documents beyond the publishing phase. Developing a schedule for these tasks as you publish the document will help you to visualize the task that lie ahead.

CHOOSING AUTHORING TOOLS AND METHODS

The vast majority of electronic documents published on the World Wide Web are Web sites, or content included as supplements as part of Web sites. Web sites can be created using a wide range of tools, including the use of markup and scripting languages with a text editor, use of Web development software programs, use of Content Management Systems, or Social Media use. In some cases, you may use multiple options, such as coding and software, to build a Web site project. A wide range of content assets is available in these programs and systems, as well as online to assist developers with use of graphics, media, templates, and scripting. Developers can use a single tool or combine the use of multiple ones to create Web sites, depending on their skills, available resources, and project needs.

Two methods commonly used in developing Web sites and supplemental electronic content are coding (content markup, scripting, and programming), and software systems (Web development software, Content Management Systems, and Social Media tools). Both methods offer developers various advantages in creating Web site content. Required knowledge of software programs or systems and coding (markup, scripting, and programming) varies widely among these methods, but ideally you should have some experience in using both programs and coding. Coding is helpful when making quick edits, when to adding customizations to sites, and when working in a content management system or Web development software programs. Conversely, when working on projects with high volumes of content, software experience can help you to automate content markup, delivery, or interactive features. Such automation saves time and effort. This section provides you with more information on both coding and software programs you may use to develop electronic content.

Markup and Scripting Languages

One method of developing Web sites involves actual coding using a text-editing program. A markup language allows content to be read, organized, and displayed in a Web browser. Scripting language allows content to be interpreted and tasks to be performed with content (or data), such as styling or interactivity. Below, is a selected list of core languages used in developing Web sites.

HTML (Hypertext Markup Language) is the basic markup languages used for the publishing of Web-based content. HTML is a Web markup language used to outline and markup content so it can be read by a Web browser. It specifies both the basic structure of individual Web pages and basic markup of individual content elements, such as paragraphs, images and hyperlinks. XHTML is an evolved, and now depreciated version of HTML, using a stricter syntax that conforms and works more seamlessly with XML (Extensible Markup Language).

XML (Extensible Markup Language) is one of the most versatile and widely compatible markup languages used in developing Web 2.0 content. XML is different from HTML in that it provides developers greater control over the document structure and customized markup of content elements on a page, including the ability to develop and define content tag and the rules that govern their use. This capability makes XML ideal for creating highly structured documents and data sources, with a high degree of versatility.

CSS (Cascading Style Sheets) is a scripting language used to specify styles and position of markup content in Web pages. CSS allows authors to create electronic stylesheets for Web pages, which address stylistic elements such as fonts, colors, margins, and text alignment, as well as positional, media, and visual formatting.

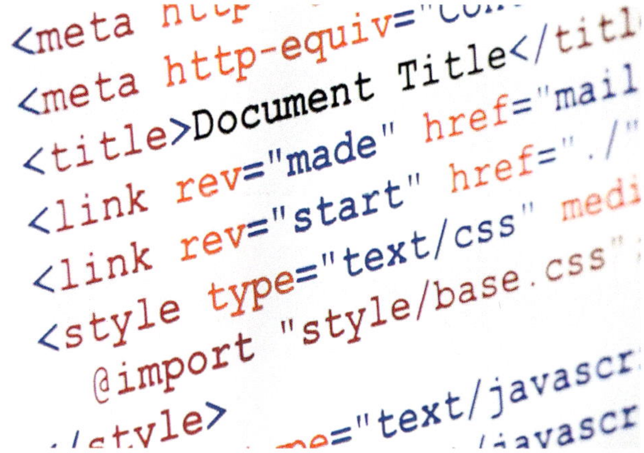

JavaScript is a client-side, object-oriented scripting language, which was created to add interactivity to Web pages and browsers. JavaScript is different from Java, a programming language used to run executable applets in Web pages. JavaScript can be used along with other markup and scripting languages to add interactive elements to pages.

Figure 13.6. Markup languages allows content to be read, organized, and displayed in a Web browser.

PHP (Hypertext Preprocessor) is a server-side scripting language, which can be used to handle and process form data or to work with other database query languages to handle and process data from servers. PHP is the backbone of many message board and content management systems. Like JavaScript, it is often used with other markup, scripting, and query languages to create interactive content in Web sites.

EXERCISE 13.2

Learning Basic Document Markup

Visit the W3 Schools' Web site (www.w3schools.com) to learn about basic HTML markup for documents. Look at some of different tags and markup examples provided on the site. Complete one of the HMTL tutorials to learn and play with basic document markup. For a bigger challenge, code a biography statement for your own Web site. Include your name, photo, a brief professional profile, and contact information.

Tasks to be completed:

1. Visit www.w3schools.com.
2. Complete one of the tutorials, such as the one on HTML.
3. Optional: code a page of your own to create a working example of markup.
4. Prepare a short presentation describing what you learned.

There are many advantages and challenges of using the coding method of electronic document development. First, markup and scripting languages are open-source, are platform independent, and, if used properly, are compliant across virtually all Web browsers. Second, codes have established standards, wide use, and many years of development behind them. Third, multiple languages can be used together to create highly customizable electronic documents. Finally, they have healthy user communities, online scripting libraries, and references available to assist developers. In terms of challenges, this method requires a high level of technical knowledge with specific languages. They require knowledge and use software to upload content to a Web server. Also, they require knowledge of basic syntax, practice, tools, and resources available to learn each language and to be able to use it successfully. Some languages require knowledge of basic programming concepts, and they often require good editing skills to locate possible errors in code, which can compromise functionality of scripts or pages loading in browsers.

Web Development Software

A wide range of software programs is available to help developers create Web sites, from companies such as Microsoft and Adobe. Also, online web development sites are available, including Squarespace, Weebly, Wix, and WordPress. A quick online search can help you locate the current products and versions available, many of which include free or trial versions for limited access. This range of software offers many advantages when producing electronic documents, including the following:

- Built-in design templates, graphic libraries, and scripting libraries, which can be used to create supplemental document content and interactive features.
- Compliance with accessibility guidelines.
- Some customization options available for developers.
- Built-in software client to publish and upload content.
- Design and code views that allow developers to alternate between using the software tools and hand-coding.
- Built-in tools for script and error checking.
- Many resources to help users learn how to use the tools, including built-in help systems.
- Wide use of tools, robust user communities, and third-party content resources.
- Technical support and help available for products from manufacturers.

Additionally, there are some challenges associated with using software to produce electronic documents. In many cases, software programs have limited customization options, which may require developers to either scale back their content design or seek out other solutions to help address the limitations. While these programs have the advantage of content libraries and resources, they are often limited and may require users to seek out other content supplements online or to create their own supplements. This software also tends to be a greater time and cost investment to learn. Additionally, many programs have updates or upgrades, some of which are necessary to keep the software current. Finally, software programs often have compatibility issues with imported content, or working with other programs.

Content Management Systems

Another option for the software development method of creating electronic documents is to use a content management system (CMS), which is "a system that approaches the problem of content management by using markup, metadata, and tools to break documents into component parts, to a level of granularity…set by organizationally defined information models, and labeling each part with metadata that describe its meaning and relationships to other content." (Clark 39). Blogs and wikis are two examples of commonly used content management system types which are widely used for a variety of purposes, including personal, educational, and commercial. Since many CMSs are out-of-the-box solutions, they come with built-in features and templates. They also afford designers the ability to customize the product, similar to Web development software programs.

Content management systems are similar to Web development software programs in some ways. They include design templates, graphic assets, and built-in and customizable scripts for things like navigation tools, banners, and interactive forms. They also often have design and code views, allowing users to drag and drop content and customize it either using tools provided, similar to word processing programs, or to enter code view to make edits. They have built-in tested templates and scripts and include software tools for uploading content. Finally, like Web development software programs, they have configurable options with some limitations.

Content management systems are different from Web development software programs in several ways. They typically provide hosting server space for developers and offer sliding scale costs, from free to pay per month. Many also provide free versions for use, but they typically include advertising banners from the host. Each content management system typically serves a particular purpose and is designed for it, such as blogging, wikis, or learning tools. Many also have robust user communities and content resources. They also include a wider range of add-ons such as widgets and social media integration tools. Among their disadvantages, many content management systems require an Internet connection for development so there are problems when working on the site when there is no access to the Internet. Also, greater customization is typically not possible without knowledge of the core development languages.

EXERCISE 13.3

Learning More about Content Management Systems

Research online content management systems to get a sense of what products are available and which ones seem to be widely used. You might even contact IT professionals you know or others who work in computer support to ask what they use. Select any two products and develop a comparison chart (or table) of their features. You might include options for free and paid subscriptions to the product, core languages used, compatibility issues, features, user community resources, and other features. Determine a list of advantages and disadvantages for each product, and identify which kinds of projects would be best suited for each tool and why. Which content management system would you be more willing to try to use in a project? Present your findings in a short presentation to your peers.

Tasks to be completed:

1. Conduct research online to learn more about the different content management system products available. If possible, contact friends or family who work in computer support roles to learn more about the tools they use.
2. Select any two content management system products and research their features, advantages, and drawbacks.
3. Develop a comparison chart of the features for each product.
4. Write a list of advantages and disadvantages for each product.
5. Present your findings.

Social Media Tools

Social media tools include a wide range of online services, which allow individuals to network with others in a variety of contexts, including personal, professional, and educational. Not all social media tools are created equal, and many users appropriate them for different uses. Distinguishing between the various purposes and your own personal needs is important in selecting the appropriate medium and message you wish to convey. Not every social media tool is the appropriate choice for every task.

Blogs, are one technological means for corresponding with others. Blogs, originally called weblogs, first appeared in 1997; by 2010, over 150 million blogs were present on the Internet. Among the most popular blogging sites in 2011 were WordPress, Blogger, and Tumblr. While blogs might be best known as a kind of personal diary, they are also important professional and business communications. Professional blogs, like distributed lists, are sites for building connections with other professionals, exchanging ideas, and building a support network.

Similarly, social networking sites like LinkedIn, Twitter, Facebook, and Google+ are used for professional correspondence. Professional networking sites like LinkedIn aim to build your professional network, and other social media are expanding their applications to make similar connections. Like other electronic correspondence, these sites allow you to search for, request connections to, and correspond with individuals for personal and business purposes.

Figure 13.7. Social media takes many forms and continues to increase in popularity among users.

Some guidelines for using social media in professional contexts include the following:

Allow your recipient to opt-in or opt-out of texting. Asking in advance of texting if text messages are acceptable gives your recipient a choice and avoids the possibility that your message is seen as spam (unwanted messages).

Consider time and costs. While many mobile users have unlimited texts, others are on limited plans that require them to pay for texts, even unwanted ones. A good rule of thumb is this: is your message valuable enough that you would spend money for a stamp to send it through the postal service? If not, then send the message via email. If the postal service is too slow, then send a text.

Avoid overly personal or inappropriate content. Because you are not face-to-face with the person with whom you are communicating, you may feel free to share overly personal or explicit information. Do not do it. Employers view these messages as misconduct, and both you and your employer are liable for any damages they cause. Not only will you harassing someone and breaking organizational policies, but you will also be leaving an electronic record behind of your misconduct.

EXERCISE 13.4

Researching Social Media Use in Business

Select a business that has an online Web site and uses social media to communicate with its customers. Examine the various kinds of tools, functions, content, and purpose of each type of social media tool used. Then, contact a representative of the business and to inquire about how they use social media tools to interact and provide services to their customers. For example, you might ask how they use social media tools to collect feedback, new ideas, or provide support for customers. Then, write a short description of the company and your findings on their use of social media tools. Include a list of specific recommendations that you feel might improve their social media presence and share your findings with peers.

Tasks to be completed:

1. Select a business with an online Web site that uses social media tools to communicate with customers.
2. Make a list of tools, functions, content types, and purposes from your observations of their Web site and tools used.
3. Contact a business representative at the company and inquire about their specific uses of social media tools, including how and why they use specific tools.
4. Write a short description of the company and its use of social media tools, including specific recommendations for improving their social media.
5. Share your findings with peers.

Chapter Summary

Creating electronic documents involves an iterative process, which includes important planning, development, quality assurance, and publishing tasks. Critical tasks in planning include determining variables related to users, content scope, and project management factors. Developing Web sites and other supplemental electronic content involves using a variety of structured authoring methods and tools. Electronic document development draws from related skills in user experience, information architecture, interface design, navigation design, interaction design, and information design. These same areas are critical tasks as part of the development process. Quality assurance involves usability and accessibility testing of the product to ensure its usefulness across a potentially wide and diverse group of users. Critical tasks in publishing include finalizing documents, determining protocols for distribution, and distribution and support for the product.

Electronic documents include Web sites, content management systems, social media, and other document formats unique to various software programs. The vast majority of electronic documents published on the World Wide Web are part of Web sites. Web sites can be created using a wide range of tools, including the use of markup and scripting languages with a text editor, use of Web development software programs, and use of content management systems. A wide range of content assets is available in these programs and systems, as well as online to assist developers with use of graphics, media, templates, and scripting. Social media tools may also be helpful in creating backchannels for Web sites, or to supplement online content.

Chapter Assignments

The exercises in this section ask you to apply what you have learned in this chapter as well as explore how this knowledge applies to and connects with other information in the textbook.

1. Research available Web development software products that are available for purchase from major sellers, such as Microsoft, Adobe, etc. Select two Web development software programs and research their capabilities, cost, ease of use, features, benefits, technical requirements, and other distinguishing characteristics. Develop a comparison chart for the two products, listing your findings from the research. Write a short description that addresses the pros and cons of each software program, by comparing and contrasting. Is one program more suited to beginners or advanced users? Is one program more likely to be useful for certain kinds of projects? Include any experience you have with using these products and answer these questions in your description, and present your findings.

2. Research the four content management system platforms you read about in this chapter, including Squarespace, Weebly, Wix, and WordPress. Develop a comparison chart evaluating the features, costs, pros, and cons of each. Include any experience you have with using these products. Develop a short presentation to share your findings.

3. Assess your skills with basic markup and scripting languages, such as HTML and CSS, which are used in developing Web site content. Visit http://www.w3schools.com and search for their quizzes on both HTML and CSS. Take each quiz, without referring to notes or other resources. Record your scores and then review the resources on HTML and CSS on the site to improve your skills. Based on your scores, write a self-assessment identifying your strengths and areas to improve upon.

4. As a developmental skills exercise in structured authoring methods, find a book or online resources, to learn the basics of HTML markup. To practice basic markup, create a short biography page for yourself, including your name, professional title, a photo, short description of skills, experiences, and any links to your favorite Web sites, and your email contact information. Use a text editor or notepad program and HTML to markup content for your biography. Save your document as a .htm file. When complete, open your document in a Web browser to see how it looks. Make any changes you feel would improve the biography. What aspects of using HTML were easiest and which presented the most challenges? What other skills might you research to help improve your work and to learn more about structured authoring and markup?

5. Select a business Web site online and explore it to see what kinds of electronic documents it provides. You might select a business that provides information or technical support on specific products, services, or processes, which are likely to include a wide range of samples. Make a list of the different document types, file formats (PDF, DOC, PPT, etc.) and uses. What supporting information does the site provide to assist users with viewing, downloading, or accessing electronic documents? What other information should it include to better assist users? What other formats for electronic documents should be included?

6. Conduct online research on either the history of the Internet or the history of hypertext. You might select a specific decade and its key influences to narrow your research scope. Collect information on early tools, feature, methods, skills required, and practices that were used. If available, collect screenshots or links to samples of electronic documents from this period. Compare these aspects to the ones that are prominent today for the World Wide Web. Prepare a presentation for your peers and share your findings and insights.

Figure Credits

Figure 13.1. © baranq/Shutterstock.com

Figure 13.2. © seamuss/Shutterstock.com

Figure 13.3. Courtesy NASA

Figure 13.4. Courtesy NOAA

Figure 13.5. Section508.gov

Figure 13.6. © Alexey V Smirnov/Shutterstock.com

Figure 13.7. © Artco/Shutterstock.com

Proposing

14

CHAPTER OVERVIEW

This chapter introduces you to proposal writing and to various types of proposals. After reading this chapter, you should be able to meet the following objectives:

- Describe the types and purposes of proposals in workplace communication.
- Identify and analyze the most common components of proposals.
- Explain the function of the various sections of a proposal.
- Identify writing situations that call for proposal writing.
- Write a proposal.

Proposals are plans for doing work. Their purpose is to offer potential solutions to a need or problem. They are preliminary documents that offer to perform work or provide a service or product. As such, they often precede other reports, such as progress reports and final reports, which follow as a project progresses or concludes.

Proposals can be categorized in many ways. For example, when organizations compete for outside projects, they submit **external** proposals. External proposals, such as those written for governmental funding, are used in many organizations—both profits and non-profits—to generate operating funds. In contrast, proposals are sometimes written for **internal** purposes to request funds to solve problems or seek money for funds for equipment or travel within the organization.

Another way to categorize proposals is to consider whether they are solicited. **Solicited** proposals respond specifically and directly to a request or call for proposals (commonly abbreviated as RFP (Request For Proposals) or CFP (Call For Proposals). In some fields, these requests are also called bids or contracts. Other proposals are **unsolicited**; they are written because a need or problem exists, but no one has yet asked for a solution. Proposals may also be categorized as **formal** or **informal**. Formal proposals typically are written in response to external solicitations or calls while informal proposals are short request written for internal approvals.

Figure 14.1. Many organizations rely on teams to create proposals for internal and external uses.

293

> ### EXERCISE 14.1
>
> ### *Thinking about Audiences for Unsolicited Proposals*
>
> Unsolicited proposals typically arise from problems that the author thinks need to be addressed. For example, if your campus library closed at 5 p.m., you may think that these hours are inconvenient and impractical for students. Or perhaps, you feel strongly that students on your campus need training in CPR in case of emergencies. In both of these examples, you see an unaddressed need, so you decide to write an unsolicited proposal to address this need or problem. This exercise asks you to take one of these situations or another similar campus issue, and consider whom you would need to convince to address the problem and what kinds of information those audiences would find convincing.
>
> **Tasks to be completed:**
>
> 1. Identify a campus problem you would like to address (or use one of the examples above).
> 2. Generate a possible solution for this problem that you could include in an unsolicited proposal.
> 3. Make a list of individuals or groups of individuals who would be the audiences for an unsolicited proposal to address this problem.
> 4. For each individual or group, list the kinds of information or evidence needed to convince the audience to support your proposal for change.
> 5. Prepare to discuss your problem, the solution you would propose, the audiences for the proposal, and the evidence needed to convince these audiences.

RFP guidelines determine content and format, which must include all of the requested information within the outlined document constraints. Informal proposals are more flexible, are shorter, and usually have fewer constraints. These categories often overlap; for example, a proposal to fund travel to a conference might be considered internal (within the organization), unsolicited (no one specifically asked for it), and informal (written as a short request in an email). When planning to write a proposal, you will find it useful to consider these categories to determine how to develop and submit it.

Whether proposals are internal or external, formal or informal, solicited or unsolicited, they typically offer to solve a problem by conducting research, providing a service, or delivering products. Each of these proposal situations requires a different kind of response. For example, after a tornado scare, city council members may decide their constituents need a better warning system and request proposals to solve this problem. If the city council wants to know its options, then the RFP will ask for proposals to investigate or research various early-warning systems and recommend one for purchase. However, if the city council has already decided it wants a severe weather text-messaging system, then the RFP might request bids for such a system. Proposals that respond to this RFP will provide details on a system, including description, specifications, features, and purchase and implementation costs. Another city may be concerned about future drought conditions and need an organization to investigate its options for water conservation. The proposal that responds to this RFP will offer to research and recommend water conservation solutions. Another RFP from the same city might result from a need to replace old transit buses. Proposals that respond to this RFP will offer to provide the requested products, new transit buses. As these examples demonstrate, requests for proposals result from varied needs and require different kinds of solutions.

Although they respond to different needs, most proposals have common structural components. They begin with an introduction that identifies the problem or need to which they are responding. This section is important because it demonstrates to the proposal reader or reviewer that you and your organization understand the situation to which you are responding. The next section explains how you will address this problem or resolve it. You can think of this section as the detailed explanation of your proposed solution, whether that solution is a service or a product. Following your explanation, the next section typically presents project management information, such as your organization's qualifications and experience, projected budget (costs of resources, time, and other financial expenses), and a schedule for completion. Finally, your proposal concludes with a discussion of any anticipated questions or objections and a request for action, urging the reader to accept your plan.

Every proposal you write will be competitive, which means that it must compete with other proposals or other activities to be accepted or approved. Because proposals are inherently competitive, they must be persuasive. They must demonstrate that the proposed solution meets the needs of the request and that it is well researched and credible. The project management section must persuade the reader that you and your organization are qualified to do the proposed work and that you have proposed a budget and schedule that is achievable and efficient. Finally, the concluding section must demonstrate that your plan has considered and evaluated other approaches but dismissed them because the proposed solution or plan is best. The proposal that best makes its case wins.

This chapter begins with an overview of guidelines for writing successful proposals, a discussion of tasks in developing proposals, and guidelines for submitting and evaluating proposals.

Figure 14.2. Almost all proposals will have these four components.

GUIDELINES AND STRATEGIES FOR WRITING A WINNING PROPOSAL

This section provides guidelines and format for writing a winning proposal. It provides suggestions for beginning the proposal writing process by carefully reading, planning, and researching the need or problem your proposal will address. After this preliminary work is done, this section recommends that you begin the writing process and offers guidance on how to develop proposal parts. Finally, it provides you with suggestions for reviewing and submitting your proposal.

Planning and Researching

Planning your proposal starts with reading the RFP carefully and researching the organization requesting the proposal. Begin by gathering as much information as you can about the organization, its needs, and the proposal requirements: What work does the organization do, or what products does it make or use? Who are the organization's clients and stakeholders? Where is the organization located? How large is it? Most importantly, what is the problem or need described in the RFP? What requirements does the RFP include for proposal development? You may be able to gather this information from the RFP itself, but, if not, you may be able to find this information on a Web site or by a telephone call to the organization itself. Legacy documents, previous proposals written to address similar RFPs or organizations, may also provide insights or answers. Finally, colleagues who have written comparable proposals can sometimes provide you with prior examples or even text that can be re-used in the current proposal. As you prepare to develop your proposal, use all of your research skills to discover all you can about the organization requesting a solution, service, or product and about previous proposals that respond to similar requests.

EXERCISE 14.2

Researching RFPs in Your Field of Study

Many professions are dependent on proposals for their income. To discover the kinds of RFPs in your profession, conduct a Web search using the kind of work you intend to do and RFP. For example, you might use these search terms: "construction RFP," "civil engineering RFP," "public relations RFP," "accounting RFP," or "service vehicle RFP." Read at least two of the RFPs that your search reveals, and then answer these questions:

1. What kinds of products or services are being requested?
2. What kinds of content must be included in the proposal?
3. Does the proposal include any limitations or constraints about content?

Tasks to be completed:

1. Conduct an Internet search to find RFPs in your field.
2. Review at least two RFP examples.
3. Answer questions about RFPs.
4. Prepare to report your findings.

EXERCISE 14.3

Reading a Simple RFP

Idealist.org is a Web site that connects non-profit organizations with potential employees and volunteers who will complete projects and provide services. The Web site is populated with requests for services. Visit Idealist.org and find a request there that interests you. Conduct preliminary research on the work requested and the organization requesting that work. When you have completed your research, write a short report discussing your findings and describing how you might respond with a proposal to complete that work.

Tasks to be completed:

1. Go to Idealist.org and find an internship or volunteer opportunity that appeals to you.
2. Read the request carefully.
3. Research the request to learn more about the organization and its needs.
4. Write a short report discussing your findings and describing how you might respond to the request with a proposal to complete the work.

Defining the Problem and Evaluating Solutions

After you have completed your preliminary research on the organization and its needs, write a problem statement that clearly defines the organization's need. Problem statements, as discussed in an earlier chapter, are concise statements that act as guides as you initiate a project. They briefly answer the following questions:

- What is the problem or need?
- Why is this problem or need important to the requesting organization? How does it affect the organization's bottom line, customers, or clients?

Figure 14.3. A problem/solution table can help you generate and evaluate problems and possible solutions.

- What is the magnitude of this problem? That is, how big or important is it to the organization, its customers, or its clients?
- What do you or your organization know or need to know about the problem or need?
- What are the real-world considerations or constraints that will affect the viability of any answer or solution you propose (financial limitations, expertise, legal/regulatory restrictions, other designs, development processes)?

After developing your concise problem statement, make a list of possible solutions to this problem or need. Your list may take many forms, depending on its complexity. For example, you might enumerate items, create a table, or generate a matrix. Figure 14.3 provides a simple problem/solution table that can help you get started with this task.

With longer proposals, you may need to collaborate closely with other team members with different expertise than yours. Such collaborations may involve face-to-face or virtual meetings where you gather information and discuss options. Depending on who is leading the team, you may assign tasks to team members or receive an assignment for developing the solution. After you or your team has identified possible solutions, then you must evaluate the proposed solutions to determine which is the best possible and why. With this information in hand, you will prepare to write the proposal.

WRITING AND DRAFTING PROPOSALS

Depending on the size and complexity of the proposal, you may need to collaborate with others to gather content. For example, you may need to gather product specifications from engineering or marketing co-workers, projected expenses from accountants, and résumés from team members who will assist with solution or service provisions. These are just a few examples of information that collaborators may need to give you.

Before writing a proposal, review the RFP carefully, noting its content and format requirements. Using the RFP as a guide, make an outline of required content, if you have not already done so. (This outline will also come in handy at the end of the process when you ask a colleague to review the proposal for completeness.) After you have a solid idea of the content you need, you should also gather and organize your research. As soon as you know what you need to write and where each bit of information goes in the outline, you are ready to begin.

As noted above, the RFP will always determine the actual content, organization, and format of the proposal; however, this section provides some general guidance on information that is typically requested in each part of a proposal. The RFP as well as the formality and complexity of the proposal you are writing determines how much of this content you will include in your proposal. More formal and complex proposals will include most of these components; less formal proposals may be shorter and less detailed in their contents. The items below are typical in most formal proposals.

Front Matter

Front matter appears in longer, more formal proposals that require a transmittal letter, a cover or title page, a table of contents, and a list of tables and/or figures. Most word-processing programs have features that allow you automatically to generate the table of contents and lists of tables and figures. To use these features, you must tag your headings and use the captioning feature for tables and figures. These features will allow the program to generate all three pages for you. Use your word-processing program's Help menu to learn the specifics for using these features.

Some proposals also require abstracts or executive summaries. (Abstracts and executive summaries are described in detail in the next chapter, and transmittal letters are discussed in the chapter on correspondence.) Front matter is not typically included in shorter, less formal proposals. The list below summarizes the most common introductory components in proposals:

- Transmittal letter
- Title page or cover sheet
- Abstract or executive summary
- Table of contents
- List of figures
- List of tables

Introductory Information

A proposal's introduction is designed to assure or persuade the reader/reviewer that you or your organization understands the problem or need stated in the RFP. The introduction overviews the problem or need and explains how your plan as outlined in the proposal resolves the problem or meets the need. The key to the introduction is to provide a few key points that describe the solution without giving too much detail. The introduction concludes with a forecasting statement that provides a brief outline of the content that follows in the rest of the proposal. This forecasting statement provides a mental map of the proposal content for the reader/reviewer. The introductions of formal and informal proposals serve very similar purposes and are comparable in content, if not in scope (length). Items in the list below identify introductory components of a formal proposal as well as the questions each component typically answers:

- Reason(s) for the proposal (Why is this proposal necessary?)
- Statement of need (What is the need or problem?)
- Background or literature review assessing current research about the problem (What do we know about the problem? How have others addressed it?)
- Summary of solution, service, or product that meets need (Briefly, what is your solution, service, or product that will meet this need?)
- Project goals or outcomes (How will your solution address this need? What are the goals or expected outcomes of the proposed project?)
- Forecasting statement, outlining proposal scope and organization (How is the rest of the proposal organized?)

Proposed Solution and Plan for Achieving It

This section of the proposal expands on the brief discussions of the solution you provided in the introduction. It includes a detailed explanation of your problem analysis. (In both formal and informal proposals, the problem analysis will be comparable in content but not in scope. Formal proposals provide more detailed explanations while informal proposals provide less.) The purpose of this section is to persuade the proposal reviewer that you and your organization have expertise in this kind of work and that you and your organization understand the problem or need. It also demonstrates that you have thoroughly considered options and identified the best one to meet the need or resolve the problem. In addition, you may need to explain how certain you are that the solution has worked. For example, if this proposal is similar to other projects your organization has completed, then past projects and their outcomes are important to mention here as well as their challenges and successes. This information will provide support for your claims that you can meet this need efficiently and effectively. Finally, you will need to discuss the methods you will use to create or develop the solution and to evaluate its effectiveness.

The list below outlines each of these components and includes questions each component should answer:

- Detailed problem analysis (What is your plan or approach to solve the problem or meet the need?)
- Solutions specifications (What are the specific details of your solution?)
- Feasibility analysis of solution (How certain are you that this solution will address the problem or need?)
- Implementation methods and proposed project duration (What methods will you use to create or develop the proposed solution? How long will the proposed project take to complete?)
- Evaluation methods (How will you assure that the solution meets the need or solves the problem?)

Proposed Project Management

This section of the proposal provides a detailed accounting of the proposed project. As the earlier chapter of this text discussed, you should use metrics from previous projects to detail how you will manage this project. These metrics will include information about your team, your track record, and your work practices. More mature teams can draw upon their previous successes to predict how long the project will take and what resources it will require. Less mature teams will have to estimate carefully to be sure they request adequate resources, including time, for the successful completion of the project. This section will be heavy in visual display of information. For example, you will likely use tables to detail your budget plan and a table or chart to detail your timeline for completion. In addition to this visual information, project management plans often require narrative explanation and justification of your proposed expenses and schedule. As with other proposal contents, the components of this section will vary depending on the project and RFP, but typically you will provide the following information:

- Budget plan (What is the total cost of this project? Use a line-item table to account for each expense.)
  - Labor (How much time in work hours is required to complete the project? How much will this labor cost you? In addition to pay, are benefits necessary? If so, how much will these benefits cost in addition to the hourly labor costs?)
  - Materials (What materials are needed? How much of each material is needed? What is the cost for each item?)
  - Equipment (What equipment is necessary? How much will this equipment cost?)

- ○ Other expenses (What other expenses are necessary? For example, does this project require travel or consultations? Will your assessment of the solution require additional labor or travel?)
- Budget narrative (Why do you need these expenses? The budget narrative provides a justification and explanation of the expenses you list in your plan.)
- Schedule (How long will this project take? What are the milestones or deadlines you will meet? What will happen in each phase of the project? Use a Gantt chart or table to outline the timeline you will keep.)
- Qualifications (What are the qualifications and the expertise of your team?)
  - ○ Personnel (Who will complete this project? Provide a brief bio of each team member and his or her expertise. Explain why the team member is qualified to complete this work. If required, you may also need to include team member's résumés in an appendix.)
  - ○ Track record (What is your team's track record with other projects like this? If your team has not worked together previously, what individual experiences do you each bring to this project?
  - ○ Facilities (Where will this project be completed, and how well equipped is the facility?)

Conclusion

The conclusion of any proposal often recaps the information previously stated. Typically conclusions are shorter sections of a proposal, reiterating important details in your proposal including a call to action and contact information. Towards that goal, a conclusion should specifically include the following details:

- A summary of the proposed project
- Answers to likely objections, if any
- A call to the readers to approve your project
- A point of contact for questions or follow-up.

In closing, focus on the positive outcomes you expect from your proposal, persuading the reader that your proposal is the best solution to the problem or need it is addressing.

Back Matter

The back matter in a proposal, like other components, responds to the RFP requirements. If your proposal includes a literature review, then it needs a list of references. Other appendices may also be necessary, such as team résumés or detailed drawings of plans or solutions. Carefully check the RFP to assure that you have included all required back matter content.

REVIEWING AND REVISING THE PROPOSAL

Although writing the proposal requires a time commitment, it is extremely important to review the proposal draft, returning to the RFP requirements and checking all content and formatting against it. When the RFP limits the number of words in the proposal, every word must carry meaning. When the RFP identifies content sections and their order, every paragraph must be in the proper location, and every heading should be in its place. The first proposals culled from the batch are those that are missing sections or difficult to read. To be competitive, your proposal must respond accurately and precisely to the RFP's requirements.

Figure 14.4. Carefully reviewing and revising proposals is critical to proposal success.

After checking your proposal against RFP requirements, you should ask another team member or an editor to review the proposal. To guide the reviewer, you might generate a checklist from the RFP that identifies required content, organization, and format. (If you developed one before writing, you can reuse it here for review.) In addition, ask the reviewer to check for poor word choice, incomplete descriptions, and badly constructed sentences and paragraphs. These are just a few of the stylistic faults that can sink a proposal, no matter how good the idea or project it proposes. A competent reviewer checking your work will assure that the proposal is well executed. A clearly organized and well written proposal sends a clear message to the proposal reviewer: you and your team are qualified and capable of producing the results your proposal promises.

SUBMITTING THE PROPOSAL

Many organizations now use electronic submission rather than printed proposal submissions. For this reason, you may discover when you submit your first proposal that the contents are uploaded into an electronic form. The form should correspond with the RFP requirements. In this situation, you will cut and paste your content into the form. Another procedure may require you to cut and paste some information into a form and then upload the document in portable file format (PDF). Review the submission requirements carefully and follow the instructions exactly to be sure the proposal is received in a timely and accurate manner.

After your proposal is submitted, then you and your team wait for approval. Often during this time, this cycle of research, writing, and review begins anew. As one project competes for funding, you seek the next project and begin again. This cycle may be interrupted when projects are funded and completed, but organizations that base their income on proposal- and grant-making are constantly seeking new sources of income for the solutions or services they provide. Their success in gaining this income is equally reliant on proposals written and solutions provided.

EXERCISE 14.4

Comparing Proposal Templates

Use the search terms "proposal template" to locate three different examples. Search for templates for different kinds of proposals—ones that propose services, products, and other solutions to needs. Compare these templates to each other and to the components discussed in this section. How do the examples you locate compare? Do they have comparable components, or are they different from those described in this section?

If you completed Exercise 14.1, return to your notes and consider whether any of the templates you located could be used to respond to the RFP you found. If so, match the required content to the template. If not, identify how the template would have to be modified to meet RFP requirements.

Tasks to be completed:

1. Locate at least three different proposal templates online.
2. Compare the templates to each other and to the components outlined in this section. How do they compare? What is similar, and what is different?
3. Compare these templates to the RFP you located in Exercise 12.2. Would any of these templates suffice for the RFP? If so, how? If not, how would you modify the template to make it work?
4. Prepare a short report on your findings or present your findings.

Evaluating Proposals

Because proposal contents are governed by the RFP to which they respond, you must evaluate them using the RFP and its requirements. RFPs will provide guidance about the proposal's contents, its organization, and the format. Carefully review your proposal to assure that it contains all required content written in the proper format. As noted in other chapters, asking another team member or editor to review the proposal is always a good idea.

Although proposals may vary widely, they are all competitive. For this reason, evaluating your proposal using the following questions will improve your chances of being most successful:

- What is the problem or need that this proposal will answer or solve?
- What is the best solution for this problem or need, and why is it the best solution?
- What are the benefits of this proposed solution?
- What process or design can most effectively arrive at this solution?
- Why are the writers of a particular proposal best qualified to design this solution?
- How much will the work cost?
- How long will the work take?

The proposal that best answers these questions and conforms to the RFP requirements has the best chance of winning the contract or opportunity to perform the work.

EXERCISE 14.5

Analyzing a Proposal Example

The following research proposal is more informal than formal. Using memo format, the proposal writers offer to conduct research for a small business in order to recommend a new communication plan that will improve the business' client base. As an informal proposal, it has fewer components than a formal proposal. It does, however, have common components found in many business proposals. Use the questions in the Evaluating Proposals section to analyze the following proposal and determine its effectiveness.

Tasks to be completed:

1. Read the following research proposal.
2. Analyze its contents using the following questions:
    a. What is the problem or need that this proposal will answer or solve?
    b. What is the best solution for this problem or need, and why is it the best solution?
    c. What are the benefits of this proposed solution?
    d. What process or design can most effectively arrive at this solution?
    e. Why are the writers of a particular proposal best qualified to design this solution?
    f. How much will the work cost?
    g. How long will the work take?
3. Prepare to discuss your findings with others.

PROPOSAL

To: Val Miller, Owner, XerEscapes
From: Li Angel And Vincent Walker
Date: November 16, 2015
Re: PLAN FOR IMPROVED CLIENTELE COMMUNICATIONS

In response to your request for a new client communication plan, we present this proposal to improve XerEscapes' communication with its clientele. Our proposed plan will allow you to communicate promotions and other information to your customers. This proposal will provide you an analysis of your current communication needs, a description of our proposed solution to meet these needs, and specific information on our project management.

Background

XerEscapes has been in business in Lubbock, Texas, for two years. The retail location specializes in xeric plants and landscaping. Although xeric landscaping has gained popularity in the Mountain West and West Coast, it is a relatively new concept in West Texas. XerEscapes is building its clientele by educating local gardeners about xeric landscaping, selling drought tolerant plants, and providing xeric landscaping services. As a relatively new business, you are concerned with growing your sales. You desire a communication plan that will boost awareness of your nursery, its products, and services. Currently, nursery business is generated primarily from drive-by customers who seek assistance about plants and products by visiting your retail location. Beyond these means, you have no formal communication plan, and you do not follow-up with customers after they purchase plants from the nursery.

Problems with the Lack of a Communication Plan

Business has declined somewhat since your grand opening in March 2014. Consequently, you seek assistance communicating news and promotions to your clientele. Others problems have resulted from XerEscapes' lack of an organized communication plan:

- You are unable to notify customers of sales and special promotions.
- You are unable to follow up with customers to suggest planting tips and landscaping solutions.
- You are unable to introduce new products to interested customers.
- You do not provide incentives for customers to refer friends and family to Xer Escapes.

In response to these problems, we offer the following plan.

Plan Objectives

In order to recommend you a communication solution, we will meet the following objectives:

- Gather data on your current marketing strategies.
- Research other nurseries' marketing strategies.
- Determine your customer demographics.
- Identify methods of communication your customers prefer.
- Determine what promotions attract customers.
- Propose a communication plan that addresses these objectives and promotes your business more effectively.

Methods

In order to meet these objectives, we will research other nurseries' market strategies online and conduct field research and surveys with your current clients.

Specifically, our team will complete this research:

- Research other nurseries' online communication
    - What forms do their communications take?
    - What kinds of information do they send to customers?
- Survey other xeric nurseries in the region and elsewhere
    - What forms of communication work best for their business?
    - What offers do customers best respond to (promotions, referral incentives, etc.)?
- Survey XerEscapes current clientele
    - What gardening information do they desire?
    - How would they prefer that information delivered?

Proposed Solution

We will provide you with a recommendation report outlining a new communication plan that will improve your business communications with your current and target clientele. More specifically, we will recommend an improved plan to communicate with your clients.

Some possible components of that plan may include the following:

- Email newsletter or company blog
- Facebook page
- Twitter feed
- Promotional ads in print and online
- Referral incentives

The team will research each solution in order to recommend the best solution(s) to you.

Project Management

This section explains our project management plan. It includes resources, budget, and labor requests.

Resources Needed

For the research the team will need a vehicle for transportation, gasoline, papers and ink, cell phones, computers, printers, word processing software, Internet access, and of course, labor.

Proposed Budget

Provided below is the projected budget that will give you more detailed information regarding the monetary value of the project.

Item	Rate	Number	Total
Software, Paper, and Ink	$.50/Page	30	$15
Gasoline	$2.50/Gallon	2	$5
Labor—Li Angel	$10/Hour	25	$250
Labor—Vincent Walker	$10/Hour	25	$250
Cell Phone Use	$.40/Min	200	$80
Computer & Internet Use	$30/Person	2	$60
		Grand Total	**$660**

Schedule and Task Management

The table below outlines the tasks the group will complete and includes a timeline for completing the tasks.

Task	Description	Assignment	Due Date
Interview Xer Escapes owners about current plan	Obtain business data, needs, ongoing communication with client	Li Angel	July 10, 2015
Conduct Internet-based research	Find local and regional nurseries and review their customer communication methods	Li Angel	July 10, 2015
Develop survey questions	Choose survey questions for customers	Vincent Walker and Li Angel	July 15, 2015
Survey customers and nurseries	Contact the customer list and nurseries to answer chosen survey questions	Vincent Walker and Li Angel	July 29, 2015
Analyze data and prepare recommendation report	Write and draft recommendation report	Vincent Walker and Li Angel	August 5, 2015
Present findings	Prepare for Final Presentation	Vincent Walker and Li Angel	August 15, 2015

Conclusion

We are more than excited to collaborate with you and your customers to provide create a new communication plan. This plan, we think, will help you inform your customers of your promotions, xeric gardening tips, and latest nursery news. Our team has experience that well qualifies us to recommend a new communication plan. One of our team members, Vincent, has worked on providing solutions for better supply chain management. He will be working on such project management problems after he graduates with degrees in Management Information Systems and Accounting. Another member, Li Angel, is an experienced technical communicator familiar with your business needs. She is also taking courses that emphasize communication and social media. We are eager to work close with you. Please grant us the permission to work on the project described in this memo by approving this proposal at your earliest convenience.

Chapter Summary

Proposals are written to gain support for a project, and, as such, they are preliminary planning documents. Proposals ask their readers to invest in ideas, services, and products. When readers review your proposal, they will typically be reading and comparing it to other proposals that are competing with it. In other words, proposals compete with others for the same resources and outcomes: funding and support. As you write proposals, always keep this competitive context in mind. To win the competition and the bid or contract that accompanies it, your proposal must convince the reader that your designs are the best possible solutions to needs stated in the RFP.

To convince the customer that your proposal is the best, keep these proposal objectives in mind:

- Your proposal should acknowledge and meet the customer's requirements for the solution.
- Your proposal should identify and specify viable solutions that meet the RFP requirements.
- Your proposal should provide a detailed plan for designing or implementing the solution (or solutions).
- Your proposal should convince the reader that you have the expertise and resources necessary to fulfill this plan.

No matter what format or order of content an RFP requests, proposals are always written to meet these objectives. Keep them in mind as you respond to RFPs, and your proposal will have an excellent chance of funding and support.

Chapter Assignments

The exercises in this section ask you to apply what you have learned in this chapter as well as explore how this knowledge applies to and connects with other information in the textbook.

1. The U.S. Small Business Administration (SBA) publishes briefs on small business economic issues. Visit the Issue Briefs at the SBA (https://www.sba.gov/advocacy/issue-briefs) and select one to review. After reviewing its contents, write a 200–300 word executive summary of the brief. After you have written the executive summary, reduce it to a 50–100 word abstract of the brief's contents. Next, create a one-sentence summary (30 words or less). Finally, select five keywords used to describe the brief.
2. Design a research project of your own, drawn from your area of study, and propose it. After your proposal is approved, conduct your research and write a final report.

Figure Credits

Figure 14.1. © wong yu liang/Shutterstock.com

Figure 14.2. © NUMAX3D/Shutterstock.com.com

Figure 14.3. © svastika/Shutterstock.com

Figure 14.4. © Gajus/Shutterstock.com

Reporting Research and Project Results

15

CHAPTER OVERVIEW

This chapter introduces you to common forms of research and decision-making reports. After reading this chapter, you should be able to meet the following objectives:

- Identify and analyze common components of technical and professional reports.
- Describe the purposes of various kinds of research and results reports in technical and professional workplaces.
- Understand content, organizational, and stylistic differences in research and project reports.

Reports are ubiquitous. Derived from Latin roots that mean "to bring" or "to carry," reports are information that you receive or give to others. In the media and in the workplace, they impact decisions. For example, you may listen to or check weather reports before deciding what to wear. You receive feedback on an assignment with a description of its strengths and weaknesses as well as a grade, in the form of an evaluation report. You read or watch news reports to learn what is happening in your hometown, state, and country. You check stock market reports to determine how your investments are doing. You skim a magazine report to identify fashion or home decorating trends. You check your email for updates on a new technology release. These are just a few of the reports that impact decisions each day. Workplace reports tend to be used to make decisions or to solve practical problems. They also have a persuasive function—to persuade others to take action, such as buying a product or service.

Some reports have established credibility; you know you can rely on them. For example, you likely do not question a meteorologist's account of yesterday's high and low temperatures. Other reports are less credible because they are predictive, such as tomorrow's forecast. In both cases, the meteorologist is providing you with as accurate a picture as possible, given the data and predictive models available. The persuasiveness of these reports depends on many factors: the quality of the data, the dependability of the models, and the meteorologist's ability to predict the forecast based

Figure 15.1. Report writers gain credibility through accuracy, attention to detail, and awareness of workplace conventions.

on this information. Over time, the meteorologist's predictions are tested or checked against the actual weather. As a user of this information, you decide whether you can trust predictive reports.

Just as a meteorologist gains credibility based on the accuracy of weather predictions, so too will you seek credibility as a report writer. You will need to collect content for reporting from the most accurate resources you can locate. You will package and present this information in a report format that demonstrates you know what a report should look like or do. Over time, if you report accurately and well, you will gain credibility or a reputation as someone who has good judgment and can be trusted to possess strong report-writing skills.

This chapter will focus on reports that are commonly used in workplaces to conclude projects and deliver research results. To create these reports, you will need to rely on skills you've gained in other chapters: researching, managing content, reusing content, and collaborating with others because reports are often written with input from others. Reports require you to bring many skills into play. This chapter explores how to do this work. It describes a common structure used in most formal and informal reports and concludes with a section describing variations on this common structure that are required to meet specific workplace reporting needs or to solve specific workplace problems.

EXERCISE 15.1

Reporting on Reports

To illustrate how reports surround us daily, track the different reports you receive or give for the next week. You can track reports either by making a list, taking pictures of them with your smartphone, or saving electronic copies. If you are not certain whether information you receive is a report, track it anyway. (You will have time in class to discuss any questionable items.) Bring your collection of reports to class with you, and be prepared to write up your findings in a paragraph or brief oral presentation. This paragraph or oral presentation, by the way, is called a report.

Tasks to be completed:

1. Track reports you receive or give for the next week.
2. Report your findings in a written or oral format.

REPORTING RESULTS

Workplace projects can range in complexity and length from government-funded grants to engineering design contracts to simple workplace research on needed equipment or services. No matter how complex the project, most of these reports are archival in nature and used to document what you have done or learned. At the end of projects, final reports are written to wrap up or summarize project outcomes, results, and lessons learned. Like proposals, results reports may be **formal** or **informal**. **Formal reports** are longer and have more structured components, while informal reports are shorter and have fewer components. Formal reports are more likely to be published; consequently, they are typically written with printed or electronic publication in mind. **Informal reports**, when delivered in writing, are shorter and take the form of memos, emails, instant messages, or texts. Both formal and informal reports can also be delivered orally. For example, academic authors frequently present formal oral reports of their research at conferences where they discuss findings and implications with their peers. These formal oral reports may later become published reports shared in journals or other periodical venues. When formal oral reports are presented at meetings or conferences, they may also be recorded, archived, and shared online with individuals who cannot attend.

You may also be familiar with TED Talks, which provide access to popular but formal presentations on a wide variety of ideas and topics. In contrast, informal reports can be delivered quickly as updates in face-to-face or virtual meetings. These updates may be formalized in meeting minutes, which are a form of short report discussed in the chapter on status and instance reports.

EXERCISE 15.2

TED Talks and Reporting

TED (technology, entertainment, and design) Talks began as a conference in 1984. Although interesting, the first event was financially unsuccessful. In the early 2000s, however, the organizers created a phenomenon when they began posting the talks online. While not all TED Talks can be classified as reports, most do contain report components. This exercise asks you to visit the TED Talks website, browse its contents, and watch a 0-6 minute video. This link (https://www.ted.com/talks) will take you to a search page where you can search the talks by duration and browse a selection of reports that meet your criteria. Choose one of those talks that you think might be classified as a report, and watch it. After watching it, decide whether the talk is, in fact, a report. If so, explain what qualifies the talk as a report or what disqualifies it. Prepare to show and report your findings to your peers.

Tasks to be completed:

1. Visit the TED Talks search page (https://www.ted.com/talks).
2. Identify a 0–6 minute video that you think might qualify as a report.
3. Watch the video and note whether it is a report or if it contains report qualities.
4. Support your conclusions with evidence from the video to explain why it is or is not a report.
5. Be prepared to show your video and to present your findings in class.

Identifying Purpose and Reader Intentions

However reports are delivered and published, the purpose of the report should always be foremost in your mind. Readers, listeners, or viewers of your reports will come to them with specific questions in mind and with different needs and intentions. Questions can vary widely, depending on the readers and their occupational perspectives. Below are a few examples of questions readers may ask as they read your reports:

- From the managerial perspective:
  - Have you successfully completed the project?
  - What do you recommend?
  - What option is the most feasible of the choices you researched?

- From the accountant/budgetary perspective:
    - How long did the project take?
    - How much did it cost?
    - Did you stay on budget?
- From a peer or competitor's perspective:
    - What were your findings?
    - What did you learn?
    - Can I apply this knowledge to projects of my own?

Figure 15.2. Each reader may have a different purpose for reading a report and bring a different perspective and questions to the document.

Thinking about these questions prior to writing your report will help you address them in appropriate report components. Some of the questions, you may note, are the same as the questions addressed in proposals. The text that answers these questions in a proposal can be recycled or reused, with slight modification, in reports. Recycling or reusing text can save time and keep focus and communication with your reader consistent.

In addition to answering each reader's questions, you should also remember that each reader will come to your report with intentions and expectations. Some readers will be thinking ahead to the start of the next project, while others will be more concerned with how well you completed this project. Your report has to answer each reader's questions no matter how disparate, and it has to support decisions readers are making as your project concludes. Consequently, addressing each reader's questions is important, but recognizing and responding to each reader's information needs is equally important.

Determining Genre Expectations

Readers not only bring questions and information needs to reports they read, but they also bring genre expectations about how reports should be organized and how they should look. Most technical, scientific, and professional final reports follow a common pattern, known as IMRD or IMRAD (Introduction, Methods, Results, and Discussion). You may have encountered this format when writing scientific lab reports, which document the results of experiments you conducted. The IMRD format developed over years of publication in scientific journals and is now a required format used for reporting research in many fields. Although IMRD format is a common research format, the format of your report will depend on the conventions of the workplace where you are employed, which may require you to use the IMRD format, some modification of it, or another form entirely.

Knowing the communication conventions used in your workplace is among your first tasks in completing a reporting assignment successfully. As you've learned with other genres discussed in this text, an important consideration before writing is discovering what these expectations are by seeking out legacy reports or asking other employees about how they write specific kinds of reports. This rest of this section will provide you with some basic guidelines about report genre expectations, but each time you write a report, you should carefully review the assignment you've been given and create a report that responds directly to it. To do so may mean modifying the basic content and organization discussed in this chapter.

The rest of this section is organized into two parts. The first part overviews report content, discusses common components or features of reports, and familiarizes you with each component's purpose. The second part discusses the similarities and differences in different types of reports and offers guidance on how to plan, write, and critique reports.

Writing Report Components

This section provides general guidance on information that readers typically expect in a report. Each section has a specific function and often addresses specific readers' questions. The purpose and delivery method of your report determines its formality and complexity; they will also determine the extensiveness of the report. As with proposals, the more formal and complex the report, the more components it will have, less formal reports will be shorter and provide fewer details. The items below are typical in most formal reports. Shorter reports will modify and even eliminate some of these items. Figure 15.3 provides a visual overview of the most common report components. The size of each component represents the proportion of the report the component takes. Towards the end of the report, documents in the back matter may vary in size, including supporting data, references, and glossaries.

Front Matter

The front matter in reports is very similar to that of proposals. Longer, more formal reports include front matter such as transmittal letters (which are discussed in the correspondence chapter), a cover or title page, an abstract or executive summary (discussed in more detail below), a table of contents, and a list of tables and/or figures. The list below summarizes the most common introductory components in reports and suggests a common organization for these components:

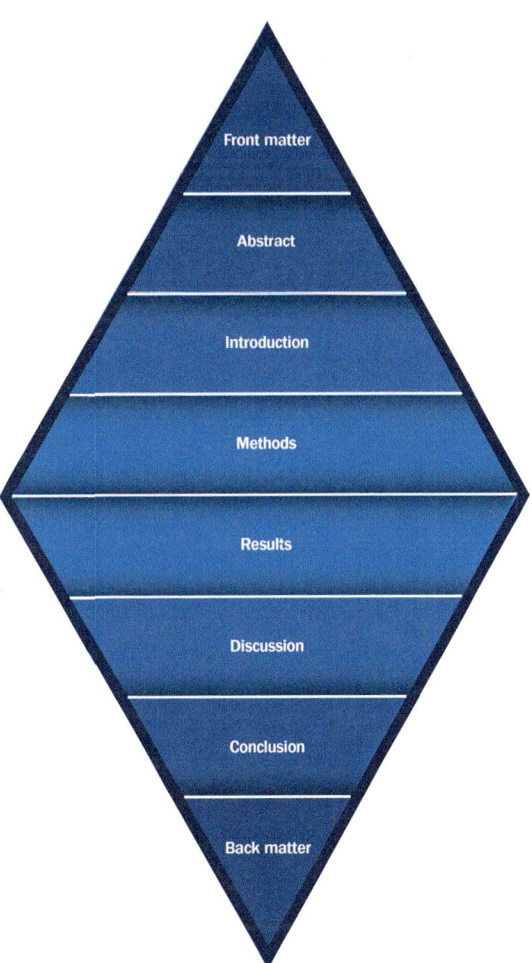

Figure 15.3. Depending on the audience, purpose, and situation, a report may include all or just some of these components.

- Transmittal letter
- Title page or cover sheet
- Abstract or executive summary
- Table of contents
- List of figures
- List of tables

Front matter is not typically included in shorter, less formal proposals and reports.

Abstracts and Executive Summaries

A key component in formal reports is the **abstract** or **executive summary**. Both abstracts and executive summaries encapsulate the contents of the report. Their purpose is to assist readers in making a decision about the report: Is the content of the report worth the time required to read it? In effect, then, both abstracts and executive summaries are time-saving features, aiding readers who have limited time to decide whether to invest that time in reading the report. They do have key differences, however.

An abstract is a synopsis of the report's main points. Abstracts appear in research reports and are short, usually only one-half to one page long. Abstracts may include technical language related to the report's subject. Think of them as the brief summaries you find when you search for an article online. When you read such abstracts, you decide whether or not the report is something you should read. Thus, the abstract provides you with an overview of contents and allows you to make a quick decision about the report and its value to you.

EXERCISE 15.3

Comparing Abstracts and Executive Summaries

Visit the U.S. Center for Disease Control's report *The State of Aging and Health in America 2013* (http://www.cdc.gov/aging/pdf/state-aging-health-in-america-2013.pdf). This report contains both a brief abstract of the report's content and an executive summary. Locate and compare/contrast both statements and make a list of characteristics of each. Be prepared to discuss your findings with others.

Tasks to be completed:

1. Visit the U.S. Center for Disease Control's report *The State of Aging and Health in America 2013* (http://www.cdc.gov/aging/pdf/state-aging-health-in-america-2013.pdf).
2. Skim the report to locate an abstract and an executive summary.
3. Note similarities and differences in the abstract and executive summary.
4. Prepare to discuss your findings.

In contrast, executive summaries are found in business reports, as opposed to research reports, and they contain less technical jargon or specialized language. They are longer, extending to a page or more. Instead of briefly summarizing key report points, executive summaries are more detailed, outlining briefly but specifically the report findings and recommendations. Executive summaries are designed to stand alone from the report and to stand in for report contents. If written well, executive summaries are all a manager or executive needs to read to get the gist of a report's contents. Many report readers will read only the executive summary of a report, while others will read the executive summary and then skip into the report for the specific details relevant to their jobs.

Introduction

Like the proposal, a report's introduction assures or persuades the reader that you or your organization understands the problem or need being addressed. The introduction provides background, overviews the problem or need, and explains how your solution resolves the problem or meets the need. It provides key points that describe the solution. (If your report begins with an executive summary, you may be able to reuse that text in the introduction to describe the problem and the solution.) The introduction concludes with a forecasting statement that provides a brief outline of the content that follows in the rest of the report. This forecasting statement provides a mental map of the report content for the reader/reviewer. The introductions of formal and informal reports serve very similar purposes and are comparable in content, if not in scope (length). Items in the list below identify introductory components of a formal report as well as the questions each component typically answers:

- Reason(s) for the report (Why is this report necessary?)
- Statement of need/problem analysis (What is the need or problem?)
- Background or literature review assessing current research about the problem (What do we know about the problem? How have others addressed it?)
- Summary of solution, service, or product that meets need (Briefly, what is your solution, service, or product that will meet this need?)
- Project status (Is it complete? Were you successful? How so?)
- Forecasting statement, outlining proposal scope and organization (How is the rest of the report organized?)

Methods

The focus of this section of your report is to describe the work completed. You will also describe the methods you used to develop the solution. The methods will likely be very similar to the series of actions (or methods) you outlined in your proposal. In the final report, you recap those methods, explaining how you conducted your research or developed the solution. If you followed your plan closely, you may recycle or reuse your methods section in the final report, but you will have to modify the tense of your steps. For example, in the proposal, your steps were stated in future tense ("I will investigate..." or "The first phase will be..."), but in the report, your steps will be stated in past tense ("I investigated..." or "The first phase was..."). Finally, if you promised evaluation methods in your proposal and used them as you completed the project, you will describe these methods as well in this section.

In brief, the list below outlines each of these components and includes questions each component answers:

- Solutions specifications (What are the specific details of your solution?)
- Implementation methods (What methods did you use to create or develop the proposed solution?)
- Evaluation methods (How did you assure that the solution meets the need or solves the problem?)

Results/Findings

The results or findings section contains new information that you gather as you complete the project. The contents of the results and findings section can vary greatly, depending on the work completed and its scope. The following list details all possible contents that may appear in this section. The explanation following the list describes how the contents may change for different types of reports.

- Details of service provided and results
- Research results (in chronological order or order of importance)
- Technical and statistical results from tests and measures conducted
- Product designs, specifications, and information about them
- Visual representations of data, designs, and other findings

If you proposed to provide a service, then this section explains when, how, and to what extent the service was provided. If the project requires empirical research, then you report your findings. Lengthier empirical reports include detailed technical and statistical data in this section. If the project required development of a product, then you describe the product, beginning with the proposed specifications as well as the final specifications. If the specifications changed from your proposal, you will need to state how they changed and explain why they changed. In some reports, the scope of this section may be very detailed and extensive; for example, in engineering reports, the details can include technical content about the product design and testing. Whatever your project required you to do or learn, you report your results here. In addition to these textual elements, this section should include the visual details of your work—diagrams, graphs, charts, and tables that illustrate the decisions you made and the work that you produced. While the textual and visual content of your results and findings section will vary greatly depending on your research question or project, this content works together to answer a central question: What did you find or do as you completed this project?

Discussion

A discussion often follows the findings and results; however, you may include discussion with the previous section. The following kinds of information are typically included in discussion sections:

- Interpretations of results of any testing conducted or data collected.
- Reasoning and explanation of discoveries or knowledge gained from experiments or design development.
- Explanations of decisions in the development or research process, challenges encountered, and solutions created.
- Insights into the process itself.
- Discussions about how well the solution resolves the problem.
- Assessment of prototypes and simulations for efficiency or effectiveness.

Just as the results vary from report to report, so too will the discussion of those results. To determine what to discuss in this section, return to the notes you made when planning your report: what will readers expect to learn and in what detail? Revisiting your plan now will help you to gauge the content that you include in the results and findings.

Conclusion

The final section of the report discusses the conclusions or inferences that can be drawn from your work. Again, depending on the type of report you are writing, your conclusion might include the following information:

- Applications for the product or solution
- Recommendations for further research
- Review of the ultimate results or final outcome of the project
- Implications or benefits of the project, product, or solution

The end of the report is a critical point where readers will need to be convinced that you fulfilled your obligations and responsibilities and credibly arrived at the answers to the questions you sought to answer. For example, if you provide recommendations, be sure that they flow logically from the conclusions you have previously stated. As you write your conclusion, be sure to review your assignment, address all key points that you were given, and demonstrate that the resulting knowledge you are reporting meets all readers' expectations for a successful outcome.

Back Matter

The back matter in a final report includes items such as a list of references, citations, supplemental data, glossaries, and other appendices. In the references section, include all reports, articles, or books that you referenced in your report. Appendices typically contain extensive data tables, charts, or numerical data. You should place any lengthy material, such as detailed specifications, drawings, or report results that would interfere with the flow of your report, in an appendix. In the text, refer readers to these appendixes, and those readers who are interested can go to the designated appendix to read further. Other readers, uninterested in these details, can continue reading the main body of the report.

Differences in Reporting Genres

Genres vary depending on organization, content, topic, purpose, and other factors. Genres are also not fixed patterns but are often customized to fit the various readers, purposes, and contexts. While reports often have comparable components, the content of the report depends heavily on the research or work you are doing. As you've learned in other chapters, your work plan relies upon an analysis of your communication's audience, purpose, situation, and constraints. From that analysis, you develop research questions, which ultimately will determine the kind of report you will write.

Figure 15.4. Research reports answer questions or provide data to support conclusions.

Different kinds of reports answer different kinds of research questions, as the following examples illustrate. You are probably the most familiar with empirical research reports. These reports answer research questions and provide facts or data to support conclusions. Types of empirical research reports include lab reports, research and scientific papers, qualitative reports, feasibility and recommendation reports, and engineering design reports (preliminary design reports and final design reports).

These reports follow the familiar IMRD organization discussed above (introduction, methods, results, and discussion) as illustrated in Figure 15.3. While these types of reports are more structured, others such as financial reports and white papers may vary widely in the organization of their contents. Each are discussed below to help you distinguish between the different types of research and results reporting types.

Feasibility reports are a common report genre and subcategory of empirical research reports. They examine several solutions in order to determine which one is best. Feasibility reports examine the advantages and disadvantages of several options in order to determine whether action or product is a feasible or viable solution. For example, you might be asked to determine whether your organization can afford to purchase tablet computers for its employees who conduct business in the field. These tablets would potentially be used to speed data entry from the field, secure the data more efficiently, and allow quicker transmission from field to home office. In order to be feasible or viable, the tablet solution has to meet certain criteria and constraints:

- The tablets must be affordable (cost less than $10,000 to outfit 10 employees with tablets).
- They must support the software needed to record data in the field.
- They must come with technical support for at least one year.
- They must be able to log data with or without Internet connectivity.
- They must require less than one day of employee training to implement.

Given these criteria and constraints, your job is to conduct the research to determine whether tablets are a viable solution for your company. This research may include a cost/benefit analysis to determine if the solution is economically feasible.

For the tablet study, your research might require you to read product descriptions; conduct interviews with technical consultants, employees, and trainers; gather other data from software and hardware manufacturers; and conduct a cost/benefit analysis. Based on this research, you will then be able to report your findings on the feasibility of this solution.

Your feasibility report will likely employ IMRD organization. The results section of the feasibility report will typically be organized by the criteria or constraints of the solution, as in the bulleted list above. You may find it easier to include results and discussion of results together under each criterion. Feasibility reports conclude by stating whether the solution is viable or not. In the example above, the report would state whether buying tablets for field workers is a good solution or not. Below is a simple outline for a feasibility report.

1. Introductions and front matter review the assignment and provide a forecast for the report contents.
2. Methods describe the research process used to reach conclusions. This section also describes the constraints and criteria used to determine feasibility.
3. Results consider each criterion separately, reporting findings for each one and discussing the potential viability of each finding.
    a. Criterion 1
        i. Findings
        ii. Discussion
    b. Criterion 2
        i. Findings
        ii. Discussion
    c. And so forth until all criteria are analyzed.
4. Discussion summarizes overall findings and leads to conclusions; the conclusions determine whether the solution is viable and provide reasoning for why it is or is not.

Recommendation reports are another subcategory of empirical research reports. Like other reports, recommendations reports support decision-making. They start with a question or problem. This question or problem usually requires you to determine the best action or actions to achieve a solution or resolve a need. To determine what action is best, you will need to establish criteria and evaluate alternatives. For example, if the tablet feasibility study concludes that tablets are feasible, then you might need to take your research one step further to recommend a specific tablet for purchase. To make this recommendation, you will need to develop criteria, such as cost, features, support, and durability. With these criteria in hand, you then compare the alternatives and decide which one best meets your organization's needs.

After you have researched alternatives, the recommendation report you write, like other empirical reports, will typically be written in IMRD format with the following content included:

> 1. Introductions and front matter review the assignment and provide a forecast for the report contents.
> 2. Methods describe the research process used to reach conclusions. This section also describes the constraints and criteria used to make the recommendation.
> 3. Results consider each criterion separately, reporting findings for each one and discussing the potential viability of each finding. You have a choice of organizations for the results section: organized by criteria or organized by alternatives.
>
> | a. Criterion 1 | d. Alternative 1 |
> |---|---|
> | i. Alternative 1 | i. Criterion 1 |
> | ii. Alternative 2 | ii. Criterion 2 |
> | iii. Alternative 3 | iii. Criterion 3 |
> | b. Criterion 2 | e. Alternative 2 |
> | i. Alternative 1 | i. Criterion 1 |
> | ii. Alternative 2 | ii. Criterion 2 |
> | iii. Alternative 3 | iii. Criterion 3 |
> | c. Criterion 3 | f. Alternative 3 |
> | i. Alternative 1 | i. Criterion 1 |
> | ii. Alternative 2 | ii. Criterion 2 |
> | iii. Alternative 3 | iii. Criterion 3 |
>
>   (OR between the two organizations)
>
> 4. Discussion summarizes overall findings and leads to conclusions; the conclusions recommend action items that help the reader decide what to do or how to act to resolve a problem.

Although both organizations are viable, the criterion organization on the left is often easier to write because it allows you to include comparison and contrast of alternatives for each criteria, concluding each section by determining which alternative best meets each criterion. In the discussion, you may simply review the alternatives or provide a simple chart that identifies which alternative best meets the criterion. That alternative becomes your recommendation. On the other hand, the alternative organization requires a more detailed discussion in which you then compare and contrast all alternatives. Without including this discussion, your readers may find it difficult to understand the basis for your recommendations. Both organizations are effective, but you must use them successfully to make your logical process of recommendation clear and credible.

White papers are another common form of report found in the research and development sector. White papers are typically written in-house and are designed to introduce and market a new product or service. Originally developed as government reports, white papers have evolved into marketing tools designed to explain an innovative

Figure 15.5. White papers are reports that describe innovative business concepts and practices in order to sell products.

process and, in doing so, recommend a new product that supports it. The ultimate purpose of most white papers is to sell the new product but, to do so, indirectly, as a means to improve some business practice. White paper contents include proof of concept or program information and overviews of the new product, program, or initiatives. They may also contain product descriptions, preliminary research reports on the product, and marketing information. (Figure 15.5's word cloud provides insights into the marketing features of white papers.) White papers are discussed in more detail in Chapter 18.

EXERCISE 15.4

Exploring White Paper Content and Structure

Working with a partner, conduct an Internet search for "white paper examples" or visit That White Paper Guy's online portfolio (http://www.thatwhitepaperguy.com/white-paper-guys-samples/), which contains many white paper examples. Find two or more examples of white papers. Sketch an outline of each white paper's content and structure, identifying the kinds of information within the white paper and the order of presentation. Then compare the two examples: Are the contents similar or dissimilar? What conclusions can you draw about white papers from your research? Prepare to present your findings to the class.

Tasks to be completed:

1. Working with a partner, conduct an Internet search for "white paper examples."
2. Find two or more examples.
3. Outline the contents and the structure of the examples you locate.
4. Compare and contrast your findings.
5. Answer the following questions:
    a. Are the contents similar or dissimilar?
    b. What conclusions can you draw about white papers from your research?
6. Prepare a short oral presentation to deliver in class.

A company, for instance, might use a white paper to promote a new search optimization feature for websites. The white paper would focus on the benefits of the new feature, explaining how it differs from other less-advanced features and how it improves findability. Other content would describe the specifications of the feature and website analytics from its use. At the end of the white paper, the final section might explain how the company's product provides this feature; this section would conclude with contact information for learning more about the product or purchasing it.

White paper organizations are typically combinations of instructional process descriptions (how something works) combined with other components, such as specifications, production descriptions, and research results. For this reason, before writing a white paper, you should consult legacy documents in your organization to determine how they are typically written.

Financial reports are common in accounting and banking sectors. These reports are primarily numerical and statistical in nature and usually focus on specific time increments. Corporate annual reports are among the reports in this category, although they may contain information that extends beyond financial accounting.

Financial reports are written for a wide range of readers—from individuals with little financial training who need to balance their bank accounts to well-informed board members at large corporations to board members and stockholders who want to verify the health of the organization or their investments. Readers can even extend to government agencies and auditors who review tax reports for authenticity and accuracy. Like white papers, financial reports take many forms and are hard to define generically because so many kinds exist. These reports may take the form of statements or reports, such as statements of financial standing, income statements, cash flow, and equity change. They are also classified by how often they are produced (daily, weekly, monthly, and annual reports). Each type of financial statement, of course, includes numerical data as well as data representations, such as charts and tables. Also, like white papers, the format for these reports varies from organization to organization. The best strategy for developing such reports is to rely on legacy documents and other internal research.

EXERCISE 15.5

Analyzing the Content and Structure of an Annual Financial Report

The U.S. Department of the Treasury reports on the Treasury's status annually to U.S. citizens. These reports are located at the Treasury's Performance and Financial Documents page (http://www.treasury.gov/about/budget-performance/annual-performance-plan/Pages/default.aspx). Visit this page and review the most recent FY (Fiscal Year) report (choose from the list). Using this report as a model, make a list or outline of its major sections, including the kind of verbal and numerical data included in it. After you have completed your list or outline, compare it to a classmate's outline, and check to see if you have included all of its contents.

Answer the following questions: How many types of financial reporting were included in the annual report? How many and what kinds of visual data representation were included? Why do you think annual reports contain so much information? Prepare to discuss your answers with the rest of your class.

Tasks to be completed:

1. Visit the U.S. Treasury's Performance and Financial Documents page.
2. Review the most recent FY report listed.
3. Outline the contents of one of the reports.
4. Compare your outline to a classmate's, and reach consensus about its contents.
5. Answer the following questions:
    a. How many types of financial reporting were included in the annual report?
    b. How many and what kinds of visual data representation were included?
    c. Why do you think annual reports contain so much information?
6. Prepare to discuss your answers with the class.

As noted in the beginning of this chapter, reports are ubiquitous in many technical and business sectors. The particular characteristics of the reports you write will depend on your career choices, but you can be assured, if you are a professional, you will contribute to or write reports wherever you are employed.

EXERCISE 15.6

Locating and Identifying Different Report Types

This exercise requires you to locate and analyze several examples of common report genres with an Internet search engine.

Using search terms, such as "recommendation report," "feasibility report," "annual report," etc., locate three or four different kinds of reports online. (Note: you may find reports that are not described in this chapter. As long as you are certain they are reports, include them in your analysis. The intent here is to locate and identify as many report types as possible.)

After you have located your example reports, bookmark or copy their locations. Now you may begin to analyze their contents:

- What kind of information is included in the report?
- How is the information ordered or organized?
- Does the content include visuals? If so, what kind and why?
- Are their components of the report all identifiable, or are there parts that are unfamiliar?

Highlight unfamiliar components for class discussion, and be prepared to discuss your findings with the class.

Tasks to be completed:

1. Locate three or four report examples online.
2. Bookmark their locations.
3. Analyze each report's contents and prepare to report your findings.
4. In particular, note any report types or components that are not discussed in this chapter.

Evaluating Reports

Like proposals, reports vary widely in content, organization, and format; however, in many cases, their contents are governed by disciplinary or organizational conventions. Because of these variations, you should always seek out legacy documents, if available, when writing reports for the first time. If these documents are not available, then you may use the following questions as basic guidelines for evaluating the contents of your reports. The contents will likely respond to all of the following questions:

- What project is discussed in this report, and why is the report necessary?
- What need or problem does it address?
- What is the background on this need or problem? What do we need to know about the problem? How have others addressed it? If so, how?

- What is your solution, service, or product to solve this problem or meet this need?
- What is the status of your project? Did it conclude successfully? How so?
- What did you find or do as you completed this project?
- How do you interpret your findings? What did you learn?
- If applicable, what is the best solution and why? Or what do you recommend and why?
- At project's end, what can you conclude about this project and its value?

EXERCISE 15.7
Analyzing a Report Example

The following empirical research report is more formal than informal. It reports the research completed after the proposal example provided in the previous chapter. As you may recall, the proposal writers offered to conduct research for a small business in order to recommend a new communication plan. The report describes the research they conducted and makes four recommendations for a new communication plan. Use the report evaluation questions to analyze the following report and determine its effectiveness. After you have analyzed the report, be sure to compare it to the proposal to identify common features (and recycled text) used in each.

Tasks to be completed:

1. Read the following empirical research report.
2. Analyze its contents using the following questions:
    a. What project is discussed in this report, and why is the report necessary?
    b. What need or problem does it address?
    c. What is the background on this need or problem? What do we need to know about the problem? How have others addressed it? If so, how?
    d. What is your solution, service, or product to solve this problem or meet this need?
    e. What is the status of your project? Did it conclude successfully? How so?
    f. What did you find or do as you completed this project?
    g. How do you interpret your findings? What did you learn?
    h. If applicable, what is the best solution and why? Or what do you recommend and why?
    i. At project's end, what can you conclude about this project and its value?
3. Prepare to discuss your findings with others.

Recommendations for XerEscapes' Communication Plan

Submitted to Val Miller, Owner, XerEscapes on November 19, 2015
Prepared by Li Angel And Vincent Walker

EXECUTIVE SUMMARY

XerEscapes has been in business in Lubbock, Texas, for two years. The retail location specializes in xeric plants and landscaping. Although xeric landscaping has gained popularity in the Mountain West and West Coast, it is a relatively new concept in West Texas. XerEscapes is building its clientele by educating local gardeners about xeric landscaping, selling drought tolerant plants, and providing xeric landscaping services. Currently, XerEscapes has no formal communication plan and, consequently, is experiencing a number of communication problems:

- XerEscapes' management is unable to notify customers of sales and special promotions.
- XerEscapes' management is unable to follow up with customers to suggest planting tips and landscaping solutions.
- XerEscapes' management is unable to introduce new products to interested customers.
- XerEscapes' management is unable to provide incentives for customers to refer friends and family to Xer Escapes.

To alleviate these problems, we conducted research by surveying local and regional nurseries, interviewing various nursery customers, and also using the Internet. Our customer survey found that the target demographic for XerEscapes is 30-39 years old homeowners who prefer to receive promotional newsletters quarterly by postal mail. We recommend that XerEscapes begin sending newsletters by mail to all their customers. We also recommend that XerEscapes include three types of information in the newsletters: promotional, informational, and an inventory summary. Furthermore, we recommend that XerEscapes post these newsletters online as soon as its website is complete and staffing capacity is increased to attract and meet the requirements of the younger demographic groups.

TABLE OF CONTENTS

Executive Summary 2

Introduction 4

Methods 4

Results and discussion 5–8

Conclusions 8

Recommendations 8

INTRODUCTION

For the past month, our team has researched means to improve XerEscapes' business communications with its clientele and target demography. XerEscapes is a nursery and landscaping business in Lubbock, Texas. Although xeric landscaping has gained popularity in the Mountain West and West Coast, it is a relatively new concept in West Texas. XerEscapes is building its clientele by educating local gardeners about xeric landscaping, selling drought tolerant plants, and providing xeric landscaping services. Currently, nursery business is generated primarily from drive-by customers who seek assistance about plants and products. The nursery has no formal communication plan, and its management does not follow-up with customers after they purchase plants. XerEscapes asked us to research and recommend a communications plan to improve it business communications with its clientele. In order to find the best means of communication, we researched other nurseries' market strategies online and conducted field research and surveys with current clients. In this report, our team recommends a plan that will improve management's ability to communicate with XerEscapes' clientele. Our plan works within two requested constraints: XerEscapes' budget and its staff availability. More specifically, it can feasibly be implemented for $500 or less per year with only two staff members. In the following report, we explain our methods for research, our results and findings, and provide recommendations.

METHODS

In this section of the report, we describe our methods of research. To complete this project successfully our team researched the best way for XerEscapes to communicate its business news, educational content, and promotions to customers.

Our team's research included the following methods:

- Researched other nurseries' online communication
    - What forms do their communications take?
    - What kinds of information do they provide to customers?
- Surveyed other xeric nurseries in the region and elsewhere
    - What forms of communication work best for their business?
    - What offers do customers best respond to (promotions, referral incentives, etc.)?
- Surveyed XerEscapes current clientele
    - What gardening information do they desire?
    - How would they prefer that information delivered?

We used the Internet to research and review a sample of six nurseries and to discover what online communication strategies they use on their websites. By phone, we contacted management at four Texas nurseries located in Plano, Austin, Tyler, and Amarillo to discover their online and direct customer communication strategies. Based on our findings from the nursery research, we developed a four-question survey and then questioned one hundred of XerEscapes's current customers as they shopped in the retail location.

Our survey included questions about customer age and preferences. We asked customers how often they wanted to receive communication from XerEscapes (frequency), how they wanted information delivered to them (delivery), and what kinds of information they wanted (information type). Our questions were all closed. We gave customers four options for frequency (weekly, monthly, quarterly, and annually) and two options for delivery (postal or electronic). We asked customers about their interest in three types of nursery information:

- Promotional: sales, seasonal promotions, clearance events, member discount days.
- Educational: landscaping and gardening tips, plant care, and types of drought-tolerant (xeric) plants.
- Product inventory: types of products and plants currently in stock.

RESULTS AND DISCUSSION

In this section, we report and discuss our research findings. The first section provides results from our online and phone nursery research. The second section reports findings from our customer survey.

Nursery website analysis and findings

On July 8, we reviewed the following websites of six nurseries in the western region of the United States:

1. High Country Gardens, Albuquerque, NM
2. Plants of the Southwest, Santa Fe, NM
3. Earth and Air Landscape, Denver, CO
4. Diggable Designs, Colorado Springs, CO
5. Sonoran Gardens, Tucson, AZ
6. The Greenhouse, Logan, UT

To find these nurseries, we used the Yelp search engine with the name of the Western state where we sought the nursery as well as the search terms "xeric," "nursery." We selected these nurseries because they met three criteria: 1) they had a viable and fully developed website, 2) they offered landscaping services, and 3) they advertised themselves as xeric landscaping and planting experts. These criteria best matched the services and products XerEscapes offers.

We focused our analysis of these six websites by asking two questions:

- What forms do their Web-based communications take?
- What kinds of information do they provide to customers?

We found that all six websites include three kinds of information:

- Promotional: sales, seasonal promotions, clearance events, member discount days.
- Educational: landscaping and gardening tips, plant care, and types of drought-tolerant (xeric) plants.
- Product inventory: types of products and plants currently in stock.

All six websites also offered plant sales and photo galleries of before and after landscaping work.

Texas nursery phone survey findings

After analyzing six xeric nursery websites, we identified four Texas nurseries that provide xeric plants and landscaping and contacted their management to discover their customer communication strategies. We chose these four Texas nurseries using the same procedures as we did for the website analysis, selecting the state of Texas and using the search terms "xeric" and "nursery." The four nurseries included in this research are the following:

1. Canyon's Edge, Canyon, TX
2. Sunset Gardens, El Paso, TX
3. The Natural Gardener, Austin, TX
4. Shades of Green, Frisco, TX

We focused our telephone survey on these two questions:

- What forms of communication work best for their business?
- What offers do customers best respond to (promotions, referral incentives, etc.)?

All four Texas nurseries we contacted have websites with comparable contents to the other nursery websites we analyzed: promotional, educational, and plant inventories; however, none of these nurseries offer online purchase or shipping of plants. In addition, two of these nurseries (Canyon's Edge and The Natural Gardener) use online blog postings to communicate tips to customers. Prior to the development of their websites, management at both of these nurseries reported that they used postal service delivery of newsletters to entice their customers to visit and purchase in-stock plants. Canyon Edge's management also noted that they sometimes use flyers delivered to homes in early spring to advertise lawn and landscaping services. In addition, all four nurseries occasionally use local newspaper advertisements to announce sales and other promotions. All four nurseries also maintain Facebook pages where they post news and promotions regularly. None of these nurseries have used referral incentives to promote their businesses.

Customer survey findings

Below you will find a series of charts and explanations that report findings from our survey of 100 customers who visited XerEscapes over two Saturdays in late July. We asked customers four questions as they shopped; our questions concerned the customer's age range and preferences about communication from XerEscapes.

Figure 1 describes the target demographic age range of XerEscapes's customers. Identifying demographics will help XerEscapes' management more effectively to target their customer communications. We found that the average age range for XerEscapes is 30–39 years old. XerEscapes has the least the amount of customers in the 20–29 range. According to the website www.marketingdemographics.com, customers in the 30–39 age range prefer to communicate with businesses electronically. The website states that customers 40 and up prefer direct contact with businesses including mailings, phone calls, or face-to-face contact.

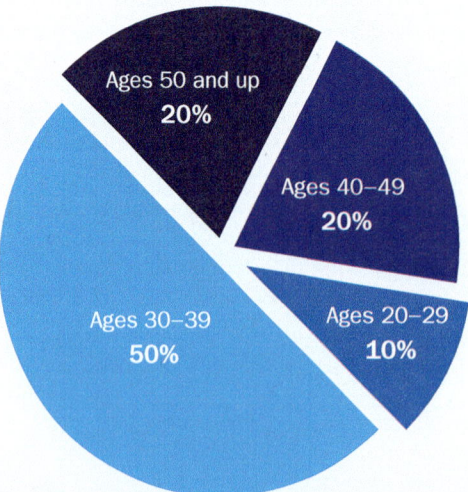

Figure 1: XerEscapes' average customer ages.

Figure 2 reflects how often the surveyed customers would like to receive a communication from XerEscapes. Sixty percent of all customers prefer quarterly communication. Less preferred were monthly (30%) and semi-annual (10%) communications. No customers preferred annual communications.

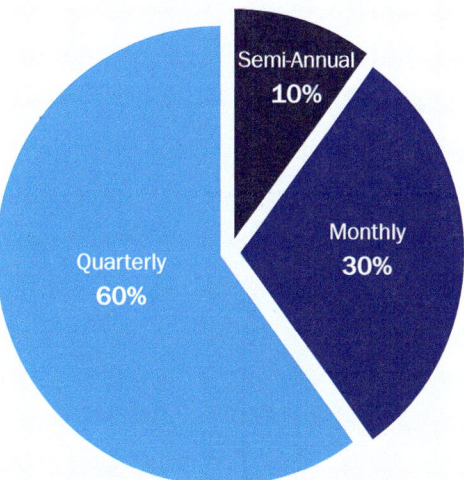

Figure 2: Customers' preferred communication frequency.

Figure 3 reports the form of communication that surveyed customers preferred. Surprisingly, 80% of all customers surveyed preferred postal mail communications and only 20% preferred online communication.

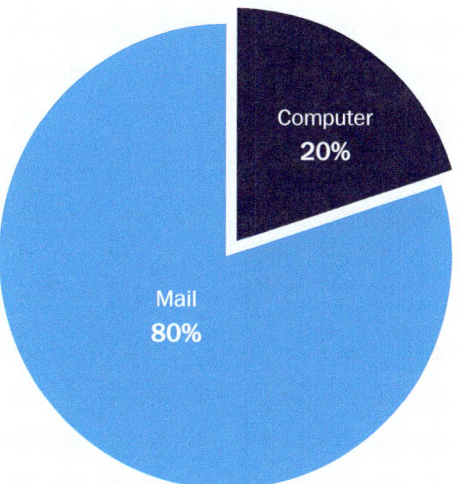

Figure 3: Customers' preferred communication delivery method.

Figure 4 identifies the type of information (promotional, educational, inventory) preferred by customers. All customers requested at least two types of information. Of the XerEscapes customers surveyed, 80% wanted promotional information included in communication from the business; 60% wanted educational information; and 40% wanted information about product inventories.

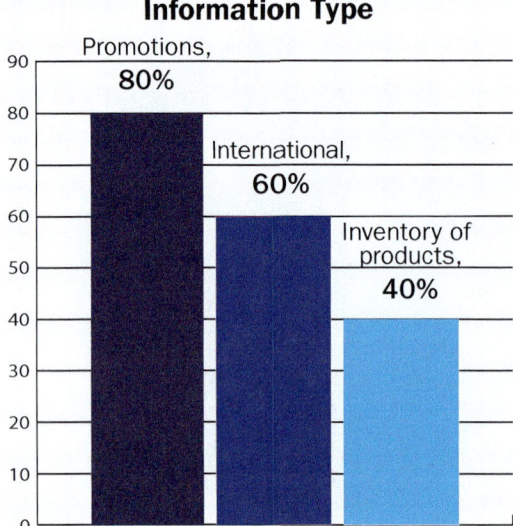

Figure 4: Customers' preferred information types.

CONCLUSIONS

Our survey of regional and Texas nurseries allowed us to identify key questions for our customer survey. We also learned that all ten nurseries have well-developed websites that advertise product inventory and services. Three kinds of information were prominently displayed on these websites: promotional information, educational tips, and product inventories. Most of the larger regional nurseries also offer plants for online purchase, but the smaller Texas nurseries did not. This information allowed us to develop a short four-question survey, which we used to survey 100 of XerEscapes' current customers.

From this survey, we arrived at the following conclusions:

- The target demographic for XerEscapes is 30–39 years old.
- Most customers prefer quarterly contact.
- Most customers prefer to receive communication from XerEscapes in the form of a newsletter by postal delivery.
- The type of information customers want to know the most is promotional information and news, but educational articles and information about services would also be welcome.

RECOMMENDATIONS

Based on our research, we recommend that XerEscapes management use the following means to communicate with customers.

1. **Immediately begin sending a newsletter by mail to customers at the beginning of each season so customers receive a communication quarterly.** By communicating with customers at the beginning

of each season, XerEscapes will be able to reach customers before they purchase seasonal plants and supplies.

2. **Include all three forms of information—promotional, informational, and an inventory summary.** Although most customers prefer promotional news, we feel including some of each category would satisfy all customer's requests. By including the additional information the customer may have questions or purchase additional products from XerEscapes.

3. **Prior to the development of a permanent website, use Facebook to publicize XerEscapes.** In addition to creating a Facebook page, post signs in the retail location asking customers to "like" you on Facebook. Use this page to provide promotional information, educational tips, and inventory notices and services.

4. **Develop and maintain a permanent website as soon as staffing is available to meet the preferences of the younger demographic groups.** In order to satisfy every customer's preferred communication type, XerEscapes should develop a website that can eventually take the place of the mailed newsletter. Publicize the new website in a final newsletter to alert customers to the transition.

These recommendations, we think, will provide customers with immediate information now and transition customers into less expensive and more easily updatable electronic communications.

If you have questions about our research or desire help in implementing these recommendations, please do not hesitate to contact us for additional assistance.

Chapter Summary

Reports are permanent accounts of how a project was designed, developed, and implemented, and its results. Reports gather key documentation into a single permanent record of the completed project. They review the project's background and customer's needs; describe alternative solutions, and explain the reasoning for the final solution. They also describe the end product and summarize its design and development process, including testing. Like the proposal, engineers or their teams write final results reports to meet established standards set by the customer or funding agency. Although these standards may vary from project to project, the general contents are often the same. Research and results reports are often the only archival documents created at a project's conclusion. Other documentation, such as the project binders, log books, and status reports, may remain in the hands of specific readers or their owners, but they are not primarily intended to be publicly reviewed documents.

Chapter Assignments

The exercises in this section ask you to apply what you have learned in this chapter as well as explore how this knowledge applies to and connects with other information in the textbook.

1. One method for organizing a report is to outline it before writing it; however, outlines can vary widely in breadth and detail. The three outlines below plan a report of three informational interviews a student conducted to learn more about working as an accountant and financial planner. Compare the three outlines below and discuss the advantages and disadvantages of each as a writing guide.

   Outline 1

   Introduction
   - Background on need
   - Research question
   - Brief strategy for answering research question
   - Forecasting statement

   Interview methods
   - Question development strategies
   - Criteria for interviewee selection
   - Strategies for scheduling, conducting, and concluding the interviews

   Interviewee #1

   Facts
   - Names and contact information of interviewees
   - Date and time of interviews
   - Information gathered from the interviewees about their work and workplaces

Discussion
- Take-away messages from the interviews
- General experiences during the interviews
- Aspects of the interviews that went particularly well
- Aspects of the interviews that did not go as well as expected

Interviewee #2

Facts
- Names and contact information of interviewees
- Date and time of interviews
- Information gathered from the interviewees about their work and workplaces

Discussion
- Take-away messages from the interviews
- General experiences during the interviews
  - Aspects of the interviews that went particularly well
  - Aspects of the interviews that did not go as well as expected

Interviewee #3

Facts
- Names and contact information of interviewees
- Date and time of interviews
- Information gathered from the interviewees about their work and workplaces

Discussion
- Take-away messages from the interviews
- General experiences during the interviews
- Aspects of the interviews that went particularly well
- Aspects of the interviews that did not go as well as expected

Conclusions
- Overall trends and conclusions
  - What I learned about informational interviewing as a result of this exercise
  - What I learned about my chosen career as a result of this exercise

Recommendations
- Things I might do differently next time I conduct an information interview
- Things I need to do to be successful in this career

Outline 2

I. Introduction
- Background
- Research question

- Names and contact information of interviewees
- Date and time of interviews

II. Methods in chronological order
- Criteria for selecting interviewees
- Strategies for scheduling, conducting, and concluding the interviews
- Question development strategies

III. Facts and Discussion
- Information generated from the interviews about interviewees' work and workplaces
  - Interview with Accounting major
  - Interview with Accounting and Finance major
  - Interview with Master's of International Business
- Take-away messages from the interviews
- Overall trends

IV. Conclusion
- What was learned about informational interviewing as a result of this exercise
- Aspects of the interviews that went well and that didn't go so well

V. Recommendations
- What I would do differently the next time informational interviews are conducted
- What I should do to prepare myself for this career

Outline 3

Informational Interview Plan

- Introduction > background, research question, date and time of interview with each person and contact information, forecasting statement
- Methods > strategies for question development; strategies for interviews
- Facts/findings and IV. discussion > information gathered; take away messages
- Conclusion > what went well; what went badly; overall experience
- Recommendations > what I learned and how to apply it; what to do differently next time

2. To learn more about how reports can be delivered in different formats, visit the U.S. Center for Disease Control's Healthy Aging podcasts (http://www.cdc.gov/aging/publications/podcasts.htm). Listen to one of the podcast reports and outline its contents. How does the podcast's contents compare to the typical report structure described in this chapter?

Figure Credits

Figure 15.1. © Ditty_about_summer/Shutterstock.com

Figure 15.2. © Dragon Images/Shutterstock.com

Figure 15.3. © Slava Kovtun/Shutterstock.com

Figure 15.4. © Creativa Images/Shutterstock.com

Figure 15.5. © dizain/Shutterstock.com

Developing Professional Profiles and Job Search Materials

16

CHAPTER OVERVIEW

This chapter introduces you to the basics of creating a professional profile and searching for a job. After reading this chapter, you should be able to meet the following objectives:

- Assess and inventory your job skills.
- Use your job skills inventory to create and design professional search materials, including a résumé, cover letter, biographical statement, profile, and portfolio.
- Read job ads and respond to them effectively with professional job search materials.
- Use effective communication to interview for a position.

College graduates can reasonably expect to be interviewed throughout their careers, but especially at the beginning. Recent employment studies indicate that most professionals in the 21st century will change jobs more than a half dozen times from the beginning of their careers until they retire. In addition, promotions within an organization often involve applying and interviewing for the new job.

At many points in your professional career, you may be required to submit a résumé and an application letter to get an interview. This chapter will give you practice in designing a résumé and writing an application letter. You will also gain experience in submitting these documents in both print and electronic formats. Additionally, you will learn about other professional job search materials that professionals commonly maintain.

This chapter is designed to give you opportunities to practice your job search skills. It is organized chronologically as a job search might be, beginning with a skills assessment and ending with interviewing. Each section will provide you with insights on how to prepare, design, and deliver effective job search materials that will improve your chances for successfully getting the job. Whether you are a recent graduate or a seasoned professional, it is important to create, develop, and maintain

Figure 16.1. Strong cover letters and résumés result in interviews. Strong interviews result in jobs.

professional materials, such as résumés, letters, biographies, profiles, and portfolios, all of which represent your most significant accomplishments and career goals.

ASSESSING YOUR SKILLS

Before any job search, you need to analyze and assess your knowledge, skills, and values. A careful analysis of these qualities is necessary if you want to find a good job match. Such an analysis will help you to generate job search materials that truly reflect what you have to offer an employer. Assessing and analyzing your skills creates an inventory that you can use to write résumés and cover letters as well as other job search materials. Creating this inventory is never easy, but it gets easier as you gain work experience. Even individuals who are looking for their first jobs have knowledge, skills, and values they can use to market themselves effectively to new employers. For this reason, the first step is creating a list or inventory of the experiences and qualities you bring to a new job.

In other chapters in this text, you have learned to start any project with a problem statement; in this case, that statement can be summarized as "I need a new job." To address this problem, you need to answer some key questions: What jobs are out there, and am I qualified for them? Assessing your skills and inventorying them is the initial planning phase of generating a professional profile and creating job search materials. Starting here will help you to determine your qualifications.

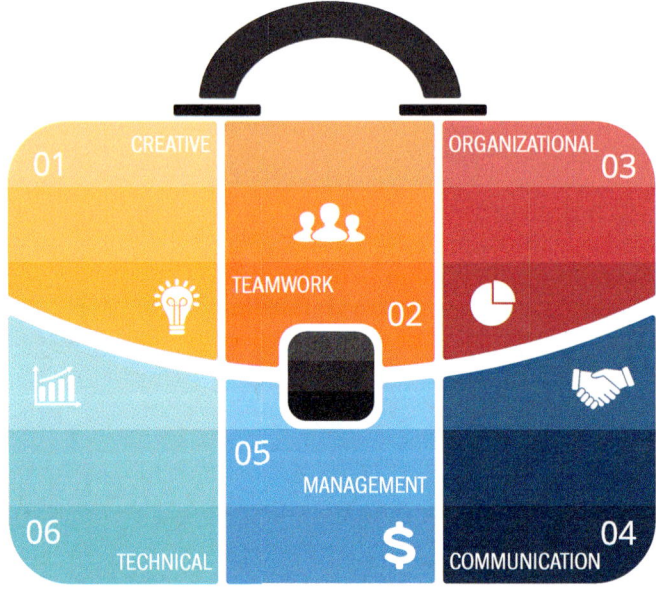

Figure 16.2. An inventory of your experiences and qualities is the first step in creating a successful résumé.

To create an inventory of your knowledge, skills, and values, you will need to think about paid and voluntary work as well as educational experiences you have successfully completed. If your work experiences are few, then you will draw heavily from educational experiences and knowledge. You may also want to consider past leadership and membership activities and duties. A skills assessment and inventory requires you to articulate those experiences in a way that showcases your strengths and abilities.

After assessing your skills and creating your inventory, review the inventory and group comparable or similar skills. For example, if you find two or three items that relate to communication, mark or highlight related items so you can group them accordingly. Groupings or categories will help you to determine how you want to shape your professional profile.

EXERCISE 16.1

Using Internet Tools to Inventory Skills

The Internet is widely populated with online quizzes and free assessments that can help you create your inventory. To begin your process, conduct an Internet search using the terms "job search skills inventory." Using this term, you will find dozens of skills inventories. Choose three of these inventory tools and complete the assessments. Print your results or save them electronically to a cloud or drive.

Tasks to be completed:

1. Conduct an Internet search using the search terms "job search skills inventory."
2. Complete at least three inventory tools.
3. Print the results of each tool.
4. Compare the results, and answer the following questions:
    a. Do you agree with the assessment you received? Why or why not?
    b. Do you have other knowledge, skills, or qualities that are not listed on these results? If so, add to the list.
    c. How are the tools alike? How are they different?
    d. How might you use the tools' findings to create job search materials?
5. Bring your findings to class and be prepared to discuss.

CREATING AND MAINTAINING A PROFESSIONAL PROFILE

Job searches today require more than résumés and cover letters. To be competitive, you will need to create a clean, professional profile. This profile includes an up-to-date print résumé that you can provide in print or via email, but it also includes other electronic documents that highlight your best qualities. This section discusses four key documents that you should create to showcase and market yourself to potential employers: the biographical sketch, online professional profile, résumé (both print and electronic), and eportfolio (or personal website). These documents build upon each other, moving from simplest and least detailed to most complicated and detailed.

Figure 16.3. An online professional profile evolves as you gain education and experience. It helps you build and connect to your personal network and market yourself to new employers.

EXERCISE 16.2

Analyzing a Job Skills Inventory

Below you will find an inventory developed by Anna Kay Boze, who will graduate from her university at the end of this semester. She has majored in accounting and will graduate with a B.S. and an M.B.A. in accounting. She has worked in several internship positions, and she has had other work experience as well. She generally takes 15 hours a semester, and she works 20–30 hours a week to support herself and pay for her education. Anna has found a job with the federal government as an auditor for which she would like to apply. So she has created the following job skills inventory. Review the inventory and answer the questions after it to complete this exercise.

Tasks to be completed:

1. Review and analyze the job skills inventory below.
2. Anna Kay, the job seeker, has already begun to categorize her inventories.
   a. How are the skills categorized?
   b. How are the skills stated or articulated?
   c. Did you note any repetition in the inventory? If so, where?
   d. How might this kind of articulation assist you as you move to the next step, creating your professional profile?
3. Using Anna Kay's inventory as an example, inventory your own skills.
4. Be prepared to discuss your findings as well as present your inventory for feedback and discussion.

Anna Kay Bose's job search inventory

Work experience
Accounting and Finance Intern, part-time 20 hours a week
Responsibilities included:
- Staff training on basic accounting practices and software use
- Recordkeeping, assisting with recording donations, reconciling accounts, and making bank deposits
- Answering phones, filing, shredding, other duties as needed
- Reporting to chief administrator and office manager
- Working with volunteers on annual fundraising dinner
- Identifying sponsors for annual fundraising event; soliciting and tracking donations
- Planning and providing oversight for annual fundraising dinner budget

S.G. Anderson, P.C., Controller, New Boston, Texas
Accounting internship responsibilities, part-time, 20 hours a week
- Reported to controller
- Produced financial reports for clients
- Reconciled accounts
- Assisted controller with monthly close-out reports

Skills

People skills
- Worked with volunteers at United Heart Fund (helped them find materials they needed to complete tasks, showed them how to use copy machine and answer phones)
- Helped with volunteers and staff to plan annual fundraising event (We planned menu, arranged for catering, made room and decoration decisions. I solicited donations from sponsors and tracked donations. On night of event, I checked in attendees and handled cash tickets to event.)
- Worked as lifeguard (interacted with parents and children)
- Worked as pizza chef and interacted with customers, taking and filling orders, sometimes handled dissatisfied customers

Communication skills
- Wrote thank-you notes for donations to United Heart Fund
- Trained staff at United Heart Fund on accounting software use and basic accounting functions
- Wrote thank-you letters to sponsors of annual fundraiser at UHF
- Wrote monthly financial reports
- Worked on financial team at SGA to divide up task and plan weekly assignments
- Used email to contact volunteers, co-workers, and sponsors regarding fundraiser

Accounting skills
- Monthly reports
- Reconciled bank accounts
- Created monthly and end-of-year donation reports

Accounting education and courses
- Will earn two degree in accounting (B.A. in accounting and MBA in accounting)
- Will take CPA test as soon as I can
- Took courses in Business Law, Beginning Accounting, Intermediate Accounting, Advanced Accounting, Accounting Systems, Professional Report Writing, Cost Accounting, Business Ethics, Advanced Auditing

Software skills
- Microsoft Office Suite, including Excel
- QuickBooks
- QuickBooks Premier for Nonprofits

Awards and Recognitions
- 2007 Awarded American Business Women's Association, Katy, TX, college scholarship for outstanding high school accounting student in Katy
- 2007 Graduated in top 10% of high school graduating class, Katy HS
- 2011 Student Accountant of the Year, Texarkana State University

Biographical Statements

Written biographical statements can provide a succinct personal overview, highlighting your background, skills, goals, and accomplishments. While such statements may summarize credentials from your résumé, they can be shorter or even longer statements, depending on what is required for their contexts of use. They can be substitutes for career objectives or career summary statements, which are featured in some résumés. Ideally, they should highlight a few significant work experiences, educational achievements, qualifications, or characteristics you possess. When possible, they should also demonstrate a diversity of skills and abilities, relevant to your career goals or interests, including some recent accolades. When writing a biographical statement, consider including the following elements:

- Your name and a professional title
- A tagline that highlights what makes you different or unique
- Summary of three to five significant or relevant work experiences, educational achievements, qualifications, or characteristics
- A personal note, such as a hobby or interest
- Visual elements, such as a photo or in some cases a unique design concept
- Links to appropriate social media content
- Contact information, such as email.

Figure 16.4 provides an example of a short biographical sketch for a soon-to-be college graduate.

Daniella Ropas
Grant and Proposal Writer

Daniella Ropas is senior at Texas Tech University, where she is earning a B.A. in Technical Communication. Through her coursework and internship opportunities, she has gained experience as a grant and proposal writer. Her first successful grant proposal was written as a class project with a team to seek funding for a local dog rescue organization. The grant won the organization $1000 to support publicity and outreach projects. This success led her to seek other grant-seeking opportunities. Since then, she has worked for a local food bank in West Texas, where she has written six grants, five of which have been funded. In 2013–2014, her grant-writing skills secured over $35,000 for the food bank. After graduation in December 2015, Daniella will seek a position as a non-profit grant writer in West Texas or Eastern New Mexico. In addition to her work, she volunteers at St. Benedict's Chapel, a local soup kitchen that feeds 80–100 individuals daily. When she is not at school or working, she enjoys outdoor sports, especially running and playing soccer.

You can learn more about Daniella at her LinkedIn profile at < https://www.linkedin.com/pub/daniella-ropas >.

She may also be reached by email at Daniella.Ropas@gmail.com.

Figure 16.4. Biographical sketches provide employers with a quick overview of your skills and experiences.

Online Profiles

Before you create a professional online profile, you will need to assess your current online persona. Employers and recruiters, like your friends, can and will access social media to see what they can learn about potential employees. If your preferred social media profiles are not as professional as they should be, you should take some time now, before you begin the job search, to scrub your profiles, clearing away and cleaning up your posts to make them as presentable as possible. Specifically, you should scrub or delete posts and photographs that are inappropriate or questionable. What kinds of posts are particularly offensive? Look for posts, shares, or photos that mention or show alcohol or drugs, nudity, or offensive behavior. When you are reviewing photos, check for photos in which you are tagged and untag your image. Delete negative comments about former friends or employers. Also edit or delete comments that suggest you have poor communication skills. Set your personal social media accounts to "private." Doing so will make it more challenging for individuals who do not know you to access your personal information. However, you should always remember that nothing on the Internet is private; everything is accessible. Scrubbing or cleaning your social media accounts is daunting, but so is competing for the best jobs.

EXERCISE 16.3

Create a LinkedIn Profile

If you do not have a LinkedIn profile, this exercise asks you to create one; if you do have one, then this exercise asks you to update it. Go to LinkedIn (www.linkedin.com), and follow the directions to create a new profile or to update a current profile. Take notes on the procedure for creating or updating a profile, and be prepared to talk about your experiences with others.

Tasks to be completed:

1. Visit LinkedIn (www.linkedin.com).
2. Create a new profile or update your current profile with new information.
3. Take notes on how the process of creating or updating works and be prepared to talk about your experience.

When your online social network accounts are scrubbed and private, then you are ready to create professional profiles. An Internet search of professional networking sites will result in dozens of possibilities. LinkedIn is among the largest and most visible online professional networking sites in the world. Even if you decide to join smaller networking sites or post to a job search site, such as Monster, you should create a LinkedIn profile for maximum coverage. Online professional profiles are similar to résumés, but they require you to engage your structured authoring skills and chunk information into relevant categories, such as a summary, volunteer experience, projects, interests, and organizations. You will enter this information into a form with fields that allows you to track and update your employment and educational accomplishments. With this profile in place, you will connect to others to build your personal network. As you add new information to your profile, your connections receive updates and can track your progress or contact you for more information. Creating an online professional profile should build on the skills assessment you completed earlier in this chapter. As you enter skills and experiences into the online form, check them off your inventory list. At the end of the exercise, you will find that you have begun to categorize and place skills and experiences into a format that will eventually become a professional résumé.

Résumés

Even if you have never applied for a professional position, you have probably completed applications to seek employment. To apply for professional positions, you will need a résumé that tells a story about your work and educational experiences and convinces hiring managers or employers to consider you for the position. A common misconception is that résumés are required to get a professional position. In reality, a good résumé will help you get an interview. The interview, ultimately, is how you get a professional position; nevertheless, the résumé is the starting point.

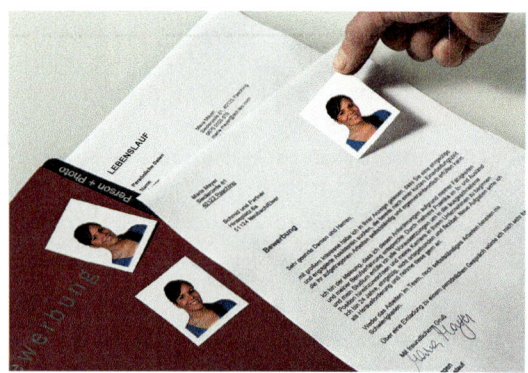

Figure 16.5. In many countries, résumés include pictures of applicants, although this practice is not advised in the United States.

EXERCISE 16.4

Researching Résumés in Your Field

Visit your campus career center, talk to a professor who teaches in your major, or search the Internet to learn more about résumés in your field. What kinds of information do résumés in your field include? What are employers' expectations about résumés in your field? Do résumés in your field have any special features? Write a short report describing your findings.

Tasks to be completed:

1. Research résumés in your field by visiting a campus career center, talking to a professor in your major, or searching the Internet.
2. Answer the following questions (and any others you generate):
    a. What kinds of information do résumés in your field include?
    b. What are employers' expectations about résumés in your field?
    c. Do résumés in your field have any special features?
3. Write a short report of your findings.

This section will provide you with basic guidance in creating and formatting a professional résumé; however, the information in this section is limited by its general focus. You may need to conduct your own research to find out how professionals in your particular field write their résumés and modify the advice from this section based on your findings.

Additionally, if you conduct online research about résumés, you will find contradictory advice. For example, the "summary" is a résumé component that many résumé coaches recommend including. This summary, located prominently at the top of your résumé, highlights personal characteristics and experiences that qualify you as the best job candidate. Although conventional wisdom recommends the summary, it is now viewed less favorably than before because it has become so commonplace. So you may find some advisors recommending it, while others do not. Consider this advice carefully, and design your résumé based on the best, most current thinking about what makes a résumé successful in today's market. One final note worth considering as you design your résumé is the amount of time—about 30 seconds—that most hiring managers or employers spend looking at individual résumés. Your résumé has only 30 seconds to make an impression, so be sure the most important information about you and your qualifications are located at the top of the page.

EXERCISE 16.5
Researching International Résumés

Use the Internet to research and locate examples and images of resumes from at least two countries. Compare to your own resume. What differences do you note in terms of content and design?

Tasks to be completed:

1. Research resumes from at least two other countries.
2. Note similarities and differences in content and design between these resumes and your own.
3. Prepare a brief document plan describing how you would modify your resume if you were searching for a job in one of these countries.

With these caveats in mind, the rest of this section provides you with some basic guidelines for résumé-building. These guidelines are divided into two categories: essential and non-essential information. Optional information is included in the essential category.

Essential Information

Your name and contact information are located in the heading at the very top of the résumé. State your full name, as it appears on your identification cards, even though you may prefer to be called by a nickname. If you are living in temporary housing that you will be leaving after graduation from college, then place both your temporary and your permanent addresses on the résumé. Label them accordingly. Following your address, include your mobile or landline telephone number, whichever is your preferred contact. This is the number the employer will use to reach you, so be sure it is one you check frequently. Finally, include your email address and any electronic profiles or websites, such as your LinkedIn profile, that contain additional information about you. Figure 16.6 illustrates a basic résumé heading.

Victoria A. Thorne

1215 Joliet St. #401 | St. Louis, MO 60433 | 314-555-5759
victhorne@gmail.com

Figure 16.6. This basic résumé heading includes name, location, and contact information.

Two other types of information are essential on the résumé: educational and work experiences. If your workplace experience is minimal, you may substitute a skills section for work experiences. Some positions may require you to demonstrate all three types of qualifications (educational, skills, and work); in this case, use all three categories. Place the category first that best qualifies you for the position. For recent graduates, a college degree is usually the best qualification, but graduates who have extensive work experience may prefer to place work information first. Whatever order you choose, each of these sections should be arranged in reverse chronological order with the most recent work and educational experience first.

Education entries should include all advanced degrees earned starting with the most recent. (College graduates do not typically include high school degrees.) In addition to the degree, each entry should include name of institution attended, location, dates of attendance, and date degree earned. Students who have not yet graduated may include an expected graduation date, rather than a graduation date. If applicable to the position for which you are applying, you may also include your grade point average (GPA) and relevant coursework. Figure 16.7 provides a basic template for each degree as well as a heading for the education section.

EDUCATION	**B.A. in Technical Communication, minor in Women and Gender Studies**
	• Texas Tech University, Lubbock, TX
	• Expected graduation date, May 2016
	• Relevent coursework: Information Design, Web Design, and Interaction Design

Figure 16.7. A basic education entry includes degree, graduation date, institution, and location. GPA and coursework are optional.

Work experience entries require more detailed information. Like education entries, they are organized from most recent to least recent. These entries must include job title, employer, location, and dates of employment. If you have experience as a volunteer, you may include these entries under work experience. For detailed work entries, you will also include a short list of job duties. These duties are usually bulleted for easy scanning, and they begin with a strong verb that describes the action required to complete the duty. (The Purdue Online Writing Center—OWL—has a great list of action verbs categorized by skill: https://owl.english.purdue.edu/owl/resource/543/02/). Résumés with work experience emphasized work well when you have sufficient job experience to demonstrate your fit for the job. Figure 16.8 provides a basic template for work entries.

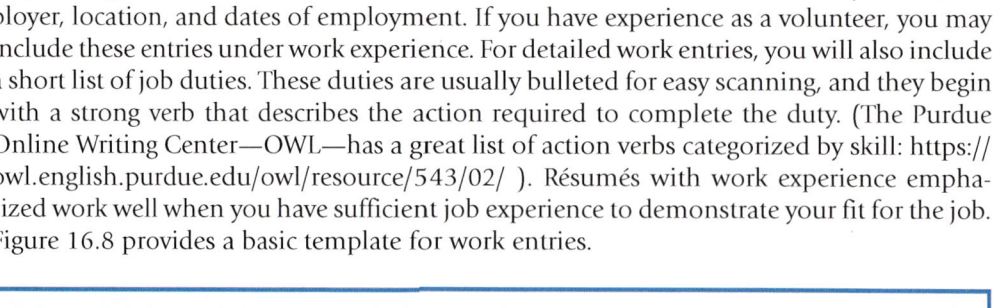

WORK EXPERIENCE	**Intern, America's Byways**
	Logan, UT 2013–present
	• Reseach national scenic byways
	• Write travel copy for Mountain West Region byways website
	• Edit travel copy for Mountain West Region byways website
	• Maintain web pages for Mountain West Region byways

Figure 16.8. A basic work entry includes bulleted job duties. These duties should begin with a strong verb.

Skills entries, like work entries, are categorized under a heading. Choose headings that reflect key qualities identified in the position announcement or ad. For example, you might showcase your communication, language, computer, financial, leadership, and/or supervisory skills. Use as many skills headings as needed to categorize key skills. Underneath the heading, you should list examples that demonstrate how you gained the skill. These examples are typically formatted just as work entries format job duties. Résumés that emphasize skills work well when you have little experience but strong educational background or when you are changing career areas. Figure 16.9 provides a basic template for a skills entry and demonstrates how work entries, as seen in Figure 16.8 can be revised as skills entries.

SKILLS

Writing and Editing Skills
- Research travel information for America's Byways
- Write and edit travel copy for America's Byways
- Wrote feature articles for the *Texas Tech Matador*

Online Content Development Skills
- Maintain web pages for Mountain West Region byways
- Designed and implemented alumni web pages for university department at Texas Tech
- Write and manage content for Texas Tech Society for Technical Communication website, including social media content

---

Figure 16.9. Like a work experience entry, a basic skills entry identifies the skill and provides evidence for it,
using strong verbs.

In addition to education, work, and skills entries, your résumé may optionally include other important information. Below is a list of entries that you may choose to include if applicable to your experience and essential to the job you are considering:

- Community activities
- Military status
- Security clearances
- Professional and service organization memberships
- Leadership, such as offices held in professional and service organizations
- Honors and awards
- Civil service ranking

While this list is not comprehensive, it illustrates the kinds of qualifications that employers may seek during a job search. Your skills assessment and inventory will help you to identify the skills you possess while the position announcement will guide you with categorical headings.

Non-Essential Information

Certain information is not essential, and it should not be included on a résumé. Most of this information is not essential because U.S. federal guidelines restrict employers from considering it when conducting a job search. In other words, most of this information is illegal for employers to use as determinants for who receives the job; for this reason, you should think carefully about including any of this information in a résumé:

- Birth date or age
- Physical characteristics (height, weight)
- Race or nationality
- Marital status
- Health status
- Home ownership
- Religion
- Political activities

As with any information, however, exceptions exist. For example, if you are seeking a job with a religious organization or a religiously affiliated organization, then including your religious affiliation may be acceptable and desirable. Similarly, if you are seeking employment with an organization known for its political connections, then political activities may be relevant. As with other documents you create, the key that guides you with non-essential information is knowledge about your audience—the specific employer who is seeking someone like you. Researching the employer or organization before you apply will help you to modify your résumé to suit that audience in ways that might not work for other audiences. More guidance on conducting employer research is included in the next section.

Organizing Résumés

As suggested in the essential information discussion, résumés are organized in one of three ways: chronologically, functionally, or chrono-functional (a combination of the two). **Chronological** résumés showcase your work experience and are organized with the most recent information first in each category. These résumés are useful when you have work experience that qualifies you for the position you are seeking. **Functional** résumés showcase your skills, highlighting the skills that the employer is seeking. These résumés are useful when you either lack work experience that qualifies you for the job or you are changing careers. For example, a functional résumé might work best if you previously worked as teacher's aide in a local school district, but, because you have now completed your MBA in accounting and finance, you are now seeking an accounting position. A functional résumé would allow you highlight the skills you have gained through education rather than skills you gained through other employment. The combination **chrono-functional** résumé includes both work experience and skills. It is appropriate when you have both kinds of experience and knowledge that qualify you for a job.

Figures 16.10, 16.11, and 16.12 illustrate the similarities and differences in these three organizations by demonstrating how the content of the same résumé can be modified to create each of these organizations.

Formatting Résumés

As you consider how to format your résumé, always keep your readers in mind. Because hiring managers and employers read résumés so quickly, your résumé should be no more than two pages long unless you are applying for a position requiring extensive experience. You can also expect these readers to receive many applications for the same position, so designing your résumé to stand out is important. Specifically, standing out will mean not using a word-processing template that results in a résumé that looks like everyone else's. If you must start with a template, modify it by changing the font, font colors, or font sizes to emphasize your information. Use easy-to-read fonts like Arial, Times New Roman, or Helvetica, and keep your font size above 9 points to improve scannability. Since many print résumés are scanned into a content management system, avoid underlining text since lines may cause misreading. Finally, plentiful white space will also create a clean and scannable design that improves résumé readability.

JULIE A. JACKSON

650 E. Center St. *jajackson@ttu.edu*
Lubbock, TX 79411 806-796-1240

EDUCATION

Bachelor of Arts, Technical Communication
Texas Tech University, Lubbock, TX
Anticipated graduation: December 2016
Minor: Instructional Technology
Current GPA: 4.0

Associate of Arts
South Plains College, Lubbock, TX
Graduation: May 2014
Overall GPA: 3.781

WORK EXPERIENCE

Tutor Aug. 2014–present
TTU Writing Center, Lubbock TX
- Design organization for Writing Center website
- Research and generate clear, usable information for site users
- Edit and write 40-page Writing Center employee manual
- Redesign educational diagnostic remediation tracking form

Technical Editor Intern May 2015–Aug. 2015
TimeForge, Lubbock, TX
- Researched, wrote, designed, and edited online help articles
- Corresponded frequently with software developers to discuss needs and goals

Technical Writing Intern May 2014–Aug. 2014
National Instruments, Austin, TX
- Wrote and edited National Instruments product documentation
- Collaborated with engineers and other technical writers

Figure 16.10. Chronological résumés are effective for job-seekers who have a strong work history related to the potential job.

Jamil Larned

253 Sheridan, Apt. #N4, Oklahoma City, OK 73101
Cell: 405.237.9489
Email: jamil.larned@hotmail.com

Education
BA in Technical Communications with a minor in Business Administration
Texas Tech University
Lubbock, TX   May 2016

Relevant Skills
Technical Communication
- Wrote and implemented SOPs at Azteca Milling Company and Flour Mills
- Created Hazard Analysis and Critical Control Points (HACCP) Organic Plan for Azteca Milling Company and Flour Mills
- Edited and updated Azteca Milling Company and Flour Mills HACCP, Good Manufacturing Plan (GMP), and Quality Assurance (QA) manuals
- Communicated with American Institute of Baking (AIB) representative to help Azteca Milling achieve the highest rating under AIB program
- Edited undergraduate research material in the area of Special Education

Computer and Internet
- Adobe InDesign and Microsoft Office software to complete assignments in technical writing courses
- Dreamweaver software and HTML to developed website for Azteca Milling Company
- Quickbooks to find financial records and generate invoices for Azteca Milling Company
- Microsoft Outlook and InDesign to create and maintain Azteca Milling Company plans and manuals
- Microsoft Outlook and InDesign to design and maintain preventative maintenance program for Azteca Milling Company and Gilt Edge Flour Mills

Document Design and Organization
- Designed product catalog for Azteca Milling Company flours and specialty products
- Created preventative maintenance system and templates for Azteca Flour Mills
- Designed technical illustrations and data displays for a document design course

Honors and Awards
- Dean's List: Spring 2013, Fall and Spring 2014, Fall and Spring 2015
- Truman and Virginia Camp Scholarship 2014

Figure 16.11. Functional résumés are excellent choices applicants seeking entry-level positions and for applicants who are changing careers or have lapses in work history.

Davis George Collins

2320 Vanguard Street, Apt. 220, Vieho, TX 79411
DavisCollins@gmail.com (786) 242-5779

Education

Bachelor of Arts, University Studies (December 2016)
With specializations Math, Speech Communication, and Technical Communication
Texas Tech University — Lubbock, Texas

Coursework in Mathematics, Education (2012–2014)
Florida International University — Miami, Florida

Associate of Arts, Mathematics (2010–2012)
Miami-Dade College — Miami, Florida

Skills

- **Computer** — Expert in MS Word, Excel, PowerPoint; QuickBooks
- **Language** — Fluent in Spanish, basic conversational French
- **Interpersonal** — Skilled in leadership in civic and educational organizations, teaching, and training
- **Communication** — Proficient in legal communication, reports, electronic communications, and blogging

Work Experience

Teaching Assistant 2012–2014
Florida International University MATHTEC Program — Miami, Florida
- Taught undergraduate mathematics labs, privately tutored.
- Assisted in mathematics education research.

Paralegal/Legal Secretary June 2010 – January 2012
Law Offices of James J. Cohen — Miami, Florida
- Performed paralegal and secretary duties for a small-sized law firm.
- Handled billing, filing and bookkeeping.

Honors and Awards

- National Spanish Honor Society, Florida International University
- National Math Honor Society, Florida International University
- Eagle Scout, Boy Scouts of America

Figure 16.12. A chrono-functional combination résumé is useful for job-seekers who have both a work history and skills that meet job requirements.

Figure 16.13. Innovative résumé design can make your résumé stand out from others.

EXERCISE 16.6

Evaluating a Résumé

In Figure 16.14, you will find Anna Boze's current résumé. Using a timer, review the résumé for 30 seconds and then close your book. Make a list of Anna's qualifications based on your memory. What ideas were you able to recall? Which ones did you forget? How might you recommend Anna modify her résumé to improve your ability to scan and remember its content?

Tasks to be completed:

1. Review Anna's résumé for only 30 seconds.
2. Close your book.
3. Make a list of what you remember about her qualifications.
4. Compare your list to Anna's résumé, and answer these questions:
   a. What ideas were you able to recall?
   b. Which ones did you forget?
   c. How might you recommend Anna modify her résumé to improve your ability to scan and remember its content?

Evaluating Résumés

After you have assessed and inventoried your skills, designed, and formatted your résumé, you are ready to evaluate it. Each job application may require you to modify your résumé to showcase your qualifications. As a result, you should get in the habit of carefully reviewing and evaluating your résumé every time you submit it. Use the following questions to evaluate your print résumé:

- Does your résumé meet the employer's most common expectations for content? Check the résumé against the job ad to make sure it documents all of the employer's requirements for a new employee.
- Is the résumé complete? Have you forgotten to include any relevant personal, educational, and experiential information?
- Is the résumé professionally designed?
- Is it persuasive, readable, and usable?
- Is it attractive and appealing to view?
- Have you checked the spelling and punctuation carefully to make sure you have eliminated all errors?
- If you are submitting an electronic résumé, use these additional questions to evaluate it:
- Have you checked the electronic résumé against the print résumé checklist?
- Did you saved the electronic résumé as a PDF?
- Did you include your name in the PDF filename?

Figure 16.14: Anna Boze's résumé illustrates why résumés must be designed for scanning and quick evaluation.

Anna Kay Boze

38122 57th St.
Atlanta, Texas 75551

Phone: (903) 930-0017
Email: annakboze@gmail.com

EDUCATION

Texarkana University — Texarkana, Texas
Major: Accounting
December 2015
GPA: 3.0/4.0

EXPERIENCE

9/14–5/15
The Best Pizza — Pizza Chef — Atlanta, Texas
- Trained new employees
- Reviewed food for quality standards
- Interacting with customers and employees

5/14–8/14
Robert N. Kauhington, P.C. — Accounting Clerk — Houston, Texas
- Interacting with clients
- Inputting tax returns
- Answering and directing phone calls
- Ability to use of Microsoft Office products

5/13–8/13
Research Assistant — Baylor College of Medicine — Houston, Texas
- Assisted in genetic research
- Interacted with patients

5/12–8/12
Lifeguard — Adkisson YMCA — Houston, Texas
- Customer service
- Performing CPR and First Aid
- Maintain pool and pool deck
- Enforcement of pool rules

ACTIVITIES

Active member of the Zeta Sigma Nu fraternity
Active member of the Accounting Leadership Council
Active member of the TSU waterskiing team

SKILLS

Knowledgeable in Microsoft Office products

Figure 16.14. Anna Boze's résumé illustrates why résumés must be designed for scanning and quick evaluation.

Professional Portfolios

Professional portfolios are consolidated collections that allow you to expand beyond the scope of a résumé and cover letter, by including important supplemental documents, examples, and even design concepts to help you stand out as a professional. Portfolios typically include résumés, work samples, biographical statements, and visual content, and they can be either print or electronic in format. Electronic or online portfolios can be created using social media tools (LinkedIn, Facebook), content management systems (blogs, wikis), or even Web development software programs (Adobe Dreamweaver, Microsoft Web Expression). The following elements are typically included in professional portfolios:

- Career profile statement, including career planning goals, specializations, skills, and significant work experience.
- Individual biography about the applicant, with email contact information and photo.
- Selected, high quality work samples that illustrate competencies and specializations, along with brief abstracts or descriptions of each.
- Awards, interests, and references.
- Updated résumé in both printable and downloadable formats, which demonstrates a solid career path.
- A professional design that demonstrates effective communication practices, skills, and creativity.

Design, in particular, is important in professional portfolios since you have an opportunity to show off work samples, photos, and your own unique design style, as part of the collection. As such, you must carefully consider your portfolio's design concept and include high quality samples of your work. Designs are often inspired by themes, photos, iconic images, color palettes, and other visuals. While many tools and programs you might use to develop a professional portfolio include design templates, you should modify or create your own design to avoid using a stock template

Figure 16.15. These two online portfolio templates illustrate how different this genre can be. Choose a template or create a portfolio design that best represents you to potential employers.

that hundreds of others might have used. One way to get inspired and to help benchmark your ideas is to research other online portfolios to see what else is out there. Remember, as with your selection of details and samples, you should strive to stand out and demonstrate your unique qualifications when making selections about the design of professional portfolios and work samples.

LOCATING AVAILABLE POSITIONS

Job seekers find positions in many ways. Traditionally, they have used newspaper classifieds, campus career centers, and employment agencies to locate positions for which they are qualified. Today, however, opportunities locally, regionally, and globally are advertised through electronic means. Job search Web sites, such as Monster.com and Dice.com, abound, and professional networking sites, like LinkedIn, help to connect employers with job candidates. In spite of these advertising methods, personal networking has been and still remains the most common means of finding employment. This section of the chapter provides insights on how to locate available positions and provides you with resources for doing so. It suggests three important methods for locating positions: networking, informational interviewing, and using job search resources.

Networking

Figure 16.16. Professional networks can extend beyond your immediate circle of friends and acquaintances.

What is networking? Networking is simply talking to people you know to discover employment opportunities. Surprisingly, most jobs are not advertised; they are filled by word-of-mouth. To find these opportunities, you need to let your network know you are seeking employment. You may not think you have a professional network, but, in fact, you do. You know family, friends, and other relationships through school, work, church, and social organizations. If you have maintained a LinkedIn or other professional social media account, then you have contacts there as well. Extending from these relations are connections with other individuals you do not necessarily know. Yet all of these individuals are potentially a part of your professional network. Figure 16.16 illustrates how professional networks function, beginning with one individual and extending well beyond.

To take advantage of your network, you will need to alert individuals with whom you have a close connection that you are job searching. Ask these individuals to let you know about opportunities and to let their networks know. Describe the kind of work you are seeking to your close connections, and tell them about your qualifications. You can contact these individuals in many ways: emails, phone calls, or face-to-face meetings. In other words, get the word out that you are looking for a position and would appreciate your network's support by letting others know.

From your close connections, you should also seek **references** if job opportunities arise. References are individuals who write or speak to employers to vouch for your qualities, skills, and talents. Ask three or four individuals, preferably people who know you or your work well, if they would be willing to serve as your references. Ideally, your references should be able to talk about more than your personal qualities; they should be able to describe how you work and what you bring to an employer.

EXERCISE 16.7

Sketching Your Professional Network and Identifying Potential References

Using Figure 16.10 as a model, draw your own professional network. In the middle of the page, draw a circle and put your name there. Draw lines outward from that circle and sketch in the names of individuals in your personal network. If possible, extend from your personal network outward, listing other individuals whom you can reach through your personal contacts. Identify as many individuals as possible as you begin to think about individuals who can speak for you if a job opportunity arises. Shade at least three or four of your personal network circles to indicate individuals who might serve as your references.

Tasks to be completed:

1. Sketch your personal network.
2. Identify your closest contacts as well as contacts that extend beyond them.
3. Shade in three or four of your personal contacts who might serve as your references.
4. Be prepared to discuss your drawing and your reference designees with others.

Informational Interviewing

After you have identified your network, informational interviewing is an excellent method of learning more about the kind of work you desire. From your network, choose two or three individuals who would be willing to be interviewed for 30 to 45 minutes about their work or workplace experiences. Set up appointments with these individuals and prepare questions for the informational interview. Informational interviews are the opposite of job interviews. In job interviews, an employer questions you about your qualifications for work; in an informational interview, you ask a professional contact questions about his or her work or workplace experiences. The object of the informational interview is to gain insights on a specific kind of job and to get advice on how to get started in this line of work.

Most professionals love to talk about their work and are very willing to help individuals get started. The informational interview allows you to take advantage of their generosity. It also lets your professional contact know that you are seeking work and provides you with the opportunity to talk about your intentions and qualifications. The key to a good informational interview is asking the right questions. You can ask about early job search experiences, getting started in a new job, advice for finding the right job, or daily tasks and duties. If you aren't sure what to ask, use the Internet to find suggested questions for informational interviews.

> ## EXERCISE 16.8
>
> ### Developing Informational Interview Questions
>
> Conduct an Internet search for "informational interview questions." Visit several sites resulting from your search. From these sites, generate a list of 10 to15 questions that you might ask during an informational interview with someone who works in your field. Bring your questions to class to share with others.
>
> **Tasks to be completed:**
>
> 1. Search the Internet for "informational interview questions."
> 2. Visit resulting sites.
> 3. Make a list of 10-15 questions that appeal to you.
> 4. Bring your list to class to discuss with others.

Other Job Search Resources

The introduction to this section noted that networking is the best method for locating unadvertised job openings, but other job search resources are also available. While your local newspaper classified ads are always a viable option for locating a job, online resources are an excellent means of finding jobs. Online resources are particularly useful for job searching after business hours. They can provide you with leads that you would not ordinarily find locally. Below is a short list of resources you should consider using as you search for professional positions:

- **University career center sites.** Most colleges and universities have career centers that assist graduates with work placement. These centers build on alumni relationships and past success from graduates to connect new graduates with satisfied employers. These centers also promote their graduates through career fairs and workshops. Connecting with your institution's career center will provide you with many opportunities and leads as you begin your job search.
- **General job sites**, such as Monster.com and Indeed.com. These sites allow you to search for specific positions and locations.
- **Specialized job sites**, such as Idealist.com and Dice.com. Sites like these allow you to search for jobs in non-profits (Idealist) and technology fields (Dice).
- **Professional organizations sites.** If your field has a professional organization and you are a member, you will often find job boards where positions are posted.
- **Government sites**, such as USAJobs and state work commissions. These sites post federal, state, and local government positions.
- **Industry and organization sites.** The Web sites of specific companies and organizations typically also provide links to job openings with them.

All of these online resources can provide you with potential leads. Because they are widely available, however, these jobs are usually very competitive. Nevertheless, individuals are hired to fill these positions; that individual might be you.

APPLYING FOR POSITIONS

After you locate a position for which you would like to apply, the next step is customizing your résumé for the position. The basic résumé that this chapter discussed earlier is always your starting point, and you should keep it up-to-date as you gain more experiences. To demonstrate your fit for a position, it will need to be modified or customized for each position. Sometimes this work is quick, requiring only a few changes in word choice or organization, but sometimes it takes more effort.

Figure 16.17. Most job ads are now pushed to job-seekers online, and often job-seekers apply for these positions through online application sites.

How do you know what modifications to make? Reading position announcements or job ads carefully will provide you with the keys to customization and will likely assist your résumé to advance in consideration. The job ad will also assist you as you write the cover letter or email that you send with the résumé. Both your résumé and your cover message should be carefully tied to the job announcement and reflect its language in an effort to convince the hiring manager or employer that you are a good fit. At the end of this section is a short set of instructions for submitting résumés and cover letters in print and through email.

Reading Job Ads

Job ads, sometimes called position announcements, contain important information that describe the company seeking an employee, the position being filled, and the qualifications and requirements to be considered for the position. Each piece of information needs careful consideration because you can use this information to shape and customize your résumé and cover letter to echo these requirements. The examples below draw from Figure 16.18, a sample job ad.

Prompts for Reading an Ad

Below are a series of questions to help you learn to read these ads as well as suggestions for how to modify a résumé and write a cover letter for it.

What kind of company is seeking an employee? To answer this question, read the ad carefully to locate the company name and location. Take notes on key words that the ad uses to describe the company. In Figure 16.18, you might note such words as "agricultural support," "environmental consultation," "environmental risk management," "project management," "technical know-how," "sensitivity," "team approach," "collaborative," "professional," and "high standards." While some of these words are more closely related to the scientific and agricultural nature of AG-TeX's business, others are clearly descriptive of the company's approach to its work. This approach could be described as team-focused, professional, and collaborative. Using words such as these to describe yourself or your skills in your cover letter will demonstrate that you understand the company and its approach to business.

AG-TeX, Inc.

JUNIOR EDITOR

AG-TeX is a West Texas agricultural support firm that provides environmental consultation and contracting services. For the past 20 years, we have taken a practical approach to environmental risk management. Our company is known for its project management skills, technical know-how, and sensitivity to environmental concerns and projects. We are an equal opportunity employer, and we believe strongly in the team approach to compliance and assessment. We seek collaborative professionals who value high standards to join our organization.

Junior editors must have B.S. in Journalism, English, Life Science, or equivalent and at least one year of experience editing technical documents. Editing skills to include proofreading technical (e.g., scientific reports) and nontechnical (e.g., newsletters) documents for grammar, spelling, consistency of ideas, sentence structure, wording, literature citation, document organization, table/figure information, document layout, and any other corrections necessary for producing publication-quality environmental documents.

Other qualifications include:
- Ability to format and incorporate editorial changes into documents using Open Office required. Working knowledge of additional software packages (InDesign, Photoshop, Excel, Acrobat) desirable.
- Ability to manage printing/copying of documents (e.g., schedule print jobs, obtain bids, prepare hard "camera-ready" and electronic copies, overseeing quality control) and conduct mailings.
- Ability to work with many different Project Managers while retaining a positive attitude during deadlines.
- Ability to multitask, organize, think analytically, prioritize, and solve problems.
- Flexibility to work additional or fewer hours depending on workload. Ability to work nights, weekends, and holidays when needed.

Position is full time with exceptional benefits. Wage will be based on experience and skills.

To apply, send résumé and cover letter to Olivia Winston, Managing Editor, AG-Tex, Inc., at vwinston@agtex.com .

Figure 16.18. Job ads contain important keywords that you can use to showcase your fitness for the job.

EXERCISE 16.9

Practice Reading a Job Ad

Using one of the online job resource sites, locate an ad for a job that you would like to have after graduation. Print or bookmark the ad, and then analyze to identify the keywords you would include in your résumé or cover letter to demonstrate you are qualified to apply for it. Make a list of the keywords, and be prepared to show the ad and your analysis of it to others.

Tasks to be completed:

1. Locate an ad for a job you would like to have after graduation.
2. Analyze the ad using the job ad analysis questions:
    a. What kind of company is seeking an employee?
    b. What kind of job is being filled?
    c. What abilities and skills does this job require?
    d. What abilities and skills are not required but desirable?
    e. How does one apply for the position?
3. Identify keywords that you should incorporate into your résumé or cover letter to demonstrate your fit for the job.
4. Make a list of keywords.
5. Be prepared to show your ad and discuss your keywords with others.

What kind of job is being filled? What abilities and skills does this job require? What abilities and skills are not required but desirable? Job ads always contain a job title; they often also contain a job number. Both the title and number, if provided, must be included in your cover letter. This information helps hiring managers and employers sort résumés and applicants. Always check carefully to make sure both are included in your cover letter. Ads will also contain short descriptions or job duties that the position requires as well as educational requirements. Required education and abilities must be addressed in your cover letter or résumé; desired abilities are optional, although the more of these desirable abilities you possess, the better your chances for an interview. In the AGTeX job ad, you will note that the successful applicant must have a college degree and strong editing skills. Additionally, the ad provides a list of abilities or skills that are required including computer software skills, collaborative skills, multi-tasking skills, and work hours. Within this list a few desirable but not required skills are mentioned, such as familiarity with more sophisticated software packages. The person's résumé and cover letter that demonstrate these skills and abilities is most likely to be interviewed.

How does one apply for the position? All job ads will provide instructions for applying. In the AGTeX ad, the hiring manager wants electronic submissions only. Other ads may require submission to a company database or postal mail to an address. Whatever the instructions, be sure to follow them so that your résumé and cover letter reach the person responsible for reviewing applications.

Carefully reading job ads will provide you with a set of keywords that should appear in your application documents. Customizing your documents with these keywords is an excellent way to assure you are qualified and considered for the position you desire.

Writing Cover Letters

With your job ad analysis complete and your résumé customized, you are now ready to write your cover letter. In this section, cover letter is used to mean both a print letter you might mail with your résumé or the email message you would send with your résumé electronically attached. The cover letter is your opportunity to turn your skills and experience into a story that demonstrates you are qualified and a good fit for the job being advertised.

As you learned in an earlier chapter on corresponding, cover letters accompany résumés. They are short letters that you write to showcase how your experiences and education have made you an excellent job candidate. They are persuasive letters meant to convince the employer that your experiences and education qualify you for the job. Strong cover letters are organized into a story or narrative that illustrates how your education and experiences have made you the best "fit," or ideal candidate, for the position. This story has to be concise and descriptive, complete within a page or two.

A common concern with cover letters occurs when applicants feel they are a good fit for the job, but they lack a specific requirement. For example, newly graduated job seekers may not have as much job experience as required. In this case, the job seeker may address this weakness in the cover letter but in a positive way. Work experience can be gained in many ways: through coursework, through internships, and through volunteer experiences, to name a few. Some employers will even consider a college degree as a kind of work experience. When faced with a missing requirement, the best approach is to note what is missing but to address it positively by offering other experiences that have made you qualified for the position. As with other components of the cover letter, this statement must be carefully argued and supported with reasons.

Figure 16.19 provides an example of a cover letter that could be formatted as a letter or an email. In it, the applicant, Jamil Larned (whose functional résumé appears in Figure 16.11) responds to the AGTeX job ad in Figure 16.18. As you read his letter, note how he incorporates keywords from the job ad into his letter and weaves his education and experience into stories that demonstrate how well he fits the job description.

Evaluating Cover Letters

Like résumés, cover letters must be carefully checked before submission. Use the following questions to evaluate your cover letter, and revise to address any imperfections your evaluation reveals:

- Does the letter respond clearly and directly to the job ad and its requirements?
- Does the letter's introduction refer directly to the ad or position notice? For example, did you reference the job number, if it's included in the ad?
- Do you describe all of your educational and employment experiences that relate directly to the job requirements?
- Does the letter clearly demonstrate your strengths as they relate to ad?
- Have you addressed any weaknesses positively?
- Does the letter refer to the résumé, request an interview, and include specific contact information?

Dear Ms. Winston:

Please accept this cover letter and attached résumé as my application for the Junior Editor position at AGTeX. I am excited to work for AGTeX, a company that provides environmental assessment and risk management services to our region. As the son of a second-generation cotton farmer, I am well aware of the challenges of environmentally friendly, sustainable farm practices, and I would enjoy working in a professional, collaborative workplace like AGTeX. As stated in my resume, I am currently attending Texas Tech University in Lubbock, and I will graduate in May with a Bachelor of Arts degree in Technical Communication. Your position requires an employee with strong communication and technical skills. I have acquired both through my education at Texas Tech and a year-long internship at Azteca Milling Company.

My computer skills are strong and wide-ranging. In my coursework in technical communication, I have used Microsoft Office to edit a thirty-page manual, with style guide, for parents and staff involved in the 4-H afterschool program. Using Photoshop, I have also worked collaboratively to design, write, and distribute a newsletter for the Tiny Tim Foundation for Kids, a foundation that specializes in helping needy families in Mexico. At my internship, I used Adobe InDesign to create and maintain company plans and manuals. I also used Dreamweaver to maintain the company website and QuickBooks to find and generate invoices. I am a quick learner with software programs, and I enjoy gaining more experience working at AGTeX.

I have also honed my technical editing skills through my coursework and job experience. I have taken courses at Texas Tech in technical editing and style. Both courses taught the importance of good writing mechanics and effective collaboration and project management skills. My internship also provided me with many opportunities to use these skills on the job. Working at Azteca, I have been able to see how technical communication works hand-in-hand with scientific and governmental work. During my internship I wrote and implemented SOPs; created Hazard Analysis and Critical Control Points (HACCP) Organic Plans; and edited and updated numerous other plans and manuals. I also worked collaboratively with a representative of the American Institute of Baking to help Azteca earn the Institute's highest rating. I work effectively on both solo and team projects, and I am well acquainted with the long hours required by looming deadlines. To assure that work is accomplished on time, I am able to prioritize tasks to manage my time effectively.

I am very interested in working with you as a junior editor at AGTeX. Please feel free to contact me at your earliest convenience. I can be reached at 806-796-1839 or via email at jamil.larned@hotmail.com. I look forward to meeting with you.

Sincerely,

Jamil Larned
253 Sheridan, Apt. #N4
Oklahoma City, OK 73101
Cell: 405.237.9489

Figure 16.19. Cover letters present a story that demonstrates why you are the best person for the job.

- Is the application letter professionally designed?
  - Is it persuasive, readable, and usable?
  - Is it attractive and appealing to view?
- Have you checked the spelling and punctuation carefully to make sure you have eliminated all errors?

Submitting Résumés and Covers Letters (Print and Electronic)

After you have customized your résumé and written your cover letter, you will need to decide whether to submit it in print or through email or other electronic delivery. Usually print résumés are delivered in person or through the postal service. In both cases, you should mail the résumé in an envelope with a cover letter. Avoid folding the résumé and cover letter by mailing them flat within a manila envelope. If you are asked to submit your résumé electronically, you can do so easily by converting your word-processed document to portable file format (PDF). To convert your résumé as a PDF for electronic delivery and send it, follow these two easy steps:

- Convert your word-processed résumé to a PDF by using the Save As function.
  - Change the document type to PDF
  - Name your PDF file so that it includes your last name.
- To package your résumé for electronic delivery, you will need to be able to copy, paste, and attach documents to an email.
  - To be sure your PDF is perfect, test the effectiveness its appearance by emailing it as an attachment to yourself.
  - When you're satisfied with your test, email the PDF with your cover letter as the message to the employer.

Occasionally, an employer will provide other directions for submission. In this case, be sure to read the submission directions carefully and follow them exactly.

INTERVIEWING

The final stage in the job search process is the job interview. If your cover letter and résumé are effective, then you will be asked to interview for the position. Interviews can be conducted with just one interviewer or a team. They can be very short or take an entire day or more. When candidates live away from the job location, they may be asked to travel to the site for an interview, or the interview may be conducted online through conferencing technologies. In some cases, organizations will conduct multiple interviews over time to get to know a job candidate

Figure 16.20. Practicing answers to sample questions can give your interview an edge over other job candidates.

well. Whatever is the case with the job you are seeking, the hiring manager or employer will contact you, usually by phone, to ask you to interview. You will be given details about the interview arrangements and asked to prepare to meet with company representatives. This section provides you with some pointers for preparing, delivering, and expressing thanks for any interview request you receive.

Preparing

Preparing for an interview takes time. It requires you to think about what you will be asked, to conduct extensive research on the company, and to consider your appearance in order to make a strong first impression.

The best way to prepare for an interview is to practice answering interview questions. As you have found with other professional documents discussed in this textbook, the Internet is populated with many examples of interview questions. Web sites, such as *Quintessential Careers* (http://www.quintcareers.com), and books, such as *What Color is Your Parachute?*, provide excellent sets of questions to help you practice answering interview questions. Take the time to gather questions from these guides, and ask your references or members of your professional network to quiz you and provide feedback on your answers. Using your network to prepare for an interview will ease your nerves and help you to brainstorm good responses to tough questions. Your college or university may also have resources to help you prepare. Most career centers offer mock interviews either in person or with software. After completing the mock interview, the career center officer will critique your interview and offer suggestions for improving your performance.

A good strategy for answering interview questions is the STAR technique. When asked a question about your job preparation or performance, begin by describing a situation (S) or task (T) that illustrates your answer to the question. Then describe an action (A) you took in this situation or while completing the task. Conclude the answer with the results you achieved (R). For example, the interviewer might ask you to describe how you managed a conflict with a coworker. You could start by describing the situation: "At my internship, I disagreed with my supervisor about how to solve a global shipping problem (situation). So I asked her to give me an hour to conduct research to prove that my solution was best (action). She agreed. I spent my lunch hour researching her solution as well as mine. At the end of this time, I found (result) to my surprise that her solution was actually better than mine in this situation. I admitted to my supervisor that I was wrong and told her what I had learned. Fortunately, we decided that I didn't completely waste my hour; the solution I suggested was an improvement over our current local shipping procedures, so we were able to implement it in these situations." This answer provides the interviewer with a clear picture of the way you manage conflict—with research and reasoned response—and it also demonstrates how you react when you are wrong—with grace. Using the STAR strategy helps an interviewer to understand how you think and react in specific workplace situations.

When you are comfortable with questions you may be asked on the interview, take some time to review what you know about the organization. Find out as much as you can about the organization and its business. Use your personal and professional network, including LinkedIn, to see what you can discover about this workplace. As you conduct your research, make a list of questions that you are unable to answer from your research. At some point in the interview, you will be asked if you have any questions. Having smart,

Figure 16.21. An interview is an organization's way of deciding if you are the right person for the job.

researched questions about the way the organization works is an excellent way to demonstrate your interest in the position.

Finally, remember that an interview is a performance of sorts. It is the organization's way of deciding if you are the right person for the job, and it is your way of learning if the organization is a good place for you to work. Both parties have to be happy at the end of the interview for it to be successful. To assure you make a strong first impression, dress appropriately for the kind of job you are applying to. Pay attention to the clothes and hairstyles of individuals in pictures on the company website, and ask members of your professional network how you should dress. Wearing jeans and a t-shirt to a company with a formal dress code is just as inappropriate as wearing a suit to an Internet social media start-up company where everyone wears jeans and t-shirts. Just as your résumé and cover letter were designed to fit the company description, so, too, must your appearance be appropriate.

Delivering the Interview

Your résumé and cover letter have made a good impression, and you are finally interviewing for the position. To prepare, you have researched the company image, and the interview provides you with opportunity to show how well you understand and can fit within this image. While you may think that your appearance is the first impression you give to the interviewer, your punctuality actually precedes it. Be sure that you are on time to the interview, and organize the materials you bring carefully. Arrive at least fifteen minutes early, and take some time to relax, if possible.

When first introduced to the person interviewing you, extend your hand, make direct eye contact, and smile. These actions send a message of friendliness, openness, and professionalism. Inside the interview room, wait until you are offered a seat to sit down. You may find that you are interviewing with one or several individuals. Address each person directly, and maintain eye contact when answering the individual's questions. Use the STAR approach to questions about your workplace behaviors, and answer questions honestly and forthrightly. You may be surprised by some questions. In these situations, take a breath and moment to think about an answer. One may come to you. If not, then answer as best you can. An honest "I'm not sure" is better than an answer that fails to address the question.

Interviews may include tours of the facility. If so, then show interest in the people and procedures you see. Ask questions, and learn as much as you can. Typically, at the end of an interview, you will be given the opportunity to ask questions. This is the time to learn more about work completed and other expectations. Use this time to emphasize your willingness, if applicable, to perform job duties that may include overtime work or travel. At the interview's conclusion, leave in the same manner you arrived: with a handshake, a smile, and gratitude for the interview.

Expressing Thanks

Companies usually interview two or more individuals for every position. If you receive an interview, you have a very good chance of getting the job, but your work is not quite concluded. The end of interview process is expressing thanks for the interview. You may decide to send the interviewer or interview team an email expressing thanks, but a handwritten note sent via postal mail will make an even stronger impression. To conclude the interview process, take a few minutes after you leave to write notes to everyone who spent time with you in the interview. The note can be a short and simple statement of gratitude, concluding with a statement of your desire to work with the person. Figure 16.21 provides a sample thank-you note.

Dear Lee Ann,

I enjoyed meeting with you today. Our interview helped me to understand TFab's work, and I am very excited to join your team. I look forward to hearing from you soon. Thank you again for your time and consideration.

Sincerely,
Alicia Vasquez

Figure 16.21. A handwritten note sent immediately after an interview is an excellent way to thank the employer for the interview.

Chapter Summary

Searching for a job requires many carefully planned and executed steps, beginning with inventorying your skills and ending, if you are successful, with an interview and a job offer. Each of these steps requires you to think about your audience—the company you would like to join—and its employees. You will also find that your researching skills are helpful throughout the process as you use them to learn about the job search process, to locate openings, and to learn more about the companies where you are applying. This process also requires you to work closely with others—individuals who make up your personal and professional networks as well as employees at the companies where you interview. You will use communication and editing skills throughout the process as you write, format, and revise your résumé and cover letter for each application and as you prepare for and engage in interviews. You will also draw upon these skills when preparing professional biography statements, profiles, and portfolios, which allow you to expand on your unique professional credentials. In essence, the task of searching for a job requires you to use every skill you have learned in this textbook. The better you use what you have learned, the more likely you are at success in finding and getting a solid job offer.

Chapter Assignments

The exercises in this section ask you to apply what you have learned in this chapter as well as explore how this knowledge applies to and connects with other information in the textbook.

1. Anna Boze is planning to apply for the job ad posted on the following page. Update her current résumé (Figure 16.14) to complete this assignment. Prepare a résumé and an application letter for Anna to submit by customizing both to address the job ad.

2. Working with a partner, compare your revisions of Anna's résumé and cover letter. Have you responded similarly? If so, what are these similarities, and why did you both include them in your documents? If not, what are the differences? Do these differences suggest areas of improvement that either of you need to consider? What are they? After comparing your work, discuss what you have found with the class, and then revise your documents once more before submitting them for evaluation.

3. Depending on the size of your college or university, its career center support information will vary. Search your institution's website for career services or career center support, or visit the actual career center on-campus. Career centers typically have print and electronic resources to help you build your résumé, and they will have opportunities, such as career or job fairs, to help you connect with corporate recruiters. If possible, schedule a personal visit or a telephone conference with a career counselor so you can learn more about the resources available at your university's career center. Prepare a brief report on your findings and deliver it in class.

4. Find a job ad for which you are currently qualified to apply. Inventory your skills and experiences. Create a print résumé and cover letter for this job.

5. After completing Exercise #4 above, modify the print résumé and cover letter for email delivery. Email the electronic versions of your résumé and cover letter to your instructor.

Figure Credits

Figure 16.1. © Africa Studio/Shutterstock.com

Figure 16.2. © seamuss/Shutterstock.com

Figure 16.3. © wavebreakmedia/Shutterstock.com

Figure 16.4. © antoniodiaz/Shutterstock.com

Figure 16.5. © Lisa S./Shutterstock.com

Figure 16.13. © Petr Vaclavek/Shutterstock.com

Figure 16.15. © plewyz/Shutterstock.com, © David Arts/Shutterstock.com

Figure 16.16. © Andresr/Shutterstock.com

Figure 16.17. © Rawpixel/Shutterstock.com

Figure 16.20. © baranq/Shutterstock.com

Figure 16.20. © Photographee.eu/Shutterstock.com

Job Title: Auditor
Department: Department Of Defense
Agency: Defense Contract Audit Agency
Job Announcement Number: 399172-11
Salary Range: $50,287.00–$78,355.00 /year

Open Period: Monday, November 01, 2015 to Monday, October 31, 2015

Position Information: Full Time

Who May Be Considered: United States Citizens

Job Summary: Are you looking for an inclusive and employee-friendly work environment, challenging assignments, specialized training, and generous benefits? At Defense Contract Audit Agency (DCAA), you will find all this in a progressive organization dedicated to continuous improvement. DCAA is looking for talented people seeking to apply their creative ideas and enthusiasm while providing a unique service to their country. Join the elite cadre of administrative professionals who have made DCAA their employer of choice.

Major Duties: You will perform a variety of assignments that involve the systematic examination and appraisal of financial records, reports, policies, and practices affecting or reflecting the financial condition and operation of Department of Defense and other Federal contractors. Work is performed in an inclusive environment which fosters teamwork, open communication, trust, and mutual respect. Our goal is to be the audit organization with the foremost reputation for competence, integrity, and customer satisfaction.

Basic Requirements: Degree: accounting or a related field (such as business administration, finance, or public administration) that included or was supplemented by 24 semester hours in accounting (may include up to 6 hours of business law).

OR

Combination of education and experience: 4 years of accounting experience or a combination of accounting experience, college-level education, and training that provided professional accounting knowledge AND 24 semester hours in accounting/auditing courses or a certificate as Certified Public Accountant or a Certified Internal Auditor.

Contact Information:
HR Customer Care Center
Attn: G. Allen
Defense Contract Audit Agency

[Position announcement adapted from USAJobs: Working for America, the Federal Government's Official Job Site: http://www.usajobs.opm.gov/, visited 12/29/10.)

17 Presenting

CHAPTER OVERVIEW

This chapter introduces you to methods and practices of developing and delivering professional presentations. After reading this chapter, you should be able to meet the following objectives:

- Describe the types of technical presentations common in professional settings.
- Identify steps in the process of planning and developing a presentation.
- Describe techniques for developing presentations.
- Explain successful presentation delivery techniques.
- Evaluate presentations using a checklist and criteria related to the content, design, style, and delivery.

PROFESSIONAL PRESENTATIONS

A presentation summarizes or provides an overview of a topic. It incorporates textual, visual, and oral communication. An effective presentation engages interested individuals in a talk about your project. Giving a presentation is an opportunity for you to discuss and illustrate your work to peers and colleagues with similar interests.

In a sense, a presentation is like a proposal or pitch. You are providing information on a topic and persuading your audience to listen, take interest, or act on your recommendations. Some presentations have the purpose of informing or educating, so they are like instructional documents. Presentations are also given on special occasions to introduce a speaker or to celebrate a special event like a retirement. The settings in which you find yourself presenting will be equally varied. You may find yourself talking about a project informally with a coworker or supervisor, updating your team in a conference room or through a videoconference, or addressing hundreds of individuals at a professional conference or trade show.

Figure 17.1. Technical communicators often prepare and deliver professional presentations in a variety of settings.

Presentations frequently draw from documents you have already produced, including résumés, reports, proposals, and job materials. Many presentations require you to use technology, such as electronic slideshows, graphics, and desktop publishing software. Regardless of the purpose or topic of your presentation, all types require you to know your subject matter and be able to communicate it effectively.

Types of Presentations

In the workplace, you will find that presentations are among the most common communication genres you use. Sometimes these presentations will be **informal** and delivered without planning. For example, a co-worker asks for an update as you walk to the break room. Your supervisor messages you, requesting a status report, so you immediately reply with a brief response. You telephone a client to ask a question about a project issue and need to explain the situation with a quick report. At other times, you may spend weeks preparing for a formal presentation at a trade show or important client meeting. More **formal** presentations like these may require a team effort to develop, design, and deliver. As you have discovered with other communication genres, presentations—whether formal or informal—require you to know your audience, purpose, and communication situation.

Figure 17.2. Presentations are typically delivered to inform, persuade, or commemorate a special occasion.

Presentation purposes vary widely. In most situations, however, your presentation will need to **inform** and **persuade**. It will inform your audience of some aspect of your work. It may even teach or instruct them. At the same, some presentations require you to persuade your audience to act or perform based on the information you provide. Finally, presentations may be delivered to **commemorate** a special event or individuals.

In addition to having various purposes, presentations can be classified by their genres, their lengths, and their delivery modes. The rest of this section further describes these classifications.

Presentations Classified by Genre

In technical or professional settings, presentations typically fall into one of five genres. Some of these genres, such as status and progress report presentations, may be delivered in intra-office settings while others, such as research report presentations, tend to delivered in more formal, extra-office settings. In other words, knowing the setting where the presentation will be delivered helps you to determine formality. Determining genre and formality of reporting are keys to successful presentations.

Status and progress report presentations give updates on projects, tasks, or team progress. They typically include a summary of the project goals or outcomes, work completed, work remaining, schedule and budgetary information, and forecasting.

Research and completion report presentations provide informative detail on a particular topic or project, but they focus on the outcomes or summative results. When these presentations are delivered to clients or experts, they require speakers to convince their audiences of the credibility of the research or effectiveness of the project's conclusion.

Analytical, feasibility, and recommendation report presentations also relate outcomes or findings, but their purpose is to convince their audience to act on the outcomes of the research. Both of these presentations include clear and convincing research methods, analysis of data, and logical conclusions.

Marketing and proposal presentations are largely informative about products, services, companies, and individuals, but they are typically designed to persuade the audience to take action on project proposals, product endorsements, hiring services, and the like. They can also be presentations given during interviews, such as job talks and pitches.

Special occasion presentations are delivered at workplace events. They include formal introductions of a speaker or a new employee, ceremonial speeches at retirement or award events, toasts, annual report speeches, and end-of-year summaries. These speeches are often motivational or honorary; they can have both informative and persuasive content.

The textual and visual content as well as organization for these different genres is discussed in other chapters in this textbook. Reviewing this information prior to developing your presentation can help you to decide what is most important to include.

While these common presentation types have remained fairly consistent, presentation formats have changed dramatically in the 21st century, thanks to technology innovations. Long lecture-like presentations with scripted narratives and hundreds of accompanying bulleted slides are less popular. Longer presentations now include stories and large graphics that illustrate key points. At the same time, shorter, more energetic presentations are gaining popularity.

Extended presentations, such as lectures and talks, are most often given to large audiences. Settings can range from meeting rooms to classrooms to auditoriums and stadiums. Lectures and other extended talks are typically scripted and lengthy. They range from 15 minutes to an hour or more. Speakers may be physically present in the room or virtual (that is, presenting from a distance via video streaming). Extended presentations include physical props, video clips, and electronic slides. Presenters deliver the talk from memory, or they use a script, written notes, or a teleprompter. These extended presentations often require teams to plan, develop, and deliver. The **TED talk** is a popular format for extended talks as are political speeches and annual reports. **Conference and class presentations** often fit into this category, depending on their length and complexity.

Brief presentations are given to audiences of all sizes. These talks are presented in meetings, conferences, boardrooms, and classrooms. They can be scripted, but they are best delivered without reading from a manuscript. Speakers may be physically present or virtual. In these presentations, presenters deliver their talks from memory or with the use of slides, notes, or notecards. They are shorter than 15–20 minutes in length, and they may include use of slides, physical props, and even brief videos. Depending on the complexity of the topic, these presentations can be developed by individuals or teams. **Elevator pitches** are among the briefest presentations. They are called "elevator pitches" because they should require no more time to deliver than it takes to go from one floor to another in an elevator. Speakers give elevator pitches when they need to summarize or describe a product or service very quickly. **Conference and class presentations** may also fall into this category, depending on their length and complexity.

Three innovative types of brief presentations are gaining popularity. These innovations have followed presentation experts' advice to limit delivery time and slide count. Experts also encourage speakers to use stories to engage audiences, and they advocate for presentation styles and deliveries that appeal to audiences rather than bore them. For example, Guy Kawasaki developed the **10-20-30 rule**: no more than 10 slides in a 20-minute talk and no smaller than 30-point font on slides. Although the newest formats all confine the time of the talk and slide counts, they vary in the amount of preparation required:

- **Pecha Kucha** talks are named after the Japanese word for "chit chat." These brief presentations consist of 20 slides. Slides are set to automatically advance every 20 seconds, and the entire presentation is over in 6 minutes and 40 seconds. Pecha Kucha presentations require preparation and practice to develop the slides and script within time constraints.
- **Ignite** talks are even shorter than Pecha Kucha. They consist of 20 slides with slides advancing every 15 seconds for a total of 5 minutes per presentation. Like Pecha Kucha, Ignite talks also require preparation and practice to develop and deliver the presentation time constraints.
- **Lightning talks** usually are limited to 5 minutes. Most lightning talks use no slides. When slides are used, no more than 3 slides are included per talk. These short talks require less time and preparation than both Pecha Kucha and Ignite talks.

EXERCISE 17.1

Lightning Talks

Lightning talks are brief presentations, which allow you to practice your presentation skills on a topic with a limited scope and with limits to time and materials. For this exercise, select a topic and give an impromptu five-minute presentation. You can select a topic that has presentation materials, or even present something that someone else has done. For an additional challenge, you might select a topic at random, by drawing topic names on slips of paper out of a hat. Once you've selected a topic, take five minutes to practice and prepare, and then present your topic. At the end, ask your audience to give you feedback on your presentation skills.

Tasks to be completed:

1. Select a short topic on which you could successfully give a presentation in less than five minutes.
2. Practice and rehearse for five minutes.
3. Present your topic.
4. After you present, solicit feedback from your audience.

Presentations Classified by Delivery Method

This classification is not as easily defined as others because it requires thinking about the physical location of the presenter and the presentation. In general, this classification divides presentations into those that are presented in person or face-to-face, those that can stand alone without a presenter, and those that are recorded or presented via the Internet. For ease of discussion, these categories are the following:

- **Present or In-person** presentations are delivered to an audience that is in the same room with the presenter during the presentation. **Conference and classroom presentations** that are given onsite fall into this category, as do **Pecha Kucha, Ignite, Lightning Talks,** and **Elevator Pitches** that are delivered to a face-to-face audience.
- **Stand-alone** presentations are delivered to an audience that is in the same room with the presentation but not necessarily the presenter. The most common types of stand-alone presentations are electronic and print **poster presentations** delivered in a class or conference setting.
- **Remote** or **distant** presentations are delivered to an audience that is not in the same room with the presenter or the presentation. **Webinars, webcasts, screencasts, podcasts, and electronic slide shows with narration and animation** are the most common of this category, but any presentation that is delivered online, rather than in person, can fall into this category.
- **Hybrid** presentations are delivered to an audience that is in the same room with the presenter and presentation as well as to an audience that is not in the same room. **Videoconference** presentations, live streamed meetings, fall into this category. As Figure 17.3 illustrates, presenters in a hybrid presentation may be located online or in the same room as some of the audience members. Similarly, presenters may be in different locations.

Figure 17.3. Hybrid presentations are useful when audiences and presenters are dispersed across distances.

Differences in developing these presentation categories are discussed in detail later in the chapter.

PLANNING, DEVELOPING, AND DELIVERING PRESENTATIONS

As you have found with other genres, presentations require you to plan first and then develop your communication. Unlike other genres, however, presentations require more than publication to deliver: They require you to rehearse and deliver them. This section provides detailed information on these steps. While you may not have much time to plan an informal presentation that takes place in a hallway or conference room, knowing these steps can help you streamline what you say and how you say it, no matter how much time you have to prepare.

Planning your presentation

Good planning always requires you to think about your presentation's audience, its purpose, and its situation. Audience and purpose considerations help you to determine the **takeaways** (key or main points) that should be the focus of your presentation. Expert presenters, such as the late Steve Jobs of Apple, focus their presentations by limiting takeaways to two or three per presentation.

Identifying the key points of your presentation first will help you to develop the rest of presentation to support those points. Your audience and purpose will also determine the **genre** of presentation you will make:

- Are you presenting on progress or completion of a project?
- Are you marketing yourself, a service, or a product?
- Are you commemorating a special event or person?

Knowing why you are presenting provides your presentation with a working generic information model that will help you shape the content and design of your presentation.

Another key planning consideration is determining the **situation** and **setting** where the presentation will be delivered. In many cases, the situation and setting will require you to think about the **technologies** you will use to develop and deliver your presentation. At the same time, you should realize that certain situations and settings allow you to deliver your presentation with the latest computer or mobile technologies available while others will limit you with no access to technology at all. Good planning includes recognizing the allowances and limitations of your delivery situation and setting. Prepare yourself by answering these questions:

- Where will the presentation be delivered: in a training or conference room, on a telephone or conference call, during a videoconference, in an auditorium?
- How many people will be present? How many people will be watching or listening remotely?
- What kinds of technology, if any, will be available to assist with delivery? For example, is the setting appropriate for an electronic slide show, such as a PowerPoint or Prezi, or is a poster a better choice?
- Will you need assistive technology, such as a microphone, to be heard by any audience members?
- If technologies or their products are not available to assist with delivery, will your presentation require other kinds of support, such as physical props or handouts?
- What other kinds of resources are necessary for development and delivery of the presentation?

Answering these questions will help you to make decisions about your presentation's delivery method, technological requirements, and audience accommodations.

Planning also assists you in assessing the **time** allotted for your presentation and the **formality** of language you should use. You will typically know your time allowance for any planned talk, but unplanned, **extemporaneous** presentations do not have predetermined time allowances or constraints. For this reason, you will need to gauge the situation and decide how long you should speak and in what detail. No one wants to be held captive with a lecture when a short two-minute update will do. You should also consider your audience's knowledge of the subject and status within the organization when determining the formality of language in your presentation. A quick status update sent as a text message, for example, might include abbreviations and textspeak, like "lol!" and emoticons. Such expressions and images in a formal presentation would be unacceptable.

All of these considerations—from takeaways to language conventions—are important for presentation success. After you have initially planned your presentation, you should be ready to move to develop it.

EXERCISE 17.2
Planning a Brief Presentation

Internet video channels like YouTube and Vimeo are populated with presentations of all kinds, and the U.S. Government also maintains a growing archive of instructional and historical videos. This exercise asks you to watch and listen to one of these videos that was produced and distributed by the Centers for Disease Control and Prevention (CDC). You can locate the presentation by searching for a video entitled "Cover and Repel: Zika Prevention for Puerto Rico," or by typing this link into your browser: http://bit.ly/2aGFK1Q.

As you watch the video, imagine that you work for the CDC and are required to develop presentations like this one. Analyze this video to learn about aspects of planning similar presentations.

Tasks to be completed:

1. Locate and watch "Cover and Repel: Zika Prevention for Puerto Rico."
2. Identify the takeaways, or main points, of the presentation.
3. Evaluate the effectiveness of the takeaways:
    a. Were the takeaways obvious?
    b. Did the presenter emphasize the takeaways?
    c. How well were the takeaways emphasized?
4. Identify the audience of this presentation. Who is the audience, and why is it important for this audience to have these takeaways?
5. Identify the kinds of technologies needed to develop the presentation. Why were these technologies selected?
6. Are any special technologies included to improve access to the takeaways? Which ones and why?
7. Note the length and format of the presentation, and consider why these decisions were made.

Developing Your Presentation

As with other genres, developing presentations requires you to research and locate content, model this content, and produce it. This section covers each of the steps in the development process. Additionally, because production methods vary depending on the technologies you use, this section includes subsections on producing slideshows, posters and recorded presentations.

Researching and Locating Content

As the introduction to this chapter noted, presentation content is often drawn from other communications. That is, presentations are typically generated from legacy content, content reuse, and content libraries, as discussed in Chapter 8. For example, a job talk (a presentation given to a prospective employer) is typically drawn from the presenter's résumé and work experience, and marketing pitches begin as white papers, product descriptions, or fact sheets. Presentations of research—whether presented orally or printed on a poster—may use the same content and images. In some cases, a presentation can take the place of a written genre, such as a proposal.

Because presentations draw from other genres, your first content development assignment is to identify content you have already created to see what you can reuse in the presentation. Look for textual content that you can reuse as well as visual content, such as images, photographs, charts, and tables. The more text and visual content you can reuse, the more quickly your entire presentation will come together.

Modeling the Presentation's Textual and Visual Content

A presentation's **information model** is simply an outline or a storyboard of your textual content. Figure 17.4 provides an example of a simple storyboard template.

To create your information model, begin with the takeaways you identified in your planning stage and identify a logical organization for presenting them. For every ten minutes of presentation time, you should have no more than two or three takeaways.

After you have noted your takeaways and organized them, then consider how to illustrate them:

- What information will your audience find useful or persuasive when considering your takeaways?
- What images can you locate to describe or support your takeaways?
- Do you have a story that explains them?
- What images can you use to illustrate your story in one or more slides?

Figure 17.4. Sketching your ideas in a storyboard is an easy way to model the content of your presentation.

Stories are perhaps the most neglected aspect of good presentations. Audiences love them, and presentation formats like TED talks depend on them. When you include stories in your presentation, you are less likely to rely on reading slides or bullet lists to your audience. Good stories engage your audience, and they provide excellent illustrations of your points. Tell stories concisely, but use them whenever you can.

Each key point you make should have one to two slides of explanation or support. In all, a ten-minute presentation should have about 9-10 slides. For each additional minute, add approximately one slide. Along with your takeaways, stories, and support, include slides at the beginning and end for introducing and concluding your presentation.

After the information model that either visually or textually outlines your presentation is complete, then it is time to consider the **visual information model**. With any visual information model, you will need to consider colors, layout, styles, and images. Images are particularly important in presentations because they both attract and reinforce the textual message you are delivering. Images options include tables, charts, graphs, photographs, illustrations, and video.

Depending on your presentation genre and delivery methods, your design may be as simple as finding an electronic slideshow template or sketching a mock-up of your visual design, as illustrated in Figure 17.5. A mock-up is a simple method for visualizing what your presentation will look like when you are not using a ready-made template. More complex presentations like video recordings may require a separate storyboard with detailed scene and prop information.

Figure 17.5. A simple mockup allows presenters to decide where to locate content, visuals, and other design elements.

After you have a model for the presentation's textual and visual content, your planning is complete. You are reading to develop this content. The next three subsections focus on how you can develop this content for electronic slideshows, poster presentations, and recorded presentations.

Producing Textual and Visual Content for Slideshow Presentations

Producing textual and visual content for your slides is an essential aspect of presenting with an electronic slideshow. Slides provide your audience with material that summarizes, supplements, and adds visual appeal to the spoken component of your presentation.

Presenters have a variety of software applications available for slideshow drafting and development. Among the most popular technologies are PowerPoint, Keynote, Prezi, Google Slides, and Haiku Deck. As with all technologies, slideshow technologies are not equal in content or delivery method. Before using one of these technologies, carefully consider its advantages and disadvantages in your particular presentation setting and situation.

Presentation slides should provide takeaways and sufficient detail on your topic. At the same time, they should not provide too much information. The following considerations can help you to draft your content and design your slides for optimum readability and audience engagement. Slideshows can be used for present, remote, and hybrid presentations.

Textual content in the presentation should be written in small bite-sized **chunks** that are easy to understand and quick to read. Remember that these chunks can be taken directly or modified from other documents that you have produced, such as reports. When using text on a slide, include a slide heading or a sentence heading that introduces or states the main point of the text. You may repeat the **heading** on several slides if they are related to one another.

> **EXERCISE 17.3**
>
> ## Technology Options for Slideshows
>
> Working in small groups, conduct a quick technology analysis search. Your goal is to identify at least ten slideshow technologies and to create a table that compares these technologies across five features. After you have completed your table and comparison, which technology option do you think would be best for an in-class presentation?
>
> **Tasks to be completed:**
>
> 1. Conduct an Internet search using the keywords "slideshow applications" or "slideshow technologies."
> 2. Make a list of at least ten applications that support slideshow creation.
> 3. Choose at least five key features of these slideshow for comparison.
> 4. Create a table with a least ten applications compared across at least five features.
> 5. Decide which technology would be best for an in-class presentation.
> 6. Be prepared to explain your recommendation.

Also, attend to your outline or storyboard when choosing textual elements, making sure that your content **organization** is logical. Think of your content as if you were telling a story: it needs a beginning, middle, and end.

In addition to these suggestions for slideshow presentation, some important content to use in an extended presentation includes the following:

- **Begin with a title slide** with your presentation title, presenter names, date, company or organization name (and logo), or any other important credentials.
- **Provide an overview** including a brief outline of the purpose, background, and topics that will be covered in the presentation.
- **Limit the content** of each slide to one idea.
- **Insert a slide number and date** on each slide.
- **Conclude with a summary** with the key takeaway points from your presentation.
- **Include a references list** if you cite sources.
- **Provide contact information** with relevant details on how presenters can contact you for more information.

Visual content in the presentation should be unified and balanced. Most slideshow applications, such as Microsoft PowerPoint, Google Slides, and Prezi, have ready-made **templates** that unify the design of your presentation. A quick internet search using the search terms "free slideshow templates" will result in hundreds more options. These ready-made templates are typically well designed, but, when they are not, you can usually make changes to design colors, fonts, and layouts. If you want to design your own template, these applications provide blank templates that you can use.

Figure 17.6. Electronic presentation software includes templates for presentation slides and other materials, which you can use for developing presentations. For example, in this graphic, you find examples (from left to right) of a title slide, a slide with text and graphic, a slide with an image and wraparound text, a slide with text and data, a two-column text slide with image, and a conclusion slide.

> # EXERCISE 17.4
>
> ## *Grid Layouts and Slides*
>
> Use the images in Figure 17.6 to familiarize yourself with grid layouts. Using a pencil or a pen, divide each of the six slide images into nine equally sized squares—three rows horizontally across and three rows vertically across each image. Then draw some conclusions about how grid images work.
>
> **Tasks to be completed:**
>
> 1. Divide each of the six images into nine squares.
> 2. Note where textual and visual content are placed within the squares.
> 3. What conclusions can you draw about how a grid layout works within a slide?
> 4. What conclusions can you draw about how grid layouts work between slides?
> 5. Present your findings to your peers.

Whatever template you decide to use—a custom or ready-made one—slide **layout** is always an important consideration. Ready-made templates provide a variety of grid layouts. A **grid layout** divides content into evenly spaced vertical columns and horizontal rows, like a table. Designers use grids to unify, balance, and emphasize slide content. Placing content in consistently sized columns and rows provides consistency across slides and balance within slides. Placing important text on locations where the lines of the columns and rows intersect creates emphasis.

Whatever you choose—to use a ready-made template or custom design your own—you should make good choices about **font types** that appear on your slides. To avoid a cluttered and chaotic appearance, use no more than two or three font families. Sans serif fonts are generally more readable in digital documents, such as electronic slide shows. When the text needs emphasis, use bold font or color to distinguish words. (Avoid using red and green colors for emphasis, however, as individuals with color blindness may be unable to distinguish between them.) When deciding on the size of text displays, consider how far away your audience is from the screen. The further they will be from the screen, the larger your font should be.

Another key consideration for graphic elements is **white space**. Similar guidelines for white space apply in electronic slide show documents as in print documents. Use white space generously in margins and between list items. Use a left-justified margin for text, and avoid centering chunks of texts as this practice makes reading more difficult.

Images, such as photographs, charts, diagrams, and tables, are particularly effective in electronic slide show presentations. Using still images instead of text allows audience members to listen to you as they look at the image. For this reason, you should use images that have rhetorical impact and assist understanding of your key points. **Video**, or moving images, can be incorporated into slideshows; however, moving from slideshow to video and back again is sometimes awkward. Short clips are best, and practice using the clips is necessary. When videos are used, they should be captioned so that all audience members can access their content.

> ## EXERCISE 17.5
>
> ### *Video Recording Comparison Table*
>
> Many free or inexpensive technologies are now available to record video clips. For this exercise, you will conduct an online search to find and compare three video technologies that are easy to access and use. Your comparison should be placed in a table and displayed on a single slideshow slide.
>
> **Tasks to be completed:**
>
> 1. Search online for free or inexpensive video technologies.
> 2. Identify three technologies to compare.
> 3. Identify the features available in each technologies.
> 4. Create a 6x4 table (like the one below) to compare the technologies and their features.
>
> | | Feature 1 | Feature 2 | Feature 3 | Feature 4 | Feature 5 |
> |--------------|-----------|-----------|-----------|-----------|-----------|
> | Technology 1 | | | | | |
> | Technology 2 | | | | | |
> | Technology 3 | | | | | |
>
> 5. Check off the features of each technology to make a comparison chart.
> 6. Place your table on a single slideshow slide.
> 7. Present your slide to your peers.

Another consideration with images and video is copyright. If you are developing your presentation for commercial use, be sure to purchase or seek permission for visuals you use. You may also find that your organization has content libraries, images, and videos that it owns, or it may employ a graphic illustrator who can create visuals for you. In some cases, you can produce your own images and videos as well or find free images and videos online. The Creative Commons (https://creativecommons.org) is a good place to begin to look for free content.

Finally, you should carefully consider how you use slideshow features like transitions, animations, and sounds. When used effectively, these features allow you to time your presentation, decide when to show and when to hide key points, and move seamlessly from one slide to the next. When used ineffectively, a serious formal presentation becomes little more than a cartoon.

> ## EXERCISE 17.6
>
> ### *Learning About Slideshow Animations*
>
> Most slideshow technologies provide tutorials to assist you with effective animation use. Choose a popular slideshow technology-- PowerPoint, Keynote, Prezi, Google Slides, and Haiku Deck, for example—search its support site for animation suggestions and tutorials, and learn how to use one animation feature. Present your findings in a brief presentation to your peers.
>
> **Tasks to be completed:**
>
> 1. Choose a slideshow technology.
> 2. Visit a Support or Help site about that technology, and locate information about its animation features.
> 3. Choose an animation feature to learn about.
> 4. Read about that feature or watch a tutorial, whatever is available on the site.
> 5. Present your findings to your peers.
>   a. Which technology did you choose?
>   b. Which animation feature did you choose?
>   c. How does this feature work?
>   d. Where did you find your information?

Producing Textual and Visual Content for Poster Presentations

Poster presentations are a common delivery method for academic and practitioner meetings and conferences. They are an opportunity for presenters to display their research or other projects to peers and potential clients. Poster presentations are typically displayed on easels or partitions in a conference room or exhibit hall. In some cases, poster presentations are delivered electronically on video screens.

Posters—whether printed or electronic—are typically designed and printed from slideshow technologies. Most slideshow applications have ready-made templates for posters or allow users to adapt single slides for poster development. In addition to slideshow technologies, like PowerPoint and Keynote, desktop publishing technologies like OpenOffice and InDesign can also be adapted for poster drafting and printing.

However they are created and displayed, poster presentations are designed to **stand alone** because presenters are sometimes available to discuss their research with the audience, but at other times, they are not. When presenters are not present, the poster provides interested individuals with an overview of the project's purpose, process or methods, and outcomes. When presenters are present, the purpose of the poster is to engage interested individuals in technical talk about the project. For this reason, in addition to the visual component of the poster presentation, presenters should also have a short oral presentation ready that provides interested individuals with a summary and demonstration of the project and its outcomes.

A poster presentation is primarily a visual document made up of both **textual** and **visual content**. Because poster presentations are more commonly presented at scientific and engineering meetings and conferences, the textual content often mirrors the structure and reuses some of the content of scientific research and completion reports. The chief constraint of the poster presentation, however, is the size of the poster display itself. Whereas the research the poster reports may extend for pages, the poster's content must be refined and summarized into approximately 1000 words.

Although the content of a poster may vary with the situation, most scientific and technical posters typically contain the following seven parts:

1. **Title:** The poster's title should identify the research conducted or product developed. If the process or approach taken to conduct this research or develop the product is important, then this information can be included as well. Most poster titles are limited to one to two lines. Because the poster will likely stand alone at some point during its display time, you should create a title that attracts the audience and piques their attention.

2. **Introduction and objectives:** The poster's introduction situates the research and identifies its purpose. Aim for a short introduction (200 words or less), and remember that your introduction spurs your audience to read on. A photograph or illustration in the introduction can sometimes provide that motivation and increase interest.

3. **Research process:** In this section, describe the major steps in the research process. Like the introduction, this section should be limited to about 200 words.

4. **Results and discussion:** This section is one of the longest in the poster presentation. It discusses the results or outcomes of your project or research. You may reuse graphics from your research report in this section to illustrate your results. Limit this section to 300 words or less.

5. **Conclusions:** This section is the other long section of text. The conclusion reviews the research's purpose and discusses what the presenter has learned from the project. The conclusion discusses how well the research met its objectives and what obstacles it encountered. Finally, conclusions sometimes discuss future research to be conducted or next steps. Like the results section, limit conclusions to 300 words or less.

6. **References and acknowledgements:** The section is optional and may not be necessary to include unless you need to thank individuals who have contributed to your work, for example, a funding source or a mentor. You may also list any significant research literature that was important to your work. This section should be very short, ranging 50-100 words.

7. **Contact information.** Include your name (or your team's names) and email contact information in case an audience member wants to learn more about your work. This section is a good location for a company logo or university seal.

> ### EXERCISE 17.7
> ### *Poster Presentations and Undergraduate Research*
>
> Colleges and universities throughout the United States use poster presentations to showcase undergraduate research. To get an idea for the variety of organizations and designs that are possible in poster presentations, conduct a quick Internet search using the keywords "undergraduate research poster presentations." Your search will results in hundreds of poster presentations that undergraduate students have developed. From this search, choose one that interests you and conduct a quick analysis of its textual and visual content design.
>
> **Tasks to be completed:**
>
> 1. Conduct an Internet search using the keywords "undergraduate research poster presentations."
> 2. Select an interesting poster from the results of your search.
> 3. Analyze the poster for textual and visual content:
>   a. What textual content is included?
>   b. How is the textual content organized?
>   c. What visual content is included?
>   d. Where is the visual content located?
>   e. How well does the textual and visual content work together?
>   f. How effective overall is the poster's textual and visual content?
> 4. Prepare to discuss your findings with your peers.

Visual content in poster presentations increases viewer interest, promotes understanding, and improves memory of the research. Effective visual choices can reduce the number of words needed to convey an idea. In addition, very few poster viewers will read every word on the poster, but they may take the time to review all of the visuals. For these reasons, you should plan wisely the visuals that you incorporate into your presentation.

Here are four guidelines to consider as you incorporate visual content into your poster:

Be strategic. Because posters are often displayed in noisy, crowded exhibit areas and viewers may have limited time with your poster, select visuals that convey the gist of your project. Viewers should be able to grasp your takeaways without having to read every word that accompanies these visuals in your poster. In addition to choosing visuals with impact, use good visual design components like bulleted and numbered lists, emphasize text with bold font and increased font size, and include white space to draw attention to key content.

Combine visual and textual information to reinforce meaning. Choose visual information that does not require significant textual explanation, but use textual cues to support viewer's understanding of the visuals. For example, legible labels and caption below visuals explain why visuals are important. Callouts and labels within visuals help viewers to identify and define significant parts. Using subheadings that convey information rather than generic section titles like "Introduction" can assist viewers' understanding of your takeaways and research process.

Size matters. Use font and image sizes that ensure that your textual and visual information is readable from at least 6 feet away, which is the approximate distance a viewer will stand from the poster.

Keep it simple. Strive for simple yet elegant graphical displays. For example, use colors, but do so sparingly. For best results, experts suggest that you use no more than two or three colors in your poster.

Figure 17.7 provides a good example of an effective scientific poster presentation. As you review it, note how the presenters use subheadings that convey information to tell the research story. The poster also has an attractive color scheme throughout and uses rules (or colored lines) to separate the poster into clear sections. Finally, the poster includes other visual content, such as logos, maps, and photographs, to reinforce and convey meaning.

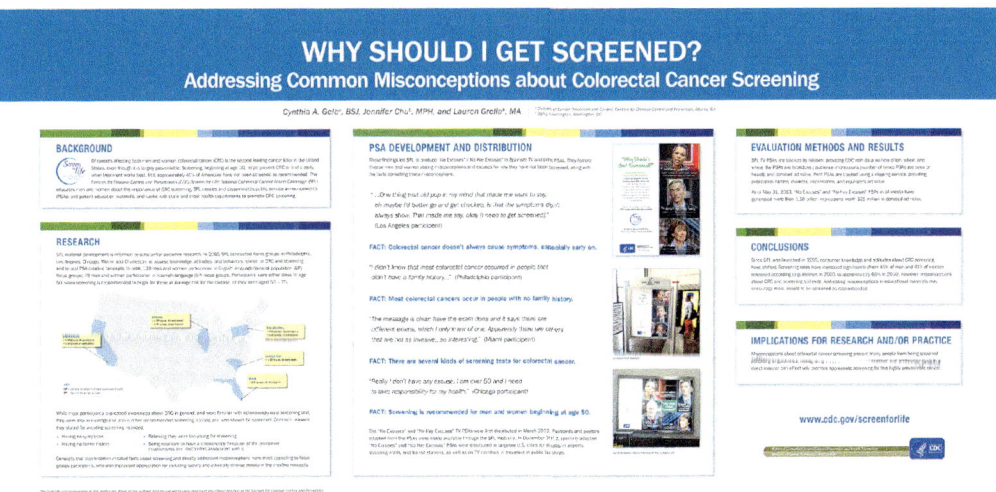

Figure 17.7. Poster presentations are designed to be viewed, not presented. Their textual and visual content works together to present information when the presenter is unavailable.

Producing Textual and Visual Content for Recorded Presentations

The newest types of presentations are hybrid recorded presentations like podcasts, screencasts, and videos. **Podcasts** are presentations delivered as audio files. Many podcasts are episodic; that is, they are part of a series. **Screencasts** are digital recordings of a computer screen; they typically have audio narration and are used to provide instructional content. **Videos** (sometimes called vodcasts or vidcasts) are recorded moving images that typically include audio tracks. Podcasts, screencasts, and videos can be used simply for archiving other types of in-person presentations, but they also can deliver stand-alone content, such as instructions and entertainment. In most cases, the textual content for these presentations is scripted and either read or memorized for presentation. Visual content must also be carefully planned to reinforce and support the presentation's overall message.

These presentations have gained popularity because they can be downloaded or streamed across the Internet at the audience's convenience. They can be archived on a company website or uploaded into channels on video-sharing websites, such as YouTube and Vimeo. To create these presentations requires both hardware and software. For example, presenters will need access to audio or video recording equipment, including cameras,

Figure 17.8. Podcasts are recorded presentations that allow audiences to listen and learn wherever they are.

microphones, and personal computers. Mobile phones and tablet technologies have made access to these kinds of hardware easier to access. After the recordings are complete, however, presentations may require editing and refining with software such as iMovie or Windows Movie Maker. Like audio and video recording technologies, screen-casting applications are becoming easier to find and download. Popular inexpensive screencasting applications include Jing and Freescreencast.

To assure that all members of the presentation's audience can access the final audio or video file, presenters should always include downloadable scripts and captions. Scripts can be provided as portable document files (PDFs), and captions can be added using software, such as Amara. Some video streaming sites, like YouTube, have captioning capabilities, but presenters should always check the captions against the presentation script for accuracy and edit the captions accordingly.

Scripting plays an important role in podcasts, screencasts, and video presentations. For this reason, the **textual content** of the script must be carefully drafted. As you learned with slideshows, outlining and storyboarding the textual content is the first step, starting with takeaways and moving to support or explanation of these takeaways. The organization of the content will depend on the genre of the presentation. For example, you should use good instructional design for do-it-yourself video presentations and effective persuasive strategies for product descriptions and pitches. Reviewing generic expectations for different genres can help you to organize the script's textual content effectively. Writing out the script will help you to keep to a prescribed time and stay on topic.

After a podcast's textual content has been planned and developed, presenters are ready to move into production of the audio file. Screencast and video presentations require another step: the production of **visual content**. Visual content in screencasts and videos ranges broadly, from images displayed on a computer monitor to movie-like sets with scenery and props. Whichever you are producing, you should plan the scenes or actions that the audience will see. You can add visual content notes to your storyboard or outline, or create a separate list of "shots," the scenes that viewers will watch. Determining when the presentation will move from one shot to another and what you will say during each shot can save you time later because videos often require more than one "take," versions of the same shot. Knowing where to start and stop each shot allows you replace just the shot, not the entire screencast or video. Post-production editing can be limited with storyboarding and recording.

A final tip for developing your content is a simple one: plan sufficient time to rehearse the presentation. The more smoothly you can deliver the presentation, the less time it will take you to produce it.

To summarize, whether you are developing a podcast, a screencast or a video, following these guidelines will help you succeed:

- **Establish your takeaways.** Make sure you know what outcome for the presentation will be.
- **Know your genre and organize accordingly.** Follow good organization and development strategies for the presentation genre you are presenting.
- **Script the textual and visual content**, dividing it into clear "shots" or scenes.
- **Rehearse and plan for multiple takes.** Plan for at least one or two trial runs.

EXERCISE 17.8

The World of DIY Video

You can find do-it-yourself or how-to videos on just about any topic. Do you want to learn how to build a doghouse or a greenhouse? Do you need some tips on making a quiche or a cocktail? Do you need help learning to edit a video or podcast? You can find the answers to these questions and many more online. This exercise asks you to watch two or three short video tutorials (less than 5 minutes each). Choose videos that interest you from streaming sites, such as Lynda.com, YouTube, or Vimeo. As you watch the video, note the textual and visual content. What strategies did the presenter use to make it effective, or, if it fails in some way, why?

Tasks to be completed:

1. Choose a topic you'd like to learn more about and search for videos online.
2. Select two or three short videos (under 5 minutes) on the topic and watch them.
3. Analyze the videos for textual and visual content:
    a. What textual content is included?
    b. How is the textual content organized?
    c. What visual content is included?
    d. Where is the visual content located?
    e. How well does the textual and visual content work together?
    f. What is effective or ineffective overall in the video's production?
4. Prepare to discuss your findings with your peers.

Delivering Your Presentation

Regardless of the presentation you are giving, there are important guidelines to follow to be successful, including preparation, communication, and stylistic techniques. This section provides tips on pre-presentation preparation and the actual delivery of your presentation. These tips can assist you with any type of presentation you are making. At the end of this section, you'll find information on three delivery situations that require additional preparation.

Pre-presentation Tips

These tips can aid you whether you are delivering your presentation as a slideshow to a live audience or recording your presentation as a podcast, screencast, or video:

Check your equipment. Equipment required for a presentation can be as simple as scripted notecards for a speech, but even the simplest notes need to be checked to make sure they are in order and easy to read. More complicated equipment, such as equipment used for a slideshow and screencast, require you to test to make sure everything is working as planned. For example, you may need to check the volume of the microphone or test the screen capture software to make sure you using it properly. Making sure all equipment, including technologies, are working correctly will assure that your presentation runs smoothly when it is time to deliver.

Set the stage. For in-person presentations, you should arrive early and note where the presentation equipment is set up. Pay attention to the seating arrangements: Will the audience be sitting at a table or in rows? Will you be presenting alone or with others? Where will you sit? Is there a podium or are you free to walk on a stage-like setting? These kinds of questions will help you to understand physically how you should delivery your presentation and address your audience.

With recorded presentations, setting the scene requires you to de-clutter your computer monitor and turn off notifications that might interrupt your recording. Making the room as soundproof as possible will also improve the quality of your audio file.

Track your time. You'll also need to know how to track your time. You can use a watch or the timer on your mobile phone. Some slideshow software includes a timer only you can see to assist with timekeeping. You can also ask a friend in the audience to give you visual timing cues.

Rehearse your presentation. Even the most practiced presenters need to rehearse and prepare materials in advance of a presentation. Your ability and skill as a presenter will improve with practice. Preparing slides and other materials for the presentation involves careful writing and editing to minimize any errors or mistakes that could compromise the success of your presentation. It is also important to prepare a backup plan in case of last minute problems with technology. Although you may not need to memorize every word of your speech, the more you practice it, the better you will deliver it. As you rehearse, remember to make eye contact with your audience and speak slowly. Avoid verbal tics like clearing your throat or repetitiously inserting "um," "like," or "you know" into your sentences. At the same, consciously vary your tone of voice to avoid monotonous delivery and add interest to your delivery. Practicing with these precautions in mind will make the actual delivery much more engaging for your audience.

Try to relax. This may be the hardest of all pre-presentation tips because speaking before an audience can be nerve-wracking. Taking a few deep breaths before your begin your presentation and rehearsing are two of the best ways to look relaxed and feel more comfortable. Remembering to smile at your audience will make you look more relaxed than you might actually feel.

Delivery Tips

During the presentation, these tips make your more confident and engaging. In turn, your audience will be better able to grasp your takeaways and follow your points.

Do not read your slides. Let the textual content come from your memorized or prepared script while the visual content reinforces your words. Remember that audiences can read slides silently faster than you read them aloud. If you insist on reading them, you may find that your audience members' minds have moved on to other thoughts, detracting from the points you are making.

Make eye contact. If your audience is in the same room as you, look at them as you speak. If you are recording your presentation, look into the camera. Eye contact with your audience makes you seem more credible and approachable. It builds good will between the audience and the presenter.

Watch your audience for physical cues. You will be able to gauge your presentation by your audience's reaction to it. Do you see audience members following your words or nodding their heads? They are engaged. Are they focused on their mobile devices or sleeping? They need to be engaged. Audience members' physical cues will tell you whether they are curious, bored, or confused. Attend to these cues and make adjustments. For example, you might conduct a quick poll by asking audience members to raise their hands or ask the audience for examples or stories to illustrate your points. Pausing occasionally or adjusting the pitch or tone of voice will also require your audience to listen more carefully. Even when you are delivering your presentation to a remote or hybrid audience, this tip can help you engage them.

Use gestures. Simple hand gestures can help you reach your audience. These gestures add emphasis when you need it. Using them mindfully prevents you from fidgeting with change in your pocket or looking stiff.

Figure 17.9. Simple hand gestures like these can add emphasis to your presentation.

Although hand gestures can provide added emphasis to any presentation, using them effectively requires you to know your audience and their cultural conventions because acceptable and unacceptable hand gestures vary across cultures. Common hand gestures in the United States—gestures like the thumbs-up, okay, and "v" for "victory" signs—have very different meanings in other cultures. Learning about hand gesture meanings in other cultures is important any time you are delivering a presentation to a multicultural audience.

Thank your host and your audience. After you have been introduced to the audience, it is good practice to thank the person who has introduced you as well as the audience for allowing you to present. Similarly, at your presentation's end, thank your audience again for their attention and participation.

Initiate discussion and questions. Because the presentation cannot include all of your research or findings, it should motivate the audience to ask you questions about your work and initiate a discussion. If your presentation results in a discussion between you and the audience, then it has done exactly what it was intended to do.

Special Presentation Delivery Challenges

This final section discusses three special delivery challenges: presenting when technology fails, presenting as a team, and presenting with a translator. Each one of these situations requires additional preparation and challenges.

Technology failure is a presenter's nightmare. After all of the work of planning and developing presentations, sometimes the delivery technologies fail. When this happens, good presenters have low-tech backups ready. Advance preparation and stage awareness can help you determine what backups are available. Among these low-tech options are handouts printed in advance of the presentation or whiteboards and flip charts that may already be in the presentation venue. Presenters do not have to be artists to use whiteboards as spaces for keywords or takeaways. Knowing your key points and having a copy of your script on hand may be all it takes to turn a nightmare into a successful presentation.

Team presentations require prior planning as well. Team members need to decide in advance what parts of the presentation each member will deliver. Deciding in advance how the team will handle questions is also important. Usually team members present for approximately the same amount of time and content. The team will need to decide how to smoothly transition from one member to another. As with all presentations, team members need to be mindful of time constraints.

Presenting with a translator or interpreter is common when working with an international audience. If you know you will be working with a translator or interpreter, plan on providing your presentation script in advance. You may also need to provide a glossary of key terms and a pronunciation guide. Before the presentation, plan on meeting with your translator to decide how you will conduct the presentation: time-delay or simultaneously. With time-delay presentation, you will speak in short bursts—sentences or paragraphs—and then stop and wait while the translator interprets. With simultaneous delivery, the translator interprets as you talk. In both methods, you will likely need to practice with your translator to understand how the translation will work. A good translator will be familiar with these methods and help to prepare you for this type of special presentation.

EVALUATING PRESENTATIONS

The following checklist will also help you evaluate presentations in terms of content, design, style, and delivery. It can be used as a valuable tool in your practice and preparation for giving a professional presentation or as a tool to evaluate presentations.

> **Textual content**
> - ☐ The presenter(s) or team identified themselves and their project at the beginning of the presentation.
> - ☐ The presentation was clearly based on the topic or project.
> - ☐ The presentation was well organized.
> - ☐ The presentation included a topic summary or overview.
> - ☐ The project or topic takeaways or objective(s) were clearly stated.
> - ☐ The presentation's takeaways were easily identifiable throughout the presentation.
> - ☐ The presenter(s) was able to answer questions effectively.

Visual content

- ☐ The presentation was based on an appropriate template or designed appropriately.
- ☐ The presentation used columns or other layout grid features effectively.
- ☐ The presentation text was designed for readability and legibility.
- ☐ The presentation used relevant and appropriate visual content to illustrate research.
- ☐ The presentation's visual content demonstrated both design elegance and simplicity.
- ☐ The presentation included adequate white space.

Style and delivery

- ☐ The presentation exhibits effective writing skills and professional style.
- ☐ The presentation contains no major grammatical or mechanical errors.
- ☐ The presentation demonstrated good time management.
- ☐ The presentation demonstrated practice, polish, and was executed smoothly.

EXERCISE 17.9

Evaluating a Presentation

Find an online video presentation on any professional or technical topic. Using the presentation checklist in this chapter, watch and evaluate the presentation. Complete the checklist and make note of any particular strengths and weaknesses in the presentation. Provide a suggestion for improvement in any weak areas. Discuss your findings with others.

Tasks to be completed:

1. Locate an online video presentation on a professional or technical topic.
2. Watch the presentation and evaluate it using the presentation checklist in the chapter.
3. Make note of specific strengths and weaknesses in the presentation.
4. For each weak area, provide a specific suggestion for improvement.
5. Share your findings with others.

Chapter Summary

Presentations are common in almost every professional setting and are an essential skill for technical communicators. Common presentations include status and progress presentations, research and completion presentations, and marketing and proposal presentations. They may vary from extended to brief presentations, and they can be delivered in-person, remotely, or a combination of these methods. The steps involved in presenting include preparatory research, developing textual and visual content, using technologies for production, and rehearsal. Finally, using a presentation checklist can help you assess the strengths in terms of a presentation's content, design, style and delivery.

Chapter Assignments

The exercises in this section ask you to apply what you have learned in this chapter as well as explore how this knowledge applies to and connects with other information in the textbook.

1. Use benchmarking to identify best and worst practices for oral presentations. To accomplish this work, watch a variety of online presentations to observe best and worst practices. Make a list of each to share with others.
2. Conduct a content inventory of a technical document you have written and create an outline for a five-minute oral presentation. As you create your outline, consider: What does your audience need to know? What research can you use? What do you need to add?
3. Choose one of the following activities to familiarize yourself with presentation visuals:
    a. Evaluate different media types and software programs (PowerPoint vs. Prezi vs. Captivate) and their visual capabilities. Create a short oral recommendation for the class.
    b. Take a report you've written and sketch visual content for it. Bring your sketches to class to present.
4. Conduct research on the use of visuals in poster presentations. What kinds of visuals are important to include? Why?
    a. Find a conference in your field and critique presentations that are online. Watch a short presentation and analyze it.
    b. Create a slide show presentation.
    c. Create a poster presentation on an instructional topic.

Figure Credits

Figure 17.1. © Andresr/Shutterstock

Figure 17.2. © Matej Kastelic/Shutterstock.com

Figure 17.3. © (right image) Andrey_Popov/Shutterstock.com, (left image) Rawpixel.com/Shutterstock.com

Figure 17.4. © lamerstudio/Shutterstock.com

Figure 17.5. © ronstik/Shutterstock.com

Figure 17.6. © Denis Cristo/Shutterstock.com

Figure 17.7. http://www.cdc.gov/cancer/colorectal/pdf/cdc_sfl_posterabstract_2013_90x44_v4.pdf

Figure 17.8. © Syda Productions/Shutterstock.com

Figure 17.9. © STUDIO GRAND OUEST/Shutterstock.com

Writing Technical Definitions and Descriptions

18

CHAPTER OVERVIEW

After reading this chapter you will be able to:

- Identify and analyze the stylistics of technical definitions and descriptions.
- Describe the purposes, document types, and genres in which technical definitions and descriptions are used.
- Understand content, organizational, and stylistic patterns common to technical descriptions and definitions.
- Explain the importance of following standards in writing accurate and consistent technical definitions and descriptions.

The main goal of technical communication is to communicate technical information clearly and accurately to both technical and non-technical audiences. As such, technical communicators must be adept in writing a wide range of document types, and in particular, technical definitions and descriptions. Definitions and descriptions are used in virtually all genres of technical documents to achieve multiple purposes, such as to inform, persuade, or instruct. They are found in abstracts, fact sheets, specifications, summaries, and white papers. They provide important background information in other kinds of technical documents as well, such as analytical reports, instructional materials, research reports, presentations, and proposals. Since many document types and genres incorporate the use of technical definitions and descriptions, they should follow consistent standards, whether they are organizational, legal, or disciplinary guidelines unique to the field. Effective technical definitions and descriptions are accurate, consistent, and written at a level of detail appropriate for the subject, audience, and informational contexts in which they are used. For these reasons, writing clear and accurate technical definitions and descriptions is an essential skill for technical communicators.

This chapter covers practices of writing technical definitions and descriptions, widely used in technical communication documents. It will introduce you to writing methods and practices of developing clear and accurate technical definitions and technical descriptions. It will cover stylistic and structural components of technical definitions and descriptions, including methods of describing, patterns of organization, and common document types that incorporate technical description. And finally, it will address the importance of following standards in writing technical definitions and descriptions.

WRITING TECHNICAL DEFINITIONS

Technical terminology is essential to almost every form of technical document, and in particular in describing technical products and processes. Since various fields and disciplines use terms to describe basic concepts and processes, terminology must be specific, accurate, and sufficiently detailed for use. In some cases, a field might use multiple terms to refer to the same basic concept. For example, the terms *user profile*, *reader profile*, and *audience* are often used interchangeably in technical communication to describe a group of individuals for which a specific document is written. As such, it is important to write technical definitions to explain terms used in a specific context.

A technical definition specifies a term and explains it in context of use, often with supporting examples to help users comprehend its proper meaning and use. A definition typically includes an identification of the term, its classification, and any distinguishing characteristics.

> term = classification + distinguishing characteristics

The examples of technical definitions below identify the term (bold), classification (underlined), and distinguishing characteristics (italics).

> A **feasibility study** is a type of <u>analytical report</u> that systematically *studies and analyzes potential solutions to a problem*.
>
> A **biologist** is a <u>scientist</u> who *studies living organisms in specific environments*.
>
> A **tablet** is a <u>mobile computing device</u> *capable of running applications and browser-based content*.
>
> A **technical editor** is <u>a type of technical communicator</u> *concerned with stylistic development and revisions to technical documents*.
>
> A **technical description** is <u>a written description</u> that *communicates technical and descriptive information to specified audiences, which can vary in their expertise, background, and demographics*.

Figure 18.1. Note how these technical definitions for "research" and "regulations" include the term, classification, and distinguishing characteristics.

Shorter versions of technical definitions in Figure 18.1 might also be written or used in documents as parenthetical abbreviations (using parentheses), or as short phrases separated by commas. The following examples of short definitions are presented in italics.

> Research *(systematic inquiry or investigation)* is essential to the planning and writing of technical documents.
>
> Regulations, *or official rules or laws*, often provide a legal context and inform the writing and development of technical documents.

Technical definitions serve a variety of purposes and convey accuracy, consistency, clarity, conciseness, and appropriate contextual application. Accuracy is essential since terms and their definitions often describe important concepts and their distinguishing features. Technical definitions should be consistent with other like terms within a given field or discipline. They should also be written clearly and concisely, to ensure their meaning is specific and to avoid potential confusion with other terms or concepts. And, technical definitions also apply terms in specific contexts, particularly when paired with examples and/or technical descriptions.

EXERCISE 18.1

Writing Technical Definitions

Briefly research the following technical communication related terms using online searches, books, or articles:

- content strategy
- data mining
- information architecture
- technological appropriation
- universal design

Using the recommended method of writing definitions, write an original definition of each term, based on your research. Each definition should include the term, classification, and any distinguishing characteristics. Compare your definitions with peers and discuss any differences based on your research.

Tasks to be completed:

1. Research the five terms listed above using online searches, books, or articles.
2. Make notes on each term, such as other uses of the term, or distinguishing characteristics.
3. Write a short definition of each, including a term, classification, and distinguishing characteristics.
4. Present and compare your definitions of the terms with peers.

Using visual content with definitions. Visuals are often used in helping add rich detail to technical definitions, particularly when the term used is a complex concept or if it involves describing a process. Visuals often complement and supplement textual definitions by illustrating a term and its use, but they also serve other important functions when used with technical definitions. Images help to illustrate distinguishing characteristics and differences when comparing and contrasting a technical term to other similar terms. They help visual learners comprehend complex concepts or processes with multiple parts or steps. When used to help define or describe technical terms, images should have a specific purpose or function, or their use should be reconsidered. Finally, images should help illustrate, rather than decorate or distract, to avoid misunderstanding or misuse. Figure 18.2 provides an example of definitions aligned with visual content (images, font weights, and colors) to illustrate distinguishing characteristics.

Figure 18.2. Visual images are used to illustrate differences in types of yoga by varying the use of colors and poses.

> ## EXERCISE 18.2
> ### Analyzing Technical Definitions
>
> Choose a chapter in this book and select any five technical definitions. You can easily spot these as bolded terms found throughout each chapter. Dissect them into their components: term, classification, and distinguishing characteristics. Then, select five technical terms of your own choosing, from another field of study or textbook. For each, begin with a list of terms, classifications, and distinguishing characteristics. Then, use your list to help you write a definition for each term. Finally, have a peer review your definition for accuracy and suggest any changes.
>
> **Tasks to be completed:**
>
> 1. Choose a chapter in the book and select five technical definitions (in bold).
> 2. Dissect each definition into its parts: term, classification, and distinguishing characteristics.
> 3. Then, choose five new technical terms, from another field of study, such as biology, chemistry, graphic design, psychology, etc.
> 4. For each, create a list of terms, classifications, and distinguishing characteristics.
> 5. Use each list to write a definition for each term.
> 6. Have a peer review your definition for accuracy and to suggest any changes or improvements.

WRITING TECHNICAL DESCRIPTIONS

Technical descriptions are extended descriptions that help define and describe a technical subject in greater detail. They typically follow one or more specific methods of development to help users understand complex topics. Some patterns used for writing technical descriptions are similar to ones you've already read about in developing paragraphs in Chapter 7. The descriptive modes commonly used to develop technical descriptions include comparison and contrast, distinguishing characteristics, part to whole, and visual illustrations. Descriptions may incorporate one or more of these methods to achieve their purpose. For example, a technical product description of a laptop computer might include details on its distinguishing characteristics (parts, capabilities, dimensions) and incorporate visual illustrations that help describe the product.

Comparing and contrasting. Often, technical descriptions will compare a product or process to other similar products or processes, identifying like characteristics to show similarity. Also, they might identify how a product or process differs from other similar products or processes as a method of describing. Side-by-side comparisons are often used in comparing and contrasting, which often incorporate information graphics such as tables or charts to highlight similarities and differences. For example, a specific model of a cell phone might be described alongside other similar models of the same product family or compared to other competing products.

Distinguishing characteristics. When writing technical descriptions for a product or process, it is common to describe how it is different or unique, or to showcase the characteristics that distinguish it from other products or processes. Lists are often good ways of identifying specific characteristics that are unique to a specific product or process. These characteristics also help to emphasize what is unique or different about a specific subject, and they help users comprehend these differences. For example, a description of a medical insurance plan might include details about the different costs, benefits, co-pays, physicians, and eligibility requirements, which make that plan different from other choices.

Part to whole. One common method of describing a product or process is to explain the individual parts in relation to the whole. This method is particularly effective for products or processes with a high degree of complexity, many parts, or steps. For example, a technical description of an automobile might incorporate a description of its major systems, these systems' parts, and their operations. Part to whole descriptions are sometimes organized from general to specific, or hierarchically. For example, a technical description that describes how a software program works might begin with general or basic functions and then move into more specialized or detailed instructions on customizing and using specific function of the product.

Visual illustrations. As mentioned in the previous section, visuals serve many important functions in helping to define and describe terms and subjects. In addition to helping define terms, visual illustrations are particularly useful in describing components or steps of a product or process in technical documents. Visual illustrations often are used to complement other methods of description. Some examples of visual descriptions include the use of information graphics, such as exploded diagrams or flow charts, which might show individual parts of a product or process. They might include the use of arrows, shading, callout boxes, or textual descriptors as supporting aids or to add emphasis to specific features. Often, the best way to visually illustrate is using photos, screenshots, or drawings, which convey realistic details which support the textual description of a product or process. Some illustrations, might be entirely or mostly visual, for example, airplane safety information cards or brochures, which may be used to describe safety features or processes to a wider range of users.

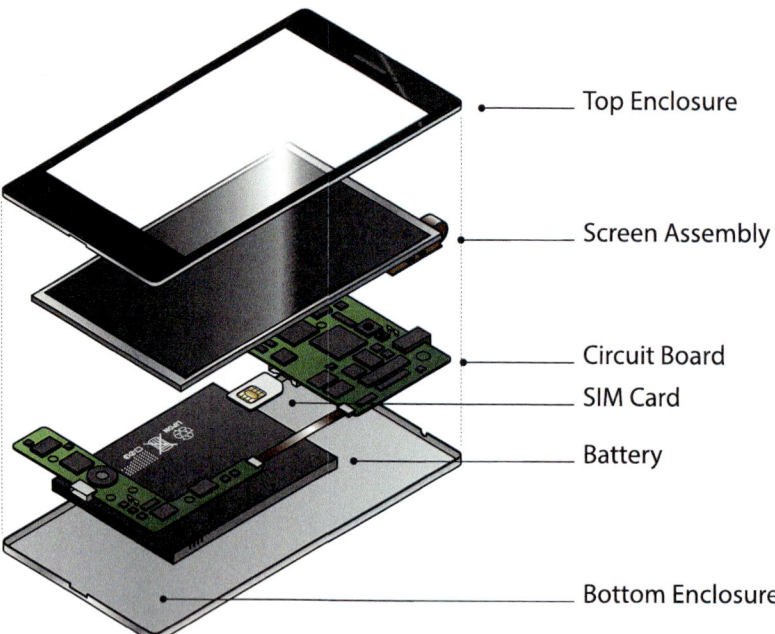

Figure 18.3. This exploded diagram of a cell phone illustrates how parts are assembled parts in relation to the whole.

> **EXERCISE 18.3**
>
> *Practicing Technical Descriptions*
>
> Using one of the four methods of description: comparison and contrast, distinguishing characteristics, part to whole, and visual, write a description of a product, such as a bicycle, computer, mixer, speaker, or any other common (or uncommon) household item. If necessary, research your product to collect specific detail or data required to write your description. Introduce your product with a brief definition and then provide adequate detail for whichever method of description you select. Present your work to peers and discuss the advantages and disadvantages of using the descriptive method you selected.
>
> **Tasks to be completed:**
>
> 1. Select a descriptive method (comparison and contrast, distinguishing characteristics, part to whole, visual) and household product as your subject.
> 2. Research the product online, collecting details needed to write your description.
> 3. Write a short definition that briefly introduces your product, and then a detailed description (approximately 250 words).
> 4. Present your work to peers, discussing the advantages and disadvantages of using the descriptive method you selected.

DOCUMENTS THAT USE TECHNICAL DESCRIPTIONS

A wide range of technical document types and genres incorporate the use of technical descriptions, but certain types function as extended descriptions. Fact sheets, white papers, specifications, summaries, abstracts, and process descriptions are all examples of extended descriptions since they use technical description to explain concepts, policies, processes, and other technical subjects. Each of these document types are described in subsections below. However, these subsections do not include generic formats because these document types may vary widely by industry and organization. If you are asked to create one of these document types, you can conduct research of published or legacy documents to help determine the format and content of your document.

Descriptions are often included or incorporated into other documents, such as abstracts, biographical sketches, instructions, process descriptions, and summaries. Analytical reports, instructional materials, research reports, presentations, and proposals may also include technical descriptions and definitions. For more information on how and where descriptions appear in these documents, refer to chapters on these documents elsewhere in this text.

Fact sheets are a type of detailed summary, providing an overview of the pertinent details of a product or program in an abbreviated form. They often summarize more detailed technical documents, manuals, and reports to present the essential facts and characteristics of their subject matter. Fact sheets typically include technical definitions of terms, statistics, information graphics, citations, and written descriptions. One distinct feature of fact sheets, as compared to marketing brochures, is they are highly technical in their description and level of detail. Fact sheets can also be mostly textual, or as in the examples in Figures 18.4 and 18.5, incorporate visual elements and styles that enhance the readability and usability of the document. They are typically a single page or a few pages in length, at most, and not a long as a white paper.

Figure 18.4. This fact sheet from USAID provides information on U.S. aid to Syria. See the full version at https://www.usaid.gov/sites/default/files/011514_SyriaFactSheet16_0.png

USGS Arctic Science Strategy 2015–2020

Background:

The United States is one of eight Arctic nations responsible for the stewardship of a polar region undergoing dramatic environmental, social, and economic changes. Although warming and cooling cycles have occurred over millennia in the Arctic region, the current warming trend is unlike anything recorded previously and is affecting the region faster than any other place on Earth, bringing dramatic reductions in sea ice extent, altered weather, and thawing permafrost. Implications of these changes include rapid coastal erosion threatening villages and critical infrastructure, potentially significant effects on subsistence activities and cultural resources, changes to wildlife habitat, increased greenhouse-gas emissions from thawing permafrost, threat of invasive species, and opening of the Arctic Ocean to oil and gas exploration and increased shipping. The Arctic science portfolio of the U.S. Geological Survey (USGS) and its response to climate-related changes focuses on landscape-scale ecosystem and natural resource issues and provides scientific underpinning for understanding the physical processes that shape the Arctic. The science conducted by the USGS informs the Nation's resource management policies and improves the stewardship of the Arctic Region.

Context:

The rapid changes facing the Arctic region resulting from climate change requires reliable scientific research and up-to-date information to help policy makers make informed resource management decisions. It is imperative that the USGS establish and undertake an Arctic science strategy that is responsive to national priorities and objectives for the region.

> *"The United States is an Arctic Nation, where we seek to meet our national security needs, protect the environment, responsibly manage resources, account for indigenous communities, support scientific research, and strengthen international cooperation on a wide range of issues."*
>
> National Strategy for the Arctic Region–Implementation Plan (January 2014)

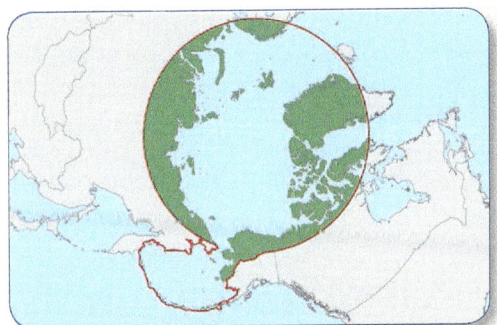

Arctic boundary as defined by the Arctic Research and Policy Act. Image Credit: U.S. Arctic Research Commission.

Focus:

USGS will provide sound and relevant scientific information that supports the goals identified in the National Strategy for the Arctic Region to pursue responsible Arctic region stewardship, strengthen international cooperation, and make decisions using the best available information.

Goals of the *National Strategy for the Arctic Region (May 2013)*

- *Pursue Responsible Arctic Region Stewardship:* "…continue to protect the Arctic environment and conserve its resources; establish and institutionalize an integrated Arctic management framework; chart the Arctic region; and employ scientific research and traditional knowledge to increase understanding of the Arctic."

- *Strengthen International Cooperation:* "…support scientific research and strengthen international cooperation on a wide range of issues."

- *Make Decisions Using the Best Available Information:* "…across all lines of effort, decisions need to be based on the most current science and traditional knowledge."

U.S. Department of the Interior
U.S. Geological Survey

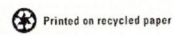 Printed on recycled paper

Fact Sheet 2015–3049
July 2015

Figure 18.5. A USGS fact sheet summarizes the U.S.'s Arctic science strategy from 2015–2020. See the full version at http://pubs.usgs.gov/fs/2015/3049/fs20153049.pdf

Specifications are typically a very detailed description of a complex product, such a computer system, or a process. They can also be longer documents, such as a construction work plan or project plan. Specifications include technical details about a product or process, explaining the functions, relationships, dimensions, and detailed methods. Specifications can be written in varied formats, including a standard report or narrative form. In some cases, they are even presented as a list of technical details, features, or steps. A work plan can also serve as a specification for a project or document, which you read about in Chapter 4. For example, Figure 18.6 is an excerpt from a specification on making a rain barrel. Note as you review Figure 18.6 that the document combines the specifications for the rain barrel with instructions for making it and tips for using it. As this chapter noted earlier, specifications like other forms of technical description are often included with other technical genres within a single document.

White papers are extended descriptions of a product, program, or study. They can be larger in scope, such as a research report or paper, and often technical in nature. They are highly descriptive and often persuasive, since they are frequently used as marketing tools and for publicity purposes. They help inform users on making decisions on issues or policies by providing the background and pertinent details on a given subject. They are much longer in length than fact sheets, but often not as long as detailed analytical or scientific reports. Some white papers are developed from longer reports or studies, and they are presented in an abbreviated form for a specific audience and purpose. While white papers may not seem to be commonly used on a daily basis, organizations and corporations use them internally (to share knowledge between groups in a company) sometimes more than externally (to share with the public).

ORGANIZATIONAL PATTERNS

Since technical descriptions can be highly complex in their level of detail and description, they must follow consistent organizational patterns, which contribute to their overall readability and usability. Organizational patterns are important to follow because they help provide a logical narrative development of a topic. Stylistically, they provide consistency and parallelism in use of language and in their narrative development. To improve readability, they might incorporate visual and spatial styles, such as the use of headings, emphasis, and grouping. To improve usability, they follow a predictable and logical pattern, which is familiar or expected based on the topic and typical user. Technical descriptions typically follow one of four organizational patterns: general to specific, sequential, topical, or customized.

- **General to specific.** This pattern of organization is typically used to describe topics and information that is hierarchically ordered, such as describing parts, steps, or components in relation to the whole. This pattern may also be used to unpack complex concepts, starting with basic terms and moving to more complex terms or processes.
- **Sequential.** This pattern is for content that is process-oriented, requiring a specific sequence or order. Technical descriptions that focus on processes or instructional typically use a sequential pattern.
- **Topical.** This pattern focuses on related topics that describe features or aspects of the subject or topics being described.

Figure 18.6. This excerpt from U.S. Environmental Protection Agency provides specifications for making a rain barrel. See the full version at: https://cfpub.epa.gov/npstbx/files/ksmo_buildarainbarrel.pdf

Water—the Nation's Fundamental Climate Issue
A White Paper on the U.S. Geological Survey Role and Capabilities

By Harry F. Lins, Robert M. Hirsch, and Julie Kiang

Introduction

Of all the potential threats posed by climatic variability and change, those associated with water resources are arguably the most consequential for both society and the environment (Waggoner, 1990). Climatic effects on agriculture, aquatic ecosystems, energy, and industry are strongly influenced by climatic effects on water. Thus, understanding changes in the distribution, quantity and quality of, and demand for water in response to climate variability and change is essential to planning for and adapting to future climatic conditions. A central role of the U.S. Geological Survey (USGS) with respect to climate is to document environmental changes currently underway and to develop improved capabilities to predict future changes. Indeed, a centerpiece of the USGS role is a new Climate Effects Network of monitoring sites. Measuring the climatic effects on water is an essential component of such a network (along with corresponding effects on terrestrial ecosystems).

The USGS needs to be unambiguous in communicating with its customers and stakeholders, and with officials at the Department of the Interior, that although modeling future impacts of climate change is important, there is no more critical role for the USGS in climate change science than that of measuring and describing the changes that are currently underway. One of the best statements of that mission comes from a short paper by Ralph Keeling (2008) that describes the inspiration and the challenges faced by David Keeling in operating the all-important Mauna Loa Observatory over a period of more than four decades. Ralph Keeling stated: "The only way to figure out what is happening to our planet is to measure it, and this means tracking changes decade after decade and poring over the records."

There are three key ideas that are important to the USGS in the above-mentioned sentence. First, to understand what is happening requires measurement. While models are a tool for learning and testing our understanding, they are not a substitute for observations. The second key idea is that measurement needs to be done over a period of many decades. When viewing hydrologic records over time scales of a few years to a few decades, trends commonly appear. However, when viewed in the context of many decades to centuries, these short-term trends are recognized as being part of much longer term oscillations. Thus, while we might want to initiate monitoring of important aspects of our natural resources, the data that will prove to be most useful in the next few years are those records that already have long-term continuity. USGS streamflow and groundwater level data are excellent examples of such long-term records. These measured data span many decades, follow standard protocols for collection and quality assurance, and are stored in a database that provides access to the full period of record.

The third point from the Keeling quote relates to the notion of "poring over the records." Important trends will not generally jump off the computer screen at us. Thoughtful analyses are required to get past a number of important but confounding influences in the record, such as the role of seasonal variation, changes in water management, or influences of quasi-periodic phenomena, such as El Niño-Southern Oscillation (ENSO) or the Pacific Decadal Oscillation (PDO). No organization is better situated to pore over the records than the USGS because USGS scientists know the data, quality-assure the data, understand the factors that influence the data, and have the ancillary information on the watersheds within which the data are collected.

To fulfill the USGS role in understanding climatic variability and change, we need to continually improve and strengthen two of our key capabilities: (1) preserving continuity of long-term water data collection and (2) analyzing and interpreting water data to determine how the Nation's water resources are changing.

Understanding change in water resources to date and predicting change into the future must be done in full recognition of the other factors that influence water availability, including changes in water use, land use, the design and operation of water infrastructure, and the depletion of groundwater. There is widespread debate about the relative importance of nonclimatic factors versus climatic factors in determining water conditions and characteristics over the coming decades (Lins and Stakhiv, 1998). Differentiating climatic from nonclimatic effects is, therefore, a critical component of any effective

Figure 18.7. White papers like this excerpt from a USGS White Paper on *Water—the Nation's Fundamental Climate Issue* showcase USGS policies on water preservation and conservation. See the full version at http://pubs.usgs.gov/circ/1347/pdf/circ-1347.pdf

- **Customized.** This pattern is more highly customized in its organization, and it might be based on other factors, such as user-specific needs or organizational requirements.

Since technical descriptions are highly organized, the basic organizational pattern or information type is often reused, as a pattern for writing descriptions about similar subjects. For example, a product information sheet for a computer might include content such as the product name, model number, price, technical specifications, and warranty information. The same organizational pattern can be reused when writing product information sheets for other makes and models of computer systems.

Content reuse is important to writing and organizing technical descriptions for a variety of reasons. First, users expect parallel content when reading descriptions on similar subjects or products, particularly within the same publication, such as company website, product catalog, or instruction manual. For example, a bookselling website might reuse author biographies, book series descriptions, return policies, and other content. Second, many technical documents incorporate multiple descriptions, which follows a similar organizational pattern. Similarly organized descriptions help users compare similar products and aid readability and usability. For example, multiple models of tablet computing devices might follow a similar organizational pattern and use of headings to organize descriptions for each product. And finally, when used across different technical documents and products, reuse of descriptions and definitions ensures greater information accuracy. Well-written and edited descriptions can save time and resources, when you can write once and reuse the same content multiple times. Careful editing is particularly essential in content reuse, since any reuse of poorly edited content could introduce multiple errors into many documents.

EXERCISE 18.4

Analyzing Technical Descriptions

Conduct online research for a technical description of a home electronics product you own, such as a cell phone, tablet, computer, or other device. The description can be highly technical, such as a list of specifications, or highly informative, such as a marketing brochure. Read the technical description and identify the methods of description (comparing and contrasting, distinguishing characteristics, part to whole, and visual) and organizational patterns (general to specific, sequential, topical, or subject-specific) used. Propose any additions or changes to the methods of describing or organizational patterns you would make to improve the document. With each change, briefly explain how and why each change would improve the technical description. Report your findings.

Tasks to be completed:

1. Locate a technical description online of a home electronics product.
2. Read the description carefully, making note of methods of description and organizational patterns used.
3. Make a list of changes to improve the technical description.
4. Explain how and why each change will improve the document.
5. Report your findings.

PERSUASIVE STYLISTICS

Despite the technical nature of many descriptions, persuasive techniques are often used to reinforce the main claims and purposes of these documents to their users. Persuasive appeals are rhetorical in nature, appealing to **logos** (logic and reasoning), **ethos** (reputation or standing), or **pathos** (emotion or values). The audience (or users), purpose, and contextual constraints will help determine which types of persuasive appeals are most effective. For example, a white paper describing a particular climatological phenomenon would likely use logos, or appeals to logic and reasoning, to persuade its audience. A written biographical statement of a political candidate might use ethos, or appeals that focus on reputation or standing, to persuade. Marketing materials for a charity might use appeals to pathos, or emotions and values, to help persuade potential donors. Multiple persuasive styles might also be used, as well, as long as they were appropriate to the audience, purpose, and contexts. And conversely, there may be situations where certain appeals might not be effective, as well.

Logos

Adults who engage in some form of exercise activity for 2.5 hours each week report reduced stress, anxiety, and better sleep.

Ethos

Only a licensed medical practitioner can provide an accurate diagnosis of the cause, symptoms, and treatments for sports injuries.

Pathos

Getting involved and volunteering in community organizations brings a great deal of satisfaction and helps individuals with the greatest need.

EXERCISE 18.5

Analyzing Persuasive Appeals

Conduct online research to locate a one-page brochure for a product or service, such as a description of a household product or a service provided by a local business. Read the document and identify the audience, purpose, and context of the document. Also, evaluate the use of persuasive appeals, including the use of logos, ethos, and pathos. Highlight each persuasive appeal using a different color or line style, to help visually illustrate the different appeals used. Make a list of any changes you would make to improve the effectiveness of the persuasive appeals used and report your findings.

Tasks to be completed:

1. Locate a one-page brochure for a product or service online.
2. Read the document and identify the audience, purpose, and contexts of use.
3. Highlight the use of logos, ethos, and pathos persuasive appeals, using different colors or line styles.
4. Make a list of any changes or improvements to the appeals used.
5. Report your findings.

USING AND APPLYING STANDARDS

Often, technical communicators write content that must be governed by specific standards or specifications, involving legal, organizational, or health and safety oriented contexts. In some cases, they will write the standards or specifications that will be used as regulatory guidelines for future publications. Standards often incorporate technical definitions and descriptions, and they can be used to explain the proper and safe use of chemical substances, equipment, safety gear, and many other items. They can also explain processes, in particular, any ethical, legal, and safety concerns that should be observed. Standards are sometimes referred to as requirements or codes, as the sample shown in Figure 18.8.

Since technical communicators often write technical descriptions and documents for other specializations and fields, their work must follow any related standards and practices. For example, a white paper on the process of using a thermal compound in mounting a processor onto a motherboard would require a writer to research and follow appropriate and related safety and quality standards, unique to the product and process.

Standards provide guidance and best practices in the use of items, products, and processes in a wide range of industries including environmental engineering, industrial hygiene, information technology, manufacturing, and the sciences. An organization that provides international standards is the International Organization for Standardization (ISO), an international organization that sets standards for proprietary, industrial and commercial processes or standards. For more information on ISO, visit the Wikipedia's encyclopedic reference: https://en.wikipedia.org/wiki/International_Organization_for_Standardization. ISO standards provide guidelines for technical communication as well, including graphical symbols (images) that are included within documents.

EXERCISE 18.6

Explore ISO Standards

ISO Standards are available for purchase, but you can browse a preview of these standards at ISO's website. The search page is located at ISO's Online Browsing Platform (OBP) located at https://www.iso.org/obp/ui/#home. To illustrate how the OBP works, type in the following search terms in the OBP: "safety signs" and click the "Graphical Symbols" button before entering. The OBP search will return hundreds of standard safety symbols. Place your mouse over the symbols to see each symbol's meaning, its type, and other information about its use. Select three to five symbols that are interesting to you and prepare a short report, explaining the meaning each symbol conveys.

Tasks to be completed:

1. Visit ISO's Online Platform Browser web page.
2. Type "safety signs" into the search engine.
3. Click "Graphical Symbols."
4. Click "Enter."
5. Find three to five symbols that interest you and research them by reading their descriptions.
6. Prepare a short report that describes your findings.

Portland's code permits rainwater reuse for potable uses at family dwellings only through an appeals process. In addition, rainwater used only for outdoor irrigation is not covered by the code and needs no treatment prior to use. Acceptable indoor non-potable uses are hose bibbs, water closets, and urinals. The code illuminates several important issues that need to be considered when developing rainwater harvesting code.

- *Water quality* – Water quality and its impact on human health is a primary concern with rainwater harvesting. This issue is comprised of two components: end use of the rainwater and treatment provided. Rainwater used for residential irrigation (on the scale of rain barrel collection) does not typically require treatment. Commercial applications and non-potable indoor uses require treatment but the type of use will determine the extent of treatment. Each jurisdiction will need to assess the level of treatment with which it is comfortable, but limiting rainwater reuse to water closets, urinals and hose bibbs presents little human health risk. Each system will require some level of screening and filtration to prevent particles and debris from traveling through the plumbing system, and most jurisdictions require disinfection with UV or chlorination because of bacterial concerns. Table 3 provides an example of minimum water quality guidelines and suggested treatment methods for collected rainwater.

Excerpts of General Requirements
Portland Rainwater Harvesting Code Guide

General
- Harvested rainwater may only be used for water closets, urinals, hose bibbs, and irrigation.
- Rainwater can only be harvested from roof surfaces.
- The first 10 gallons of roof runoff during any rain event needs to be diverted away from the cistern to an Office of Planning & Development Review (OPDR) approved location.

Rainwater Harvesting System Components
- Gutters – All gutters leading to the cistern require leaf screens with openings no larger than 0.5 inches across their entire length including the downspout opening.
- Roof washers – Rainwater harvesting systems collecting water from impervious roofs are required to have a roof washer for each cistern. Roof washers are not required for water collected from green roofs or other pervious surfaces. The roof washer is required to divert at least the first 10 gallons of rainfall away from the cistern and contain 18 inches of sand, filter fabric, and 6 inches of pea gravel to ensure proper filtration.
- Cisterns – Material of construction shall be rated for potable water use. Cisterns shall be able to be filled with rainwater and the municipal water system. Cross-contamination of the municipal water system shall be prevented by the use of (1) a reduced pressure backflow assembly or (2) an air gap. Cisterns shall be protected from direct sunlight.
- Piping – Piping for rainwater harvesting systems shall be separate from and shall not include any direct connection to any potable water piping. Rainwater harvesting pipe shall be purple in color and labeled "CAUTION: RECLAIMED WATER, DO NOT DRINK" every four feet in length and not less than once per room.
- Labeling – Every water closet or urinal supply, hose bibb or irrigation outlet shall be permanently identified with an indelibly marked placard stating: "CAUTION: RECLAIMED WATER, DO NOT DRINK."
- Inspections – Inspections are required of all elements prior to being covered.
- Maintenance – Property owner is responsible for all maintenance.

A review of treatment standards among various jurisdictions shows a wide range of requirements from minimal treatment to reclaimed water standards. A recent memorandum of understanding from the City and County of San Francisco allows rainwater to be used for toilet flushing without being treated to potable standards. Texas requires filtration and disinfection for non-potable indoor uses, and Portland requires filtration for residential non-potable indoor uses, but requires filtration and disinfection for multi-family and commercial applications. Treatment requirements ultimately come down to risk exposure with risk of bacterial exposure determining the most stringent levels of treatment. However, San Francisco's Memorandum or Understanding indicates a belief in a low exposure risk with rainwater when used for toilet flushing. Likewise, testing conducted in Germany demonstrated that the risk of *E. coli* contact with the human mouth from toilet flushing was virtually non-existent, resulting in the

Figure 18.8. This white paper excerpt from the U.S. Environmental Protection Agency describes rainwater harvesting and treatment standards. See the full version at https://www.epa.gov/sites/production/files/2015-10/documents/gi_munichandbook_harvesting.pdf

In addition to regulatory and organizational compliance, there are many advantages of using standards in technical descriptions and documents. Their primary purpose is to ensure technical documentation follows appropriate legal and regulatory standards and practices; however, they serve a number of other important functions. They provide consistency across technical documents written on similar or related subjects. Standards also rely on field-specific common knowledge of terms, concepts, and practices. The use of standards also helps ensure proper use of terminology within a given field or discipline. Following standards also helps create sustainable processes and practices across organizations and disciplines. Standards also help novices learn how to communicate using proper and consistent terms, concepts and practices. Using standards facilitates a transfer of information between professionals, ensuring consistency and error reduction in the production of technical documents. And they can help reduce the possibility of miscommunication and misuse of information.

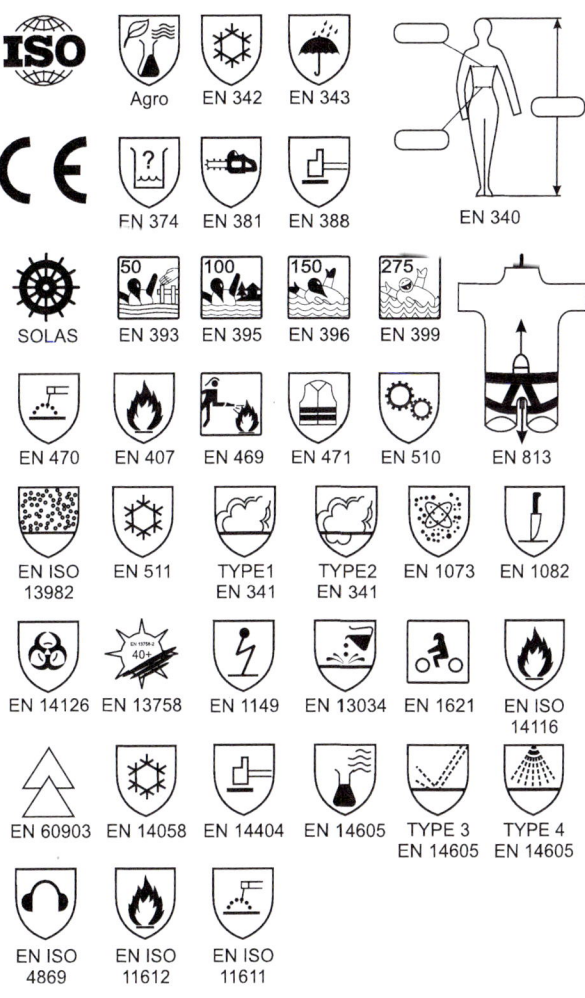

Figure 18.9. In this collection of European Standards icons for personal protective equipment, each standard is depicted with its alphanumeric code for use.

EXERCISE 18.7

Analyzing Technical Standards and Regulations

Conduct online research to find information on a technical standard from the International Organization for Standardization (ISO). Since there is a wide range of topics to choose from, try to select a topic of interest or something related to technical communication. Read the description of the standard and make note of its use of technical definitions and descriptive modes. Then, write a short 250-word summary of the standard for a standard layperson audience. Be sure to include the name and number of the standard, its title, and a short overview of its scope and application. Report and present your findings.

Tasks to be completed:

1. Find an ISO technical standard on any topic by conducting an online search.
2. Read the description of the standard, making note of the use of definitions and descriptive modes.
3. Write a short 250-word summary for a general audience, including the title, number, and short description of its scope.
4. Report and present your findings.

Chapter Summary

Technical definitions and descriptions are used in virtually all technical document types and genres. They provide detailed background information in a wide range of technical documents, including analytical reports, instructional materials, research reports, presentations, and proposals. Technical definitions explain key technical terms and concepts to specialized audiences. Definitions typically identify the term, its classification, and any distinguishing characteristics. Shorter versions of technical definitions can also be used parenthetically or as short phases separated by commas.

Technical descriptions serve a variety of purposes; they can inform, persuade, and instruct. Fact sheets, white papers, specifications, summaries, abstracts, and process descriptions are all examples of technical documents that use technical description to explain concepts, policies, processes, and other technical subjects. Types of description common to technical documents include: comparison and contrast, distinguishing characteristics, part to whole, and visual illustration. Technical descriptions typically follow one of four organizational patterns: general to specific, sequential, topical, or subject-specific. They also typically incorporate one or more modes of persuasion, including appeals to logos, ethos, and pathos. Content reuse is important in writing technical descriptions because users expect parallel content, many technical documents incorporate multiple descriptions, and reuse of descriptions and definitions ensures greater information accuracy.

Since technical communicators often write technical descriptions and documents for other specializations and fields, it is important that their work follows any related standards and practices. These standards or specifications might cover legal, organizational, or health and safety oriented contexts, which must be followed when writing technical documentation. The primary purpose of using standards is to ensure technical documentation follows appropriate legal and regulatory standards and practices; however, they serve a number of other important functions.

Chapter Assignments

The exercises in this section ask you to apply what you have learned in this chapter as well as explore how this knowledge applies to and connects with other information in the textbook.

1. Find and select a common technical term used in any field or industry. Locate at least three different technical definitions for that term. Compare the definitions for how they are similar and different. Decide on which definition is the most accurate for the term, or if none are satisfying, write your own definition of the term and present your findings.

2. Select a common electronics product (computer, phone, speaker, television) and collect technical descriptions from at least two different manufacturers. The descriptions can be in any form marketing-oriented, technical specifications, brochures, etc. Compare and contrast the two technical descriptions in terms of their content, descriptive methods, organizational patterns, and use of visuals. In each of those four areas, evaluate and select which description is superior, and briefly explain why. Finally, make a decision as to which product you would buy, and provide a rationale. Present your findings.

3. Research online to locate a white paper on any given subject. Read and analyze the paper for its use of descriptive methods and organizational patterns. Note in particular, the use of technical terms, definitions, standards, and examples given. Present a summary of your findings and compare your results with another white paper.

4. Locate a technical paper online that includes the use of technical definitions, and specifically the use of graphics to explain technical terms and processes. Read and evaluate the use of visuals in helping to explain those terms and processes. Identify which techniques are most effective and offer any suggestions for adding or changing visuals to improve how technical terms and processes are explained. Report and compare your findings with other technical papers that use visuals to explain terms and processes.

5. Visit the IKEA website (http://www.ikea.com) and search for a set of visual instructions on assembling a product. Examine how visual images are used to explain objects, terms, or to describe processes for users of the instructions. Also, make note of the limited use of numbers or words. Determine the effectiveness of these visual instructions and what additions or changes you might make to help improve their descriptive value for the intended audience. Compare your findings to other visual instructions you have used or found online.

6. Visit the USGS website at http://www.usgs.gov and select a white paper on any topic that interests you. Read the white paper in its entirety. Identify any technical definitions and descriptive modes used in the document. Look closely at the use of persuasive techniques used in describing and evaluate their effectiveness.

Figure Credits

Figure 18.1. © Tomislav Zidanic/Shutterstock.com

Figure 18.2. © Sergey Shenderovsky/Shutterstock.com

Figure 18.3. © Zern Liew/Shutterstock.com

Figure 18.9. © EmptySD/Shutterstock.com

References

Albers, M. (2009). Design for effective support of user intentions in information-rich interactions. *Journal of Technical Writing and Communication, 39*(2), 177–194.

Allen, N., & Benninghoff, S. T. (2004). TPC program snapshots: Developing curricula and addressing challenges. *Technical Communication Quarterly, 13*(2), 157–185.

Arnheim, R. (1969). *Visual thinking*. Berkeley: University of California Press.

Asimov, I. (1978). "My own view." The Encyclopedia of Science Fiction, ed. Robert Holdstock New York: Octopus. Reprinted in Asimov on Science Fiction (1981), New York: Doubleday, 5.

Baehr, C. (2002). Conceptualizing the whole: Using visual-spatial thinking in the interpretation and design of hypertext systems. Ann Arbor: UMI.

Baehr, C. (2007). *Web development: A visual-spatial approach*. Upper Saddle River: Prentice Hall.

Baehr, C. & Lang, S. (2012). Hypertext theory: Rethinking and reformulating what we know, Web 2.0. *Journal of Technical Writing and Communication, 42*(1), 39–56.

Baehr, C., & Alex-Brown, K. (2010). Assessing the value of corporate blogs: A social capital perspective. *IEEE Transactions on Professional Communication, 53*(4), 358–369.

Barry, A. M. (1997). *Visual intelligence: Perception, image, and manipulation in visual communication*. New York: SUNY Press.

Bureau of Labor Statistics (2014). U.S. Department of Labor, Occupational Outlook Handbook, 2014–15 Edition. Technical writers. Available online: http://www.bls.gov/ooh/media-and-communication/technical-writers.htm. (Accessed June 12, 2014).

Campbell, K. S. (1999). Qualitative research methods for solving workplace problems. *Technical Communication, 46,* 532–545.

Clark, D. (2008). Content management and the separation of presentation and content. *Technical Communication Quarterly, 17*(1), 35–60.

Dalkir, K. (2011). *Knowledge management in theory and practice*. Cambridge: The MIT Press.

Gardner, H. (2006). *Multiple intelligences: New horizons in theory and practice*. New York: Perseus Books Group.

Garrett, J. (2011). The *elements of user experience: User-centered design for the web and beyond*. Berkeley: New Riders Press.

Golbeck, J. (2005). *Art theory for web design*. El Granada: Scott/Jones Inc.

Goodman, E., Kuniavsky, M., & Moed, A. (2012). *Observing the user experience: A practitioner's guide to user research*. Boston: Morgan Kaufmann/Elsevier.

Governor, J., Hinchcliffe, D., & Nickull, D. (2009). *Web 2.0 architectures*. Sebastopol: O'Reilly Media, Inc.

Hackos, J. A. (2007). *Information development: Managing your documentation projects, portfolios, and people*. Indianapolis: Wiley Publishing, Inc.

Hart-Davidson, W. (2001). On writing, technical communication, and information technology: The core competencies of technical communication. *Technical Communication, 48*(2), 145–155.

Hoft, N. L. (1995). *International technical communication: How to export information about high technology*. John Wiley & Sons, Inc..

Horton, W. (2012). *E-Learning by design, 2nd ed.* San Francisco: John Wiley & Sons/Pfeiffer.

Hughes, M. A., & Hayhoe, G. F. (2009). *A research primer for technical communication: Methods, exemplars, and analyses*. London: Routledge.

Johnson, R. R. (1998). *User-centered technology: A rhetorical theory for computers and other mundane artifacts*. New York: SUNY Press.

Johnson-Sheehan, R., & Baehr, C. (2001). Visual-spatial thinking in hypertexts. *Technical communication, 48*(1), 22–30.

Lee, W., & Owens, D. (2004). *Multimedia-based instructional design, 2nd ed*. San Francisco: John Wiley & Sons/Pfeiffer.

McLuhan, M. (1964). *Understanding media: The extensions of man*. New York: McGraw-Hill.

Moriarty, S. (2005). *Visual semiotics theory. Handbook of Visual Communication: Theory, Methods, and Media*. Malwah: Lawrence Earlbaum Associates, Inc.

Morville, P. (2005). *Ambient findability: What we find changes who we become*. Sebastopol: O'Reilly Media, Inc.

Nardi, B. A., & O'Day, V. L. (1999). *Information ecologies: Using technology with heart*. Cambridge: MIT Press.

Nielsen, J. (1995). 10 usability heuristics for user interface design. NN/g Nielsen Norman Group: Evidence-Based User Experience Research, Training, and Consulting. Retrieved from: http://www.nngroup.com/articles/ten-usability-heuristics/.

Paretti, M. C., McNair, L. D., & Holloway-Attaway, L. (2007). Teaching technical communication in an era of distributed work: A case study of collaboration between US and Swedish students. *Technical Communication Quarterly, 16*(3), 327–352.

Pringle, K., & Williams, S. (2005). The future is the past: has technical communication arrived as a profession? *Technical Communication, 52*(3), 361–370.

Rainey, K.T., Turner, R. K., & David, D. (2005). Do curricula correspond to managerial expectations? Core competencies for technical communicators. *Technical Communication,* 52(3), 323–352.

Raskin, J. (2000). *The humane interface: New directions for designing interactive systems*. Boston: Addison-Wesley.

Richey, R., Klein, J., & Tracey, M. (2011). *The instructional design knowledge base: Theory, Research and Practice*. Routledge: New York.

Rockley, A. (2001). The impact of single sourcing and technology. *Technical Communication, 48*(2), 189–193.

Rockley, A., & Cooper, C. (2012). *Managing enterprise content: An unified content strategy*, 2nd ed. Berkeley: New Riders.

Rosenfeld, L., & Morville, P. (2007). *Information architecture for the World Wide Web*, 3rd ed. Sebastopol: O'Reilly Media, Inc.

Slack, J. D., Miller, D. J., & Doak, J. (1993). The technical communicator as author meaning, power, authority. *Journal of Business and Technical Communication, 7*(1), 12–36.

Slattery, S. (2007). Undistributing work through writing: How technical writers manage texts in complex information environments. *Technical Communication Quarterly, 16*(3), 311–325.

Smith, G. (2008). *"Tags, Metadata, and Classification Systems," Tagging: People-powered metadata for the social web*. Berkeley: New Riders.

Society for Technical Communication Web site, http://www.stc.org/about-stc/the-profession-all-about-technical communication/defining-tc.

Steinfeld, E., & Maisel, J. (2012). *Universal design: Creating inclusive environments*. Hoboken: John Wiley & Sons, Inc.

Trying out the new assembly line. (1913). Retrieved from National Archives and Records Administration, Records of the Bureau of Public Roads (30-N-49-1482) [VENDOR # 17]. Retrieved from http://www.archives.gov/exhibits/picturing_the_century/newcent/newcent_img5.html

Unger, R., & Chandler, C. (2009). *A project guide to UX design*. Berkeley: Peachpit Press

Whiteside, A. (2003). The skills that technical communicators need: An investigation of technical communication graduates, managers, and curricula. *Journal of Technical Writing and Communication, 33*(4), 303–318.

INDEX

A

Abstract words, 142
Accessibility, 182, 208–209
Adaptive content, 179, 198
Additive color, 204
Adult learning theory, 188–189
Aesthetic considerations, 210
Agendas and minutes, distributing, 91
Agile
    communication, 9
    definition, 9
Agile communicators, 2, 36, 72
Agile development cycles, 7
Agile development models, 7
Agility, twenty-first century workplaces, 8–9
Analytical report
    genre, 60
    presentations, 377
Animations, 388
Assessment and revision task, editing, 157
Assignment, 272
Asynchronous communication, 92
Asynchronous meetings, 92
Attitudinal questions, 115
Audience
    definition of, 30
    generic identifiers, 30
    multimedia product, 30
    person with disability, 30–31
    technology usage, 31
    writing content for, 31–34
        classroom conversations, 31
        job search materials, 32–33
        marketing documents, 33–34
        personal conversations, 31
        speeding citation, 32
        workplace communications, 31
Audience analysis
    cultural differences, 36–37
    definition of, 34
    document and project plans, 73
    user profiles, 34–35
    use scenarios, 35–36
Authors, 134
Automotive production lines, early, 3–4

B

Background information, 261–262
Bad news responses, 226–227
Behavioral questions, 115
Benchmarking
    information models, 171
    with legacy documents, 123–124
    research, 258
Bite-sized chunks, 383
Blogs, 289
Blue-and white-collar workers, job stability of, 6
Brief presentations, 377–378
Brigham Grid for Learning (BGfL), 188
Bulleted lists, 156
Business operations, process maturity impact on, 102
Business writing, 2–3

C

Captioning, information graphics, 213
Charts (information graphics), 212
Chrono-functional résumé, 352, 355
Chronological résumés, 352, 353
Chunking, 153
Citation, 70–71
    information graphics, 213
Clickstream measures, 120
Client interviews, 111
Closed questions, 114
Coding method of electronic document development, 285–287
Cognitive design, 202
Cognitive learning, 201
Cognitive overload, 202
Cognitive process, 203
Cognitive theory, 201–202
Coherent paragraphs, 152–153
Collaborative authoring, 166
Color composition terms, 205–206
Color composition theory, 204–205
Color schemas, 206–207
Communication, 5
    project-based, 9
    and writing situations, 134
Communication documents, 40
Communication professional, 3
Communication situations, carefully assessing, 1
Communication skills, adapting, 1
Communication theory, 30
Communicator, 30
Communities of inquiry (CoI), 87
Communities of practice (CoP), 86–87
Complex information graphics, 212
Complex sentences, 144

Compound-complex sentences, 144
Compound sentences, 144
Concrete words, 142
Conference and class presentations, 377
Connotation and denotation, difference between, 142
Constraints, 41
Consumer information, 6
Consumer products, 4
Content and multiple media, 173
Content authoring, 134–138
   employment entry page from Monster.com, 138
   résumé, 137
   structured, 135–136
   unstructured, 135
Content delivery, 135–136
Content designers, 199
Content development considerations, 134
Content editing, 265
Content management, 165
   content reuse. *See* Content reuse
   information modeling. *See* Information modeling
   information planning tools, 167–168
   metadata development, 167
   practices, 166
   and process maturity, 166–167
   single-sourcing, 167
   tacit and explicit knowledge, 167
Content management system (CMS), 166
   blogs and wikis, 288
   built-in features and templates, 288
   definition of, 287
   purposes of, 288
   vs. Web development software, 288
Content reuse, 14, 20–22
   as content strategy, 20
   guidelines for, 20–21
   importance of, 172
   levels of revision
      customized and personalized content, 174
      identical content and multiple media, 173
      static content with multiple media, 173–174
   plagiarism and citation issues, 22
   reusability and usability considerations, 179–182
      accessibility testing, 181–182
      usability testing, 180–181
   strategies for product description, 180
Content strategy, 15, 82
Copyright
   considerations, 387
   and intellectual property issues, 70–71
Copyrighted material
   citation rules, 70–71
   permissions for, 71
Correctness, 141
Correspondence
   electronic, 220
   meaning of, 219
   printed, 220
   professional. *See* Professional correspondence
   role in organizational communication, 220
   used in organizations, 219
Courteous of others, 89
Cover letters, 33, 227, 341, 368
CPR, procedures for, 268
Creative play, 116–117
Cross-functional teams, 86
   respecting disciplinary differences on, 89
CSS, 286
Cultural differences
   constraints, 41
   respecting, 89
   in teams, 90
   and technical documentation, 36–37
Culture, localizing for, 70
Customer focus, 101
Customized and personalized content, 174

D

Data displays, 210
Deliverables
   document and project plans, 73
   purpose of, 40
   user analysis, 73
Denotation and connotation, difference between, 142
Descriptive titles and headings, 177
Designers, 82
Design principles, visual information, 207–210
   accessibility considerations, 208–209
   aesthetic considerations, 210
   factors influencing, 207–208
Design process, 198
Developed paragraphs, 152
Diction
   definition of, 138
   importance of, 138–139
   levels of
      colloquial diction, 140
      formal diction, 140
      informal diction, 140
      slang, 139
      word choices, 140–141
Dictionaries, 141
Digital technical content
   creation, 136
   delivery, 135–136
Disciplinary differences, respecting, 89
Discipline-specific or professional regulations, 122
Distributed work teams, 81
   and workplaces, 83–93
Document development, 16
Document ecologies
   and activity cycles, 15–16
   definition of, 15
Document plans, 53
   audience and user analysis, 73
   definition of, 72

deliverables, 73
overview and outcomes, 73
parameter setting for, 72
planning document, 73
preliminary planning, 73
professional resume, 75–77
request for approval, 75
resource allocation, 75
roadmap for, 72
tasks and milestones, 74
Document templates, 65–67
Document variation, 60–61
Drafting of paragraphs
conclusions, 156
introductory paragraphs, 155
middle sections, 155–156

E

Editing
assessment and revision task, 157
design of document, 159
general background of document, 158
genre conventions and content organization, 158–159
overall effectiveness of document, 160
style, 159–160
Editors, 82
Electronic communication
technologies, 81
tools, 81
Electronic content
development and publication of, 275
pull content, 275
purposes and genres, 275
push content, 275
Websites, 275–276
Electronic correspondence, 220
emails
guidelines for writing, 233–234
potential problems, 234–235
guidelines for writing, 236–237

Electronic documents
development of
authoring tools and methods for, 285–290
development process, 280–281
planning process, 276–279
publishing process, 283–284
quality assurance process, 282–283
skills and abilities for, 276
user experience, 277
writing for, 277
Electronic networking, 137
Electronic presentation software, 67
Electronic publications, 122
Electronic publishing technologies, 13–14
Electronic tools, 166
Emails
guidelines for writing, 233–234
potential problems, 234–235
Empirical research reports, 320
E-server Technical Communication Library, 177
Ethos, 412
European Standards icon, 415
Expense reports, 242, 244–246
Experiential design theory, 202–204
Explicit and tacit knowledge, 167
Expressive words, 142
External resources, 121
Eye-tracking technology, 120

F

Face-to-face teams, 86
Fair use laws, 71
Feasibility report presentations, 377
Feasibility reports, 320–321
Feasibility studies, 60
Field observations, 117
File naming conventions, 177–178

Financial reports, 323–324
Financial writing, 2–3
Findability, 176, 177
Focus groups, 113
Folksonomies, 178
Font types, 386
Ford automobiles, assembly line of, 3
Forecasting statements, 155
Formal reviews, 101
Functional paragraphs, 152
Functional résumés, 352, 354
Functional teams, 86

G

General etiquette suggestions, 88–90
General words, 142
Geographically dispersed users, 69
Gestalt theories, 200–201
Good news responses, 226
Grammatically correct words, 141
Graphic placement, 213
Graphs (information graphics), 212
Grid layouts and slides, 386
Groupthink, avoiding, 90

H

Handouts, 271
Headings, 156, 383
Health and safety issues, 258
Heuristics
information product evaluation by, 180–181
process maturity assessment, 99–100
web site design evaluation using, 181
Higher maturity teams, 101
High level maturity, 98–99
HTML, 285
Hue, 205
Hybrid presentations, 379
Hybrid teams, 86

I

Idea development and construction, 5
Ignite talks, 378
Illustrations (information graphics), 212
Impressive words, 142
IMRD format, 314
Informational interviewing, 361–362
Information architecture, 277
Information design, 197, 199, 277
Information ecologies, 15
Information gathering, options for, 44
Information graphic analysis, 214
Information graphics. *See* Visual information graphics
Information in company directory, 169
Information modeling, 93, 167
    as content planning tool, 169
    content topics, relationship between, 20
    outlining and, 20
    user-centered approach to, 168
    working mechanism of, 168
Information models, 135
    benchmarking, 171
    developing, 170–171
    functions of, 168
    scaling, 171–172
    significance of, 169–170
    simple and complex, 168
    trip proposal content, 175
    trip report, 176
Information Process Maturity Model (IPMM), 96
Information technologies, 6
Information types, 115
In-house legacy documents, 121
Innovation, 95, 99
In-person interviews, 111
In-person presentations, 379

Instance reports
    expense reports, 242, 244–246
    functions of, 241
    meeting agendas, 246–248
    meeting minutes, 248
    trip reports, 242
Instructional content, 166
Instructional design, 182
Instructional development
    analysis phase, 183
        adult learning theory, 188–189
        learning modalities, 185–186
        learning objectives, 183–184
        learning styles and theories, 185
        multiple intelligences, 186–187
        technology considerations, 189–190
    definition of, 182
    design and development phases, 183, 190–191
    implementation and evaluation phases, 183, 192–193
Instructional documents
    characteristics of, 256
    definition of, 255
    instructions, 256, 265–266
    learning materials, 256–257, 265
        activities, 271
        assignment, 272
        handouts, 271
        instructions for writing, 271
        media and interactive content, 271
        organized by topics, 271
        purposes, 270–271, 273
        tutorials, 271
    objectives of, 255
    procedures, 256, 265, 267–270
        for CPR, 268
        elements in writing, 267

        improving, 270
        for tornado preparedness, 269
        user research for developing, 255–256
        written instructions, 265
Instructional documents, writing
    researching task for, 257–260
        benchmarking research, 258
        design, layout, and graphic content, 259–260
        health and safety issues, 258
        organizational structure, 259
        reusable content, 258–259
        standards or practices, 258
        subject matter, 257
        user research, 258
    testing and reviewing tasks for, 265
    writing and designing tasks for, 260–265
        background information, 261–262
        introductory information, 261
        procedural steps or topics, 262–263
        supplemental content, 263–264
Instructional products, 166
Instructions, 256, 265–266
Intangible benefits, 102
Intelligent content, 197
Intermittent Internet service, 108, 109, 126, 128
Internal documents, 120–121
Internet search, 47, 343
Interview answers, 33
Interview questions, 369
Interviews, 113, 341
Introductory information, 261
Inventorying, 342–343
ISO standards, 413
Iterative development cycles, 7
Iterative process cycles, 9, 13

Iterative work processes, 101
   advantages, 14, 15
   causes and needs for, 13–14
   challenges, 14
   collaborations, 14, 15
   definition of, 13
   process maturity, 14
   and project management, 15–16

J

JavaScript, 286
Job ads, reading, 363–365
Job interview, 368
   delivering, 370
   expressing thanks for, 371
   preparing for, 369–370
Job opportunities
   applying for
      cover letters, writing, 366–368
      job ads, reading, 363–365
      résumés and covers letters, submitting, 368
   identifying. *See* Positions, methods for locating
Job search materials, 32–33
   job interview, 368–371
   job opportunities. *See* Job opportunities
   job search resources. *See* Positions, methods for locating
   résumé. *See* Résumé
Job search skills, 341
Job skills inventory, 344–345

K

Keywords
   as metadata, 176
   and tagging, 178
Kolb's cycle of experiential learning, 204

L

Labeling, information graphics, 213
Layouts, 215–216

Leader, designating, 88
Learning
   environment, control over, 189
   modalities, 185–186
   non-traditional forms of, 189
   objectives, 183–184
Learning materials, 256–257, 265
   activities, 271
   assignment, 272
   handouts, 271
   instructions for writing, 271
   media and interactive content, 271
   organized by topics, 271
   purposes, 270–271, 273
   tutorials, 271
Learning process, model of, 204
Learning styles
   multiple intelligences as, 186–187
   and theories, 185
Legacy content research, 61
Legacy documentation, 60–61
Legacy documents, 70–71
Lessons learned review, 47–48
Letters, formatting of, 229–231
Lightning talks, 378
Linear processes, 6
Listener, 30
List management tools, 236
Listserv, 236
Localization and translation, 69–70
Logos, 412
Lower maturity teams, 101
Low level maturity, 97

M

Main clause, 143–144
Mapping statements, 155
Marketing documents, 33–34
Marketing presentations, 377
Markup and scripting languages
   CSS, 286
   HTML, 285
   JavaScript, 286
   PHP, 286
   XML, 285

Media and interactive content, 271
Meeting agendas, 246–248
Meeting minutes, 248
Messages of appreciation or thanks, 227–228
Metadata
   definition of, 176
   developing, 167, 176
      descriptive titles and headings, 177
      file naming conventions, 177–178
      folksonomies, 178
      keywords and tagging, 178
      taxonomies, 178
   importance of, 176–177
   keywords, 176
Metrics, 23
Milestones, 48
Mixed media forms, 166
Moderate-level maturity, 97–98
Monster.com, employment entry page from, 138
Multiple intelligences, 186–187
Multiple media, static content with, 173–174

N

Naming conventions, 68–69
Networking, 360–361
Numbered lists, 156

O

Objectives of task, 42–43
   purpose, requirements, and, 43
   sequential/hierarchical, 42
   templates for, 42
Observation methods, 116–119
   creative play, 116–117
   field observations, 117
   protocol or plan, 119–120
   think-aloud protocols, 117
   usability tests, 118–119
Offshoring, 84
Online content citation rules, 70–71

Online networking and researching tools, 81
Online publication, 14, 165–166
and writing, 172
Online resources, 362
Open-ended questions, 114–115
Operating expenses budget request, 52
Organizational structure, 259
Ornithology proposal, style sheet for, 64
Outlining and information modeling, 20
Outsourcing, 84
Overview and outcomes, document and project plans, 73

P

Paragraphing strategies, 154
Paragraphs, 138, 151–157
   brief descriptions of, 156
   chunking, 153
   coherent, 152–153
   developed, 152
   drafting of
     conclusions, 156
     introductory paragraphs, 155
      middle sections, 155–156
   functional, 152
   functions of, 155, 157
   transitional words and phrases, 153–154
   unified, 152
Pathos, 412
Pecha Kucha talks, 378
Perception and cognition, 202
Perceptual theory, 200–201
Periodic reports, 249–250
Permissions, research rules for acquiring, 71
Personal identity, establishing, 87
Persuasive appeals, 412
Persuasive stylistics, 412
Photographs (information graphics), 212
PHP, 286
Pilot test, 125

Plagiarism and citation issues, 22
Planning revision strategies, 160–161
Podcasts, screencasts and videos, 391, 393
Positions, methods for locating, 360–362
   informational interviewing, 361–362
   networking, 360–361
   online resources, 362
Poster presentations, textual and visual content for, 388
   guidelines for visual content, 390–391
   parts, 389
   poster size constraints, 389
   undergraduate research, 390
Post-project review meeting, 26
Post-publication activities, 26
Predictive product development cycle, 7
Presentations
   classified by delivery method, 378–379
   classified by genre, 376–378
   delivering, 393
     challenges in, 396
     delivery tips, 394–395
     pre-presentation tips, 394
   developing, 381–393
     content, researching and locating, 382
     poster presentations, 388–391
     recorded presentations, 391–393
     slideshow presentations, 383–388
     textual and visual content. *See* Textual and visual content
   evaluating, 396–397
   extended, 377
   formal, 376
   informal, 376
   planning, 379–381
   purposes of, 375–376
Presentation software program, 60

Primary research, 111
   definition of, 112
   observation methods, 116–119
     creative play, 116–117
     field observations, 117
     protocol or plan, 119–120
     think-aloud protocols, 117
     usability tests, 118–119
   question-asking methods, 112
     attitudinal questions, 115
     behavioral questions, 115
     characteristic questions, 115
     closed questions, 114
     focus groups, 113
     information types, 115
     interviews, 113
     open-ended questions, 114–115
     research protocol, 114–115
     surveys, 113–114, 116
   user data collection methods, 120
Printed correspondence, 220
Printed memos, formatting of, 232–233
Print publications, 122
Problem statements
   formulating, 108–110
   writing, 112
Procedural steps or topics, 262–263
Procedures, 256, 265, 267–270
   for CPR, 268
   elements in writing, 267
   improving, 270
   for tornado preparedness, 269
Process improvement. *See* Team process improvement
Process mature iterative work practices, 101
Process mature organization, 102–103
Process maturity, 82–83, 101
   and content management, 166–167
   definition of, 93

Index

impacts on business operations, 102
impacts on return on investment, 102
strategies for improving, 102
Process maturity assessment
  heuristic assessment, 99–100
  potential problems, 101
  workplace, 101
Process maturity model, 93
Product description, content reuse strategies for, 180
Product design, 3, 7
Production models
  21st century. *See* Twenty-first century workplaces
  twentieth century. *See* Twentieth century workplaces
Product stability, 94
Professional correspondence
  complaints, claims, and adjustments, 222
  critiquing request message, 224–225
  formatting, 229–233
    letters, 229–231
    printed memos, 232–233
  recall notices, 222–223
  recommendations, 223
  requests, 222
  response messages, evaluating
    response to request checklist, 228–229
  response messages, writing, 225
    bad news responses, 226–227
    cover letters, 227
    good news responses, 226
    messages of appreciation or thanks, 227–228
  structure, 221
Professional networking sites, 289
Professional portfolios, 359–360

Professional profile, creating and maintaining, 343
  biographical statements, 345–346
  online professional profiles, 347–348
  professional portfolios, 359–360
  résumé
    design, 349
    education entries, 350
    evaluating, 356–357
    formatting, 352
    innovative design, 356
    misconception about, 348
    name and contact information, 349
    non-essential information, 351–352
    online research about, 348–349
    organizing, 352
    skills entries, 351
    work experience entries, 350
Professional résumé document work plan, 75–76
Professional style guides, 65
Progress reports, 250–251
Project assessment, 102
Project documentation, 173
Project management, 81
  content strategy, 82
  document types, 16
  and iterative processes, 15–16
  part of, 15
  process maturity, 82–83
  process maturity assessment. *See* Process maturity assessment
  responsibilities and tasks, 38
  strategies, 37–38
  team roles. *See* Team roles
  tracking metrics, 38
Project managers, 38, 82
Project metrics, 101–102
Project plan, 53
  audience and user analysis, 73
  deliverables, 73

overview and outcomes, 73
parameter setting for, 72
planning document, 73
preliminary planning, 73
professional resume, 75–77
request for approval, 75
resource allocation, 75
roadmap for, 72
tasks and milestones, 74
Project postmortem, 47–48
Proposal presentations, 377
Proposals
  categorization of, 293
  competitive, 295
  content and format, 294
  definition of, 293
  evaluating, 303–308
  formal, 293
  functions of, 294
  guidelines and strategies for writing
    evaluation of solutions, 297–298
    planning and researching, 296–297
    problem statements, 297
  informal, 293
  reviewing and revising, 302
  solicited, 293
  structural components, 295
  submitting
    electronic/printed, 302
    wait for approval, 302
  templates, comparing, 303
  unsolicited, 293
  writing and drafting
    back matter, 301
    conclusion, 301
    content gathering, 298
    front matter, 298–299
    introductory information, 299
    proposed project management, 300–301
    proposed solution, 299–300
    RFP review, 298
Proposal writers, problems with, 109, 110, 126, 129
Protocol or plan, 119–120

Published materials, acquiring permission for use of, 71
Publishing checklist, 25
Punctuation
  commas, 146–147
  end punctuation, 145–146
  importance of, 148
  semicolons, 147
Purpose statements, 88

Q

Quality assurance, 265
Quantitative metrics, 102

R

Reader, 30, 73
Receiver, 30
Recommendation report presentations, 377
Recommendation reports, 321–322
Recorded presentations, textual and visual content for
  hardware and software requirements, 391–392
  podcasts, screencasts and videos, 391, 393
  popularity, 391
  scripts and captions, 392
Recordkeeping, 91
Recruitment protocol, 125
References, 141
Referencing, information graphics, 213
Relative pronouns, 143
Remote/distant presentations, 379
Reports, 121
  archival nature, 312
  case study, 327–335
  components
    abstracts, 316
    back matter, 319
    conclusions, 319
    discussion, 318
    executive summaries, 316–317
    front matter, 315–316
    introduction, 317
    methods, 317
    results/findings, 318
  content of, 319
  credibility, 311–312
  definition of, 311
  evaluating, 325–326
  formal, 312
  genres, differences in
    factors influencing, 319
    feasibility reports, 320–321
    financial reports, 323–324
    IMRD organization, 320
    recommendation reports, 321–322
    research questions, 319–320
    tablet study, 320
    white papers, 322–323
  guidelines for writing
    communication conventions, 314
    genre expectations, 314–315
    purpose identification, 313–314
    reader intentions identification, 313–314
  impact on decisions, 311
  informal, 312–313
  oral delivery of, 313
  persuasiveness of, 311
  reporting on, 312
  TED talks and, 313
Report writer, 312
Request for approval, 75
Research and completion report presentations, 376–377
Research methods, 111–124
  classification of, 111
  primary research, 112–120
  research questions, aligning, 124
  secondary research, 120–124
Research protocol, 114–115
Research questions
  formulating, 110
  and methods, aligning, 124
  methods for asking, 112
    attitudinal questions, 115
    behavioral questions, 115
    characteristic questions, 115
    closed questions, 114
    focus groups, 113
    information types, 115
    interviews, 113
    open-ended questions, 114–115
    research protocol, 114–115
    surveys, 113–114, 116
  writing, 112
Research reporting responsibilities, 124–129
  when planning research, 124–126
  when writing findings, 127–129
Resource allocation, 75
Resource planning, 48–53
  grocery list preparation, 48–49
  resource allocation
    distribution of shared costs, 53
    documenting and reporting, 51–53
    estimating, 49–51
    importance of, 49
    operating expenses budget request, 52
Response messages
  evaluating, 228–229
  writing, 225
    bad news responses, 226–227
    cover letters, 227
    good news responses, 226
    messages of appreciation or thanks, 227–228
Résumé, 32–33, 137, 341
  design, 349
  education entries, 350
  evaluating, 356–357
  formatting, 352
  innovative design, 356
  misconception about, 348
  name and contact information, 349
  non-essential information, 351–352

online research about, 348–349
  organizing, 352
  skills entries, 351
  submitting, 368
  work experience entries, 350
Return on investment, process maturity impacts on, 102
Reusability considerations, content reuse, 179–182
  accessibility testing, 181–182
  usability testing, 180–181
Reusable content, 198, 258–259
Review assessment strategies, 160–161
Reviewing, testing, and editing, 23
RGB and CMYK color mixes, 205

S

Scaling, information models, 171–172
Scientific writing, 2
Scripting, 392
Scripts and captions, 392
Secondary research, 111
  importance of, 120
  resources for
    benchmarking with legacy documents, 123–124
    categories of, 120
    evaluating and authenticating, 122–123
  resources, identifying and locating, 120–122
    discipline-specific or professional regulations, 122
    electronic publications, 122
    in-house legacy documents, 121
    print publications, 122
    reports, 121
    single-sourced texts, 121
    white papers, 121
Section508.gov Web site, 282–283

Sender, 30
Sentence, 138
  choices and audience, 145
  construction, improving, 151
  economy, 149–150
  emphasis, 151
  faults, 147
  punctuation. See Punctuation
  variety, 150
Sentence structure, 143–148
  main clause, 143
    arrangements of, 144
  relative pronouns, 143
  subordinate clauses, 143
  subordinating conjunctions, 143
Session-based measures, 120
Shared costs, distribution of, 53
Shorter style sheets, 64
Simple sentences, 144
Single reuse strategy, 172
Single sourcing content, 14, 20, 70, 166, 167
  guidelines for, 174–176
  level of
    customized and personalized, 174
    identical content and multiple media, 173
    static content with multiple media, 173–174
  process for, 175
  single-sourced texts, 121
Single-sourcing methods, 173
Site-wide measures, 120
Skills assessment, 342–343
Slideshow presentations, textual and visual content for
  animations, 388
  bite-sized chunks, 383
  copyright considerations, 387
  font types, 386
  grid layouts and slides, 386
  heading, 383
  images, 386
  templates, 385
  unified and balanced, 384
  videos, 386
  white space, 386

Social capital, 102–103
  process mature organizations, 102–103
  understanding value of, 103
Socially mediated communication, 235
  instant messaging (IM), 236
  SMS (short message service), 235–236
Social media
  in business, 290
  guidelines for using, 290
Social media tools, 289–290
Social networking sites, 289
Software engineering, 4–5
Special occasion presentations, 377
Specific words, 142
Speeding citation, 32
Stand-alone presentations, 379
Standardization, 68–69
Standards, 413–416
  advantages of using, 415
  ISO standards, 413
  or practices, 258
  rainwater harvesting and treatment, 414
  and regulations, 416
STAR technique, 369
Static content with multiple media, 173–174
Status and progress report presentations, 376
Status reports, 241
  periodic reports, 249–250
  progress reports, 250–251
Structured authoring, 135–136, 166, 168
  vs. unstructured authoring, 138
Structured content delivery, 136
Style guides, professional, 65
Stylesheets, 64, 198, 215
Subject matter research, 257
Subordinate clauses, 143
Subordinating conjunctions, 143
Subtractive color, 204
Supplemental content, 263–264
Support and help, 90
Surveys, 113–114, 116

Sustainability, 94, 99
Sustainable work practices, 81
Synchronous meetings, 92
Syntax, 143–148
System-centered approach, 94

T

Tables (information graphics), 212
Tablet study, 320
Tacit and explicit knowledge, 167
Tangible benefits, 102
Task analysis
    advantages of, 40
    in communication design and planning, 39
    definition of, 38
    project scoping with, 38
        deliverable's purpose, 40
        obstacles and constraints, 41
        steps to complete the task, 44–45
        task completion. *See* Task completion
        task requirements and documents, 41, 42
        task's objectives, 42–43
Task completion
    organization for, 45–48
        evaluation step, 47
        objectives, 45
        parallel or tandem tasks, 45–46
        project postmortem, 47–48
        visual representation of plan, 46–47
Task objective, steps to complete, 44–45
Tasks and milestones, 74
Taxonomies, 178
Team
    categories of, 86–87
    defining project roles for, 84
    experiences, 85
    failure reasons, 85
    interactions, ground rules for, 88
    structure, 93
    working as, 88
Teaming
    advantages and disadvantages of, 84–85
    definition of, 83
    importance of, 83–84
    technologies promoting, 91–93
Team leader
    roles of, 91
    suggestions for
        agendas and minutes, distributing, 91
        keep in touch, 91
        recordkeeping, 91
Team members, conflict among, 85
Team player, strategies for successful
    general etiquette suggestions, 88–90
        being trustworthy, 90
        courteous of others, 89
        cultural differences, respecting, 89
        disciplinary differences, respecting, 89
        good listener, 89
        groupthink, avoiding, 90
        support and help, 90
    getting started, 87
    ground rules for team interactions, 88
    leader, designating, 88
    personal identity, establishing, 87
    purpose statements, 88
    working as team, 88
Team processes, strategies for improving, 101–103
Team process improvement
    innovation, 95
    process maturity levels
        factors influencing, 96
        high level maturity, 98–99
        incremental process, 96
        low level maturity, 97
        moderate-level maturity, 97–98
        structure, 93
        sustainability, 94
        usability, 94–95
Team projects, 85
Team roles
    definition of, 82
    and skills for project, 82
    in workplace communication projects, 82
Technical communication, 133
    agility in, 8–9
    applications, 2
    definition, 1
    forms of media covering, 1–2
    goal of, 399
    in locations, 2
    principles and key values, 21st century, 8
    situations, 8
    skills and jobs in, 3
    variations of, 2
Technical Communication Body of Knowledge (TCBOK)
    information map for, 20, 21
    tagging, 179
    use scenario, 35–36
Technical communication documents, 57
    content reused in documents, 172
    conventions, 61–62
    copyright and intellectual property issues, 70–71
    genres
        importance of, 59
        literary, 59
        status reports, 59
        and types, 58–59
        variations of document types within, 60–61
    persuasive stylistics, 412
    stylistics
        document templates, 65–67
        localization and translation, 69–70
        naming conventions, 68–69
        style guides, 62, 63, 65

style sheets, 62, 64
version control, 67–68
technical definition. *See* Technical definition
technical descriptions. *See* Technical descriptions
Technical communication documents, planning of, 29
 audience. *See* Audience
 importance of, 30
 project management
  responsibilities and tasks, 38
  strategies, 37–38
  tracking metrics, 38
 project plan writing, 53
 resource planning. *See* Resource planning
 responsive to changes, 30
 scoping with task analysis, 38
  deliverable's purpose, 40
  organization for task completion, 45–48
  steps to complete the task, 44–45
  task requirements and documents, 41
  task's objectives, 42–43
Technical communication iterative process, 14, 17–26
 development phase, 17
  content reuse, 20–22
  execution of project, 19
  outlining and information modeling, 20
  single-sourcing, 20
  tasks, 19–20
 planning phase, 17
  activities, 17–18
  documenting, 18–19
  gantt chart, 19
  planning tasks, 18
  project plan, 18
  research, 19
 publishing phase, 17
  complexity, 23
  organization, content, and design, 24
  post-project review meeting, 26

post-publication activities, 26
publishing checklist, 25
tasks, 23–24
technology issues, 24–25
quality assurance phase, 17
 goals, 22
 reviewing, testing, and editing, 23
 tasks, 22–23
Technical communication product
 purposes of, 57
 types of, 57
Technical communicators, 57, 133
 job titles, 2–3
 roles and responsibilities, 2–3
 technical documentation, 6
Technical definitions, 400–403
 analyzing, 403
 definition of, 400
 examples of, 400–401
 writing, 401–402
Technical descriptions, 403–408
 comparing and contrasting, 403
 content reuse and, 410
 definition of, 403
 distinguishing characteristics, 403–404
 documents using
  fact sheets, 405–407
  specifications, 408, 409
  white papers, 408, 410, 414
 laptop computer, 403
 organizational patterns, 408, 410
 part to whole, 404
 visual illustrations, 404
Technical documentation, 6
Technical document projects, 13
Technical information, 6
Technical information product, iterative approach to
 advantages of, 15
 challenges of, 14
Technical staff, 82

Technical standards and regulations, 416
 ISO standards, 413
 rainwater harvesting and treatment standards, 414
Technical terminology, 400
Technical writers, 5–6
 waterfall process and, 6
Technical writing, 2
Technology considerations, 189–190
TED talk, 377
Templates, 65–67, 198, 215, 385
Testers, 82
Textual and visual content
 information modeling
  storyboard template, 382
  visual information model, 383
 for poster presentations, 388
  guidelines for visual content, 390–391
  parts, 389
  poster size constraints, 389
  undergraduate research, 390
 for recorded presentations
  hardware and software requirements, 391–392
  podcasts, screencasts and videos, 391, 393
  popularity, 391
  scripts and captions, 392
 for slideshow presentations
  animations, 388
  bite-sized chunks, 383
  copyright considerations, 387
  font types, 386
  grid layouts and slides, 386
  heading, 383
  images, 386
  templates, 385
  unified and balanced, 384
  videos, 386
  white space, 386
Thematic or decorative elements, 210

Thesauruses, 141
Think-aloud protocols, 117
Topic sentences, 156
Tornado preparedness, procedures for, 269
Transitional words and phrases, 153–154
Trip reports, 242
Trustworthy, 90
Tutorials, 271
Twentieth century workplaces
   assembly line production, 3–4
   cohesive process, 4
   construction logic, 3–4
   predictive nature of, 6
   product designs, 3
   prototyping, 4
   waterfall development process, 4–5
Twenty-first century workplaces, 6–9
   agile development models, 7
   agility in, 8–9
   constraints, 41
   cross-cultural teaming, 6
   cross-functional teaming, 6
   cyclical processes, 7–8
   iterative development cycles, 7
   skills and competencies, 7
   vs. 20th century development model, 7
   workplace change, 7

U

Unified paragraphs, 152
University career center sites, 362
Unstructured authoring *vs.* structured authoring, 138
Usability considerations, 94–95, 99, 179–182
   accessibility testing, 181–182
   usability testing, 180–181
Usability tests, 118–119
User analysis, 73
User-based measures, 120
User-centered approach, 15, 94–95
User data analysis, 120
User-driven content, demand for, 166
User experience, 277
User feedback, 101
User-friendly approach, 94–95
User-generated training materials, 166
User profiles, 34–35
User research, 258
Use scenarios, 35–36
U.S. Government's Printing Office Style Guide, 64

V

Version control conventions, 67–68
Videoconference presentations, 379
Videos, 386
Viewer, 30
Virtual teams, 86
Visual content. *See* Textual and visual content
Visual cues, 156
Visual design, 202
   choices, theoretical approaches to, 199
   elements, 199
Visual design theories, 199
   cognitive theory, 201–202
   color composition theory, 204–205
   color schemas, 206–207
   design principles, 207–210
   experiential design theory, 202–204
   perceptual theory, 200–201
Visual evidence, 210
Visual identity, 215–216
Visual information, 198
   design conventions, 215–216
   stylesheets, 198
   templates, 198
   types of, 198
   visual design theories. *See* Visual design theories
Visual information graphics
   development of
      using raw data, 211–212
   functions of, 210–211
   integration into technical documents, 213–214
   kinds of, 211
Visual information model, 383
Visual interpretation, 200
Visual perception, 200
Vocabulary, 138–139, 141

W

Waterfall development
   predictive product development cycle, 7
   process, 4–5, 7
   visualizing, 7
Web development software, 287
Web sites
   authoring tools and methods for, 285–290
      CSS, 286
      HTML, 285
      JavaScript, 286
      PHP, 286
      XML, 285
   publishing protocols, 284
   Web development software, 287
Web usability and accessibility icons, 58
Wheel spinning, 85
White papers, 121, 322–323
White space, 386
Word choices
   abstract words, 142
   concrete words, 142
   expressive words, 142
   general words, 142
   grammatically correct, 141
   impressive words, 142
   levels of diction, 140–141
   making good, 143
   specific words, 142
Word-processing templates, 67
Words, 138
   denotation and connotation, difference between, 142
   functions of, 139
   references, 141
   selecting the right, 138–139

Working processes, agile approaches to, 14
Workplace communication documents
   job search materials, 32–33
   marketing documents, 33–34
   planning of. *See* Technical communication documents, planning of
   speeding citation, 32
Workplace communication projects
   reporting results, 312–335
   team roles in, 82
Workplace process maturity assessment, 101
Workplace research
   problem statements, formulating, 108–110
   research methods for, 111–124
      primary research, 112–120
      research questions, aligning, 124
      secondary research, 120–124
   research questions, formulating, 110
   situations driving, 107–108
Workplaces, 1
Work teams, 83
Writers, 82
Writing process, 96
Writing situations, 134

X

XerEscapes' communication plan, recommendations for, 327–335
XML, 285